To Boldly Go

ALSO EDITED BY NADINE FARGHALY

Gender and the Modern Sherlock Holmes: Essays on Film and Television Adaptations Since 2009 (2015)

Unraveling Resident Evil: *Essays on the Complex Universe of the Games and Films* (2014)

EDITED BY NADINE FARGHALY *and* EDEN LEONE

The Sexy Science of The Big Bang Theory: *Essays on Gender in the Series* (2015)

FROM MCFARLAND

To Boldly Go

Essays on Gender and Identity in the Star Trek *Universe*

Edited by Nadine Farghaly
and Simon Bacon

McFarland & Company, Inc., Publishers
Jefferson, North Carolina

ISBN (print) 978-1-4766-6853-6
ISBN (ebook) 978-1-4766-2931-5

Library of Congress cataloguing data are available

British Library cataloguing data are available

Printed in the United States of America

McFarland & Company, Inc., Publishers
Box 611, Jefferson, North Carolina 28640
www.mcfarlandpub.com

Table of Contents

Introduction

"Space: the final frontier. These are the voyages of
the starship *Enterprise*. Its five-year mission: to explore
strange new worlds; to seek out new life and new
civilizations; to boldly go where no man has gone before"
—*Star Trek: The Original Series*

You do not need to be a die-hard *Star Trek* fan to know what this introduction signifies. It was the beginning of a new era of television. The beginning of the first fandom that actively fought for a television show. The beginning of an epic (b)romance between Kirk, Spock and Bones. The beginning of slash fanfiction. The beginning of a franchise that would last for the next 50 years.

Recent years have brought back and reinvigorated the characters of the beloved original crew of the *Enterprise* in three new movies, various graphic novel issues, books, audio plays, board games, PC games, console games, you name it. With this reboot a renewed interest in the *Star Trek* franchise arose which led to the conceptualization of the newest *Star Trek* installment—*Star Trek Discovery*—a television show that will air in 2017. Its main protagonist will be a woman; a lieutenant commander serving as Number One. Personally, we (the editors) are very excited about this information and are counting the days until we can get a look at this new show.

Neither of us were originally *Star Trek* fans, though like many we knew bits and pieces, references like the Vulcan salute and the fact that Captain James T. Kirk had a girl on every space station, planet, ship, asteroid ... you get the picture. However, what really got both of us into *Star Trek* was the series *Voyager*. It was a show to instantly love. Featuring so many wonderful and strong female characters and great interpersonal dynamics and in, what we would later discover is the best *Star Trek* tradition, they always seemed to make the worst possible decisions but survived to make them again, all with the best intentions. And of course, it has a happy ending.

Returning to *TOS*, it is difficult not to be enchanted by the overboard to barely there acting, the cheap backgrounds, the sometimes flimsy and silly story lines, and the great friendship of the main crew and the possibility of a love story between two men (yes, we are Spock/Kirk shippers), the great episodes, the sad ones, the unexpected ones. The show that gave everything it had and aimed for so much more. It contained the most recognized and memorable, though not the first, on-screen kiss between an African American woman and a white American man.[1] It looked closely at ideas such as gender, women's rights, slavery, the promises of utopia; it exposed mankind's greatest weaknesses and faults and elevated its greatest strengths and infinite possibilities. After the disillusionment of wars in Asia and a seemingly never-ending conflict with the Soviet Union, it created a picture for mankind that was worth striving for; one of unity and enlightenment.

The stories *Star Trek* has to tell and the lessons it has imparted has made it one of the most successful and enduring science fiction franchises, not just for the possibilities it constructed for the future but for those that it visualizes for the present. It has taught us to strive for equality in all things—beyond gender, race and even species—and to recognize that differences can bring us together rather than keep us apart. This collection was created to demonstrate how these ideas have been presented but also to highlight their shortcomings and complications.

This collection actively engages with theoretical constructs of gender, feminism, the crisis in masculinity, transgender, and others, and focuses on the ways in which the franchise not only introduced these issues but made them accessible to mainstream media. Perhaps the most startling of these is seen in the episode "Plato's Stepchildren," which has subsequently proven to be a game changer in interethnic relationships. Despite initial concerns about conservative viewers, the episode featuring a kiss between Captain Kirk and Lieutenant Uhura was filmed. To be on the safe side, NBC ordered two different versions: one with and one without the kiss. After the kiss was successfully shot, Shatner and Nichols allegedly, yet very deliberately, made every other shot unusable by very terrible acting. As Nichelle Nichols writes:

> Knowing that Gene was determined to air the real kiss, Bill shook me and hissed menacingly in his best ham-fisted Kirkian staccato delivery, "I! WON'T! KISS! YOU! I! WON'T! KISS! YOU!" It was absolutely awful, and we were hysterical and ecstatic. The director was beside himself, and still determined to get the kissless shot. So we did it again, and it seemed to be fine. "Cut! Print! That's a wrap!"[Nichols 195–7]

Nichols went on to say that the fan reaction to the kiss was dominantly favorable (196–7). This kiss, aired in 1968, represents a milestone in the portrayal of interracial relationships as represented by mainstream media.

While the depiction of interspecies as well as interethnic relationships has been commonplace in the *Star Trek* franchise, not all non-normative identities have been treated equally well and the depiction of LGBT themes has been largely pushed to the margins. When any type of non-heterosexuality is portrayed, it happens in a mirror verse or other sphere separated from the main reality portrayed in the franchise. Although Gene Roddenberry had promised to introduce an LGBT character to *ST:TNG*, he never made good on his promise. Indeed ideas about a script featuring two homosexual crew members was benched in 1986. The episode "Blood and Fire," written by David Gerrold, was supposed to address the public's fear of donating blood during the height of the AIDS crisis while also featuring a positive portrayal of an openly homosexual partnership. However, that episode was never filmed and Gerrold quit after the cancelation. It would take an additional 22 years before it was finally filmed by what is known as Phase II—a fan created science fiction web series (Kay).

The marginalization of non-normative relations first started with Captain Kirk and Commander Spock, a couple that, according to Gene Roddenberry, can be linked to that of Alexander and Hephaestion "Yes, there's certainly some of that—certainly with love overtones. Deep love. The only difference being, the Greek ideal—we never suggested in the series—physical love between the two. But it's the—we certainly had the feeling that the affection was sufficient for that if that were the particular style of the 23rd century" (Shatner 147–8). Thousands of fans wholeheartedly agree with him. The relationship between Spock and Kirk has always been one that was easily interpretable to be linked to homosexuality. Statements such as the one above made by Roddenberry or the one made by Spock when he states that "I have been and always shall be yours" (*Star Trek II: The Wrath of Khan*) have always encouraged fans (such as ourselves) to see beyond the relationship aimed for on the show and to incorporate every gesture, physical contact, and, more often than enough, every flirtatious gaze which resulted in the incredible homoerotic subtext delivered between these two characters and realize them for what they could be—the deep love and affection between two men. Even attempts made by Roddenberry and Captain Kirk (the TV character) could not dissuade fans from their own interpretations. In the Editor's Note of the novel *Star Trek: The Motion Picture* (1979), Gene Roddenberry had a pretend interview with Admiral Kirk.

> *Editor's note*: The human concept of *friend* is most nearly duplicated in Vulcan thought by the term *t'hy'la*, which can also mean *brother* and *lover*. Spock's recollection (from which this essay has drawn) is that it was a most difficult moment for him since he did indeed consider Kirk to have become his brother. However, because *t'hy'la* can be used to mean *lover*, and since Kirk's and Spock's friendship was unusually close, this has led to some speculation over whether they had actually indeed become lovers. At our request, Admiral Kirk supplied the following comment on this subject:

> "I was never aware of this *lovers* rumor, although I have been told that Spock encountered it several times. Apparently, he had always dismissed it with his characteristic lifting of his right eyebrow which usually connoted some combination of surprise, disbelief, and/or annoyance. As for myself, although I have no moral or other objections to physical love in any of its many Earthly, alien, and mixed forms, I have always found my best gratification in that creature *woman*. Also, I would dislike being thought of as so foolish that I would select a love partner who came into sexual heat only once every seven years" [Roddenberry 358].

Kirk/Spock shippers used this short excerpt as another bit of proof regarding their favorite couple. The whole exchange, while seemingly putting an end to the homoerotic subtexts, in reality, however, just sparked more discussion. While we are not going to dissect this short text, dozens of people have done so … dare to have a look.

Producers, writers, actors—no one was able to dissuade fans from their own perceived ideas and perceptions on fandoms. Fanfiction is the ultimate vehicle to live through these ideas and concepts and to realize what has not been realized in the source text. Fanfiction not only offers a way to fill the gaps for some fans, but it is also a tool that engages the readers in a conversation with each other. Fans are able to bring their own emotions, hopes, insecurities, and fears into the story. It is here that mainstream culture offers a place for non-mainstream expressions. Fanfiction, therefore, offers readers and fanfiction writers alike the possibility to explore dormant possibilities in the source texts. In "Keeping Promises to Queer Children" Ika Willis argues:

> Fan fiction, then, is generated first of all by a practice of reading which, rather than expressing its latent meanings, reorients a canonical text, opening its fictional world onto a set of demands determined by the individual reader and her knowledge of the (fictional and nonfictional) world(s)…It is through writing fan fiction that a fan can, firstly, make space for her own desires in a text which may not at first sight provide the resources to sustain them; and, secondly, recirculate the reoriented text among other fan without attempting to close the text on the "truth" of her reading [155].

Other authors such as Sarah Gwenllian Jones agree with this idea by adding that slash is not a "perverse 'resistance' to a given text's presumed heteronormativity but rather 'an actualization of latent textual elements'" (Jones 79–90). It can, therefore, be said that fanfiction functions as a kind of written speculation. Fanfiction writers are writing about the "what if…" What if all the gazes between Spock and Kirk portray more than friendship? What if the casual touches mean more between a human and a Vulcan touch-telepath? In fact, the whole series is very heteronormative and does not encourage any other reading, an aspect that is emphasized by the fact that "Heteronormative reading practices dominate in our culture: … even where characters' sexualities are not indicated in the … text, a wider cultural logic dictates that heterosexuality can be assumed while homosexuality must be proved" (Jones).

This suggestion may very well be the basis on which all slash fanfiction is written. Since every "text does not exist," and the logic of reading "is not deductive but associative: it associates with the material text … *other* ideas, *other* images, *other* significations" (Willis 158). Therefore, the practice of reading is a quality that affects fanfiction because readers are guided by their own responses and desires as they create a new text; a text is not simply "queer" but it can be interpreted as such. Hans-Georg Gadamer wrote in *Truth and Method* that "Not occasionally but always, the meaning is not merely reproductive but always a productive activity as well" (qtd. in Westphal 26). The reader may interpret the text differently than it was intended by the author, and even more importantly, some fans consider their work to be a conversation with the source text. This idea is also emphasized by Sandvoss Cornell in his essay, "The Death of the Reader," where he writes about the impossibility to separate content from meaning, but stresses that meaning can change in different forms of communication. He also endorses the idea that fans need to "rely on intertextual knowledge to interpret text and context" (25). Furthermore, Barthes states that:

> the modern scriptor is born simultaneously with the text, is in a way equipped with a being preceding or exceeding the writing, is not the subject with the book as predicate; there is no other time that that of the enunciation and every text is eternally written here and now … [and] that text is … a multi-dimensional space in which a variety of writings, none of them original, blend and clash [Willis 157].

Therefore, it could be argued that it is the duty of the reader to complete a text with his or her own knowledge and associations. In fanfiction, this aspect is facilitated by anonymity. In his essay "Kierkegard and the Anxiety of Authorship," Merold Westphal writes that Kierkegaard wrote under pseudonyms because he wanted to give his readers the space they would need to explore the text for themselves. He did not want to constrain them by being present as an author (Westphal 36). Anonymity, therefore, plays a role in the notion of authorship. To be anonymous offers internet users, including fanfiction authors and readers, the freedom to do what they want without "outing" themselves to the world. Nobody needs to provide their real name, address or birthday to the public. They are instead able to create a new identity. A new name. A new background. And moreover, the possibility to write and read whatever they want. These readers and authors can pursue their own interests and sexual preferences without having to fear being castigated or affronted. Fanfiction offers them not only the possibility to live out their fantasies and desires but also to explore and discover these desires. This idea also speaks to another reason for the interest in slash pairings.

By writing slash fanfiction women can experience the male part of a relationship. It is not just about writing pornography, it is about exploring the emotional factors, the reasons and the reasoning behind the actual occurrence. Willis explains that it is not only about eroticism but about criticism as well. Many other scholars share this interpretation. Catherine Driscoll explains in her essay, "One True Pairing—The Romance of Pornography and the Pornography of Romance," how pornography and romance cannot be divided. She explains that fanfiction plays with our fantasies and desires and that fanfiction writers project themselves into their stories. In "Normal Female Interest in Men Bonking," the authors say that slash is a way to "rewrite traditional masculinity" (Green, Jenkins and Jenkins 19). Slash, for many fans, is just the next step to explore the closeness and feelings between two characters. They literally do not care if what they do is the norm or if it is a reading that goes against the grain; they write about pairings that make sense to them, pairings whose attraction to each other appears obvious and inescapable. Writers of slash fanfiction often project their beliefs and insecurities into their assimilation of the source text; they use it not only to immerse themselves in their own desires but also to make their desires visible for others. The fans are operating inside their own "canonical law" (Foucault 37), they take the discourse and transform it into something new; an innovative unique text. The death of the author levels the way for the readers. It offers them the opportunity to express their own desires and beliefs and to reach millions of people at the same time. *Star Trek* fans successfully picked up where Roddenberry and others like him dropped the ball on LGBT relationships portrayed in this massive and influential franchise. This collection hopes to shed a bit more light on the subject of gender and sexuality as portrayed in *Star Trek*.

Many scholars contributed to this collection and we want to thank all of them for their dedication, faith, and hard work. Without their patience and their determination, this collection would have been lost.

The first essay in this collection, "The Bad Boy and Feminism: Analyzing Captain Kirk," by Suzan E. Aiken, analyzes the connection between Captain Kirk and feminism, challenging the traditional masculinity portrayed in the *TOS*.

Next Andrew M. Butler examines the shifts from a liberal or radical text of the Lyndon B. Johnson 1960s to a neoliberal or neoconservative text of the Reaganite long-1980s in his essay "Reinscribing Patriarchy in *Star Trek* Films, 1979–1994." Butler looks closely at images of patriarchy within the *Star Trek* motion pictures.

Teresa Cutler-Broyles addresses sexuality and power in her text "What We See When We Look in the Mirror: *Star Trek*'s Alternative Sexuality." She discusses how dark subjects such as rape, death and pain are only visualized in alternative universe scenarios such as the mirror verse.

The essay "On How to Overcome Nonfunctional Attachment Bonds in Outer Space" by Nadine Farghaly focuses on Aeryn Sun and Seven of Nine. Farghaly delves further into the ideas of attachment theory and the construction of new identities that were suppressed by outside forces.

Jack Fennell discusses gender issues in the *Star Trek* universe and what it means to be a transgender *Star Trek* fan in his essay "Infinite Diversity in Infinite Combinations: The Representation of Transgender Identities in *Star Trek*."

Andrew Howe, in "Deep Space Gender: Miles O'Brien, Julian Bashir and Masculinity," focuses on two very different male characters and how the show *Deep Space Nine* treats their masculinity.

Ken Monteith argues, in "From Supercrip to Assimilant: Normalcy, Bioculture and Disability in the *Star Trek* Universe," that to be a part of the Federation means to be willing to experience pain to a certain degree. He uses disability studies to write a compelling argument.

In "Mothering the Universe on *Star Trek*," Ericka Hoagland discusses instances of femininity and motherhood, highlighting that these concepts are more often than not shrouded in stereotypes or by absentness.

Eleanor Dobson looks upon Captain Janeway through the lens of a gothic heroine with a twist in "Photons and Phantoms: Kathryn Janeway as Gothic Heroine."

In "Strange New Worlds: Gender Disparity in *Star Trek: TOS*," Michael Pringle dissects *TOS*'s fresh take on heroic masculinity while it simultaneously fails to do the female crew members (and therefore viewers) justice.

Addressing the issue of female leadership within the Federation is Lorrie Palmer in her essay "Female Leadership, Sacrifice, and Technological Mastery on *Star Trek: Voyager*." She looks upon *STV*'s main female characters and villains to combine the show's narrative, its active circle of fandom, and society's evolving negotiation of gender roles.

In "'This is me cargo': The Commodification and Hyperreality of Women in 'Mudd's Women,'" Haley M. Fedor and Derek Frasure analyze *TOS* episode "Mudd's Women" to demonstrate the relationship between the female characters as well as the female viewers of this particular episode.

In "Hybrids: Interspecies Intercourse and Biracial Identity in *Star Trek*," Kevin J. Wetmore, Jr., declares that the hybrid characters in the *Star Trek* franchise function as a mirror of society's tension over mixed race identity. Focusing on Spock, Worf, and B'Elanna, Wetmore examines the idea of the hybrid from a cultural construct point of view.

Zara T. Wilkinson discusses the focus on the shift of women in her essay "Where No Girl Has Gone Before? Teenage Girls in *Star Trek*'s Strong Female Future." She looks closely at the transition to single officers, to families and family structures.

Lastly, Simon Bacon, in his piece "To Boldly Go Where No Undead Have

Gone Before: Comparisons between Gene Roddenberry's *Star Trek* and Bram Stoker's *Dracula*," showcases the similarities and connections between particular aspects of the franchise and the novel, respectively, and where the concerns of the British Empire in the late 19th century are oddly prescient of those of the Federation in the 23rd century.

We hope you enjoy the journey of reading this book, and that you will recognize it for what it is: an honest and appreciative look at 50 years of *Star Trek*.

Happy Birthday, *Star Trek*. May this be just the beginning of your journey.

Notes

1. Recent evidence suggests that the first kiss happened in the TV show *You in Your Small Corner* which aired on British television in 1962 (McKenzie).

Works Cited

Driscoll, Catherine. "One True Pairing—The Romance of Pornography and the Pornography of Romance." *Fan Fiction and Fan Communities in the Age of the Internet*. Eds. Karen Hellekson and Kristina Busse. Jefferson, NC: McFarland, 2006. 79–96. Print.

Foucault, Michel. *The History of Sexuality*. Trans. Robert Hurley. Vol. 1. New York: Random House, 1978. Print.

Jones, Sarah Gwenllian. "The Sex Lives of Cult Television Characters." *Screen* 43 (2002): 79–90. Print.

Kay, Jonathan. "Gay 'Trek.'" *Salon.com RSS*. N.p., 30 June 2001. Web. 03 Nov. 2016. Web.

McKenzie, Sheena. "Uncovered Footage Reveals 'First' Interracial Kiss on TV, Before Star Trek." *CNN*. Cable News Network, 21 Nov. 2015. Web. 07 Nov. 2016.

Nichols, Nichelle. *Beyond Uhura: Star Trek and Other Memories*. New York: Boulevard Books, 1994. Print.

Roddenberry, Gene. *Star Trek, the Motion Picture: A Novel*. New York: Simon & Schuster, 1979. Print.

Sandvoss, Cornel. "The Death of the Reader." *Fandom: Identities and Communities in a Mediated World*. Eds. Jonathan Gray, Cornel Sandvoss, and C.L. Harrington. New York University Press, 2007. 19–32. Print.

Shatner, William, Myrna Culbreath, and Sandra Marshak. *Shatner: Where No Man: The Authorized Biography of William Shatner*. New York: Grosset and Dunlap, 1979. Print.

Westphal, Merold. "Kierkegaard and the Anxiety of Authorship." *The Death and Resurrection of the Author?* Ed. William Irwin. Westport, CT: Greenwood Press, 2002. 23–45. Print.

Willis, Ika. "Keeping Promises to Queer Children." *Fan Fiction and Fan Communities in the Age of the Internet* Eds. Karen Hellekson and Kristina Busse. Jefferson, NC: McFarland, 2006. 153–170. Print.

The Bad Boy and Feminism
Analyzing Captain Kirk

Suzan E. Aiken

These Are the Voyages

The 1960s, rife with upheaval and change, offer many potential topics for analysis in political, industrial, and social arenas. Feminism entered a Second Wave, moving from suffrage to women in the workplace, pioneering new professional roles for women and the ideal of "equal pay for equal work" (Breaking Down Barriers for Women). Political organizations such as the National Organization for Women (NOW), founded in 1966, helped to lobby for change, advancing the adoption of the Equal Rights Amendment, which has yet to be added to the Constitution. Meanwhile, television reflected the variant sets of social and political values in its program offerings. Popularly rated primetime programs included variety shows (*The Lawrence Welk Show*, *The Red Skelton Hour*), sitcoms (*The Lucy Show*, *The Beverly Hillbillies*), episodic westerns (*The Virginian*, *Bonanza)* and police dramas (*The Man from U.N.C.L.E.*, *The F.B.I.*). Most shows, such as *Bewitched* and *The Lucy Show* featured the so-called nuclear family, while others like *My Three Sons* and *The Andy Griffith Show* featured a single-parent household, but a household in order with traditional roles for men and women. *Star Trek* appeared in the fall lineup in 1966 and featured a crew of diverse people on a ship exploring "strange new worlds" in outer space. The program lasted only three seasons, but captured larger audiences while in syndication, launched other series and films, and is now recognized as being very influential. While *Lost in Space*, *The Time Tunnel*, *The Invaders*, other science fiction programming was available, the program *Star Trek* and its crew have long remained the focus of attention for multiple, diverse audiences.

James T. Kirk (William Shatner), Captain of USS *Enterprise*, leads his crew of 428 on many adventures as they advance their mission (Charlie X). While Captain Kirk is not always onscreen, he is widely known as a friend to the ship's doctor, Bones, played by DeForest Kelley, and to Science and First Officer, Spock, played by Leonard Nimoy; he is known as the narrating voice of the Captain's log portions and the opening sequence of the show. In popular culture, descriptions of Captain Kirk often discuss his masculinity, his bad-boy characteristics, and his swagger. These Alpha male qualities appear prominent in the re-launch of the Captain Kirk character in the 2009 *Star Trek* film. However, the *implied* overall nature of the show explores diverse ways of thinking and being in the future as well as undiscovered star systems. Noting the diversity of characters in the historic context, Dockterman identified an audience perception that "*Star Trek* gave life to that future where skin tone, gender and nationality did not matter" (17). Further, theater critic Richard Zoglin notes the adventures of the *Enterprise* "were often thinly disguised allegories for very current social problems" (12). Potentially, audiences can see the struggles of feminism and the gendered character, the stereotypical male.

The rise of Second Wave feminism sought to change the way that the female gender is framed, constructed, and limited, and these changes resulted in challenges for men. Thus, within the complexity of gender and politics of a varied crew of humans and non-humans alike, Captain Kirk's character is challenged. Kirk's masculinity is constrained by the interplay of oppositions, questions, and problems set in motion by the feminist movement. The evidence for these constraints play out onscreen in characters, settings, and plots of *Star Trek*. Analyzing Kirk in the context-specific *Star Trek* can provide an opening for additional perspectives and ongoing conversations. With close viewing of the first episodes, this study will seek out the constraints or juxtapositions of the historic context of feminism and traditional masculinity as characters are introduced to television audiences. Considering Second Wave feminism's attention to women, this study unearths additional challenges to traditional masculinity in the exploration of the Captain Kirk character. By examining Kirk as a traditional male, this essay discovers more about the historical shift in feminist thinking and the resulting challenges confronting the stereotypical male.

The Scope of the Mission

Feminism is a movement concerned with socially constructed binaries applied to gender and sex. To imagine a specific definition of feminism would be insufficient in depth and breadth, and beyond the scope of this essay. Instead, I carefully suggest there are some concepts that could be contemplated as broad enough to summarize feminist ideals, paired with the understanding that there are many feminisms and none should be discounted. Second Wave feminism in the 1960s first provoked thought and action about roles available to women, challenging the social norms, and then feminism turned its attention to equality in the workplace, in hiring practices, and in pay. Frequently linked to Simone de Beauvoir's suggestion that women were possessions or property (Breaking Down Barriers for Women), 1960s feminist thought was stimulated by Freiden's *The Feminine Mystique*. Friedan introduced a problem "which throws into question the standards of feminine normality, feminine adjustment, feminine fulfillment, and feminine maturity" (31). Frieden interrogated the roles available to women, suggesting that the socially accepted nuclear family was, in some ways, offensive. Similarly, Greig suggests that "changes in the gender order as a result of challenges [...] to the division of labour are [...] undermining men's masculine identities predicated on the subordination of women" (1). Essentially, roles for women undermine masculinity because new roles for women, even non-gendered roles, are established in compliance with a masculine structure. Important moments for gender equality included, but were not limited to: the Equal Pay Act of 1963; Title VII of the Civil Rights Act of 1964 became law in the U.S.; and, in 1966 Barbara Jordan, the first African American woman in the Texas legislature, was elected to the Texas Senate in 1966. The decade that launched *Star Trek* also brought Second Wave feminist activism, whose roots from the 1940s lasted beyond the 1960s, and gave rise to new branches of feminist thought. For the purposes of this research, references to Second Wave Feminism aim to invoke the concepts of new roles for women outside of the home, women in the workplace, and equal hiring practices. These concepts presented new challenges to roles and spaces previously and comfortably held by men.

During the Second Wave, masculinity was treated as a binary, opposite to femininity. Much more deeply connected is the idea of masculinity as "a continuously and contested set of interlocking hierarchical social relations" (Elias and Beasley). Masculinity is contested during the Second Wave, and questioned what it meant to be "real" men and women; thus the tensions multiplied between an *either-or* binary rather than opportunities for a *both-and* existence. Cixous said "A man is always proving something; he has to "show off," show up others. Masculine profit is almost always mixed up with a success that is socially defined" (87). Any invasion of the typically masculine spaces, roles, or responsibilities is considered a threat to masculine dominance, and any divergence is a potential threat. So-called threats perceived in political and social structures, using an either/or binary, a feminine/masculine opposition, would undermine the inherent hierarchy in those structures and thus redistribute the power inequalities that serve those masculine structures. Concrete examples of those institutional structures in the program

Star Trek manifest in the military rank of officers, the Federation, and Starfleet. There are masculine structures and masculine bodies. The perceived physical nature of gender can be undermined. Pilcher and Whelehan idealize that "the physical differences between men and women should not adversely affect their ability to take on roles more traditionally associated with one sex or the other" (28). The historic context claimed new roles for women, and further challenged female stereotypes. Feminist claims and ideals surfaced, conceptually, in the qualities and behaviors of Captain James T. Kirk. So, the character is at the center of this study, focusing on his traditional leadership role and obedience to socially-constructed boundaries for gender roles. The very first episodes invite viewers to become acquainted with characters, and Captain Kirk in particular, prior to longer story arcs and development of character growth and change. For the purposes of close-reading, the corpus is narrowed to the first four episodes: "The Man Trap," "Charlie X," "Where No Man Has Gone Before," and "The Naked Time."

To Explore, to Seek Out

The First Episode—A Routine Medical Examination

Star Trek's pilot episode was created and reviewed by the network in November 1964, introducing Captain Christopher Pike, Dr. Phillip Boyce, Mr. Spock, and other characters. The original episode does not resemble the cast or crew with which historic and modern audiences are most familiar. The first episode proper of *Star Trek*, "The Man Trap," aired on September 8, 1966, and featured Captain James Tiberius Kirk, Dr. Leonard "Bones" McCoy, and Commander Spock—as well as Lieutenant Nyota Uhura. Some audiences also remember the Captain's Yeoman, Janice Rand, who takes a significant part in the plot points of the first four episodes. Other favorite characters such as Lieutenant Hikaru Sulu, Lieutenant Commander Montgomery "Scotty" Scott, and Ensign Pavel Chekov were introduced in the second, third, and fourth episodes. The first episode brings audiences to another world, introduces the roles and relationships of the crew of the starship *Enterprise*, and demonstrates the potential meanings and ethics for the mission of exploring "strange new worlds" and seeking "new life and new civilizations." "The Man Trap" has the crew beaming down to a planet to bring supplies and to conduct a health check on the two Earth inhabitants, an archeologist and his wife. As the episode begins, audiences hear Kirk's narration of the Captain's Log, but see Commander Spock in the Captain's chair, the ship's bridge and crew before seeing Captain Kirk.

This juxtaposition of authority figures begins the analysis of Captain Kirk's character: a subordinate officer in the captain's chair, a captain away on a mission. Captain Kirk's disruption of an expectation allows this study to consider the ways disruption and disobedience may be productive forces used to interrogate gendered roles and stereotypes. The best place to start is this opening sequence of the first episode, during which Captain Kirk's voice narrates but Mr. Spock is in the captain's chair on the bridge. Arguably, a character's introduction typically places that character in the front and center. Here, audiences only hear Captain Kirk's voice explaining the scene and setting the tone:

> On board the *Enterprise*, Mister Spock temporarily in command. On the planet the ruins of an ancient and long-dead civilization. Ship's surgeon McCoy and myself are now beaming down to the planet's surface. Our mission, routine medical examination of archaeologist Robert Crater and his wife Nancy. Routine but for the fact that Nancy Crater is that one woman in Doctor McCoy's past ["The Man Trap"].

Audiences discover that Kirk has gone on this undertaking, not only for the purposes of the *Enterprise*'s mission, but also because Kirk is supporting his friend, Dr. McCoy, at an emotional meeting with a cherished ex-girlfriend: "that one woman in Doctor McCoy's past." Considering traditional masculine roles of the 1960s, viewers may have been surprised that the leadership of the vessel is in subordinate hands, the main character is away and supporting his friend during an emotional reunion. Audiences hear Kirk's voice within 5 seconds of starting the episode, but do not see him until 25 seconds after that—after audiences have seen the exterior of the *Enterprise*, the planet, Mr. Spock, the bridge, and Lt. Uhuru. This ship's captain is, potentially, a leader who trusts others to lead ethically in his absence, and a leader who is physically and emotionally present for his crew (or, one who is absent). Audiences expect a masculine leader to be first on screen, in command on the bridge, separate from and above the crew as well as emotionally detached or aloof. Captain Kirk has given audiences some insight to the potential disruptiveness of Kirk's character.

The First Episode—As Commander of the Ship

Captain Kirk's voice narrates the captain's log as well as the series' opening credits, controlling the delivery of information to the audience. The show's opening theme is a combination of the narration of the starship's mission underscored by composed music:

> Space: the final frontier. These are the voyages of the starship *Enterprise*. Its five-year mission: to explore strange new worlds, to seek out new life and new civilizations, to boldly go *where no man has gone before* [The Man Trap"].

The starship's purpose is also cited by the captain and crew of the *Enterprise* many times during the course of the original series and subsequent spinoffs. This mission is key to the audience's understanding the structure of the Starship, the directives for Captain Kirk, and to introducing the future organizational, political structures known as the United Federation of Planets and Starfleet Command. The point is that the *Enterprise* has rules, has a governing body, and thus falls under the leadership of Captain Kirk who must also uphold rules, procedures, and protocol of these governing bodies. The mission is part of the Captain's character and his masculinity. These roles and structures are masculine stereotypes, and in context, are generally expected by audiences.

When Captain Kirk and Dr. McCoy first see the archeologist, Dr. Crater, there is resistance to conforming to the rules. Dr. Crater, on the planet with his wife for approximately five years, wants to be left alone to his work. The tense exchange between Dr. Crater, Dr. McCoy, and Captain Kirk contribute to Kirk's interests in following orders:

> CRATER: Doubtless the good surgeon will enjoy prodding and poking us with his arcane machinery. Go away, we don't want you.
>
> MCCOY: What you want is unimportant right now. What you will get is required by the book.
>
> KIRK: Quote. All research personnel on alien planets are required to have their health certified by a starship surgeon at one year intervals. Like it or not, Professor, as commander of the starship, I'm required—
>
> CRATER: To show your gold braid to everyone. You love it, don't you ["The Man Trap"].

The role of the ship's captain is clear: to declare and enforce rules, to execute orders, to lead and complete missions; so, Kirk asserts and performs this aspect of his position. Both Dr. Crater and Dr. McCoy are emotionally invested in their own agendas, and in a battle of wills: a stereotypical, competitive exchange. Kirk is obedient to social norms, and upholds his gendered role; Kirk is "showing his gold braid," a military rank, as Crater implied. From a different perspective, it is possible that Kirk's interjection is an emotional support to Dr. McCoy. While Kirk and McCoy exhibit a close friendship onscreen, Kirk's authority supersedes both Dr. McCoy as the ship's doctor and Dr. Crater as the lead scientist on the planet. McCoy's role as doctor-subordinate and Crater's role as archeologist-subject are both roles that exist and fall under the scope of Kirk-as-captain. This example shows audiences a traditional leader that knows, follows, and supports traditional structures of power. However, this example of authority and protocol is key to later considering Captain Kirk as one who disobeys, since this example shows Kirk using his authority to advance the primary mission on the planet: a routine medical examination.

In a later interaction between Kirk, McCoy, and Crater, the mission of the Starship *Enterprise* comes in to question. At this point in the plot, Crewman Darnell, has died mysteriously. Kirk and McCoy express concern for the safety of the Craters, but Dr. and Mrs. Crater only want the requested supplies and to be left alone. Dr. Crater, again, opposes the imposition and intrusion of the crew on the couple's lives and routines:

> CRATER: Captain, considering the inescapable fact that you are a trespasser on my planet—
> KIRK: Your complaint is noted, sir. Look, something we don't understand killed one of my men. It could prove to be a danger to you and Mrs. Crater, too.
> CRATER: We've been here for almost five years. If there were anything hostile here we would know about it, wouldn't we? ["The Man Trap"].

Crater aggressively resists, and in response Kirk is seemingly sympathetic. Here, Crater asserts himself as inhabitant and Kirk as a trespasser. In doing so, Crater places himself in a position of power outside the roles and structures of the *Enterprise*; he threatens Kirk's authority. Conversely, in the exchange of words, Captain Kirk tries to find common ground with Dr. Crater. Kirk suggests there is good reason to worry and gives Dr. Crater an opportunity to shift his resistant masculine role to a protective masculine role with the potential danger to Crater's wife, Nancy. Kirk offers Crater an alternate standpoint, and presents the position as a suggestion rather than an order, a less aggressive approach than the previous example of Kirk simply using authority to overcome Crater's resistance.

In contrast, Crater does not change his position, and Crater verbally jabs with a question of logic. Crater's challenge to Kirk is answered as the conversation continues:

> KIRK: One of the missions of the Enterprise is to protect human life in places like this. I'm going to have to ask you and Mrs. Crater to stay aboard my ship until we find out what killed that crewman.
> CRATER: But you can't do that.
> KIRK: But I can, Professor ["The Man Trap"].

Kirk's authority removes any possible arguments from Crater. As the captain, Kirk has the power to make a decision that impacts the lives and routines of Dr. and Nancy Crater. Kirk is supported in his role by the Starfleet and Federation, masculine structures which give power to the masculine role. At first, Kirk presents an alternative to allow Dr. Crater a position of masculine guardian: Kirk suggests there is a danger, Crater can be a protective, dominant male and still yield to Kirk's authority. Yet, Dr. Crater refuses Kirk's offer of this face-saving role. So, when his authority is threatened, Kirk applies his jurisdiction to force Dr. and Mrs. Crater to leave the planet. Audiences expect a traditionally masculine role to take charge, and now see a captain using conviction and agency to gain control of a situation.

This scene uncovers a disruption of the *Enterprise*'s missions. At this point in the series, audiences only know the mission of the starship to "explore," "seek out," and "boldly go." In the combative conversation with Dr. Crater, Kirk *adds*: "to protect human lives"; Kirk uses his authority to interpret and expand the mission. Disobedience implies that there is a structure of rules or authority which must be followed, and that those structures are refused, manipulated, or ignored. For example, a masculine stereotype might take the woman, and leave the man on the planet to eliminate the challenge to authority. This use of authority is a disruption—to protect is a masculine action, but the addition of "human life" is inclusive, feminist thought. Captain Kirk does not use his authority to "protect *my* men" or "protect *my* crew," instead, he "protects human life," expanding the scope of the mission to be inclusive of *all* human life. His masculine role is stretched, perhaps, uncomfortably, to include the challenges to his role.

Further, and logically, it would be a bad idea to bring aboard persons (or, aliens) who are not among the crew as it may endanger the rest of the crew or the ship, undermining the protection of all. Kirk, instead, extends his concern for humankind to those persons he does not know, even when those persons are not likeable, are not compliant with rules, and are different from him. The tension in Kirk's motivation may include the worries of his friend, Dr. McCoy, for Nancy, but protecting a friend from suffering is a masculine task. Nonetheless the authority used here to disrupt and extend the mission of the ship and to disrupt the human lives on the planet are a stretch for a masculine captain. He is abrupt, direct, and conclusive, and, at the same time, he cares for the crew, the planet's human inhabitants, *and* his friend, Dr. McCoy. It is with anxiety, the perceived threat to his authority, that Captain Kirk expands his masculine role as upholding the safety and well-being of others within a frame of rule-following as he concludes the argument using his authority.

The First Episode—My Demonstration of Concern Will Not Change What Happened

Captain Kirk's emotions, his ability to care, are often on display in the episodes of the original series, disrupting the concept of a stoic commanding officer, and challenging the expectations for male stereotypes and gender roles. In the first episode, Kirk's narrative explains that the visit to examine Dr. and Mrs. Crater is going to be emotionally challenging for Dr. McCoy because of McCoy's connection to Nancy Crater. Kirk supports Dr. McCoy on this "routine visit." During the first moments that the audience sees Captain Kirk, he fondly teases Dr. McCoy. The first interaction between Kirk and McCoy can be interpreted as playful, even juvenile:

> KIRK: Shall we pick some flowers, Doctor? When a man visits an old girlfriend she usually expects something like that.
> MCCOY: Is that how you get girls to like you, by bribing them? There doesn't seem to be anybody around, does there.
> KIRK: They'll be along. You rushed us down ten minutes early ["The Man Trap"].

This is not the authoritative male that audiences would expect landing on a planet, on alert. Traditional masculinity dictates that a "real man" would not be openly emotional, even though there is a sarcastic tone. Being emotional means being vulnerable and deferring power. Kirk begins by teasing Bones with the suggestion of picking flowers, and then he belittles Bones' sensitivity by remarking that they arrived too early because Bones was in a rush. Kirk's face smiles, his eyes twinkle, his tone sardonic. The first time viewers see him they do not see a professional, military personality: this display of lighthearted, mischievous affection introduces a less-than-serious Captain Kirk. Kirk values McCoy as a friend, and the nature of the friendship is clear. At this point, audiences do not see a captain who is emotionally connected with his team of officers, but there is potential because Kirk's actions suggest he may be the kind of person who is emotionally connected and supportive. In a modern perspective, the scene between the two may even evoke the term "bro-mance": a romantic-like relationship between two heterosexual male friends. In context, this friendship is how the captain is introduced to the audience: playfully teasing his friend, playing on romantic stereotypes, making eyes with and offering flowers to Dr. McCoy.

In spite of the playfulness, Captain Kirk wields authority and demands professionalism. For example, later when the captain and doctor are discussing poison as the cause of the crewman's death, audiences see the complex character's roles:

> McCoy: Jim, don't tell me my business. He could not have swallowed any. My instruments would have picked up any trace of it whatsoever.
> Kirk: Then what kills a healthy man.
> McCoy: I'll tell you something else. This man shouldn't be dead. I can't find anything wrong with him. According to all the tests he should just get up and walk away from here. I don't know. I'll have the tests double-checked. My eyes may be tricking me. I swear, Jim, when I first saw her she looked just as I'd known her ten years ago. Granted, for a moment I may have been looking at her through a romantic haze.
> Kirk: How your lost love affects your vision, Doctor, doesn't interest me. I've lost a man. I want to know what killed him.
> McCoy: Yes, sir ["The Man Trap"].

In this exchange, Kirk and McCoy end the conversation on a recognition of their respective roles to each other and to their professional roles. Kirk calls McCoy by "Doctor," yet Dr. McCoy is calling Captain Kirk by his first name,

Jim, and concludes by saying "Yes, sir." Kirk performs as a traditional masculine leader, and, when challenged, Kirk maintains order by guilt-shaming Dr. McCoy: his lost love clouds his professional ability. In the first example, McCoy was on the planet to perform the duties of a ship's doctor—as he is in this exchange. In this scene, however, Kirk's emphasis is on emotional distance and professional conduct. In this example, Kirk is not a friend but a commanding officer assessing McCoy's work, and placing McCoy's role into the hierarchy. Friendship and loss both threaten Kirk's authority and his ability to maintain control. Kirk exudes tension between his roles of friend and captain. So, instead of a caring friend (more feminine), Kirk takes a stable position of masculine authority and control, demanding facts and answers. Kirk's behavior suggests that Kirk is an emotional being and capable of openly demonstrating those emotions to others *unless* his authority is challenged. Kirk's emotional displays are one way that feminist tensions play out onscreen.

By contrast, Kirk's other primary officer, Commander Spock, who is half-Vulcan and half-human, shows little if any emotion. Spock's culture as a Vulcan places emphasis on logic, not human emotion. This contrast between logic and emotion is often featured as a means of exploring themes and creating conflict on the television program. At the beginning of the episode, after the crewman dies, the doctor and captain return to the ship. Viewers see Spock's response in this scene on the bridge:

> CREWMAN: Transporter room to Bridge. Landing party returning. They report one death.
> SPOCK: Bridge acknowledging.
> UHURA: I don't believe it.
> SPOCK: Explain.
> UHURA: You explain. That means that somebody is dead and you just sit there. It could be Captain Kirk. He's the closest thing you have to a friend.
> SPOCK: Lieutenant, my demonstration of concern will not change what happened. The transporter room is very well-manned and they will call if they need my assistance ["The Man Trap"].

In this scene, Uhura, a woman in a professional role on the bridge, remarks on Spock's lack of emotion. The crewman on the intercom reports that someone on the planet died, and Spock "acknowledges." Spock responds by thinking logically: the death has already happened, he cannot change it, and his responsibility is to the crew and ship. In this scene, lack of emotion is the performance of male leadership. Spock and Uhuru's conversation is a direct contrast to Kirk's emotions and the intensity with which Kirk wields the sense of responsibility as an authority figure to Dr. McCoy and the rest of the crew. Spock's lack of emotion upholds the gendered role of male to Uhura's feminine claim that death requires an emotional response. In either case, whether

Spock's logic or Kirk's hierarchy, masculine authority is claimed and wielded as superior to the challenges posed.

When faced with the death of a crewman, Kirk's tells McCoy he needs answers. Kirk tries to maintain control by pursuing fact, though the contrasts of emotionally intense wording and his masculine behavior display anxiety. Earlier, at the point when they find the body of the crewman, Kirk is demanding as he exclaims, "I've just lost a crewman, Mrs. Crater. I want to know what happened." The loss of a crewman symbolizes a loss of control, and, therefore, a shift in power. Kirk personalizes and then internalizes the loss as part of his jurisdiction. Later, as he is insistent on finding the root cause of the death, Kirk expresses not just an emotional response but a physical one, "We're all aware of the need for salt on a hot and arid planet like this, Professor, but it's a mystery, and I don't like mysteries. They give me a bellyache and I've got a beauty right now" (The Man Trap). Kirk's claim to his authority, his masculine role, has been undermined by the mystery of the loss and he has reached "an uneasy equilibrium with respect to his male dominance" (Schwartz). The "mystery," unknown and feminine, results in Kirk's instability. Thus, anxious, he exhibits unstable bodily symptoms. Male emotions and the masculine body are a part of the performance of traditional masculinity which defines itself by the opposite: feminine emotions and female body.

The First Episode—"I'm sorry, Bones"

What is of interest, though, is the use of emotions instead of logic. Rather than respond with the logic that Spock demonstrates, Kirk's need for knowing is in tandem with his emotional state. Kirk demonstrates a kind of anxiousness that mimics grasping at knowledge, at the power that comes from undoing the mystery. Oddly, at this point, he is not a detached captain waiting for the facts and reports to come from others; Kirk is anxious, with a bellyache. The tension between Kirk's role as "caregiver-friend" and "captain" destabilize the solid ground of traditional masculinity. These interactions are a concrete connection to his claim of protecting human life while also exemplifying and embodying the anxiety produced by challenges to his masculinity. Kirk's emotions appear at different times and in different ways, often to serve masculine structures and roles. The real conflict appears when feminine and masculine motives clash resulting in Kirk's anxiety.

The value of masculine emotions and the gendered roles are explored further at the end of the episode. In one of the very last scenes, McCoy, Spock, and Kirk confront the alien aboard the *Enterprise*. The alien that has killed crewpersons, that is the last of its kind, and that has taken the form of Nancy Crater. With the alien cornered, ready to attack, this scene exposes several threats to masculinity:

McCoy: I won't shoot Nancy.
Spock: This is not Nancy. (punches repeatedly) If she were Nancy, could she take this?
McCoy: Stop it! Stop it, Spock! Stop it! (Nancy sends Spock flying with one slap)
Spock: Is that Nancy, Doctor?
McCoy: No. (Nancy moves to Kirk again) No! (She transforms into the alien body. Kirk screams, McCoy fires the phaser, the alien changes back into Nancy).
Nancy: Leonard. Leonard, no. Leonard, please.
McCoy: Lord, forgive me. (He fires again and she dies)
Kirk: I'm sorry, Bones ["The Man Trap"].

In this scene, Kirk's authority is physically challenged as the alien overpowers him. The woman/alien is going to kill Kirk, thus removing him from the hierarchy, symbolic of the imagined struggles of women in the workplace. Again, both literally and figuratively, Kirk's masculine role relies on support structures and roles. This scene, as Kirk is attacked and subdued by the alien, externalizes the challenges to Kirk's dominance and his place in the traditionally masculine hierarchy. Kirk's screams embody the anxiety produced by the upheaval of gendered roles and in gendered spaces.

Once the alien is dead, Kirk's attention does not shift to the ship, the crew, the dying of an alien species, or his own masculine role and authority. There is not a traditional celebratory and congratulatory scene with men high-fiving. The scene closes with Kirk's emotional declaration to McCoy, when he says, simply, "I'm sorry, Bones." The tone is familiar, using the Doctor's nickname; the line conveys tenderness and sympathy: aspects of Kirk's character echo the historic context and the conflict of feminist struggles which result in masculine anxieties. Instead of masculine face-saving after crying out in fear, or bravado claims about championing a win over the alien, Kirk reaches out, emotionally, in support of his friend who faces two losses. McCoy, as a doctor, preserves life, and in a laser's blast, he has killed the whole of an alien lineage *and* his lost love, Nancy. Kirk's utterance is not an apology, but is sympathy. The episode begins with the friendship of McCoy and Kirk, and ends with their friendship. The episode is the first time audiences meet Captain Kirk, and this scene resonates feminist thinking concerned with gendered power and relationships.

The Second Episode— Is There Nothing You Can Do?

"Charlie X," the second episode, which aired September 15, 1966, has Captain Kirk in a battle of mind and body with a teenager aboard the starship. Charlie X, a rescued teen who follows his emotions, is omnipotent, and he begins eliminating obstacles by killing crew and taking over the *Enterprise*. Yet, when Charlie's "caregivers" come to take him away, Kirk's compassion overrules his own desire to have the threat to his crew and ship eliminated:

> CHARLIE: I won't do it again. Please, I'll be good. I won't ever do it again. I'm sorry about the Antares. I'm sorry! When I came aboard! Please, I want to go with you. Help me!
>
> KIRK: The boy belongs with his own kind.
>
> THASIAN: That would be impossible.
>
> KIRK: With training, we can teach him to live in our society. If he can be taught not to use his power
>
> THASIAN: We gave him the power so he could live. He will use it, always, and he would destroy you and your kind, or you would be forced to destroy him to save yourselves.
>
> KIRK: Is there nothing you can do?
>
> THASIAN: We offer him life, and we will take care of him. Come, Charles.
>
> CHARLIE: Oh, please, don't let them take me. I can't even touch them! Janice, they can't feel. Not like you! They don't love! Please, I want to stay ["Charlie X"].

As he did with Dr. Crater, Kirk extends his jurisdiction to those persons outside of his own crew. Kirk challenges an omnipotent alien being to allow Charlie to stay aboard a starship that Charlie nearly destroyed, and the opposition between masculine structure and feminine spaces is made visible. Kirk struggles between his ability to care (feminine) and his masculine responsibilities: Kirk must protect his ship and crew. Yet, after nearly losing all control of ship, crew, and his own body to Charlie's powers, Kirk feels compassion for the teen. His emotional femininity seemingly takes precedence over his traditional masculinity. Perhaps, Kirk demonstrates that the hierarchy of order and control can be set aside to create a space for compassion. However, Charlie is on Kirk's ship, under Kirk's jurisdiction. Thus, Kirk's compassion is a masculine action that maintains order by keeping roles aligned. Kirk suggests the boy stay with "his own kind" and that Charlie's powers can be controlled, that masculine structures and authority could teach and train the teen to submit to social mores. Even though Kirk and his crew just faced certain destruction, Kirk cannot release the boy from the masculine structure of the ship. The juxtaposition between what *can* and what *cannot* be controlled is argued onscreen. As long as the misuse of power and emotions are properly controlled, and the being (in this case, Charlie X) finds a place in the norms of socially defined behavior, then compassion is appropriate to display or "show off" as Cixous would suggest. The Thasian, an alien being/race beyond the scope and jurisdiction of humanity and masculine structures, removes and controls Kirk's struggle by removing Charlie from the *Enterprise*.

The Third Episode—It Is My Duty to Listen

Earlier, dialogue examined from the first episode shows a point where Kirk deems himself "commander of the ship." By contrast, in the opening scene, viewers did not see Kirk in his captain's chair, they saw Spock who is not the commander. Then, viewers saw Kirk enforce the rules of routine medical exams, and later, in contrast, interpret and extend the ship's mission to protect human life. Within the scope of masculine roles, Kirk modifies his power but also experiences anxiety. Other characters fall under the jurisdiction and control of Kirk's masculine authority, and they are assigned their gendered functions within the frame that traditional masculine structures afford: Spock is less emotional, Crater is resistant and controlling, McCoy is curious, Charlie X needs training to fit in. Yet, in some places, the lines between gendered stereotypes are blurred. Audiences are introduced to a captain that believes in rules but will interpret them, and who will leave the captain's chair. Kirk's character varies from traditional masculinity, and becomes anxious; the masculinity seems malleable, but ultimately is not.

In a scene from the third episode, "Where No Man Has Gone Before," which aired for the first time on September 22nd, 1966, audiences see the ship's leaders in a round table discussion. The episode does not feature the characters Dr. McCoy or Lt. Uhura (as seen in the other episodes) because it was written and produced before those two characters were created and cast. The episode features a cast that includes other characters such as helmsman Lieutenant Commander Gary Mitchell, ship's psychiatrist Dr. Elizabeth Dehner, ship's physician Dr. Mark Piper (instead of McCoy), Communications Officer Alden (instead of Uhura), Navigator Lee Kelso, Yeoman Smith (instead of Yeoman Rand) and Lieutenant Leslie. The third episode is credited, too, as the official moment that "Scottie" was introduced as Chief Engineer Montgomery Scott. In the plot of the episode, the crew discovers a ship's recorder. Subsequently, in playing the recording, and following the lost ship's coordinates, some crew members are killed, but Gary Mitchell and Dr. Elizabeth Dehner are affected with psychic powers. Mitchell begins to transform in aggressive and dangerous ways, causing concern; and in response, Kirk assembles a meeting of his core advisors to discuss the events (as he does in many episodes). Included in the meeting are Spock, Sulu, Scott, Navigator Kelso, Dr. Piper, and Dr. Dehner. During the round table discussion, Kirk suggests that listening is part of his role:

> SPOCK: (to Dehner) Our subject is not Gary Mitchell. Our concern is, rather, what he is mutating into.
>
> DEHNER: I know those from your planet aren't supposed to have feelings like we do, Mister Spock, but to talk that way about a man you've worked next to for years is worse than—

KIRK: That's enough, Doctor.
DEHNER: I don't think so. I understand you least of all. Gary told me that you've been friends since he joined the service; that you asked for him aboard your first command.
KIRK: It is my duty, whether pleasant or unpleasant, to listen to the reports, observations, even speculations, on any subject that might affect the safety of this vessel, and it's my science officer's duty to see I'm provided with that. Go ahead, Mister Spock ["Where No Man has Gone Before"].

Kirk shifts the conversation back to Spock. Kirk, again, takes control of the meeting and uses his authority to assert a value set. During the meeting, a woman calls out the objectivity of a man, defies Kirk, and by virtue of doing so calls "into question the masculinity of the man's interest simply by showing an interest in it" (Schwartz). This scene exemplifies the challenges of men "being unable to adhere closely enough to their prescribed masculine roles" (Greig). It is Kirk's job to listen to reports, but Kirk asserts his role in the hierarchy, the subsequent roles of those present, and addresses the autonomy of Dr. Dehner. Spock's point, "what he is mutating into," draws attention to the chaos of unknown changes. So, when the responsibilities of women change, roles are questioned, and there is tension on the responsibilities of men. While Kirk implies that both of Spock and Dehner are vital to the conversation, Kirk is only genuinely listening to Mr. Spock. Kirk's authority identifies and categorizes the roles, and leaves truly alternative voices out of the hierarchy. In this case, the unpleasant perspective is coming from a man, and conforms to the logical and unemotional male code that identifies another man as a "mutating other." The scene exposes the conflict in the changing roles of men and women.

Alternatively, this example shows some complexity as, in theory, Kirk is asking for all of the leaders to provide information, and Kirk is advocating for listening to all of the perspectives, including those of a woman. In this meeting, viewers see an engaged and heated discussion that includes a woman in a position of leadership, and a woman able to stand her ground. Dehner speaks assertively and defiantly to her commanding officer, Captain Kirk, with little or no official consequences. Once Kirk interrupts Dehner's verbal exchange with Spock, and Kirk's position in the hierarchy is established, Kirk allows Dehner to finish her statements *when* those statements are directed at Kirk. Dehner is in a position of authority, and asserts her contrasting opinions and ideas openly, challenging the gendered space of the meeting. This small part of the whole exchange emphasizes a unique investment in identifying and playing through masculine-feminine tensions. Kirk could easily silence the women, people of color, and non-humans in the meeting, and devalue the importance and complexity of their insight. So, the assertion of power is to place participants in a hierarchy but not to silence them fully.

This space is a different sort of workplace: a masculine space with some non-traditional elements that creates some anxiety.

The Fourth Episode—A Few Days, No Braid on My Shoulder

During the fourth episode "The Naked Time," which first aired on September 29, 1966, the crew of the *Enterprise* fights an unknown pathogen brought aboard after a recovery mission. Overcome by the disease, Kirk becomes uninhibited, drunk with emotions while trying to rescue his own ship from certain disaster:

> KIRK: I've got it, the disease. Love. You're better off without it, and I'm better off without mine. This vessel, I give, she takes. She won't permit me my life. I've got to live hers.
>
> SPOCK: Jim.
>
> KIRK: I have a beautiful yeoman. Have you noticed her, Mister Spock? You're allowed to notice her. The Captain's not permitted.
>
> SPOCK: Jim, there is an intermix formula.
>
> KIRK: Now I know why it's called she.
>
> SPOCK: It's never been tested. It's a theoretical relationship between time and antimatter.
>
> KIRK: Flesh woman to touch, to hold. A beach to walk on. A few days, no braid on my shoulder ["The Naked Time"].

Spock is also fighting the disease, trying to remain logical and provide solutions, while Kirk succumbs, and struggles between emotional needs and professional responsibilities. As he did with interpretation of the ship's mission in the first episode, Kirk interprets his identity within a masculine hierarchy, responsible for his feminine ship and his crew. Further, his responses to females—whether the ship or his crew—must remain subverted by the masculine structure of his role as Captain. Kirk dreams of a time with "no braid on [his] shoulder" because love is the disease, and he is "better off" without it. Kirk appears to be exploring the masculine-feminine opposition in an either-or existence. His ability to be uninhibited does not match the "drunkenness" of others; his anxiety is anchored in the instability of masculinity. The role of the feminine, and of emotions, is to be subverted for masculinity and a traditional place in the hierarchy. However, instead of feminine emotions (care, love, desire), what Kirk *feels* is masculine responsibility, the weight of his "gold braid." The struggle is the categorization of needs and desires subordinate to masculine structures, and Kirk works to align the masculine and feminine in a familiar, socially defined, masculine structure. The role of feminine emotions such as love and compassion, as long as they are in a familiar arena, appreciated and controlled by men, and connected with masculine structures makes Kirk superior as a leader, even if Kirk seems inconsistent, unstable.

Where No Man Has Gone

The selected examples in this study are few among many rich patterns that position Captain James T. Kirk as an anxious masculine character in a context of outer space that is always changing, a context that challenges his role. Kirk symbolizes an interesting point in the history of feminism as the conceptual and activist realms evolved and the resulting anxiety about gendered roles and gendered spaces invaded typical and traditional masculine arenas such as the bridge of a starship. At the beginning, I posited that Kirk couldn't be a simple, traditionally masculine character. Rather, Captain Kirk is a unique character that possesses both traditional masculine (strength, leadership) qualities and traditional feminine (nurturing, compassion) qualities that also exemplify anxieties about the stability of a masculine character. Captain Kirk exhibits qualities that challenge a traditionally masculine set of circumstances: a man who places "others" (women, persons of culture or ethnicity, non-humans) in roles of leadership, a man who is emotional and compassionate, especially with those close to him. Kirk is surrounded by challenges to his authority: Bones, his friend; Crater, who questions; and, Spock, who lacks emotion. The program *Star Trek* often shows characters that challenge traditional roles, but Captain Kirk is at the helm of that vessel. He cries, mourns, worries, discerns, interprets—Kirk, in body and in conversation, expresses a range of actions that challenge the masculine ideas of roles in the workplace as the show challenges the traditional and anxious male leader with the chaos of change.

The challenges that feminism faced make visible some of the problems that socially-constructed gender identity produced. If the 1960s produced a humankind that Cixous suggested would change "ways of relating that are completely different from the tradition ordained by the masculine economy," then traditional masculinity faced a confusing transformation (78). The conflicts and tensions created by these problems played out in the episodes of *Star Trek*, and in our hero, Captain James T. Kirk. In this futuristic setting, Kirk does not often embody feminist ideals. He instead exhibits anxiety and tensions when the boundaries of institutionally-defined and socially-defined gender roles are blurred. Kirk asserts his authority and aligns others in the hierarchy regularly, especially when his masculine power is challenged. However, his disruption of masculine authority, though often fraught with anxiety, leads viewers to see a man with emotions, unafraid to exhibit caring or support, and potentially willing to listen to multiple viewpoints. In Kirk's case, he is a man with qualities on a sliding continuum, rather than limited to specific points of an on-off switch. Kirk acknowledges "others" are more than examples to be tolerated, but instead are integral and key components to Kirk's view of existence in the universe, even when those roles and spaces being challenged are creating anxiety.

Works Cited

"Breaking Down Barriers for Women." *The 1960s–70s American Feminist Movement.* The E-Collaborative for Civic Education. TAVAANA.org. 2016. https://tavaana.org/en/content/1960s-70s-american-feminist-movement-breaking-down-barriers-women. Accessed March 25, 2016.

"Charlie X." *Star Trek*, created by Gene Rodenberry, performance by William Shatner, DeForest Kelley, Leonard Nimoy, Nichelle Nichols, season 1, episode 2, CBS Network. September 15, 1966.

Cixous, Helene, and Catherine Clement. *The Newly Born Woman.* USA. Series: Theory and History of Literature, Volume 24. Betsy Wing, Translator. University of Minnesota Press, 1986.

Dockterman, Eliana. "Diversity on the Bridge." *Star Trek: Inside the Most Influential Science-Fiction Series Ever.* Time Special Edition. Ed. Thomas E. Weber. New York, Time, Inc., Books, 2016. p. 17.

Friedan, Betty. *The Feminine Mystique.* New York: W.W. Norton and Company, Inc. 1963.

Greig, Alan. "Anxious States of Masculinity." June 1, 2011. http://www.alangreig.net/text/anxious-states-of-masculinity/anxious-states/ Accessed July 23, 2016.

"The Man Trap." *Star Trek*, created by Gene Rodenberry, performance by William Shatner, DeForest Kelley, Leonard Nimoy, Nichelle Nichols, season 1, episode 1, CBS Network. September 8, 1966.

"The Naked Time." *Star Trek*, created by Gene Rodenberry, performance by William Shatner, DeForest Kelley, Leonard Nimoy, Nichelle Nichols, season 1, episode 2, CBS Network. September 29, 1966.

"1966–67 United States network television schedule." Wikipedia, the free encyclopedia. Last modified on 26 December 2015. Wikimedia Foundation, Inc. https://en.wikipedia.org/wiki/1966 percentE2 percent80 percent9367_United_States_network_television_schedule. Accessed March 27, 2016.

Pilcher, Jane, and Imelda Whelehan. *Fifty Key Concepts in Gender Studies.* London: SAGE Publications, 2004.

Rodenberry, Gene, creator. *Star Trek Original Series.* CBS and Paramount Studios, 2014.

Schwartz, David J. "Masculinity Is an Anxiety Disorder: Breaking Down the Nerd Box." *Uncanny: A Magazine of Science Fiction and Fantasy.* Issue 6; September/October 2015. Uncanny Magazine. http://uncannymagazine.com/article/masculinity-is-an-anxiety-disorder-breaking-down-the-nerd-box/ Accessed July 23, 2016.

"Where No Man Has Gone Before." *Star Trek*, created by Gene Rodenberry, performance by William Shatner, Leonard Nimoy, Nichelle Nichols, season 1, episode 3, CBS Network. September 22, 1966.

Zoglin, Richard. "A Bold Vision." *Star Trek: Inside the Most Influential Science-Fiction Series Ever.* Time Special Edition. Ed. Thomas E. Weber. New York: Time Inc Books, 2016. p. 6–13.

Reinscribing Patriarchy in the *Star Trek* Films, 1979–1994

ANDREW M. BUTLER

There is a moment in *Star Trek VI: The Undiscovered Country* (Nicholas Meyer, 1991) when the Klingon Chancellor Gorkon toasts "The undiscovered country—the future." Captain Kirk later repeats the chancellor's words, firstly to Gorkon's daughter—"Your father called the future the undiscovered country"—and then in the film's closing voiceover:

> This is the final cruise of the Starship *Enterprise* under my command. This ship and her history will shortly become the care of another crew. To them and their posterity will we commit our future. They will continue the voyages we have begun and journey to all the undiscovered countries, boldly going where no man—where no *one*—has gone before.

While Spock notes that Gorkon has quoted *Hamlet* he does not note that he has misinterpreted the line. Hamlet's words are part of the "To be or not to be" soliloquy:

> Who would fardels bear,
> To grunt and sweat under a weary life,
> But that the dread of something after death,
> The undiscovered country from whose bourn
> No traveller returns, puzzles the will
> And makes us rather bear those ills we have
> Than fly to others that we know not of?

The "undiscovered country" is the afterlife rather than the future—perhaps heaven, perhaps hell—the location of "existence" after life. Gorkon lives in an era of uncertainty as the Federation-Klingon war may be ending, just as in the extradiegetic world the Cold War was. Kirk, repeatedly coded as a cold warrior, notes that "Some people think the future means the end of history," surely a reference to Francis Fukuyama's 1989 article "The End of History," which argues liberal democracy is the final form of rule for all countries. The Capitalist-Communist battle was declared over; a free market utopia would eclipse a socialist utopia one, while in the *Star Trek* universe the United Federation of Planets would expand.

In this essay, I explore *Star Trek*'s shifts from a liberal or radical text of the Lyndon B. Johnson 1960s to a neoliberal or neoconservative text of the Reaganite long–1980s. Rick Worland describes the original *Star Trek* as "the single most revealing popular culture document of American social and political actions of the 1960s" ("Captain Kirk" 116–17), as it engages with a variety of Cold War, racial and sexual politics. Mike O'Connor argues that "the show spoke in a confusing and contradictory voice that embraced both Cold War liberalism and countercultural pacifism" (186), going on to note that "Considering the racial tumult in the United States during the period in which *Star Trek* aired, its cast alone made a progressive statement on race and gender relations that few in the late 1960s would have missed" (191). This liberalism is normally associated with creator, producer and regular writer Gene Roddenberry. A fannish campaign had helped bring *Star Trek* back for a final, third, season, and this must have contributed to its resurrection in animated form (8 September 1973–12 October 1974). There was still an ongoing demand for a new version in the mid–1970s, initially envisaged by Paramount Pictures as a film, then as a television series on their mooted Paramount Television Service, then again as a film. Eventually *Star Trek: The Motion Picture* (Robert Wise, 1979) was made and in this essay I will focus on this and its six sequels, which mark a partial retraction of Roddenberry's utopian vision as the franchise producers increasingly excluded him. I will examine images of patriarchy within the sequence, as well as reflecting upon connections between death and the future, in part drawing upon the writings of the philosopher Emmanuel Levinas—although I do not expect that the filmmakers knew of him.

Emmanuel Levinas: Being and Concern for the Other

Levinas sought to establish an ethics of being in which the self becomes a self through its concern for an other—typically, but not necessarily, the widow, the orphan, the stranger (*Totality* 77). This for-the-other relationship maintains the distinctness or alterity of the other rather than reducing it to a tool for the self and thus an extended part of the self. It is through this relation for the other that the self enters into time, into a present. This ethical relation seems somewhat the antithesis of the Reaganism that I describe later in the essay, in which social groups such as "women, children, the elderly, minorities [...] who most acutely suffered from the contradiction between the logic of capitalism [...] and the humanist principles that lie at the core of liberal democracy" (Hamamoto 125). In his early work *Time and the Other* (1947), Levinas argues that "our relationship with death [...] is a unique relationship with the future" (71) and "This future of death determines the future for us" (80). As a phenomenologist, Levinas believes that sense data mediates reality. Death, by definition, marks the end of perception and so Levinas considers death to be a kind of impossibility—the self cannot experience it as it is a move beyond being, a final frontier of the senses. Death marks the end of mastery over being, the end of virility. In the same work, Levinas discusses Hamlet's soliloquy, arguing that:

> Death is thus never assumed, it comes. Suicide is a contradictory concept. [...] *Hamlet* is precisely a lengthy testimony to this impossibility of assuming death. Nothingness is impossible. [...] "To be or not to be" is a sudden awareness of this impossibility of annihilating oneself [73].

In *Existence and Existents* (1947), he notes Hamlet's horror as he "recoils before the 'not to be' because he has a foreboding of the return of being ('to dye, to sleepe, perchance to Dreame')" (62). *Something* can come from nonbeing and impose upon the self. In "Bad Conscience and the Inexorable" (1981), Levinas muses "To be or not to be—this is probably not the question par excellence" (40), which chimes with his observation in "Ethics as First Philosophy" (1984): "To be or not to be—is that the question? Is it the first and final question?" (86). In that case, he adds: "The question par excellence or the question of philosophy. Not 'Why being rather than nothing?,' but how being justifies itself" (86). Levinas insists on a being-for-the-other against a being-towards-death, in which the being of the self is justified by their treatment of the other.

Star Trek's *Political Contexts*

Like many sf texts, *Star Trek* uses encounters with others as metaphors for the extradiegetic encounters between a given culture and a group marked as different—for example, an ethnic minority. Roddenberry produced the original television series in an era where a number of groups challenged traditional social structures—Robin Wood identifies "radical feminism, black militancy, gay liberation, the assault on patriarchy" (164). Network censorship limited Roddenberry's liberal vision, but this was a time when Hollywood could produce a more radical cinema. Wood sees the 1970s "as the period when the dominant ideology *almost* disintegrated" (69). As a quasi-neo-Western, in the era of Vietnam, the series of *Star Trek* re-enacted and critiqued the era of colonialism and the frontier myth, with an ethical veneer of non-interference that smacks much more of paternalism. The other seems to have to adopt the United Federation of Planets' white, American, Protestant, patriarchal values. Wood, writing of *Star Trek II*, notes "the American-led crew of the spaceship (with its appropriate collection of fantasy-ethnic subordinates)" (169), whereas Thomas B. Byers argues "a black captain (Terrell), an Asian (Sulu), a Russian (Chekhov), and a woman (Saavik) [...] have been successfully assimilated; all admire and [...] work loyally for Kirk, the white male supreme" (331). Despite the use of female and non-white actors as minor characters—even as captains of other starships—white patriarchy rules.

By the late 1970s, the limited gains of radicals triggered a rear-guard action in culture, most obviously seen in the unproblematic heroic figure of Luke Skywalker in *Star Wars* (George Lucas, 1977), after half a decade of anti-heroes. A good guys vs. bad guys morality returns. It is in this context that America elected Republican Ronald Reagan on November 4, 1980. Reagan's policies were in favor of deregulation of the economy and the lowering of taxes to spur growth. As a result, government spending would drop and the state would have less responsibility for the welfare of the people, who should provide their own insurance and safety net. On the other hand, he increased spending on weaponry, stoking up the Cold War against the Soviets, perceiving them as an evil empire; in March 1983, he proposed the Strategic Defense Initiative that would defend the West from Soviet missiles using laser beams fired from orbiting satellites. Reagan won a landslide second victory on November 6, 1984, inaugurating a term in which Libya was bombed on November 15, 1986, and money from weapon sales to the Iranians was diverted to Contra Rebels in Nicaragua, circumventing Congress's rulings. The Soviet Union began to crumble, with General Secretary Mikhail Gorbachev attending four summits with Reagan. It was not until the presidency of George H.W. Bush, however, that the Berlin Wall came down. The film critic Andrew Britton, writing in 1986, envisaged mass pauperization ahead, along with greater inequality and a more coercive state apparatus with Reagan's freedom for business. For Britton, the new American radical right looked back "from a position of [...] recently humiliated and increasingly embittered hegemony [...] to a vanished golden age in which the national was great and the patriarchal family flourished in happy ignorance of the scourges of abortion and a soaring divorce rate, gay rights, and the women's movement" (109).

Hollywood seemed to fall in line with Reaganite ideology. Remakes, sequels and film cycles came to dominate, with fantasy in the broadest sense being the chief mode. Britton argues that "The ritualized repetitiveness of

Reaganite entertainment goes with its delirious, self-celebrating self-reference—its interminable solipsism" (99): films explicitly refer to or quote other films. Britton's mentor Wood characterizes the 1980s cinema as one of "reaction, recuperation, and reassurance" (69). Like Britton, he identifies the restoration of the father as a key element of films that nostalgically return us to an easier age—pre–Jimmy Carter, pre–Watergate, pre–Vietnam. We repeatedly see the triumph of the good father over the bad. Wood explains:

> The Father must here be understood in all senses, symbolic, literal, potential: patriarchal authority [the Law], which assigns all other elements to their correct, subordinate, allotted roles; the actual heads of families, fathers of recalcitrant children, husbands of recalcitrant wives, who must either learn the virtue and justice of submission or pack their bags; the young heterosexual male, father of the future, whose eventual union with the "good woman" has always formed the archetypal happy ending of the American film, guarantee of the perpetuation of the nuclear family and social stability [172].

These are the fathers in the *Star Trek* films.

The Families of Star Trek

In the original series, crew members rarely had family. Ilsa J. Bick notes that they were introduced and then killed off: "Some representative examples include Kirk's loss of his brother and sister-in-law in 'Operation, Annihilate' (1967), a wife and unborn child in 'The Paradise Syndrome' (1968)" (47). *The Wrath of Khan* (Nicholas Meyer, 1982) introduces Kirk's son, David, to whom I will return, and Sulu (to everyone's apparent surprise) has a daughter, Demora, in *Generations* (David Carson, 1994). Scotty has a (possibly non-canonical) nephew in *Wrath*, Peter Preston, who dies. Meanwhile, Spock's father Sarek appears in the episode "Journey to Babel" (17 November 1967), as well as in *The Search for Spock* (Leonard Nimoy, 1984), *The Voyage Home* (Leonard Nimoy, 1986) and *The Undiscovered Country*. McCoy's father appears in *The Undiscovered Country*. Alongside biological fathers, there are father and authority figures, and, of course, there is Kirk.

E. Anthony Rotundo traces the role of the father from frontier times to the present day of the mid–1980s. In the era of the frontier, the father owned all land and thus controlled the property of the entire family, including that of any children. Fathers were responsible for the moral and spiritual growth of their sons, punishing any transgression. Rotundo argues that the industrial world relocated the father-son relationship to one of competitiveness: "in this wide-open race for success, young men strove mightily to outdo their fathers" (11). In the shift from the frontier to the factory or the office, the father was increasingly absent from home, whether he was at or travelling to work, and his power became compromised. In the meantime, the growth of divorce rates through the twentieth century led to the establishment of more second households. In the era of the Federation, Kirk and his crew largely leave biological family behind, with the regular cast forming a surrogate family. Starfleet have promoted Kirk to admiral as a reward for the success of the original five-year mission. This temporarily unmans him, but he reasserts his masculinity in the lengthy sequence during which Scotty takes Kirk on a tour of the exterior of the *Enterprise*. As Vivian Sobchack writes, the two nostalgically gaze "at the refitted but still familiar (and now technologically old-fashioned) starship *Enterprise* for what seemed to some less nostalgic spectators an interminable length of overreverent screen time" (276). The two admire the ship as if they were men objectifying a pin-up model. She is theirs to control, to ride and to possess. As Britton says of Reaganite space fiction, it combines "the awe-inspiring and the banal" (116). Worland compares Kirk's promotion to the treatment of Captain Brittles (John Wayne) in the western *She Wore a Yellow Ribbon* (John Ford, 1949) as it allows them to become mentors to the next generation rather than to fade into sorry retirement: "Kirk, like Brittles, is supposed to pass command to a younger generation of officers but similarly must step in to save them, proving his continued effectiveness and vitality" ("New Frontier" 28). Willard Decker, the new captain of the *Enterprise*, should deal with the deadly energy cloud that is headed toward the Earth.

Fathers and Sons: The Future of Filiality

Roddenberry had created Decker for the television series *Star Trek: Phase II*—the son of Commander Matt Decker who sacrifices himself in "The Doomsday Machine" (20 October 1967)—but instead he was used for the film. Kirk and Decker thus have a history relating to fathers and sons, and, while Decker respects Kirk, he is better qualified to look after the refitted ship. Nevertheless, Kirk demotes Decker to commander, insisting he take the place of a science officer killed in a transporter accident. The returning Spock then usurps him from that position. The old characters drive out the new—with the tacit support of the audience who are there to see Kirk and his crew. The energy cloud emanates from an ancient *Voyager* probe, a successor to the solar system exploration craft that had been launched in 1977, *Voyager 1* having flown by Jupiter in January 1979 and *Voyager 2* in July 1979. In the intervening centuries, it has been modified and upgraded by an alien civilization. Now it searches for its creator on Earth, seeking the approval of its "father" and wanting to download its information. Further, it wants to merge with its father, having first absorbed a beautiful Deltan empath Ilia (first created for *Phase II*) and turning her into an electronic simulation. In the original series, Kirk would have been attracted to such an exotic female, but Decker is the more fertile lover and elects to merge with her. By this point, he has started calling Kirk Jim, a privilege reserved for Spock and McCoy. The substitute son faces the not-to-be and transcends being; meanwhile the crisis rejuvenates Kirk, restoring his patriarchal powers. This transcendent offspring brings us back to Levinas, who writes "The relation with the child [...] establishes relationship with the absolute future, or infinite time" (*Totality* 268). The child is the product of the self and not the self: "The father does not simply cause the son. [...] The son resumes the unicity of the father and yet remains exterior to the father: the son is a unique son" (278–9). In Levinas's account of what he calls "filiality," the son need not be biologically related—he could be a pupil or mentee, with the identity of the self being carried on by non-genetic means.

In *Wrath*, fatherhood becomes at stake, as consequence of two incidents from Kirk's past—the events of the episode "Space Seed" (16 February 1967) and his fathering of David. The film begins with the apparent death of Spock, in a training exercise for the next generation of Starfleet cadets, overseen by Kirk as instructor. Kirk suspects "These kids don't know how to drive." Ina Rae Hark observes, "The younger, usurping generation again and again proves inadequate or unable to perform the galaxy-saving assignments that inevitably fall to the *Enterprise*" (1978). The aging Kirk faces his own not-to-be, his own mortality, and now has to wear glasses (McCoy's birthday gift) to read *A Tale of Two Cities* (Spock's gift). David is not what Levinas would describe as someone who "can be brought up, be commanded, and can obey" (*Totality* 279), rejecting the "Boy Scout" that his mother used to hang around with. Byers notes that "David has pacifist tendencies, and his pacifism seems to be both a consequence of his having been raised by his mother, without a properly virile, violent role-model [...] He reacts both against the father he really 'is a lot like' (as his mother says) and against his Oedipal hostility towards that figure" (332). David Greven takes David's pacifism, absent father, close mother, sensitivity and lack of romantic subplot to indicate that David is gay: "With his lithe Adonis physique, soft, curly blond tendrils, and sensitivity bordering on the hotheadedness" (147). David at one point does engage in the sort of hand-to-hand fight with Kirk familiar from the original series, using a knife, but is defeated. David must ask his father's forgiveness and confesses to his pride in his father. Kirk's filial relations are here genetic and he is established as the good father despite his absence from child-rearing. That father/son conversation points towards death:

> DAVID MARCUS: Lieutenant Saavik was right: You never have faced death.
>
> JAMES KIRK: No. Not like this. I haven't faced death. I've cheated death. I've tricked my way out of death and patted myself on the back for my ingenuity. I know nothing.

> DAVID MARCUS: You knew enough to tell Saavik that how we face death is at least as important as how we face life.

Death itself remains unknowable, beyond perception and comprehension. This is the cheating of death that Levinas saw in *Hamlet* and *Macbeth*:

> Prior to death there is always a last chance; this is what heroes seize, not death. The hero is the one who always glimpses a last chance, the one who obstinately finds chances. Death is thus never assumed, it comes. Suicide is a contradictory concept [*Time* 73].

By this point we have seen Spock sacrifice himself to save the *Enterprise*, with Sidney Carton's words on the way to the guillotine in *A Tale of Two Cities* (1859) ringing in our ears: "It is a far, far better thing that I do, than I have ever done; it is a far, far better rest that I go to than I have ever known" (Dickens 466). Spock's is a good dream. It transpires that Spock has transferred his *katra* into McCoy shortly before his death and so a vestige of his spirit still lives—the third film becoming an account of the attempt to resurrect Spock. Good father Kirk contrasts to the bad father Khan, abandoned by Kirk twenty years before *Wrath*. Khan's son dies in the course of the narrative, giving further revenge grist to his mill. Wood notes Khan's contrast to Kirk's white identity: "It can scarcely escape notice that the arch-villain Khan of *Star Trek II* is heavily signified as foreign (and played by a foreign actor, Ricardo Montalban)" (169), and places him within a then recent tradition of villains misusing a power that the heroes also want: the Jedi and the Empire want to use the Force, Indiana Jones and the Nazis want the Ark of the Covenant and now Starfleet and Khan want the Genesis device, which will bring barren planets to fertile life. Britton declares *Raiders* and *Khan* to be "parables of the redemptive and regenerative properties of the weaponry of annihilation in American hands" (125). The film endorses Kirk's actions and reaffirms traditional bourgeois values.

Fraternity vs. Paternity

In *Search for Spock*, Kirk's fraternity outweighs his paternity, as he barely pauses to mourn the death of his son David at the hands of the Klingon Kruge. He is prepared to sacrifice everything, including his career, to rescue Spock, as he hijacks the ready-to-be-decommissioned *Enterprise*. Levinas notes how the self is part of a fraternity: "The human I is posited in fraternity: that all men are brothers is not added to man as a moral conquest, but constitutes his ipseity [selfhood]" (*Totality* 279–80). Spock as alien and other is of course a prime example of the Levinasian other, even if Kirk is hardly an altruistic Levinasian self. Indeed, in resurrecting his friend/brother, it is almost as if Kirk fathers Spock. Bick reads the *Enterprise* as "the comforting womb of civilization" (46) and in Freudian terms, of course, the home becomes the substitute for the womb. The *Enterprise* is the only place that the crew see as home, but it is necessary that it be destroyed in order that Spock may live. Presumably, the crew would prefer to sacrifice themselves rather than suffer the ignominy of being decommissioned.

Kirk in is conflict with Sarek as influence on Spock. Spock had joined Starfleet against his father's wishes, leading to an estrangement between the two of them only resolved in "Journey to Babel" when Spock saves Sarek's life. Bick argues that "Consistent with *ST*'s emphasis upon male solidarity, Spock's relationship with his father, Sarek, is preserved; however, this bond is strained, distant, and formal, leaving Spock no alternative but to return to Kirk's side" (47). The logic of the Vulcan and their alleged lack of ego might suggest that a "strained, distant, and formal" relationship is preferable, but Spock's human heritage desires Kirk's friendship. Spock wants his father's approval, but constantly returns to the side of the arch-patriarch Kirk. It is not until the later scenes of *Voyage* that a full reconciliation is affected; Sarek tells Spock: "Your associates are people of good character." The culture of the other approves of the values of the dominant ideology after all.

Coming Home: The Comforting Womb

The crew return to their theoretical home of Earth on board the Klingon Bird of Prey to face trial for their actions—in other words, the arch-patriarch is to face the rule of law. They encounter a further crisis en route: another alien probe threatens Earth when humanity cannot reply to it. Spock realizes that it is broadcasting whale song, adjusted for the distortion that it will undergo when being heard under water. Unfortunately, the humpback whales that the probe is trying to communicate with have been extinct for at least two hundred years—the inevitable conclusion of hunting. Kirk and his crew work out how to travel back in time to the twentieth century, in hope of finding and then rescuing whales. The tone of *Voyage* is considerably lighter than the previous three films, being played as broad comedy, despite being more overtly political in its culture clash between the utopian twenty-third century and the dystopian twentieth. Chekov and Uhura's search for nuclear vessels—at the height of the Cold War—demonstrates again the dichotomy of good and bad uses of technology, with Starfleet on the side of the good. While *Wrath* had contained several references to Captain Ahab and the Great White from *Moby-Dick* (1851), the *Enterprise* crew are good whale hunters. Britton notes how *Wrath* had adjusted the novel's politics of the white patriarch Ahab chasing the whale to Khan chasing the *Enterprise* and that "for the purposes of *Star Trek*, the whale may be indistinguishable from the starship *Enterprise*"

(126). In *Voyage*, the crew negotiate linguistic and cultural differences and evade military and policing organizations—not to mention *bad* hunters—to transport two humpback whales to the twenty-third century. The whales communicate with the probe and it "relents, showing it to be an omnipotent god-like creature who has demanded proof of humanity's right to live and in so doing reaffirmed the message in *Star Trek*'s original ethos of human progress that we must learn from history" (Geraghty 237). The god-likeness is rather an Old Testament–style God the Father, defeated by the intelligence of the resurrected Spock. The likelihood of humpback whales surviving as a species from two specimens is not questioned—even as Dr. Gillian Taylor, their carer from the twentieth century, abandons them for a space mission of her own in the twenty-third. Taylor is a potential love interest for Kirk, but for once, a woman retains control by saying that she will be the one to get back in touch. Kirk as patriarch, in the meantime, is mostly outside the law—in recognition of his services, Starfleet drop all charges against him aside from his failure to obey the orders of a superior officer and demote him to captain. In audience terms this is a restoration as the character is always already *Captain* Kirk and the title of Admiral feels wrong. Sulu hopes that they will be assigned the USS *Excelsior*, the ship with the new transwarp drive that they had disabled in *Search*—and which he will command in *The Undiscovered Country*—but this is a "newfangled, hence unreliable starship" (Worland "New Frontier" 28) inappropriate for this crew. Instead, Starfleet restores them to the (rebuilt) *Enterprise*, to which Kirk's response is "We've come home." Home is not twenty-third century Earth and its civilization, but rather this comforting womb.

God the Father

If *Voyage* returns us to the end of the original series—*Captain* Kirk on board the *Enterprise*—then the title of the fifth, *The Final Frontier*, points us back to its recurrent spoken prologue; later in the film the words "To boldly go where no man has gone before" can be seen engraved beneath an old ship's wheel. The title also hints at the western genre that underpins the franchise, although as Daniel Bernardi notes, *Star Trek* depicts "a final frontier that is explored and domesticated for a dominantly white imagination" (92). Pilkington argues that "*Star Trek V* not only has the 'heart and soul' of one of the television episodes, it also very nearly has the plot of one of them ["The Way to Eden," 21 February 1969] and that the film should really be subtitled *The Search for God*.

God, in Levinasian terms, is the infinitely other, the other that cannot be assimilated, but is encountered in the face of the other: "The dimension of the divine opens forth from the human face. [...] There can be no 'knowledge' of God separated from the relationship with men" (*Totality* 78). This is a God who is defined by his absence—because of his infinite otherness—but who may lie in the faces of the stranger seeking aid. We have already seen the technological transcendence of being in *The Motion Picture*, and I have discussed the interconnection of death and the future—now we have a God who is located beyond the final frontier, beyond being. Early in the film, Kirk observes that men like him do not have families, although through the course of the narrative he learns that the *Enterprise* is a family—he is its patriarch—and explicitly acknowledges Spock as his brother. It is Spock's half-brother, Sybok, who provides the plot engine, wishing to take a starship to Sha Ka Ree beyond the Great Barrier, and find God. In doing so, Sybok wrests the sympathies of the crew from Kirk as good father to himself, by showing them painful family memories and using the Vulcan mindmeld techniques to cathart them. Sybok is in search of the ultimate father, the creator God. As in *The Motion Picture*, God is not all he seems: here he is a highly evolved alien, who also wants a starship. Kirk, so attached to his own, is skeptical. Bick, in her psychoanalytic exploration of the franchise, notes the cyclic narrative of *The Wizard of Oz* (Victor Fleming, 1939):

> Escaping from the drudgery and persecution of her home and borne aloft upon a tornado representative of her fury, Dorothy [Judy Garland] wanders in the primitive, mystical wilderness of Oz, meeting and eventually reconciling her disparate, contradictory images of mother, father, and self only to conclude that home is best [45].

Home is obviously the *Enterprise* and there is a lot of the humbug of the supposed Great Oz in this God. Professor Marvel's (Frank Morgan) eventual granting of wishes in *Wizard* is in the form of acknowledging that the Scarecrow, Tin Woodman and Cowardly Lion already have the qualities they seek within themselves; it is surely no coincidence that Kirk, speaking of God to McCoy says, "Maybe he's not out there, Bones. Maybe he's right here," and points to his heart. If the films assert the rightness of Kirk as the patriarch, they also seem increasingly keen to do so. *The Undiscovered Country* is made at the point when the U.S.–Soviet Cold War allegory of Earth-Klingon collides with glasnost, perestroika, the fall of the Berlin Wall and the end of history. The Klingon, General Chang, observes, "In space, all warriors are cold warriors," but now détente is about to be reached. The explosion of the Klingon moon destroys their ozone layer and now the species seek peace with the Federation; they are the other seeking the protection of the self. Kirk, Cold War relic, does not trust the Klingons because they killed his son—whose photo he places on his desk. During the peace conference, two unknown parties from the *Enterprise* beam aboard the Klingon ship and massacre much of the crew, including Gorkon. McCoy fails to save Gorkon, and he and Kirk are sentenced to labor in the gulags on the frozen asteroid Rura Penthe. Naturally, Kirk is not guilty. Federation members, Klingons and Romulans, including Spock's protégée Valeris, Chang, the Romulan Ambassador Nanclus and Fleet Admiral Cartwright, have conspired to try to thwart the peace. The white Americanness of the good warriors is ranged against the alienness (including an alien female) and African Americanness of the evil. Meanwhile, Spock compares Kirk to Richard Nixon, the U.S. president elected in 1968 who was brought down by the scandal of the Watergate Building break-in and subsequent cover-up in his 1972 re-election: "There is an old Vulcan proverb: only Nixon could go to China." This is a long way from the 1960s Kennedy/Johnson liberal Kirk: "Interestingly, if Kirk were once implicitly 'Kennedy' (whose cold warrior credentials were in any case secure) by 1991 he had explicitly become 'Nixon': the staunch anti-communist and red-baiter who nonetheless made the historic opening to Maoist China" (Worland "New Frontier" 31). Kirk saves civilization but elects not to return to it as he has the *Enterprise*—instead he instructs Chekov to set a course "Second star to the right and straight on 'til morning," in an explicit reference to the directions to Neverland in *Peter Pan; or, The Boy Who Wouldn't Grow Up* (1904), a play in which Pan says "To die will be an awfully big adventure."

The Deaths of Kirk

Kirk's own death comes not once but twice in *Generations*—released in the second year of Bill Clinton's presidency—as it did for Spock in *Wrath*. Kirk, Chekov and Scott have finally retired but attend the launch of another *Enterprise* on its maiden voyage. The *Enterprise* responds to a distress signal from El-Aurians who are endangered by an energy ribbon and Kirk dies in an explosion on the *Enterprise*. A century later, Captain Jean-Luc Picard of the *Enterprise-D*, having just learned that his brother and nephew have been killed, responds to a distress signal from an observatory near the star Amargosa and rescues an El-Aurian, Dr. Tolian Soran. Soran wants to re-enter the Nexus—a realm beyond normal time and space that conflates the future, death and nonbeing into one transcendent domain. Picard attempts to stop him, but he and Soran are absorbed into the Nexus as the *Enterprise* crashes onto the planet. First Picard encounters the family he never had and his dead nephew—in a Reaganite throwback to what Britton described as "the Victorian hearth in which the household gods are celebrated not around the pianoforte but around the computer" (109). Picard then finds a married Kirk, living on a ranch, and the two team up to defeat Soran. Kirk dies heroically in the process. Soran sees time as a predator: "Aren't you beginning to feel time gaining on you? It's like a predator. It's stalking you. Oh, you can try and outrun it with doctors, medicines, new technologies, but in the end, time is going to hunt you down and make the kill." The heroes Kirk and Picard, in contrast, always see one more chance. Picard believes that "time is a companion who goes with us on the journey, and reminds us to cherish every moment…," and time is of course the dimension in which the concern for the other is demonstrated. The baton passes from one generation to another, Picard being Kirk's non-biological filial successor. Picard, meanwhile, perceiving himself as the end of his line, indicates to his First Officer William Riker (a double to Decker) that someone would take over the chair of another *Enterprise*. The film thus guarantees the franchise—it was made as the television series *The Next Generation* was coming to an end and was followed by another three movie outings of that cast.

Patriarch Reinscribed, Reborn, Rebooted

Of course, the *Enterprise* would have another or, rather, earlier captain. Captain Jonathan Archer takes the helm in the prequel, *Enterprise* (September 26, 2001–May 23, 2005). As Greven observes, the new series debuted in the year that George W. Bush took office and a few weeks after the attacks on the World Trade Center and the Pentagon. Cold War peace had given way to the War on Terror. I have already noted how Kirk, in *The Undiscovered Country*, said, "Some people think the future means the end of history." He adds: "Well, we haven't run out of history quite yet." Greven feels that "*Enterprise* was a neoconservative reimagining of *Trek* that not only 'corrected' the politically correct stances of the previous recent *Trek* shows but even retooled the concepts of Original *Trek* to refashion *Trek* in its entirety as monolithically conservative vision, a fictive universe opposed to diversity and tolerance" (118). But this was already there in the *Star Trek* films of the long 1980s. Kirk's concern for the other is repeatedly a concern for himself. The films justify the patriarchal worldviews of Kirk and retool him as a reassuring, heroic figure in a neoconservative landscape. Worland compares him to the septuagenarian Reagan, who had been declared by the Democrats as too old for high office and yet won landslide victories. As Britton argues, "Good is affirmed through the spectacle of its robustness and its pre-given triumph" (113). In Kirk's continued "pre-given triumph" we see "Maturity, retrenchment, and defense of tradition became valued over youthful vitality, progress, and the new" (Worland "New Frontier" 28). The nods to feminism and diversity might be summed up in Uhura's strip tease and Sulu and Chekov's lusting after female Klingons in *The Undiscovered Country*; in both cases we are shown the male gaze at work, even if the tone might be knowing and ironic. Meanwhile, Kirk has been resurrected, rebooted, in three more films to date in an alternate timeline, the first set "before" the events of the original series. Shatner's Kirk might have been missing from the screen since the dawn of the age of Clinton, but, as Philip Strick observes, the Nexus "is the simplest possible way of endlessly reviving Kirk, Spock, Tasha Yar, or any other lost colleagues for further adventures" (55). This is a reassuring trope—the hero waiting to be woken, the once and future king. Both Kirk and Spock have already returned once from the undiscovered country—of death, if not of the future—and Kirk's patriarchy can be endlessly reinscribed.

Works Cited

Bernardi, Daniel L. *Star Trek and History: Race-ing Towards a White Future*. Rutgers University Press, 1998. Print.
Bick, Ilsa J. "Boys in Space: *Star Trek*, Latency, and the Neverending Story." *Cinema Journal* 352 (1996): 43–60. Web.
Britton, Andrew. "Blissing Out: The Politics of Reaganite Entertainment." Ed. Barry Keith Grant. *Britton on Film: The Complete Film Criticism of Andrew Britton*. Wayne State University Press, 2008. 97–154. Print.
Byers, Thomas B. "Commodity Futures: Corporate State and Personal Style in Three Recent Science-Fiction Movies." *Science Fiction Studies* 14.3 (1987): 326–39. Web.
Dickens, Charles. *A Tale of Two Cities*. Ed. Andrew Sanders. Oxford: World Classics, 1988. Print.
Geraghty, Lincoln. "The American Jeremiad and *Star Trek*'s Puritan Legacy." *Journal of the Fantastic in the Arts*, 142 (2003): 228–45. Web.
Greven, David. *Gender and Sexuality in Star Trek: Allegories of Desire in the Television Series and Films*. Jefferson, NC, McFarland, 2009. Print.
Hamamoto, Darrell Y. *Nervous Laughter: Television Situation Comedy and Liberal Democratic Ideology*. New York, Westport, CT, and London: Praeger, 1989.
Levinas, Emmanuel. "Bad Conscience and the Inexorable." Ed. Richard Cohen. *Face to Face with Levinas*. New York University Press, 1986. 35–40. Print.
_____. *Ethics and Infinity: Conversations with Philippe Nemo*. Trans. Richard A. Cohen. Duquesne University Press, 1985. Print.
_____. "Ethics as First Philosophy." Ed. Seán Hand. *The Levinas Reader*. Oxford: Basil Blackwell, 1989. 75–87. Print.
_____. *Existence and Existents*. Trans. Alphonso Lingis. The Hague: Martinus Nijhoff, 1988. Print.
_____. *Time and the Other, and Other Essays*. Trans. Richard A. Cohen. Duquesne University Press, 1987. Print.
_____. *Totality and Infinity: An Essay on Exteriority*. Trans. Alphonso Lingis. The Hague: Nijhoff, 1979. Print.
O'Connor, Mike. "Liberals in Space: The 1960s Politics of *Star Trek*." *The Sixties* 5:2 (2012): 185–203. Web.
Pilkington, Ace. "*Star Trek V*: The Search for God." *Literature/Film Quarterly* 24.2 (1996): 169–76. Web.
Rotundo, E. Anthony "American Fatherhood: A Historical Perspective." *American Behavioral Scientist* 29 (1985): 7–23. Print.
Sobchack, Vivian. *Screening Space: The American Science Fiction Film*. New York: Ungar, 1987. Print.
Strick, Philip. "*Star Trek: Generations*." *Sight and Sound* 5.3 (1995): 55–6.
Wood, Robin. *Hollywood from Vietnam to Reagan*. Columbia University Press, 1987. Print.
Worland, Rick. "Captain Kirk: Cold Warrior." *Journal of Popular Film and Television* 16.3 (1988): 109–17. Web.
_____. "From the New Frontier to the Final Frontier: *Star Trek* from Kennedy to Gorbachev." *Film and History* 24.1 (1994): 19–35. Web.

What We See When We Look in the Mirror

Star Trek's *Alternative Sexuality*

TERESA CUTLER-BROYLES

From its inception, *Star Trek* has dealt with the issues of each new iteration's political, social, and cultural times. No subject was sacred; Gene Roddenberry and the *Star Trek* franchise writers and crew were happy[1] to tackle them all. Often, the issues each crew faced and resolved were actively being debated at that particular historical moment in the cultural milieu—witness, for instance, one of the first interracial kisses on television[2] that aired just a few months after the assassination of Martin Luther King devastated the American Civil Rights movement which, to that point, had been a strong force in American culture.[3] The war in Vietnam and the Cold War and its effects were certainly backdrops for *The Original Series* (*TOS*); *The Next Generation* (*TNG*) dealt in large part with post–Cold War realities; many have seen the Arab-Israeli conflict informing the episodes in *Deep Space Nine* (*DS9*); and neoliberal philosophies, imperialism, famine, bio-diversity, love, gender-normative assumptions, bio-ethics, tolerance, bigotry, and germane to this analysis, morality have all been tackled by *Star Trek* in its fifty-year existence. A common thread throughout the franchise's lifetime has been an ongoing interest, and indeed an almost doctrinal belief, in the development or evolution of humankind. However problematic this belief,[4] the universe of the original *Star Trek* as envisioned first by Gene Roddenberry and adopted as doctrine by its writers, producers, and fans, was seen as *evolving*, moving toward a better, less war-like, kinder, and importantly for this analysis, a more *moral* future peopled with moral creatures. Roddenberry "had a very positive view of mankind; he saw the future as a place of endless possibilities."[5] Humans, of course, would lead the way and by default this meant human men.

As noted, one of the tenets of this future was the premise that human evolution would include a component of morality, and the questions that arise include: what does an evolved morality actually mean? What constitutes morality in a universe where war and famine and disease are outmoded, and where love and acceptance are the goals, even to the extent of kissing—and more, one would assume—between different races is commonplace?[6] For the writers and producers of the show, it was not enough to simply contrast the morally "good" characters viewers knew and loved with Others—most often extra-terrestrial aliens—whose actions and beliefs identified them as dubious at best, and morally corrupt at worst. It was far more effective to employ a Mirror universe in which both familiar and unfamiliar incarnations of known characters transgressed those semi-rigid bounds set up by the United Federation of Planets under Roddenberry's vision.

Star Trek's Mirror universe is a canonical[7] alternate one that runs parallel to the traditional *Star Trek* storyline. In it, "familiar characters are given reversed characteristics. Heroes might be evil, or at least far more ruthless and aggressive. This is often indicated visually by more sexually revealing clothes, longer hair and/or facial hair...."[8] In this alternate universe, visited for the first time in *The Original Series* and revisited by characters from various subsequent series, episode writers were able to "depict dark subjects such as torture, death, rape, dubiously consensual sex, or fantastical/unsafe BDSM practices."[9]

Fans, critics, film and culture theorists alike have commented on the Mirror universe, in particular the juxtaposition of the upright citizens of Kirk's *Enterprise*—or later the *DS9* station or the earlier-in-the-timeline *Star Trek Enterprise* (*ENT*) commanded by Jonathan Archer—and those who inhabit the darker space. The common through-line is the Mirror universe's moral ambiguity and the sexual nature of those who live there, and how these made for erotic possibilities not appropriate for the morally advanced, peaceful, non-warlike members of the Federation. Writer and producer of *Star Trek: Deep Space Nine* (*DS9*) Robert Hewitt Wolfe tells us that people in this universe are, "prone to do evil and wrong things."[10] And "the basic idea was that everyone would be somewhat the opposite of who they were or sometimes *a more extreme version of who they were, showing a buried part that might have come out*"[11] (emphasis added). In other words, Freud's theories made manifest.

What remains problematic about the simple formulation that Mirror characters are opposite to their moral selves is how each of those mirror-denizens evidences some draw or tendency toward, or outright practice of, *deviant* sexuality, as noted in almost every description of them, from fansites to the writers of the characters themselves. "Deviant" in this context is taken to mean non-normative, and that itself is a socially constructed concept.

Roddenberry's underlying assumption seems to have been that in the morally upright (uptight?) universe of the 23rd century, when peace reigns and the motto is Infinite Diversity in Infinite Combinations,[12] sexuality will be a non-controversial subject, perhaps open, always vanilla.[13] In this universe, Kirk's lovers become an extension of his masculinity and exist merely for his and the viewing audience's pleasure. As Karin Blair contends, "The *femme-objet* appears in many *Star Trek* episodes. In almost every one of them we have a different female guest star ... who is 'disposed of' at the end of the episode."[14] Anne Cranny-Francis[15] tells us that "The female characters in *Star Trek* are limited to passive, non-threatening, non-assertive roles; when assertive or aggressive, female characters signify, and are signified as, evil." She offers examples from a number of episodes to show that aggressive, assertive females in the series, especially those whose aggressiveness includes sexuality, inevitably get put in their place by male characters, specifically Kirk and Spock. This exorcism, as Cranny-Francis styles it, is performed via the stereotypical hyper-masculinity attributed to Kirk, and the restrained, unemotional, i.e., also stereotypically male characteristics attributed to Spock. In a reflexive move, these hyper-male characteristics define the proper role for women by virtue of exhibiting all that women are not supposed to be: aggressive, confident, imperious, self-serving, sexual, and predatory. While Cranny-Francis does indeed make a case for her conclusion, she neglects to take into account the Mirror universe and the women who reside there. Admittedly only one episode, "Mirror, Mirror," out of the eighty-three in *The Original Series* was available for analysis at the time of her publication (1985), and it is perhaps only in light of later forays into the Mirror universe that the role of strong, aggressive women was developed fully; still traces of it were there from the start in 1967 in the character of Science Officer Marlena Moreau, the Captain's Woman in the Mirror universe that viewers—and the *Star Trek* crew—were first introduced to. Unafraid to use her sexuality to persuade, or ascend the political or military ladder, Moreau undergoes no pacifying metamorphosis at the hands of Kirk or Spock.[16] When the crew returns to their own universe, details of which will be discussed below, she remains behind. In the Mirror timeline she continues to advance using all means at her disposal.

The implications are intimated here and only fully developed in later series; powerful and sexually aware females who cannot be tamed cannot exist in the philosophically and morally advanced 23rd century world of the Federation. But they thrive in the Mirror universe, a space in which all this presumed "morality" turns on its head in a kind of carnivalesque move that allows viewers, fans, and analysts, to examine the underpinnings of this representation, and its eventual recuperation. Not surprisingly, the burden of representation of this morally deviant space rests squarely on the shoulders—or, more accurately, the bare midriffs—of the female characters. In the *DS9* episode "Crossover" that aired in 1994, nearly thirty years after the *Enterprise* crew, and viewers, first encountered the Mirror universe, Kira Nerys, *DS9*'s Executive Officer, is transported to the Mirror universe with the station's Doctor Julian Bashir. Almost immediately they are confronted with the woman who rules that universe's Alliance space station Terok Nor: Kira's counterpart, Mirror Intendant Kira who is "ruthless, sadistic, hedonistic, bisexual and sexually aggressive—characteristics common in Mirror Universe females."[17] Writer and movie critic Jordan Hoffman says about Mirror Kira: "Intendant Kira Nerys oversaw the operation of Terok Nor for the Klingon-Cardassian Alliance, and was a violent and sexually voracious woman. In addition to having an eye for (Mirror) Sisko and Ezri Tegan, she found a true object of her lust in herself, naturally, when our Kira crossed over."[18]

Another important Mirror character is Hoshi Sato from the *Star Trek Enterprise* series, who in the Prime *Star Trek* timeline is a sometimes fearful, relatively sexless communications officer. Her Mirror character, however, is of a different sort. She goes from sexual companion to Empress using all the wiles at her command. "At first, she seemed merely to be the "Captain's Woman, but after a few crosses and double-crosses (and poisoning Mirror Jonathan Archer[19]) she comes out on top and in command. And wearing a half-shirt."[20] The role of Captain's Woman is an important one and goes to the question of whether the women portrayed in *The Original Series* were indeed helpless, passive and non-threatening as posited. We have Soto's example above, and she is a direct descendant of the 1967 episode that started it all, in which the Captain's Woman is Lieutenant Marlena Moreau; she is also a ruthless assassin willing to use her wiles for advancement.

TOS's "Mirror, Mirror"[21] starts with James T. Kirk and his landing party made up of Commander Montgomery Scott (Scotty), Dr. McCoy (Bones), and Lieutenant Uhura,[22] in the last stages of an unsuccessful negotiation with the Halkans on their home-world. The party beams back to the *Enterprise* but due to a passing ion storm materializes instead on the transporter pad in a theretofore unknown and unsuspected parallel universe. They recognize immediately, due to visual cues such as First Officer Spock's goatee and various differences in uniform that resemble pirate costumes, and of course Uhura's famously bare belly, that they have arrived in quite a different space than their own. It is established soon thereafter that this Mirror universe is violent, predatory, and almost diametrically opposed morally to their own. After thwarting an assassination attempt on his own life, and condemning Commander Chekov to the "agonizer" for trying to kill him, Kirk enters the Captain's quarters to find the beautiful—and bare-midriffed—Lieutenant Moreau reclining on his bed. It becomes clear almost immediately that she is his confidant and his Mirror counterpart's equal in intelligence and ambition. And, his lover. Her ruthlessness is demonstrated halfway through the episode when she reveals to Kirk her bloodthirsty willingness to wipe his rivals out of existence using a piece of technology. This moment is counter-balanced by her obvious sexual desire for Kirk in the next scene. When he rebuffs her advances—reluctantly but effectively—she demands to be transferred, telling him, whom she still believes to be her own Captain/lover, that on another ship she can "hunt fresh game." She goes on to tell him, significantly, "I've been a Captain's woman and I like it. I'll be one again if I have to go through every officer in the Fleet." In other words, she will use her sexuality as power, and will get what she wants without guilt and without shame. Power and sex intimately entwined.

It is in fact this moment that reveals the sexuality and power at the heart of the Mirror universe; this becomes the early foundation for the later manifestations of the same impulses in Mirror Intendent Kira and Empress Sato, as well as other Mirror women who, while not discussed herein because their roles are smaller, just as successfully own their sexuality and their power. Hidden though it may be in its germinal state in "Mirror, Mirror," this combined sexuality and power in the Mirror universe is what allows each person is to be at her—and sometimes but not nearly as often his—strongest when she is deploying sex as weapon. And doing so is not only accepted but expected. Even Lieutenant Uhura in this episode acts in ways that run counter to the behavior we have come to expect of her, and by extension of all 23rd century Federation citizens. Paralleling Moreau's behavior, Uhura uses sexuality as a way to obtain her goals and accomplish her purpose. Dressed in her be-sashed, midriff-revealing uniform, carrying a knife, and holding herself in a much more sexually aggressive way, Uhura lures Mirror Commander Sulu with promises of a sexual game he just might stand a chance in if he only learns the rules. She diverts his attention using herself as bait, and when he responds to her in kind with physical desire, she threatens him with bodily harm. Sex, power, and violence all coming together in the Mirror universe in the body of a woman.

Uhura in fact has adapted more fully than the other, male (and white) characters out of place in this Mirror universe.[23] She is participating in, and succeeding at, the overt sexuality that permeates this space and performs her part far more effectively than her companions manage to perform theirs. This connection between female sexuality and power is endemic to the Mirror universe, and illustrated in the *DS9* and *ENT* episodes previously mentioned.

In "Crossover," the Mirror Intendent Kira Nerys is "such a strong character that she's very clearly aware and in charge of her sexuality."[24] She uses it to intimidate, to rule, and to seduce, and her seductions occur in the context of power imbalances between herself and her objects of desire, including Mirror Commander Sisko and her own doppelganger, *DS9* Kira.[25] At the end of the episode her ambitions are thwarted by her lover Sisko, but her sexuality and power are not diminished within the Mirror world, nor used as a means to degrade, demote, or otherwise downgrade her relative status as, arguably, they might have been in the Prime *Star Trek* universe. She has not been put in her place, she has not been exorcised and turned into one of the Prime universe's "passive, docile creatures."[26] When next we encounter the Mirror Kira one year[27] later in the *DS9* timeline, we find her reclining against a handsome (dark-skinned) male lover, next to a beautiful (also dark-skinned) woman Kira is also sexually involved with. The trappings of sex and power are clear: pseudo-slave imagery that viewers would identify immediately in the clothing of both the man and woman, their subservient positions in relation to Kira on the couch, and their absolute attention to her every move and word. Classic dominant/slave dynamics, i.e., all the expected visual indicators of power in the Mirror universe as related to women. Throughout the episode, power either stays with Kira or, in situations where she is momentarily placed into a subservient or dangerous position, she flips the dynamic using her sexuality—and her black, painted-on latex jumpsuit.

Two seasons later[28] in "Resurrection," Mirror Kira travels to the Prime *ST* universe, and uses, no surprise, her sexuality to con her way around the station. At the end of the story she is temporarily incapacitated by a lover but doesn't lose her potential for power and all it entails. Even unconscious, she exerts enough influence that he chooses to stay with her, despite the possibility that she might kill him upon waking. And in "The Emperor's New Cloak," Mirror Kira continues to wield her sexuality as a weapon across (humanoid) species, and in relation to both men and women, making explicit the implied same-sex pairings from earlier seasons. She seduces her way through the episode and though the last scene takes place without her, it keeps the female sexuality and power center stage as her female ex-lover and another woman make clear their upcoming pairing.

The Mirror universe would appear twice more, in the prequel *Enterprise*[29] in two parts in 2005. Hearkening back to the Mirror universe's roots, in "In a Mirror Darkly" we encounter again a Captain's Woman, Hoshi Sato, dressed in similarly revealing clothing. Her bare midriff differentiates her from her counterpart on the "real" *Enterprise*, and signifies that she is, like her predecessor Marlena Moreau, sexually available, ruthless, and willing to use both those characteristics to get what she wants. She is companion-lover to not one but two Captains, moving between Jonathan Archer and Maximilian Forrest, and back to Archer as the two men move up or down in the ranks. Archer confides in her that he wants to be emperor and as the two-part episode approaches its conclusion Sato schemes to kill him. During a postcoital celebration of a space battle Archer has won, she hands him a glass of poisoned wine. During his death throes she brings in his guard, Mayweather and kisses him passionately while staring at the dying Archer, making it clear that she is responsible for the poison, and that Mayweather is under her thumb. At the end of the episode she strides onto the bridge of the ship she now controls and opens a channel to the Fleet admiral and threatens his world. She introduces herself as Empress Sato, and her last words to him reverberate across space and time. "Prepare to receive instructions," she tells the entire Mirror universe—and the standard universe as well. The last image is of her face center screen, with Mayweather, out of focus, behind her. She is in control of the man, the ship, and the empire. The message is clear: Mirror women are powerful, sexual, unbeatable, and unapologetic to the end. They get rewarded for their ambition and their sexual prowess instead of punished or disappeared, and have their choice of lovers.

However, while the Mirror universe appears to function largely as a space where writers, fans, and characters can explore their sexuality, it works in other ways too. It requires knowledge of, and familiarity with the *Star Trek* Prime universe in order to work. "The mirror universe is not just a variation on the familiar diegetic universe but, at least in its intention, its diametric reversal. Its unique features emerge in contrast to the familiar universe, and, through this intertextuality, its function is predominantly didactic in regard to values and ideals of behavior and conduct."[30]

For viewers in the 1960s watching Uhura and Moreau in *The Original Series*, for those in the 1990s watching Kira Nerys from *Deep Space Nine* and again for those watching Hoshi Soto in the prequel *Enterprise* in the early 2000s, the Mirror women were not just exhibiting power, and not simply wearing leather or baring their bellies, they were in fact embodying and performing power in ways not easily available to women in those time periods, and most certainly not in the closely constrained future envisioned by Roddenberry and his legion of writers and producers; in a moral universe, female power is problematic, and distinctly separate from sexuality. And when it occurs, the logic of storyline and culture tells us that it will be eradicated / reabsorbed back into the traditional trappings of power. It will be recouped, and the status quo restored in a distinctly Bakhtinian move. The Mirror universe eradicates this last step, allowing it to not only exist but to flourish, subverting this restoration.

In light of this tendency toward the righting of the status quo, it is perhaps not surprising that the crew of *Voyager* never found their way to the Mirror universe. In a future where a woman can be a Starship Captain (Kathryn Janeway), a full alien female can become the ship's trusted Medical Assistant (Kes), a half–Klingon, ex-criminal resistance fighter can become the ship's trusted Chief Engineer (B'Elanna Torres), and an overtly sexualized—and infantilized[31]—member of the Borg collective and still-partly-assimilated woman/machine can become the ship's trusted Science and

Astronomy expert (Seven-of-Nine), a trip to a Mirror space in which female strength, power, violence, and sexuality are linked was unnecessary.

Not coincidentally, *Voyager* is often cited as the most disliked of all the *Star Trek* series, and the predominance of strong women and its concomitant critique of male authority, war-like aggressiveness, and often trigger-happy commanders is a large part of why it is panned.[32]

> It was a rare heavy-hardware science fiction fantasy not built around a strong man, and more audaciously, it didn't seem to trouble itself over how fans would receive this. On *Voyager*, female authority was assumed and unquestioned; women conveyed sexual power without shame and anger without guilt. … it was the most feminist show in American TV history.[33]

Two particular theoretical constructs come into play in discussing the representation of women in the Mirror universe and of at least two of the powerful women on *Voyager*, Seven-of-Nine and Captain Janeway: the concept of performativity, and a kind of return of the repressed. Judith Butler applied the theory of phenomenology to gender and identity in her seminal work *Gender Trouble* in 1990. Phenomenology is a "theory of acts" that suggests that, among other things, identity is formed through the performance of actions; in other words, social agents are constructed through the actions they perform. Butler uses this formulation to posit that gender identity specifically is constructed by repeated performative acts. Performative acts are those that create as they are being enacted. Strictly and originally speaking, performativity was an adjective that described a speech act, i.e., it was "the capacity of speech and communication not simply to communicate but rather to *act or consummate an action*, or to *construct and perform an identity*" (emphasis added). This has been expanded to include actions that work toward the same ends. As many film scholars and cultural theorists have noted,[34] representation and identity are in a feedback loop and, informed by the culture in which a given representation occurs, in large part construct concepts as fundamental as race, gender, normative, deviance, and identity itself in conversation with the connections viewers make between what they see on screen and how they exist in the world. Identity, then, is a complex fusing of actions, and beliefs about those actions; a character's performance becomes not only a window into his or her identity, but a window into the world from which their identity is drawn. For the inhabitants of the *Star Trek* universe, this formulation becomes both problematic and boundless—or perhaps, problematic *because* of its boundlessness. With all of space and time to draw from, with all possibilities of gender and sexuality to write into characters, the fact that *Star Trek*'s Mirror universes frequently feature women who are hyper-sexual, clothed in fetish-wear and/or exhibiting lots of skin, and often have a ruthless or sadistic streak, is striking. As Mike Johnson, author of a number of books set in the rebooted *Star Trek* universe of JJ

Abrams, says about the original incursion into the Mirror universe, and which holds true throughout others' returns, "I think it embraces and explores a key part of what it means to be human: *our Id*. For all of Trek's wonderful and vital optimism, humanity will always possess less noble instincts, and 'Mirror, Mirror' is an example of the show's willingness to confront that"[35] (emphasis added).

Sigmund Freud, in the early 1900s, famously suggested that human development toward a more civilized state required the continued repression of primitive desires. These primitive desires include selfishness, violence, and sexual impulses.[36] Importantly, this assumes that such an evolution is in fact taking place, a view that Roddenberry embraced wholeheartedly, and used as the foundation for both the canonical "rules" followed by subsequent writers, producers, and fans, and the representation of the future presented in virtually all the *Star Trek* series. The ongoing repression of those desires in most of the series is successful most of the time, but as Freud suggested and as the Mirror universe attests, those desires are too strong to keep a lid on forever, and *Star Trek* returns both characters and viewers to their own primitive natures—embodied by women often marked as non-white—within a space coded as the opposite of a normative male-dominated one. Therefore, the performance of gendered power is understood within the Mirror world to be the opposite of the world found in Roddenberry's posited future, and that of daily life of the viewers in any decade. When this topsy-turvy, carnivalesque space is eventually righted by the characters' return to their not-nearly-as-sexual norm, and power returns to the male, everyone and all things fall back into their proper place.[37] But the Mirror universe continues to run parallel to the Prime universe; women there continue to be powerful, sexual, and resistant to the morality of Roddenberry's future; and just as Freud might have predicted, it continues to return. In an imagined future within which humans are supposed to have reached a point of civilization beyond their base impulses, women who embrace their power and their sexuality and, when it suits them, make this combination part of their repertoire for achieving their goals, are relegated to a space that is "less civilized," "more primitive" and thereby acceptable.

It could be argued that all of this boils down to a fear of women's sexuality and power; more specifically, the fear of what happens when those two are combined. Women, the *Star Trek* of the future seems to be saying, will be voracious sexually and ambitiously given the chance to express their unbound natures. They will overwhelm, they will break the bonds, break the rules. But it's not that simple. When these characters identity is constructed from their actions, which are deliberately set up to be opposite of, and yes threatening toward, the normative, accepted behavior, they can be seen to be actually reinforcing the very roles they seem to challenging so successfully. And they *are* successful. Lieutenant Moreau gets her Captain back and gets to keep her death ray machine, Hoshi Soto rises to the position of Empress of the Empire, Mirror Kira keeps her command of the Mirror *Deep Space Nine*. All these things shake up the viewers as well as the *Star Trek* characters in the normative universe.

But before it becomes too uncomfortable the Prime universe characters find their way back to their rightful places, the status quo is reinstated, and everyone breathes a sigh of relief. Through the pseudo-science of ion storms and gravitational vortices, the universe has shifted and the Mirror is obscured, reflecting nothing back to viewers.

Ergo, women don't have to be feared because they're only aggressive and sexual in that other space; sexuality isn't threatening because it is controlled and so accepted it's become a non-issue in the 23rd century; desire itself has been relegated to pushing boundaries by venturing into inter-species relationships rather than S and M; and power has reverted to its rightful spot.

Ergo, inevitably *Star Trek* is a muti-textual cultural product which asks us to look at ourselves. Its transgressive nature is a staple and continues to push the boundaries in each subsequent iteration. When those boundaries are breached, the only acceptable reaction is one of recuperation—for the characters, for the show, and for the viewers. And if the residual effects of that Mirror space linger, it is only until the next episode begins and viewers are reassured that their understanding of power and place are stable once more. But that Mirror universe is still out there, and chances are good that its power dynamics continue to exist in opposition to those in the standard *Star Trek* universe. As catharsis or as carnival, that space exerts a gravitational pull on viewers and likely on any new crew of any new series. The questions it asks haven't been answered, and the morality it upends hasn't been reached. And as *Star Trek* continues to rewrite itself and its viewers' assumptions, its continuing mission will be to keep reflecting back to us what we still need to face: ourselves.

Notes

1. "Happy" is a hyperbolic term here, perhaps. And yet in one particular and exemplary instance, that of one of the first interracial kisses on television between a white man, William Shatner (James T. Kirk) and Nichelle Nichols (Lieutenant Uhura), Shatner did indeed make a point to make the kiss a real one, and not as some of the censors and others hoped, merely a token.

2. See previous note.

3. The Civil Rights movement continued after his death, though with less visibility until recently. School desegregation occurred in the 1970s, and advancements in the rights and representations of black Americans has continued. The Black Lives Matter movement is a direct descendant, and in a way a hearkens back to the visibility of the movement in the late 1960s.

4. For the purposes of this essay, Roddenberry's guiding principle will be accepted as a starting point from which to examine the dichotomy between the Prime and the Mirror

Star Trek universes. However, much work has been done in the fields of anthropology and psychology, as well as historical analyses, that suggests that the human race is *not* evolving toward a more peaceful state. Elizabeth Cashdan, professor of anthropology at the University of Utah, posits that, "Evolution didn[apost]t just shape us to be violent, or peaceful, it shaped us to respond flexibly, adaptively, to different circumstances, and to risk violence when it made adaptive sense to do so." In essence our ability to react, to respond, suggests that there is no overall tendency toward more, or less, violence—or peace—over time, but that those attitudes and actions will reflect context and environment. See for instance: Heather Whipps. "The Evolution of Human Aggression." http://www.livescience.com/5333-evolution-human-aggression.html.

5. Rick Berman, writer/producer of a number of *Star Trek* films and series. In *Gene Roddenberry's Vision*, Paramount Pictures, 2009. https://www.youtube.com/watch?v=9jBr6lZYsco.

6. Black and white Federation citizens were just the beginning, of course; in the future, the term "race" has real meaning and refers to beings that originated light years from Earth and may or may not share actual human DNA or be able to procreate together with them.

7. Canonical in the sense that as the individual series have progressed, and various series' characters have visited this alternate world, a full back-/alternative-/parallel story and history was created to explain what started out as a one-episode adventure in the lives of the original crew. The Mirror universe is, however, also non-canonical in that it has been co-opted by fanfic writers and artists, given more inhabitants with characteristics to suit the moment, and used as a foundation for adventures and events that wouldn't fit into the canon. This is another subject altogether, and is part of what makes the *Star Trek* phenomenon unique.

8. Uncredited. http://fanlore.org/wiki/Mirror_Universe.

9. *Ibid.*

10. Robert Hewitt Wolfe. In *Star Trek—Alternate Realities—Mirror Universe, Part 1.* https://www.youtube.com/watch?v=1tqZ32v8AEc

11. Robert Hewitt Wolfe, in Granshaw, Lisa. "A loOk Through *Star Trek*'s Mirror Universe." 2015. http://boingboing.net/2015/04/01/a-look-through-star-treks-m.html.

12. Mentioned only once in one episode, this has become one of the lasting credos of the *Star Trek* world.

13. I use this term advisedly, and tongue-in-cheek. Readers of James' *50 Shades of Grey* books will be overly familiar with it, and arguably as a result, its meaning and use in the BDSM world is suspect and has become somewhat of a no-go zone.

14. Karin Blair and R.M.P. "Sex and *Star Trek*." *Science Fiction Studies*, Vol. 10, No 3 (Nov. 1983), pp. 292–297.

15. Anne Cranny-Francis. "Sexuality and Sex-Role Stereotyping in *Star Trek*." *Science Fiction Studies*, Vol 12. No. 3 (Nov. 1985), pp. 274–284.

16. Though she may be the only character ever to be sexually involved with both. In the Mirror universe storyline she marries Spock after he takes over the Mirror *Enterprise* and helps him rise to rule the empire.

17. Uncredited. https://en.wikipedia.org/wiki/Mirror_Universe#Deep_Space_Nine.

18. Jordan Hoffman. "One Trek Mind: 10 Most Awesome Things About The Mirror Universe." http://www.startrek.com/article/one-trek-mind-10-most-awesome-things-about-the-mirror-universe#sthash.AxO99TXE.dpuf. 2013.

19. Accomplished through seduction of Archer's guard, an important point to note in that it illustrates and exemplifies the specific characteristic that the Mirror universe is known for—that of sexually-charged power.

20. Jordan Hoffman.

21. Season 2, Episode 4.

22. The question of why the *Enterprise*'s landing parties often consisted of the most valuable and essential crew members, thereby virtually ensuring that should some disaster befall them the entire ship and its mission would probably fail, is another issue entirely, one I do not address here, but note.

23. In this alternate universe this sexual woman's body is exclusively marked by color,

Uhura as a black woman and Lieutenant Moreau as indeterminately olive-skinned and thereby "exotic," is significant though not part of my particular analysis. Academics and scholars, notably Daniel Bernardi and including professors Peter Decherney, Michael C. Pounds, and Michael Green, among others, have explored race and its functions within the *Star Trek* franchise. From the beginning, the *Star Trek* universe was decidedly white and male, with people of color, women, and aliens being the Others, and as such often violent, sexual, voracious in appetite, and threatening.

24. Handlen.

25. In this aspect, and not developed in this essay, her use of power hearkens back to Kirk's oft-noted use of his own position as Captain to gain the attention of yeomen assigned to him on the bridge.

26. Cranny-Francis, p. 275.

27. And twenty-two episodes.

28. An interim episode, "Shattered Mirror" plays out many of the same dynamics. Essentially, when Sisko returns to the Mirror universe, Kira has become a prisoner but she hasn't lost either her power or her sexuality, and when she escapes she keeps it all intact.

29. With a new TV series about to launch as of this writing, it will be fascinating to see whether the Mirror universe will receive a visit from the new crew. Chances are it will. After all, as all the writers and many fans note, having an oppositely charged universe in which to play out scenarios that would not be possible in a morally upright, Federation-controlled future is compelling.

30. Steffen Hantke. "*Star Trek*'s Mirror Universe Episodes and U.S. Military Culture Through the Eyes of the Other." *Science Fiction Studies*, Vol. 41, No. 3 (Nov. 2014), pp. 562–578.

31. Again, not an area I plan to examine in this essay, but a fertile one.

32. A number of online sources, mostly fan sites but with some critics' chiming in, discuss this. A few follow, accessed July, 2016: http://www.denofgeek.com/tv/star-trek-voyager/23099/why-do-star-trek-fans-hate-voyager; http://jmtresaugue.blogspot.com/2012/05/11-reasons-why-i-hate-star-trek-voyager.html; http://www.wewantinsanity.com/am2/publish/Peter_Dawson/When_Bad_Shows_Go_Good_Star_Trek_Voyager.shtml; http://entertain-o-rama.com/6-reasons-star-trek-voyager-was-unsuccessful/.

33. Ian Grey. "Now, *Voyager*: In Praise of the Trekkiest Trek of All." 2013. http://www.rogerebert.com/balder-and-dash/now-voyager-the-least-beloved-star-trek-offered-some-of-the-franchises-strongest-feminist-messages.

34. See for Example: Richard Dyer, Laura Mulvey, Stuart Hall, Toni Morrison, James Snead, Graham Turner, Fatimah Tobing Rony, etc.

35. In Granshaw.

36. This development parallels that of children, according to Freud, who must be civilized by learning to repress those desires, just as the human race as a whole must learn to do. A future examination into how this is in play with *Voyager*'s Seven of Nine character's child-like innocence in all things sexual is forthcoming.

37. When *Voyager*, however, doesn't allow for the return—when the carnival continues after the episode ends—it is more than unsettling; it requires a repression of another sort. Namely, criticism and dismissal.

Works Cited

Bernardi, Daniel Leonard. *Star Trek and History: Race-ing Toward a White Future*. London: Rutgers University Press, 1999.

Blair, Karin, and R.M.P. "Sex and *Star Trek*." *Science Fiction Studies*, Vol. 10, No 3 (Nov. 1983), pp. 292–297.

Butler, Judith. *Gender Trouble*. New York: Routledge, 2008.

_____. "Performative Acts and Gender Constitution: An Essay in Phenomenology and Feminist Theory." *Theatre Journal*, Vol. 40, No. 4 (Dec. 1988), pp. 519–531.

Cranny-Francis, Anne. "Sexuality and Sex-Role Stereotyping in *Star Trek*." *Science Fiction Studies*, Vol 12. No. 3 (Nov. 1985), pp. 274–284.

Deeherney, Peter. "Race in Space." *Cinéaste*, Vol. 26, No. 3 (Summer 2001), pp. 38–39.

Freud, Sigmund. *Moses and Monotheism*. Knopf, 1939.
Handlen, Zach. "Star Trek: Deep Space Nine: Crossover/The Collaborator." http://www.avclub.com/tvclub/star-trek-deep-space-nine-crossoverthe-collaborato-81222.
Hantke, Steffen. "*Star Trek*'s Mirror Universe Episodes and US Military Culture Through the Eyes of the Other." *Science Fiction Studies*, Vol. 41, No. 3 (Nov. 2014), pp. 562–578.

On How to Overcome Nonfunctional Attachment Bonds in Outer Space

NADINE FARGHALY

Aeryn Sun and Seven of Nine are two female characters who, while not situated in the same universe, both overcame nonfunctional attachment bonds, and a lack of a secure base they had been subjected to during their childhood and teenage years. The connection between those characters might not be apparent at first glance, but once one looks deeper, it becomes clear that these characters not only share a very similar upbringing, but also have had to face the same challenges and experienced the same difficulties while integrating into other societies. Both manage to leave emotional constraints caused by their upbringing behind them in order to become functional as well as emotionally accessible members of society.

These two characters both starred in SFF television shows, *Star Trek Voyager* and *Farscape*, that aired in 1995 and 2001. This essay demonstrates how both characters overcame the lack of attachment bond relationships, the lack of a secure base, as well as an absence of expressing and sharing their emotions; how these aspects managed to influence their adult relationships, and how these women overcame their misgivings in order to become fully functional, accessible, and integrated members of their respective societies. But before these ideas can be discussed in detail, it is necessary to have a closer look at attachment theory.

Attachment Theory

Attachment theory explains the concept of long-term relationships between individuals. The main premise is that children need to form a bond with their primary caregivers in order to establish a secure base from which they are able to explore the world around them. If the secure base is lacking or missing, the child's future might be complicated by an inability to function properly in a social environment. The child's social, as well as emotional and behavioral development can be severely limited if this base and the attachment are unsatisfactory.

The origins of attachment theory lie with John Bowlby and Mary Ainsworth and draw on the fields of ethology, cybernetics, information processing, developmental psychology, and psychoanalytics (*Bowlby* 1). Bowlby states that the mother figure functions as a child's superego and ego: "she orients him in space and time, provides his environment, permits the satisfaction of some impulses, restricts others. She is his ego and superego.... Ego and superego are thus inextricably [b]ound up with the child's primary human relationships" (*A Secure Base* 53). Bowlby concluded that in order for children to grow up healthy and to develop all the social skills needed to become functional members of society they should "experience a warm, intimate, and continue[d] relationship with [a primary caregiver] in which both find satisfaction and enjoyment" (84). Furthermore, Bowlby claims that attachment behavior, while at its peak in early childhood, continues to be present throughout one's life. He concludes that his theory of attachment is "an attempt to explain both attachment behavior, with its episodic appearance and disappearance, and also the enduring attachments that children and other individuals make to particular others" (18).

Officer Aeryn Sun, Peacekeeper Commando, Icarion Company, Pleisar Regiment

To understand the extraordinary character development Aeryn Sun underwent, one needs to be aware of not only Sebacean, but also Peacekeeper Society.[1] Sebaceans are a race that never mixes with other species; individuals who do so are expelled and punished for their transgression. Not only is it forbidden to engage in interspecies relationships and to conceive hybrids, but Sebacean parents are helpless to stand up to Peacekeeper Rule as well. Captain Bialar Crais and his brother were taken from their parents when they were teenagers to serve in the Peacekeeper army. One can speculate on the reasons for their conscription, but it seems to be plausible that the brothers, and many more like them, were taken for two main reasons: first, to increase the Peacekeeper forces and second, to extend the already existing gene pool since most Peacekeepers are not taken like Crais and his brother; rather, Peacekeeper soldiers are bred. Although the Peacekeepers employ active breeding programs, where women are inseminated to ensure steady

Peacekeeper replenishments, offspring are also secured through "recreation." Peacekeeper Command encourages their armed forces to be discrete but uninhibited with their sexual urges. Once a child is conceived from recreation, which is considered to be a healthy outlet for stress, it is taken away from the parents. Peacekeeper Command assumes that the mothers do not want their children anyway, since this kind of emotional attachment is forbidden. Developing positive feelings for one's child is regarded as a weakness and needs to be punished severely. Although the children inherit their mothers' last name, there is no form of family connection attached to it. After being born, the mini soldiers are raised by specially trained Peacekeeper staff that prepare them for a life of battle and obedience. The mothers, having been raised in the same fashion, do not object to this procedure. In addition, after Peacekeepers were taken from Earth centuries ago,[2] the Idalons altered the genetic code of the female soldiers, resulting in an acceleration of the pregnancy process. The precise duration of the growth period is unknown, though it is described as a "geometric pregnancy" ("Peacekeeper Wars"). Having the pregnancy last a few weeks rather than a few months effectively diminishes the mother-child bonding time, resulting in a lack of emotional attachment. Furthermore, Peacekeeper children also do not get any kind of emotional encouragement or support from their caretakers.

As was explained earlier, Bowlby states that children need a strong secure base while they are growing up. He also proposes that the first bonds an individual forms will have a lasting impact on all future relationships. The first secure base is provided by the primary caregivers. It can be said that every child feels safest around the person who looks after the child the most. Toddlers use their primary caregivers as a centre from which they explore their surroundings (*A Secure Base* 120). Peacekeeper community does not offer any of these features. They do not provide any kind of secure base at all. On the contrary, the strict command structure does not encourage their soldiers to think and act independently; Command expects but one thing, complete obedience.

It was an act of disobedience that brought Aeryn Sun into this universe. Her mother, Xhalax Sun, and her father, Talyn Lyczac, committed insubordination in more ways than one. First, they fell in love, an emotion regarded as weak and a nuisance, second, they entered an exclusive relationship, and third, they deliberately conceived Aeryn, as a daughter who should be the living embodiment of their feelings and devotion to each other. Xhalax, unwilling to give her child over without some kind of emotional bond, seeks her daughter out when Aeryn is still a child. Aeryn remembers this incident as a dream, but later this dream gets validated by a recording Crais shows her:

AERYN: When I was very young, one night a soldier appeared over my bunk. Battle-hardened. Scarred...
JOHN: Cool. Your father.
AERYN: My mother. She told me I wasn't merely an accident, or a genetic birthing to fill the ranks, that she and a male that she had cared about had chosen to yield a life. Mine ["Family Ties" *Farscape*].

Xhalax wanted her daughter to have some kind of knowledge of her origin. She wanted Aeryn to know that she was not a by-product of a random recreational act, but that she was "conceived in love. Our love. I wanted you to know this. It makes you special. We wanted you and we love you" ("Thanks for Sharing" *Farscape*). It is this knowledge that predestines Aeryn to stray from the strict path Peacekeeper training wants her to follow. The fact that she was indeed a child conceived in love with parents that cared about her allowed her to exceed her Peacekeeper training. As Bowlby states, "the powerful influence on a child's development, of the ways he is treated by ... the mother figure" (*A Secure Base* 120) predestines all other kinds of attachment this child will form later in life. And while Aeryn lived her life under Peacekeeper rule and oppression, a life without emotional attachment and security, the short interaction with her mother might have been the sole reason for her ability to "be more" ("Premiere" *Farscape*). Aeryn changes from a stone cold warrior without time for tender feelings into an emotionally mature woman who feels comfortable about herself, but can still kick ass with the best of her regiment. In the first episode "Première" the audience gets a good idea of Aeryn's state of mind during a conversation she has with Crichton; they discuss what they should do with the prisoners once they are able to flee.

JOHN: Sabotage? Give me a break—they haven't hurt us! How about we show them a little compassion?
AERYN: Compassion? What is compassion?
JOHN: Compassion? Wh- you're kidding right? It's a feeling that you have when you see someone else's pain and instead of taking advantage of their weakness you help 'em.
AERYN: Oh. I know this feeling.
JOHN: Yeah well it is a fairly *common* human feeling.
AERYN: I hate it ["Première" *Farscape*].

As was stated, an inability to balance and express (positive) emotions, is the result of a nonfunctional attachment bond. It is therefore no surprise that Aeryn, who grew up knowing that positive feelings by compassion are a hindrance, is unaccustomed to think about other individuals in a positive manner. Although Aeryn dislikes this feeling, considering such emotions a sign of weakness, she matures more and more into a woman who can appreciate it. When Crichton tells her in the series' pilot that she can be so much more

("Première" *Farscape*), she does not believe him. Even though Aeryn knew that she was special, Peacekeeper training was so ingrained into her subconsciousness that she is unable to imagine that her life could be different. To develop meaningful connections with other individuals is deeply frowned upon in Peacekeeper society, and therefore, Aeryn is very wary of Crichton's offer. Gradually, over the course of four seasons, the miniseries, as well as the graphic novel series, Aeryn becomes so much more: friend, sister, role model, teacher, daughter, lover, wife, and mother. The most impressive aspect here is that her character develops naturally and slowly; there is nothing forced or fake about her personality growth. While it was the relationship with Crichton that originally made her aware of her emotional cravings, the close friendships that she made with the other members of Moya also helped her to restructure her nonfunctional attachment bonds. Aeryn's close interaction with the crew of Moya, as well as Moya herself, help to restructure, repair and rebuild her ability to form attachment bonds. The change happens gradually; while Aeryn had experienced emotional attachment to men before, emotional attachment to strictly platonic friends are completely new to her. Once Aeryn realizes that she could trust her crew members to not leave her behind, she herself becomes more open in exploring her own personality. It is this feeling of security, that helps her to leave the parameters of her upbringing behind her. Once she is fully integrated into the crew of Moya, she is able to use them as a secure base. Not only to explore herself, her emotions, but also the world around her. This feeling of security also enables her to form attachments, as well as personal relationships with other individuals. This emotional security likewise allows Aeryn to mourn not only for Valorek, a former lover she had betrayed, but also for her lost childhood and the nonfunctional bond between *her and her mother.*

Another aspect of Aeryn's character which makes her character development very credible is her motivation. She does not change because society demands it from her, neither does she change because certain individuals expect it; Aeryn changes because she wants to. She wants to be so much more than just a Peacekeeper prowler pilot who expects the following stations in her life, "Service. Promotion. Retirement. Death" ("Bad Timing" *Farscape*). She strives to become a better Sebacean when she realizes that once she was free from the Peacekeeper regime and its rigid militaristic code of behavior, she is free to do as she pleases. It takes her a long time to reach that conclusion, but once she does nothing could can stop her. Even after she and Crichton openly acknowledged their feelings for each other, she does not mold her life around him. On the contrary, Aeryn leaves him at the end of the third season even though she discovers that she is pregnant. Even as Crichton pleads with her to stay with him Aeryn decides to leave.

AERYN: Do you love Aeryn Sun?
JOHN: Beyond hope.
AERYN: Then don't make me say good-bye and don't make me stay ["Dog with Two Bones" *Farscape*].

In the end he accepts her decision and she flies away in her prowler, alone, pregnant and without goal. His acceptance of the decision, is one of the reasons why she comes back to him. Aeryn realizes that whatever happens, their attachment bond was strong enough to survive the separation, and Crichton's willingness to let her go not only exhibited his readiness to accept her for *whom* she had become, but also that he would be there for her if she should choose to come back. Eventually, Aeryn returns to Moya; she does so after she came to terms with her own feelings and desires. Aeryn realizes that she can very well be attached to someone without losing or compromising herself. However, Aeryn's biggest challenge takes place after the television series ends. The graphic novel series, which continues the narrative of the televison show, demonstrates how she is slowly growing into her role as a mother. During the first story arc, which consists of four separate installments, "The Beginning of the End of the Beginning," the readers can accompany Aeryn as she gets used to motherhood. The reader witnesses how uncomfortable she seems to be around the child. There are many instances when she is shown holding, and struggling with, the screaming infant whereas Crichton seems to take to fatherhood naturally. Keeping Aeryn's upbringing in mind, her inability to bond with the child is very believable. While she has achieved a remarkable progress in her ability to form bonds with other individuals, becoming a mother must have brought up the failures and fears of her own childhood. This imbalance is a source of great discomfort to Aeryn; however, it is one she overcomes by the end of the first story arc. She and John attempt to discuss Aeryn's uneasiness with the child several times during this story arc; however, they are always interrupted and nothing fruitful comes of these conversation attempts. Thankfully, at the end this issue is resolved:

JOHN: How're you doing, Aeryn?
AERYN: Better now that I have figured it out. Deke [their son] was reacting to me being unsure of myself-and being anxious and frightened of being a poorer mother than my own. Deke sensed that. But when I was myself...
JOHN: Kicking ass and taking names.
AERYN: Exactly—then he was fine. So from now on, I'll just be myself.
JOHN: Best person for you to be ["Hynerian Rhapsody"].

Aeryn realizes that all she needs to do is to be herself. She does not need to pretend to be some kind of über-mother or even a completely different person. The person that she is proves to be more than sufficient for the job she has to do, being a mother. Her son recognizes this from the start and in time so does Aeryn. In the end, all she has to do is to find a way to feel comfortable with herself again; accepting her changed status as a parental figure is the final step for her to becoming not only a good mother, but also to completely regain her ability to form emotional attachments and not only be functional member of her own family, but of the society she lives in as well. Aeryn realizes that she can indeed be a secure base for her own child. Contrary to her own upbringing, she has developed enough compassion and nurturing instincts to not only keep her child alive, but also happy. After she acknowledges to herself that she will be a far better mother than Xhalax, Aeryn is able to embrace motherhood. The Soldier moved beyond her challenging upbringing and the lack of nurture she had to endure; despite everything, she has managed to become a whole person in her own right, one who is more than able to function as a secure base for others.

Her role as a mother is not the only aspect of her new "self" with which Aeryn has to struggle. Her new status as a mother affects her relationship with Crichton, who seems to regard her in a different way now that she is a mother and he is, according to his own lived experiences, the head of the family. During the first story arc, when the two try to decide who is going to rescue the others from a trap on Hyneria (Rygel's home planet) Crichton and Aeryn have the following heated discussion:

> Aeryn: In any case.... I'll ready a transport pod so I can effect a rescue.
> John: Whoa. So you can effect a rescue.
> Aeryn: Someone has to stay behind with Deke.... I am a trained soldier-if there's going to be a rescue I should be the one who goes.
> John: Look, Aeryn, I'm not just gonna sit on my ass changing diapers while you go off on some harebrained rescue mission.
> Aeryn: Yet, you expect me to do likewise.
> John: Yes! Well, no! I mean it should be both of us ["Dungeons and Dominars"].

And so it happens that they go together and take their son along for the ride. The fact that Aeryn has become a mother causes Crichton to change tack from his otherwise very unpatriarchal, almost feminist character. With the birth of the baby, he suddenly expects Aeryn to conform to his idea of the stereotypical woman/mother, someone who would like nothing better than to stay at home with the kids waiting for her husband to return from work. However, Crichton's lapse in judgment (and memory) was very brief, given that he soon agrees that all of them should go rescue their comrades. Neither Crichton nor Aeryn is the type to just stay at home and wait for something to happen, although Crichton finds that forgetting ingrained cultural standards is a difficult process as he repeats his mistake in a different form shortly thereafter. Aeryn discovers that John has been lying to her about the potential threat and her reaction makes it very clear what she expects of her partner:

JOHN: Look, I didn't want to worry you, and-
AERYN: I do not need you to protect me!
JOHN: Dammit! Protecting my family is my job!
AERYN: It's our family, John, and I'm perfectly capable of protecting it, too! You will not keep dangers from me- ever! Is that understood?
JOHN: You're right, Aeryn. I'm sorry.
AERYN: Yes, I am right. And yes, you are sorry ["Dungeons and Dominars"].

There is no doubt for the readers, the producers, or the writers that Crichton's plan would never have worked. The quote above illustrates how Aeryn must negotiate a new space, wherein the fact that she is a mother does not diminish her other roles, such as warrior, friend, lover, or wife. The fact that Aeryn is able to embrace her new role as mother and to align with her other character aspects, if the ultimate proof that she has found her secure base. John Crichton became Aeryn's primaries secure base, secure in his love and support, she is able to work through her new status as a mother, knowing, that even if she should stumble or fall, he would be there to catch her.

Seven of Nine, Tertiary Adjunct of Unimatrix Zero-One

Seven of nine was born as Annika Hansen. Her parents were exobiologists who embarked on a long-term trip to study the Borg, a mixture of different species that are being captured and then transformed using cybernetic organisms which changes them into drones who reside in a collective they call the hive. The Hansens took their four-year-old daughter with them, a fact that Seven later describes as highly irresponsible ("Dark Frontier" *STV*). They followed the Borg for three years before they were finally captured. Seven's parents were assimilated while she was put into a Borg maturation chamber. These maturation chambers are used to accelerate the development of adolescent humanoids until they are ready to be functional members of the Borg collective. In the episode "Mortal Coil," it is stated that the drones stay in their maturation chambers until they are biologically 17 cycles old. Seven of Nine spent several years of her life in a Borg maturation chamber, and although she was able to form positive emotional attachment bonds to her parents before they were captured by the Borg, it is safe to assume that the years in isolation, being held captive in the maturation chamber right after being implanted with cybernetic nano probes, did not help her emotional development. Furthermore, Jeri Ryan, who plays Seven of Nine, said in an interview "that [Seven] has no memory whatsoever of humanity or emotions or any of that" (*Voyager* Time Capsule Season 6 Extras). An idea that is later mirrored in the television series. A confrontation between

Janeway and Seven of Nine in the second episode of Season Four demonstrates that, although Seven was born as human and was raised as such, for the first six years of her life, her newly liberated self has no idea about human emotions.

> SEVEN: Take me back to my own kind!
> CAPT.: You are with your own kind—humans.
> SEVEN: I don't remember being human. I don't know what it is to be human! ["The Gift" *STV*].

Seven of nine was liberated from the Borg against her will, much like she was assimilated into the Borg years before. Therefore, her relationship to Capt. Janeway is a very difficult one, Janeway starts out as being Seven's liberator, and their relationship gradually changes until it resembles that of mother and daughter, complete with all the arguments and disagreements that usually accompany a normal mother-daughter relationship (especially during puberty). While Seven seems to be one of very few people who are able to defy Janeway and her ideals, Janeway also functions as a secure base for Seven of Nine. In fact, Capt. Janeway functions as a secure base for all *Voyager* crew members. While Starfleet captains are usually advised to keep a certain form of emotional distance from their crewmembers, Janeway is different. This difference arose from the situation they were in and is explained by Janeway in her personal log "Here, in the Delta Quadrant, we are virtually the entire family of man. We are more than a crew, and I must find a way to be more than a captain to these people, but it's not clear to me exactly how to begin" ("The Cloud" *STV*). Janeway gradually became more than a captain and a friend, she became some kind of mother replacement for her crew. But in no other of her relationships does she function more prominently as a mother figure as in the relationship between her and Seven of Nine.

Although Seven is often portrayed as a foil for Janeway, their relationship is more similar to that of mother and daughter. Seven uses Janeway as a kind of role model, even when they disagree on certain topics, and even though Seven is not beyond going behind Janeway's back if she deems it necessary, she still looked up to her. It can easily be argued that Seven's deassimiliation functions as her rebirth, therefore the fact that she regards Janeway as some kind of mother figure is highly important. As Bowlby states, children need a primary caregiver, and in this case, the caregivers are obvious, Capt. Janeway and the Doctor. Capt. Janeway offers Seven the possibility to safely explore the world around her. Seven, knowing that Janeway will be there to help her, teach her, and more importantly catch her, gains more and more confidence, not only where her own emotional state is concerned, but also about her place among humans. Seven's close relationship to Capt. Janeway can be observed multiple times throughout the series and their strong emotional bonds manifests often during times of stress or emotional turmoil. Seven often comes to her when she has questions regarding humanity:

> Seven: I am finding it a difficult challenge to integrate into this group. It is full of complex social structures that are unfamiliar to me. Compared with the Borg, this crew is inefficient and contentious, but it is capable of surprising acts of compassion.
>
> Janeway: Unexpected acts of kindness are common among our group. That's one of the ways we define ourselves ["Day of Honor" *STV*].

Janeway often helps Seven when the young woman is in need of advice. In the episode "Dark Frontier," Janeway could can also be observed performing other motherly aspects. At the end of this episode, Janeway performs the equivalent of putting a child to bed, when she argues with Seven about the time when Seven should start to regenerate, up to the point when Janeway guides Seven to her alcove and watches her fall asleep. Janeway fulfills her motherly duties in more ways than one, besides offering Seven of Nine a basis from which she could safely explore not only herself, but also the world around her; she often functions as someone Seven could go to in times of need and more importantly, someone who cares for her unconditionally. By entering this relationship, Seven makes her first step towards regaining her ability to function successfully with other individuals, laying the groundwork for future attachment bonds.

Besides Janeway, the holographic Doctor also functions as a caregiver for Seven of Nine. Starting out as a serial hologram without any remarkable character traits, the Doctor had to gain his humanity as much a Seven did. Having developed his own humanity within the four seasons before Seven joined the crew of *Voyager*, he is in the unique position to understand both sides. He knows where Seven is coming from and where she is headed to. It is therefore logical that the Doctor assumes the role of mentor for Seven of Nine. He worked out a multi-step program for Seven, which guides her step by step through the various phases of reintegrating herself in humanoid society. These steps consisted consist of how to have small talk, how to behave during a date, after jokes, and many other aspects. He also encourages her to experiment with hobbies, tastes, and so on. The Doctor becomes more than a friend for Seven and in various episodes it can be seen that he is someone she goes to when she is feeling insecure or is in need of counsel; their relationship gradually passes through different phases like father figure, mentor, and friend. Remember that Bowlby states that individuals crave their caregivers, especially when they are "frightened, fatigued," or in need of comfort (A Secure Base 27). The doctor's most remarkable accomplishment, however, may be that he finally got Seven to indulge. In the episode *Body and Soul* the Doctors program is transferred into Seven's Borg implants, resulting in him taking over her body. For the first time the Doctor is able to experience sensations such as eating and drinking. Needless to say, he completely indulges himself, and to say Seven is not amused would be an understatement; she highly resents the Doctor for over-indulging while in her body:

> The Doctor: When did it become a crime to enjoy a sensation or two? Of course, you'd be the last person to understand that.
> Seven: What do you mean?
> The Doctor: The whole world is full of experiences and sensations, but you insist on denying yourself. Instead of replicating caviar, you choose nutritional supplement thirteen alpha.
> Seven: Caviar is an indulgence.
> The Doctor: Indulgences are what make life worth living! ["Body and Soul" *STV*].

This scene reveals that although Seven has gradually accepted her role as a human being, she still does not see any value in experiencing unnecessary joy. This episode is important for multiple aspects: first of all Seven's ability to actually have an argument with someone is a huge step forward in her development. The fact that she is completely open with the Doctor and does not fear any repercussions for speaking her mind demonstrates that she has a close personal relationship to that person. It becomes clear that her emotional attachment to the Doctor is strong enough to survive the small argument unharmed. This feature serves as another validation for the Doctor's function as secure base. This awareness is reinforced towards the end of this episode when Seven enters the Doctor's sick bay carrying a tray of Foie gras with truffles as well as wine. When the doctor informs her that the mess Hall is three decks up, she replies, "it's come to my attention that nutritional supplements don't fully meet my needs" ("Body and Soul" *STV*). Because of the argument, Seven was willing to reconsider her choices in food intake. This does not seem to be an important aspect for any other characters, but for Seven of Nine who was a raised after Borg principles, that every indulgences is unnecessary and cannot be tolerated, this kind of indulgence is an impressive task. If it would not have been for the Doctor, Seven would not have been following his advice to indulge once in a while. Through the interaction with the Doctor and the Captain, Seven was able to rebuild her ability to form attachment bonds to individuals. Moreover, without the constant validation and support that she was offered by her to primary caregivers, Seven would not have been able to explore her humanity in the way she did.

One of the most important factors that enables Seven to be able to form attachment bonds, as well as function as secure base for others, are the Borg children *Voyager* adopts over time. In the episode "Drone," Seven experiences motherly feelings for the first time. In that particular episode, during a transporter malfunction, Seven's nanoprobes interact with the Doctor's mobile transmitter, and with the help of an innocent bystander creates an actual

Borg baby drone. The drone matures very quickly, and after almost one or two days he is completely grown. Capt. Janeway commands Seven to look after the drone and to help it to discover his individuality, and One, the name he gave himself, does just that and decides at the end of the episode that he should not be alive. This is one of the rare moments in the series where Seven expresses feelings for another individual, when One was dying she was pleading with him not to hurt her. When *Voyager* later adopted four Borg children, Seven makes them her responsibility. Not only does she devise schedules for learning and activities, she also helps them to discover their heritages. The process of looking after those children who were so much like herself, expedites Seven's ability to form attachment bonds. Knowing that she does not want those children to experience the same emotionless upbringing she had to endure, she tries her best to offer them an emotionally stable environment. Seven wants them to be able to express themselves, knowing that she would be there if they need her. Almost against her will, Seven can be observed changing from an emotionally unavailable Ex–Borg drone into a fully-fledged crew member. A short interlude between her and Lieut. Tuvok, demonstrates that Seven started to care about the crew of *Voyager* almost without her noticing it. The following scene is from the episode *The Raven*; Tuvok and Seven are stranded on the planet where her parents' ship had crashed years ago. Here, Seven is plagued by flashbacks of her childhood and her assimilation, hallucinations which leave her frightened and overwhelmed. In this state, she can be observed falling back into Borg behavioral patterns:

> TUVOK: We've scanned this entire region for Borg. There are none.
> SEVEN: You're wrong. They are here. Vulcan. Species Three Two Five Nine. Your enlarged neocortex produces superior analytical abilities. Your distinctiveness will be added to our.
> TUVOK: Seven?
> SEVEN: No. I will not assimilate you. Once I return to the Collective, you will go back to *Voyager* and tell Captain Janeway what's happened to me. Thank her for her patience, for her kindness.
> TUVOK: Curious. Your behaviour demonstrates affection and sentiment. Traits of humanity. Hardly Borg. You've been experiencing hallucinations, flashbacks.
> SEVEN: Yes.
> TUVOK: Does that usually occur when a resonance signal is activated?
> SEVEN: No.
> BORG [OC]: Seven of Nine. Grid nine-two of subjunction twelve.
> SEVEN: But I can hear them calling me. I'm frightened
> TUVOK: That's understandable. Lower the forcefield. We can return to *Voyager* and find out what's happening to you. I am your shipmate. We can return to *Voyager* together. ["The Raven" *STV*].

This scene is important for multiple reasons: it is the first time that someone besides Janeway refers to Seven as a member of the crew; it is also a turning point because Seven experiences dread, as well as angst for the first time after her liberation from the Borg. But apart from these aspects, this episode also is important because this is the first time that Seven of Nine admits to her becoming attached to the members of *Voyager*. The crew of *Voyager* starts to function as a surrogate family for Seven.

While Seven finds a new family on *Voyager*, her old life refuses to let her go easily. In almost every encounter with the Borg Queen, the Queen tries to not only persuade Seven to come back to her and the Borg collective, but she also insists on the fact that Borg is family. The last of these exchanges happens in the episode *Endgame Part II*:

> THE BORG QUEEN: Seven of Nine, Tertiary Adjunct of Unimatrix 01. It's been too long.
> SEVEN OF NINE: What do you want?
> THE BORG QUEEN: Do I need a reason to visit a friend?
> SEVEN OF NINE: We're not friends.
> THE BORG QUEEN: No. We're more than that. We're family ["Endgame II" *STV*].

Although the Borg Queen is more than persistent in this episode, Seven decisively cuts all bonds to her former society. This dialogue marks the first occasion where Seven does not feel the need to comply or to engage in a conversation with the Borg Queen at all; another step for her in leaving her old life behind and to finally and completely accept her own humanity. But the episodes *Endgame Part I and II* also include the last step Seven takes towards her full recovery.

The final endeavor Seven undertakes in her journey to completely regain the whole facets of human emotions and capabilities is her decision to date one of the crew members. While Seven could be observed in romantic relationships before, those relationships are usually in either dreams sequences or otherwise unreal settings. Her relationship with Commander Chakotay is the first one Seven enters into consciously as well as in charge of her human emotions. During the episodes *Endgame Part I and II* the audience learns that Chakotay and Seven of Nine eventually married and lived happily ever after, until one of them died. With this final act of entering a romantic relationship, Seven completes the cycle of regaining and repairing all the possibilities that have been diminished by the lack of a secure base of attachment bond during her early years. The attachment bond that she forms with Chakotay functions successfully as an addition to the attachment bonds she formed with her primary caregivers, the Captain and the Doctor. As Bowlby states, "as an individual grows older, his life continues to be organized the same kind of way, though his excursions become steadily longer both in time and space" (A Secure Base 62). Bowlby believes that according to how we live our life, it is completely natural to form new attachment bonds. Seven of Nine was able to form a romantic attachment bond to commander Chakotay because of the positive experiences she made on *Voyager*. As Fraley verifies, "whether an adult is secure or insecure in his or her adult relationships may be a partial reflection of his or her experiences with his or her primary caregivers." Having had the opportunity to almost start with a blank slate and to recover not only her humanity, but also built and reconstruct attachment patterns and bonds, Seven left her unfortunate childhood upbringings behind her. By first becoming a daughter, then a friend, a teacher and mentor herself, and finally a partner in a romantic relationship, Seven successfully demonstrated that she is more than capable of offering herself as an attachment bond partner as well as a secure base.

Aeryn Sun and Seven of Nine: Two Sides of the Same Coin?

As shown above, these two individuals are not that different. While Aeryn was raised by the Peacekeepers, Seven was raised by the Borg collective; Aeryn's growth was accelerated, while Seven was put into a maturation chamber; Aeryn comes from a society that breeds their members indifferent of emotional attachment, and Seven comes from a society which assimilates and does not partake in any emotional behaviors whatsoever. Both of them were liberated against their will: John Crichton rescued Aeryn and Capt. Janeway rescued Seven. Equally, both of these characters are regarded as traitors and can never return to their respective former societies. At the beginning, both of these characters reject emotional feelings as inefficient and superfluous. They insist that they do not need other individuals in order to lead functional lives; an idea that works well with Bowlby's claim that a false impression of maturity functions as a defence mechanism. It is not until later that both of them realize that their emotional attachments and connections to others are not only assets, but that they also help them to enrich their lives and to make it easier to socialize with other individuals. Both of them have to learn to find meaning from sources other than the collective and Peacekeeper Command, and by doing so, they find not only a way to reconnect with themselves, but they are also enabled to reconstruct, rebuilt, and regain their ability to form attachment bonds to others.

Aeryn and Seven also differ from other female SFF characters in a number of ways. For one, they are not involved in stereotypical fights with other women. Whenever Aeryn is confronted with a possible rival for Crichton's affections, she refuses to fight with the other woman. Instead, she decides to take the responsible way and resolve her tension in another fashion. While this behavior could be interpreted as passive or even cowardly, I think it demonstrates Aeryn's unwillingness to compromise her own integrity for something she thinks every person needs to decide for him or herself. In addition, due to her upbringing Aeryn, does not place much faith in emotions; therefore, fighting over a man would be a very trivial affair and a waste of time for her. As a result, she is also not burdened by the idea that she can increase her self-worth or social standing if she is attached to a male partner. Since Seven is not seen in a real romantic relationship until the series ends, it is not possible to say how she would react; however, it is doubtful that Seven would engage in the above mentioned behaviour as well.

However, there are a few aspects in which Aeryn and Seven differ: for one, the way in which they are integrated in society and in which they reconstruct their abilities to form attachment bonds. While Aeryn's main mentor is John Crichton, her love interest, Seven of Nine was first guided by Capt. Janeway and the Doctor. Both of these female protagonists acquire friendships that help them to reshape, rebuild, and reconstruct the attachment bond that should have been formed while they were growing up. Whereas Aeryn befriended Pilot and the rest of the crew of Moya, Seven's first foray into the realm of friendships occurred with children and a non-humanoid life form. It is here, where the main difference between those two characters lies, Aeryn Sun becomes a lover and a friend before she is ready to accept her role as mother. In contrast, Seven of Nine becomes a daughter, a friend, and mother figures before she is able enter into a romantic relationship. These two characters also differ in the way they are portrayed on the screen. When comparing the way Aeryn's appearance on screen is staged with other female SFF characters, such as *Star Trek Voyager*'s Seven of Nine, Aeryn almost seems to be prudish. Whereas Seven of Nine's presence can be attributed to low ratings and the producers' plan to incorporate more sexuality into the series in order to increase audience numbers (Snierson), Aeryn's presence on *Farscape* was incorporated as an important part of the plotline from the series' conception. Despite the fashion in which they are dressed, the camera shots for these two women also differ from each other. Seven of Nine wears various colored cat suits, but Aeryn is rarely shown out of her Peacekeeper uniform, made of black leather. It can hardly be called enticing or inviting, although the black leather vest she wears for much of Seasons Three and Four is low-cut and bares her midriff. The audience rarely sees Aeryn in plain clothes. During those rare episodes when Aeryn is sexualized through her clothing, she is usually acting in dream sequences, alternate realities, or in need of a disguise. Farscape's producers seemed eager to ensure that Aeryn was seen as a warrior, especially at the beginning of the series. Later, Aeryn's character changed, but it was not until the Fourth Season that this change was mirrored in her outer appearance. Unexpectedly, Aeryn wore a lot of make-up and also appeared to be much slimmer. This increased focus on her female attributes was presumably the producers' way of portraying "the dichotomy in [Aeryn's] character" (Ginn 99). Nonetheless, the fact that Aeryn did not wear make-up during the earlier seasons as well the lack of an "inviting" clothing style demonstrated that the character was constructed in a way that made sexualizing her unnecessary. *Farscape*'s writers and producers reinforced this concept—that Aeryn is more than an attractive woman—in the ways in which they wrote and filmed her character. For example, Aeryn is rarely the object of body-focused camera shots. She is usually filmed without heavy influence on her breasts, backside, or other gender attributes, suggesting that she is not as sexualized as Seven. In fact, one can see no difference in the way the male characters on *Farscape* are staged in contrast to Aeryn. This is also true in the few sex scenes the audience is treated to: Aeryn rarely shows naked skin and she is even concealed in the bedroom scenes. In contrast, Chiana is not restrained in the same way. The audience can witness a lot of naked skin when she and D'argo have sex in "Look at the Princess Part 1." Female crew members were generally not filmed without their clothes on, with the notable exception of a naked praying Zhaan in earlier seasons. Even when giving birth during the sequel mini-series, *The Peacekeeper Wars*, Aeryn was fully dressed, using a knife supplied by Crichton to split her pants when the baby was born. In contrast, Seven of Nine offers the audience two possibilities to look upon her topless upper body, and while the audience is just able to see her backside, Seven still shows more skin than Aeryn. Both of these characters were brought to the screen by two very talented actresses who enjoyed bringing these complicated and multidimensional characters to life.

Both of these actresses, Jeri Ryan and Claudia Black, contributed wonderful characters to the genre of speculative fiction, both of them managed to portray multidimensional characters, who not only accomplished to leave their emotionally and unsatisfying upbringings behind them, but who were able to overcome these disadvantages by completely rebuilding their emotional background situations. They became completely functional members of their respective societies; friends, teachers, and women in successful romantic relationships. More importantly, both of them were able to become a secure base as well as an emotionally stable attachment bond partner for others. As a result, these two characters added their own unique achievements to the television gene pool. John Bowlby's and Mary Ainsworth's work on attachment theory demonstrates how important it is not only for infants, but for individuals in general, to form emotional secure attachment bonds to other individuals throughout their lives. Their theories demonstrate that integrating oneself into society is a necessity, and that a failure to do so can have dire consequences. In addition, these theories reveal how individuals experience the first few years in their lives; create patterns, on how they interact with other people, and how these relationships can influence all future relationships that an individual has. As was established throughout this essay, their theories are not only relevant for physicians, psychologists, parents or other potential caregivers, but they can also be used to explain the behavioural development of fictional characters. This essay gives an insight into what can happen when the need for an emotional attachment is disregarded, and how difficult it is to repair and to reconstruct the ability to form attachment bonds in the first place. Utilizing Aeryn Sun, as well as Seven of Nine, this study demonstrates how individuals can overcome nonfunctional attachment bonds, as well as the lack of a secure base, during their childhood. Though this analysis offers a thorough insight into how attachment theory can be applied to two of the, in my opinion, most interesting female characters SFF television has to offer, there is much more to say about these two characters than how they overcame their unfortunate childhoods and how they regained their ability to form lasting and successful attachment bonds to others. However, this is a good start.

Notes

1. Sebacean being the race and the Peacekeepers being the military branch of that race.
2. This information was released in the *Peacekeeper Wars.* There it was revealed that an ancient race of aliens, thousands of years ago, took humans and relocated them to other planets in order to grow new populations.

Works Cited

"Body and Soul." *Star Trek Voyager.* Perf. Jeri Ryan, Kate Mulgrew. Paramount Home Entertainment, 2011. DVD.

Bowlby, John. "Maternal Care and Mental Health." World Health Organization (Print 1951), Web. 1 June 2012.

_____. *A Secure Base Parent-Child Attachment and Healthy Human Development.* New York: Basic Books, 1990. Print.

"The Cloud." *Star Trek Voyager.* Perf. Jeri Ryan, Kate Mulgrew. Paramount Home Entertainment, 2011. DVD.

"Dark Frontier." *Star Trek Voyager.* Perf. Jeri Ryan, Kate Mulgrew. Paramount Home Entertainment, 2011. DVD.

"Day of Honor." *Star Trek Voyager.* Perf. Jeri Ryan, Kate Mulgrew. Paramount Home Entertainment, 2011. DVD.

"Drone." *Star Trek Voyager.* Perf. Jeri Ryan, Kate Mulgrew. Paramount Home Entertainment, 2011. DVD.

"Endgame Part 1." *Star Trek Voyager.* Perf. Jeri Ryan, Kate Mulgrew. Paramount Home Entertainment, 2011. DVD.

"Endgame Part 2." *Star Trek Voyager.* Perf. Jeri Ryan, Kate Mulgrew. Paramount Home Entertainment, 2011. DVD.

"The Gift." *Star Trek Voyager.* Perf. Jeri Ryan, Kate Mulgrew. Paramount Home Entertainment, 2011. DVD.

Ginn, Sherry. *Our Space, Our Place: Women in the Worlds of Science Fiction Television.* Lanham, MD: University of America, 2005. Print.

Hanania, Joseph. "SIGNOFF; Intergalactic Generation Gap." *New York Times.* New York Times, 07 Feb. 1999. Web. 12 June 2012.

Jancelewicz, Chris. "Jeri Ryan of 'Body of Proof' Recalls Her Days as Seven of Nine on 'Star Trek: Voyager'" *The Huffington Post.* TheHuffingtonPost.com, 11 Apr. 2012. Web. 12 July 2012.

"Mortal Coil." *Star Trek Voyager.* Perf. Jeri Ryan, Kate Mulgrew. Paramount Home Entertainment, 2011. DVD.
"The Raven." *Star Trek Voyager.* Perf. Jeri Ryan, Kate Mulgrew. Paramount Home Entertainment, 2011. DVD.
Rockne, O'Bannon S., Keith R.A. DeCandido, Tommy Patterson, Michael Babinksy, Marshall Dillon, Andrew Dalhouse, Zac Atkinson, and Ed Dukeshire. *Farscape: The Beginning of the End of the Beginning.* Los Angeles: Boom! Studios, 2010. Print.
Snierson, Dan. "Lust in Space." *Entertainment Weekly* (1997). E.com. 19 Sept. 1997. Web. 01 Aug. 2011.
"Voyager Time Capsule Season 6" *Star Trek Voyager.* Perf. Jeri Ryan, Kate Mulgrew. Paramount Home Entertainment, 2011. DVD.

Infinite Diversity in Infinite Combinations

The Representation of Transgender Identities in Star Trek[1]

JACK FENNELL

Introduction

Following letter-writing campaigns orchestrated by the Gaylactic Network fan organization, as well as numerous public criticisms, in 1991 *Star Trek* creator Gene Roddenberry publicly reiterated his position on the issue of LGBTQ inclusion in the series: he did not want to make a specifically gay-themed episode, since he believed that in *Star Trek*'s utopian future, such labels would not exist anymore. However, he compromised on the necessity to actually normalize queer relationships within the *Star Trek* universe—season five of *Star Trek: The Next Generation*, he asserted, would include glimpses of gay crew members in day-to-day circumstances (Drushel 31–3). Roddenberry died in October 1991, "leaving his promise of queer representation on *ST: TNG* unfulfilled" (33).

In *TNG*'s feature-length pilot episode, "Encounter at Farpoint," two physiologically male crewmembers can be seen wearing short-sleeved mini-dress uniforms similar to those worn by Deanna Troi and various other female crewmembers. One can be seen in the background of the engine room scenes, wearing the gold-and-black "operations" color scheme, and the other, wearing a red-and-black "command" variant, can be seen during the evacuation scene, as Captain Picard prepares to give the order to separate the *Enterprise*'s saucer from the rest of the ship. Most of the physiologically female crewmembers wear pantsuits as well, suggesting that the different styles of uniform are either down to personal preference or otherwise arbitrary, but the audience is clearly meant to notice the unnamed character in the command colors: he crosses the foreground during a wide shot with plenty of chaotic background action, and the camera pans with him until he walks out of frame. This clip highlights the problematic aspect of Roddenberry's protestations that sexuality and gender would no longer be remarked upon in the 24th century of his imagination. Certainly, the other characters in the scene appear oblivious to this individual, indicating their social evolution beyond our current assumptions about gendered clothing and which kinds of bodies that can wear certain articles. At the same time, though, the scene was originally staged for an audience of the late 20th century, and the presentation of a male-bodied person in a "female" uniform is clearly meant to be startling (it was in keeping with this intention that male pronouns were used to describe this character).

This study aims to find out how trans* people (the asterisk indicating a broader catch-all encompassing all kinds of "gender variance") responded to *Star Trek*. Socially transitioning from one gender to another in the *Star Trek* universe would seem to pose no problem, for, as pointed out above, nobody in that fictional world would even think to comment on another's gender presentation. Since in the same world humanity no longer uses money and practically any medical procedure can be performed quickly and safely, transitioning medically would not pose any significant issues either: unlike today, gender-confirmation surgery would cost nothing and take only a couple of minutes, with practically no time needed for recovery. Thus, in *Star Trek*, nobody needs to be visibly gender-variant unless they want to be (such as the aforementioned crewmembers in female attire); it is very possible to pass as one social gender or the other, and it seems that most trans* people do. Subsequently this study proposes to question what it means to be a transgender (or otherwise gender-variant) *Star Trek* fan, when the utopian nature of the franchise's fictional universe more or less prevents the appearance of openly trans* people with whom that fan can identify? As part of this inquiry an online survey was produced to do just that.

Survey Issues

One of the big issues with this plan was this author's own status as an "aca-fan," which was something that would have to compensated for in trying to convince people to respond. An "aca-fan" is a theorist who, as the term suggests, purports to speak from within fandom, as a participant in the fan subculture. They are often very forthright about their self-identification as fans, criticising those who theorise about fandom without getting involved; however, as Zubernis and Larsen point out, these same people often do not participate themselves, or their fandoms are acceptable to "mainstream" culture—such as a sports team, for example (45). Another issue is that academic practice sometimes contravenes fans' expectations of privacy (51), and aca-fans, regardless of their good intent, occupy a perceived position of social power by virtue of their academic employment, meaning that they can unwittingly do damage to the fan communities they study (58–9). Sometimes, motivated by a perceived need for "objectivity" in their research, they distance themselves from emotional fan behavior and thus contribute to the stigmatization of fandom as a whole (47). Consequently, aca-fans are quite often regarded with suspicion by non-academic fans (11). It does not suffice to merely make note of these as difficulties or obstructions to research: this author has to come clean and admit to many of the hypocrisies outlined above, describing himself as a *Star Trek* fan (among other things), but rarely attending conventions or frequenting fan sites. By writing in an academic register, this author casts himself in the role of an objective observer and attempts to project expertise, and in the past, has minimized his emotional investment in science fiction for fear that his "research interest" in the genre would not be taken seriously (by colleagues and, more crucially, by research-funding bodies). Added to all of the above, of course, are the privacy concerns of the subjects regarding their gender identity. This author had no way of knowing whether these respondents were out and openly presenting as their preferred gender identity, or if they were keeping that aspect of their identities secret, but for safety's sake the study had to err on the side of protecting those in the latter category. The descriptor "transgender *Star Trek* fans" describes a perfect overlap—not so much a Venn diagram as a circle—of factors that might make a respondent nervous about being publicly identified. This author's awareness of these issues notwithstanding, the fact remains that the respondents to this survey took a gamble by doing so, and the author is grateful to them for it.

Design

The survey was designed to be as comprehensive as possible without soliciting any information that could be used to identify respondents. No questions were asked about the respondents' medical histories. The demographic questions were instead focused on respondents' identities. Following recommendations made by the UK Equality and Human Rights Commission (see Balarajan et al., 2011), respondents were asked how they were described at birth ("Female," "Male," "Intersex" or "Prefer not to say") and how they currently identify. The list of identity options was somewhat long, but probably not comprehensive, so respondents were asked to "select all that apply" and were provided a text box in case any other possible identities were omitted through forgetfulness or ignorance. "Cisgender" was one of the options here, even though cisgender people (i.e., individuals whose personal gender identity is consonant with the societal/cultural genders attached to their physiology) were not the focus of the study. The purpose of including them in the data-gathering was as a kind of "control group," or a useful contrast to the trans* respondents, should any unexpected correlations emerge from the data. This was also intended to be a safety-valve measure in case well-meaning allies took the survey in order to have their say on this issue, and in doing so misrepresented their actual gender identity and skewed the results. With this precaution in place, the study proceeded on the good-faith assumption that, given the "cisgender" option, allies would choose it and the results for trans*-identified people would not be impacted.

Respondents were then asked to select their age range. For practical purposes, this study did not solicit responses from people under the age of 18: had it done so, this author would have been legally required to seek the written permission of the respondents' parents, which in some cases could have amounted to asking those respondents to out themselves. While the author had no control over who could respond, following consultation with the Arts, Humanities and Social Sciences (AHSS) Ethics Committee at the University of Limerick, under–18s were specifically told not to participate. Again, the study proceeded on a good-faith assumption that respondents would not misrepresent themselves. Respondents were asked whether their first language was English, but because this author did not want to gather data that might identify them, they were not asked what their first language was or anything that would indicate a geographical location—this was also the logic behind collecting culture-specific identities under a general "Third Gender" category in the gender identity question, rather than listing them as separate entries. This may have been a mistake, since cultural identity can obviously influence the reception/interpretation of a TV series or film, but this area is open for future researchers in this area. For the purposes of this study, this author was simply interested to see if there were any broad correlations between certain responses and a non–Anglophone perspective. In the next section, sample statements and scales were used to gauge respondents' attitudes to social issues in popular fiction. On a scale of 1 (Don't agree at all) to 5 (Strongly agree), they were asked to rate the following statements:

- ☐ "I like to see real-world issues explored in the fiction I read/watch/listen to"
- ☐ "I read/watch/listen to fiction primarily to be entertained"
- ☐ "It is important to me that trans* issues be acknowledged in the fiction I read/watch/listen to."

One potential problem, which only occurred to this author after the survey was disseminated, was that the final statement could be interpreted as absolutist (i.e., that the respondent will *only* consume fiction about trans* people and issues). To avoid this, the question should have been worded "*occasionally* acknowledged" or something similar (since for the respondent, it might suffice to have one well-crafted episode about trans* issues, or a single well-written trans* character). The section after this concerned the respondents' involvement in *Star Trek* fandom. They were asked to rate their own participation in fan activities, their enthusiasm for "expanded universe" material (i.e., narrative spin-offs in the form of licensed books, video games and so on), and their enthusiasm for fan-created works. they were then asked to rate the various *Star Trek* series and films according to how much they enjoyed them, from 1 (Didn't like it at all) to 5 (I love it), with an additional "N/A (I haven't seen it)" option.

A little bit trickier was the issue of self-identification as a *Star Trek* fan, and whether being a fan entailed any friction with the respondents' gender identities. Respondents were asked to rank their agreement with three sample statements on a scale of 1 to 5, with an additional "N/A" option as required. The first statement was, "*Star Trek*'s vision of the future is utopian/aspirational for me": this was intended to gauge the emotional resonance of the series with the individual respondent—do they earnestly want that future to become a reality, or do they regard it as an antiseptic, sanitised future to be avoided at all costs? Unfortunately, the question did not take into account the pejorative meaning attached to "utopia," in the sense of pie-in-the-sky wish-fulfilment fantasies, which may very well have impacted the responses. The next statement was, "I feel comfortable expressing my *Star Trek* fandom openly to my family and friends." This question was included for reasons outlined earlier: some fans learn to internalise shame about their enthusiasms and go to some lengths not to be identified as fans. For symmetry's sake, this statement could have been worded to be specific to trans* social spaces rather than a general "friends and family," but this would presuppose that the respondents had access to such spaces, which might not be the case. There is also the consideration that being bullied on account of one's fandom is, for the most part, not as potentially life-threatening as abuse and discrimination based on gender identity, especially in light of the current furore over trans* bathroom-access laws. By and large, it is safer to "come out" as a *Trek* fan than as a trans* person (though that's not to say there are no circumstances, contexts or even specific locations where the chances of physical assault or familial abandonment on either account are somewhat similar). After this, the next statement to be evaluated was "I feel comfortable expressing my gender identity in physical fan spaces (e.g., conventions, meet-ups, specialist retail outlets)," followed by "I feel comfortable expressing my gender identity in online fan spaces (e.g., forums, Facebook groups, subreddits)." As is the case with any large community, within sf fandom there is a reactionary element that occasionally lashes out at visible minorities. The key difference, of course, is that online interactions facilitate a greater degree of depersonalization: it is easier to bully someone else when one does not have to do it face-to-face.

Having gathered this data, respondents were then asked to consider how trans* issues have been handled in *Star Trek* thus far. Again, this was done via a number of statements with five-point scales for respondents to rate how closely they agreed with them. The statements were:

- ☐ "I feel that trans* themes and issues have been adequately addressed in the *Star Trek* franchise"
- ☐ "More could be done to adequately address trans* themes and issues in the *Star Trek* franchise"
- ☐ "I feel that certain *Star Trek* episodes speak to my own personal experience of issues related to gender identity"
- ☐ "In terms of gender identity, I feel I can identify with particular *Star Trek* characters"
- ☐ "I have found the depiction of trans* themes and issues in *Star Trek* to be even-handed, positive, or personally beneficial"
- ☐ "I have found the depiction of trans* themes and issues in *Star Trek* to be dismissive, negative or upsetting."

After going through the entirety of the film and broadcast facets of the *Star Trek* franchise (excluding *The Animated Series*), this author came up with three broad tropes that were regularly invoked in instances where a character changed (or appeared to change) their gender presentation or biological sex. These tropes were:

- shape-shifting aliens (for convenience's sake, this category included beings with the power to "psychically camouflage" their true appearance, though in retrospect it seems clear that those should have been listed separately)
- mind-body duality, encompassing stories involving body-swaps and "possession"
- the symbiosis of two sentient minds—in *Star Trek* terms, this most obviously refers to the Trill species, but it encompasses the Vulcan "mind meld" and other instances where it happens by some other means. {/BL}

As these were the most common recurring gender-changing tropes in *Star Trek*, respondents were asked if they found any of them useful as metaphors for their own gender identity. For instance, one description of a trans* person is "a man trapped in a woman's body" or vice-versa, which might resonate with storylines that rely on mind-body duality. A bi-gender or two-spirit person might very well relate to the different aspects of their identity as separate personas in symbiosis. Someone who changes their gender presentation regularly or does not identify in any particular way might see something of themselves in the various shape-shifters that have cropped up in *Star Trek*. Lastly, the study included a free-response text box for respondents to write down their own thoughts on the subject, or on the content/structure of the survey.

Dissemination

From the beginning, it was decided that responses to the survey would be solicited through online transgender forums, rather than *Star Trek* fan forums. There were two reasons for this: first of all, because at the time of writing only a very small proportion of the overall population of the West is believed to be trans*, this author hypothesized that the chances of finding *Star Trek* fans on a trans* forum would be higher than the chances of finding trans* people on a *Star Trek* forum; secondly, with larger communities come higher likelihoods of attracting "trolls," and it was thus more likely that the survey would attract transphobic bullies on a *Star Trek* forum than *Star Trek* "anti-fans" on a trans* forum. As an added safeguard, this author would contact the forums' moderators to ask permission before posting any links, and would not do so without a very clear signal of approval.

In a very unfortunate coincidence, the survey was published on surveymonkey.net and messages were sent to forum moderators on June 12, 2016, this author being unaware of the mass murder that had taken place at the Pulse LGBT nightclub in Orlando, Florida, six hours earlier. Having spent the day putting the survey together after receiving authorization from the Ethics Committee, the author did not become aware of the incident until at 4 p.m. that evening (GMT). At the time of writing, the incident is being described as the worst terrorist attack on U.S. soil since September 11, 2001, and the worst anti–LGBT hate crime in U.S. history. It was not reasonable to expect the trans* community to participate in this research at a time when the LGBT community was in mourning worldwide; the moderators were contacted again and it was agreed that, all things considered, it would be best to leave the survey for a couple of weeks.

With the deadline approaching, this author contacted those moderators again on July 9, and disseminated the survey link through his own Facebook and Twitter accounts while awaiting a response; some colleagues were kind enough to share the link as well. The survey was closed on July 29, having gathered 168 responses. This author then filtered out the incomplete surveys, a couple of trolls and a small number of people who did not appear to understand the premise of the survey—i.e., they did not seem to be aware of the distinction between gender and sexuality, and entered "Gay" or "Straight" as their gender identity. After this filtering had been applied, the sample size had been rounded down to 126.

The Sample

Most of the respondents reported that they had been designated male at birth (DMAB), i.e., they were described as male when they were born and were socialized as boys throughout the early years of their life, regardless of how they later identified; this accounted for 84 of the 126 respondents (66.67 percent). Thirty-eight respondents (30.16 percent) were designated female at birth (DFAB), and four respondents (3.17 percent) chose not to disclose this information; none of the respondents reported that they had been described as intersex when they were born. Of these, 35 described themselves as cisgender, meaning that their inner gender identity was consonant with their outer "designation." As was expected, the majority of respondents placed their identity somewhere in the trans* sphere. Because respondents had been instructed to "Select all that apply" when it came to describing their gender identity, there was a significant amount of overlap between those other categories: 59 (46.46 percent) described themselves as "Transgender," while only one person each (0.79 percent) described themselves as "Dual gender" and "Third gender." The other respondents reported themselves as having gender identities that are not exclusively masculine or feminine, with some identifying more as an admixture of the two, others mixing-and-matching aspects of different gender presentations or switching back and forth as the mood takes them, and others identifying as neither. Some respondents picked as many of these "gender-expansive" options as they felt necessary, and while a few of them linked these identities to the "Transgender" option, others did not, indicating that they perceive a clear difference. Where necessary, this author has grouped these various identities together under the umbrella term "gender-expansive," though future researchers may wish to concentrate on investigating these identities with greater nuance. A number of respondents objected to the category "Transgender" instead of more specific ones such as "Trans Male" or "Trans Female"; the primary reason for organizing the gender identity question in this way was to respect the privacy of respondents who did not want to disclose the gender they had been assigned at birth. In the end, only four respondents chose not to give this information, all of whom opted to describe themselves as Transgender (with one further specifying a Non-binary/Agender identity).

The majority of the respondents were between the ages of 22 and 34 (50.39 percent); the next highest age bracket was 35–44 (25.98 percent), with the 18–21 age group (12.6 percent) coming in third. Only nine respondents (7.09 percent) were aged between 45 and 54, and only five (3.94 percent) were between 55 and 64 years of age. None of the respondents were over 65 years old; neither did any of them decline to give their age via the "Prefer not to say" option. This age profile may explain the results outlined in Table 1. Respondents were asked to rate their enjoyment of the various *Star Trek* TV series and films, on a scale of 1 ("I don't like this series at all") to 5 ("I love this series"), with an N/A option for those not seen. Respondents were free to "love" more than one series if they so wished, since this was not an either/or option.

Table 1: Series Rankings

Series	*Loved it*	*Didn't like it at all*	*Haven't seen it*
Star Trek: TOS	28 (22.05%)	5 (3.94%)	7 (5.51%)
Star Trek: TNG	69 (54.76%)	1 (0.79%)	1 (0.79%)
Star Trek: DS9	73 (57.48%)	1 (0.79%)	14 (11.02%)
Star Trek: Voyager	25 (19.69%)	4 (3.15%)	13 (10.24%)
Star Trek: Enterprise	13 (10.24%)	16 (12.6%)	28 (22.05%)

The best-regarded of the TV series in this survey appears to be *Star Trek: Deep Space Nine* (1993–1999), which has historically been regarded by *Trek* fans as one of the weakest of all the franchise's iterations. The oldest respondents currently in the 22–34 age bracket would have been 11 years old at the time when it was first broadcast, while the youngest would only have been born the following year. If we assume that these respondents are mostly American, there is a reasonable chance that they watched *DS9* during its original broadcast run, which would have made it a regular fixture of their childhoods and perhaps predisposed them to regard it with fondness. Other factors may pertain to fans outside of the USA. For example, this author personally likes *DS9* very much, and now attributes this appreciation to the fact that while it was being broadcast in Ireland, the Northern Irish Peace Process was underway, and there was a definite resonance between the news stories of the day and the show's backdrop of territorial dispute, sectarianism and ethnic conflict. Of the 126 respondents, 122 (96.06 percent) responded that their first language was English, with five (3.94 percent) indicating that it was not. None of the latter group identified themselves as "Third gender," which may indicate that none of the respondents belonged to specific culture-bound trans*-spectrum identities, such as the Omani *khanith*, the Samoan *fa'afafine* or the different kinds of "two-spirits" belonging to various American Indian and Aboriginal Canadian nations. On the other hand, it may be that the "Third gender" category as summarised in this survey simply did not suffice.

One of these respondents identified as cisgender, one as genderqueer/genderfluid, one as transgender/non-binary, and two solely as transgender.

The other aspect of the sample, of course, was *Star Trek* fandom. As noted previously, the survey included a number of questions pertaining to licensed narrative spin-offs and fanfiction in order to offset some of the potential drawbacks of comparing self-assessments. The working hypothesis was that the higher a respondent rated their participation in fandom, the more likely they were to enjoy this kind of "extraneous" material. Thirty-five people said their enthusiasm for *Star Trek* extended to official licensed narrative spin-offs. Fifteen of these described their participation in *Star Trek* fandom as Occasional/casual, with another 12 saying their participation was Moderate/semi-regular. Eighteen of the same people said that they also enjoyed fan-created works, and nine reported that while they were generally not interested in fanfiction, there were some particular fan-created pieces that they liked. These numbers were largely reflected in the answers to the separate question on fan-created works: of the 32 respondents who said they enjoyed fanfiction, 15 rated their fandom participation as Occasional/casual, 12 as Moderate/semi-regular; 18 said that they also enjoyed licensed works (with six saying that they enjoyed some but otherwise had no interest), and only three respondents who enjoyed fanfiction also said that they did not like such works. Twenty-seven respondents reported that they did not like licensed material at all. Twelve of these described their fandom participation as "Minimal," while 11 said that their participation was Occasional/casual. The same sub-sample, for the most part, did not like fan works either, with 15 answering "No" compared to just three saying "Yes." Seven people out of this sub-sample said that they enjoyed specific fan-created works, but otherwise had no interest in such things. Again, these numbers were largely the same for the 30 respondents who answered that they did not like fan-created works: 15 professed Minimal/no involvement in fandom, with 12 rating their fandom participation as Occasional/casual; 15 said that they did not like licensed works either, though six said there were some licensed narratives that they liked, and another six said they enjoyed licensed works in specific formats.

It would seem that the hypothesis was proven for this particular sample: those who enjoyed licensed works were also more likely to enjoy fanfiction, and for the most part these people rated their fandom participation as Occasional/casual or Moderate/semi-regular. Those who rated their involvement as "Minimal" were less likely to enjoy third-party narratives, licensed or unlicensed. This author was initially concerned that respondents might be under-reporting their involvement with fandom, but the argument could be made that science fiction and *Star Trek* are no longer minority interests, or that "fandom" does not fully account for respondents' enthusiasm. Though 25 people overall stated that they were not involved in fandom, four of them still enjoyed licensed narratives, another four enjoyed spin-offs in particular formats, five enjoyed particular licensed spin-offs and three of them said that they enjoyed fanfiction. One respondent explicitly linked her enjoyment of fanfiction to her gender identity: "This isn't a super important thing for me but trans girls are rare in fiction and I do seek out stories (especially fan stories) that include them in the main cast."

What the above demonstrates is that the respondents' self-assessment of their enthusiasm for *Star Trek* was consistent. Now, the two strands of data can be combined.

Table 2: Fandom by Gender Identity (Broad)

Fandom involvement	*Transgender*	*Cisgender*	*Gender-expansive*
None/minimal	12	6	7
Occasional/Casual	22	20	22
Moderate/Semi-regular	8	7	13
High	2	2	2
Very High	0	0	1

For the purposes of this table, I separated those who identified as Transgender from those who additionally identified as Genderqueer, Genderfluid or otherwise "Gender-expansive." The Transgender column on this table consists of respondents who identified themselves as Transgender alone, which is broken down further in the table below.

Table 3: Fandom Among Self-Identified Transgender Individuals:

Fandom involvement	*Trans Men*	*Trans Women*	*Not disclosed*
None/minimal	2	9	1
Occasional/Casual	4	17	1
Moderate/Semi-regular	1	6	1
High	0	2	0
Very High	0	0	0

Among self-identified Transgender respondents, the highest number was of trans women (to recap: female-identified individuals designated male at birth). There were far fewer trans men (male-identified, designated female at birth), and while those in the third column could in theory have all been DFAB as well, their addition to that column would not have balanced the numbers at all. Among the self-identified trans women, the largest number consisted of those who described themselves as occasional/casual *Star Trek* fans; only two described their fandom involvement as High, and none said their participation was Very High. In fact, the *only* respondent in the survey to describe their fandom participation as "Very High" was in the Gender-expansive category, which is broken down in the next table:

Table 4: Fandom Among Self-Identified "Gender-Expansive" People:

Fandom involvement	*DMAB*	*DFAB*	*Not disclosed*
None/minimal	5	2	0
Occasional/Casual	12	10	0
Moderate/Semi-regular	3	9	1
High 1	1	0	
Very High	1	0	0

As can be seen here, the Occasional/Casual fandom category wins out again, though this time the overall numbers of those designated male and designated female at birth are equal, and interestingly, more DFAB gender-expansive individuals were inclined to describe themselves as Moderate/semi-regular fandom participants. The survey's only respondent with a self-described Very High level of fandom participation highlights the need for a larger sample. This individual identified as Genderqueer, gave their age as somewhere between 45 and 54, and said that English was their first language. They strongly agreed that they consume fiction primarily for entertainment purposes, and that they like to see real-world issues explored in that fiction, but they were equivocal on the issue of whether it was personally important to them to see trans* issues explored to a similar extent. They were enthusiastic about both licensed *Star Trek* narratives and fanfiction, "loved" each one of the TV series and loved all of the films, with the exception of 1989's *The Final Frontier* and 2002's *Nemesis* (both of which were ranked at the equivocal "It's okay"). They strongly agreed that *Star Trek*'s vision of the future was utopian/aspirational to them, and strongly agreed that they felt comfortable expressing their fandom to their family and their gender in both physical and online fan spaces. They strongly disagreed with the statement that *Star Trek*'s treatment of trans* issues has been satisfactory thus far, but they were equivocal about whether more could be done, about whether certain stories spoke to their own personal experience, about whether they identified with particular characters, and whether *Star Trek*'s handling of trans* issues thus far has been even-handed. They strongly disagreed with the statement that the franchise's handling of such issues has been hurtful or upsetting. This respondent found all of the tropes/archetypes "Extremely useful" as metaphors for describing their own gender identity, but declined to use the free-response box to contextualize their answers any further. This respondent is, literally and figuratively, in a category by themselves, and this author regrets that this survey did not draw in more respondents like them.

Politics in/and Entertainment

Among the 27 respondents who said they "strongly agreed" that trans* issues should be explored in popular fiction, all similarly agreed (22 "strongly," 5 "mostly") that they liked to see real-world issues addressed in the fiction they consumed, and 21 agreed (11 "strongly," 10 "mostly") that they consumed this fiction primarily for entertainment purposes, with six equivocating. The overall number of people who liked to see social issues included in their fiction was 107 (57 strongly agreeing, 50 mostly agreeing), and of this overall number, 84 nonetheless agreed (35 strongly, 49 mostly) that entertainment was their primary concern. In fact, this author would have been surprised if the majority of respondents to a *Star Trek* survey indicated anything else: the combination of entertainment with "serious issues" has been *Star Trek*'s stock-in-trade for most of its existence.

Among the 57 people who strongly agreed that they liked to see social issues explored in popular fiction, twenty mostly agreed with the importance of exploring trans* issues as well; none completely disagreed, and only two "mostly disagreed" by ranking the statement at "2" on the scale (though 13 were equivocal on the issue). Of the 43 who strongly agreed that they prioritized entertainment in their popular fiction, 24 likewise agreed (11 strongly, 13 mostly) with the inclusion of trans* issues in that fiction; among the 100 who agreed that entertainment was their primary concern in this regard (43 strongly, 57 mostly), 51 agreed (21 strongly, 30 mostly) with the inclusion of trans* issues.

Of those who agreed that trans* issues should be explored in popular fiction, 16 were cisgender (5 strongly agreeing, 11 mostly agreeing) and 50 were transgender and/or gender-expansive (22 agreeing strongly, 28 agreeing mostly). Of the 66 respondents expressing agreement with the exploration of trans* themes in popular fiction (27 strongly agreeing, 39 mostly agreeing), only ten agreed (two strongly, eight mostly) that *Star Trek*'s handling of trans* issues thus far has been adequate, while 46 disagreed (19 strongly, 27 mostly). Sixty-three of the respondents agreed (48 strongly, 15 mostly) that more could be done to address these issues properly in the franchise. Some of the difficulties in doing so could be structural, though. As one respondent pointed out, quite rightly, "[*Star Trek*'s] general self-assigned role as regards social commentary tends to limit its treatment of issues of that sort to one-shot episodes; ongoing arcs featuring recurring characters are difficult to place in such a Utopian setting." Only two respondents "completely disagreed" with the inclusion of trans* issues; both of them also mostly disagreed with the inclusion of general real-world issues in fiction, while mostly agreeing that entertainment was their primary motivation in consuming said fiction. Going by the numbers alone, it seems clear that on the whole, entertainment value is not inversely proportional to engagement with social issues, and a significant proportion of these respondents would like to see trans* issues engaged with as part of that rubric.

Representation

The survey included a question about whether respondents saw *Star Trek*'s future as a utopian or "aspirational" one, thinking that those who answered in the affirmative might be more likely to identify with particular characters or storylines. As it turned out, even though the majority of trans*-identified respondents conceived of the series' depicted future in this way (38 agreeing mostly, 43 strongly agreeing), they were no less critical of what they see as the franchise's shortcomings. Below is a table of respondents' ratings detailing how well they feel they can identify with particular plots and characters, whether they feel that *Star Trek*'s treatment of trans* issues has been positive/beneficial, or if they find it to be negative/hurtful:

Table 5: Trans Representation/Identification Scores:

	Disagree	*Neither*	*Agree*	*N/A*
Plots/episodes	30	16	44	1
Characters	28	20	41	2
Positive/Beneficial	28	36	24	3
Negative/Hurtful	38	30	19	4

On this table, the respondents are agreeing or disagreeing with statements outlined earlier. By and large, the majority said that they personally identified with certain characters and storylines, and the majority seems bigger for characters. This indicates that trans* *Star Trek* viewers are more likely to identify with individual characters than to see something of their personal experiences reflected in a given episode. All things considered, though, the difference between the positive and negative scores is not very wide for either of these, and the number of respondents who feel they cannot identify with either is significant. More encouraging is the fact that twice as many respondents disagreed than agreed with the statement that *Star Trek*'s treatment of trans* issues is hurtful or negative: it seems that although opinion is divided on plots and characters, the majority of trans* respondents are not actively upset by the franchise. This author would be wary of taking this result as widely representative, however, given the relatively small sample size. After all, more people disagreed than agreed that the franchise's depiction of trans* issues was positive or beneficial.

One particular story worthy of attention is episode 5.17 of *TNG*, "The Outcast," in which Riker falls in love with Soren, a member of an alien race that has renounced gender. The J'naii reproduce by inseminating a "fibrous husk," and they sleep together only to stay warm; when they dance, the taller one leads. The main minority among the J'naii are transgender in nature, and Soren reveals that *she* is one of them, having discovered her female identity as an adolescent. The gendered J'naii associate with each other in secret, and if they are caught, they are tried in a court of law and subjected to "psychotectic" therapy to remove all traces of their gender identity (though there is no indication that this therapy actually does anything other than traumatizing the subject into conformity, the apparent effect is similar to brainwashing). When Riker and Soren act on their mutual attraction, Soren is found out, tried and given the therapy; Riker tries to intervene, potentially risking his career, but arrives too late to save her. "The Outcast" struck a chord with a number of respondents. Some understood the episode as a depiction of gender-based persecution, with one respondent describing it as a favorite of theirs and another calling it "problematic" and "quite upsetting," both for the same reason. Some were upset that the J'naii's genderless society was depicted as oppressive. "The J'naii [...] were the first exposure I ever had to gender that wasn't binary and cisgender," said one respondent, "[and] I remember being very upset that their culture shamed and 'treated' any members [...] who *did* identify as a particular gender." Another respondent, who identified as agender, said "I would have liked to see a more progresive [sic] J'naii who lived in the gendered world outside their home planet and accepted people who were different from them while accepting themself [sic] as a genderless person." Three of the respondents who commented on this episode criticised the studio's decision to "play it safe" by casting a female actor as Soren, with one respondent saying that this "effectively robbed [the episode] of any didactic value."[2] A number of respondents also pointed out that "The Outcast" was intended as an allegory for gay rights, not for trans* identities, and by the time it was broadcast, one respondent said, "*TNG*'s refuge in allegory was well behind the curve of what other mainstream shows had done in that vein."

Closely related to the issue of plot/character identification are the responses pertaining to the various tropes identified as having potential significance for trans* viewers, outlined here in table 6:

Table 6: Combined Trope Rankings:

Trope	*Not useful*	*Sort of useful*	*Useful*
Shape-shifting aliens	55	24	11
Mind-body duality	29	30	31
Symbiosis	41	24	25

The "usefulness" invoked here was a measure of how well these things served as metaphors for respondents' own experiences or identities, and shape-shifting aliens are clearly the biggest losers in this regard.

The symbiosis trope, most clearly figured in the Trill species, fares a good bit better than the shape-shifters, but is still found lacking by quite a stretch. One respondent said that they specifically identified with the Trills' combination of male and female perspectives from their past hosts. Another identified with Jadzia Dax "even before I realized I was transgender," but qualified that statement by saying "While it isn't the best depiction of transgender topics, I do find it to be the closest thing within the *Star Trek* canon." Other respondents were much more critical of Trills: one respondent dismissed them as "just memories and sexual orientation," while another noted that "Trills in general never seem to feature in any other plotlines that explore how shifting genders between hosts feels or whether there's any agency in the practice." Another respondent said they "never really got the vibe of 'this is a trans character'" from Dax, and pointed out that gender is meaningless to Trills, further distancing them from the actual experiences of trans* people. The issue of whether or not Trills can actually be transgender generated some interesting responses. One respondent argued that since host-changing is a natural process for the Trills, changes of sex or gender are normal for them: therefore, they are not likely to experience gender dysphoria, which this respondent seems to feel is a defining characteristic of transgender existence. A different respondent agreed with this in broad strokes, but asserts that this view of the Trills invalidates the only identifiable character in the franchise. Dax is "in every right a gender-fluid individual," but since she is an alien, this never rises above the metaphorical level, and she can be safely excluded from the trans* category by viewers who would rather not acknowledge such issues. Among the tropes, mind-body duality came closest to an overall winner. However, the winning margin comprised just two people, and a roughly equal number were equivocal about its usefulness. None of the respondents responded freely about this trope either, apart from one knowledgeable individual who brought up *TOS* episode 3.24, "Turnabout Intruder" (in which one of Kirk's ex-girlfriends forcibly switches bodies with him in order to commandeer the *Enterprise*): "apart from expressing hilariously outdated views about gender roles in the general sense," the respondent said, "[the episode] associates the transposition of biology and self-identification with mental illness and moral turpitude, in an all-too-familiar pattern."

Avenues/Suggestions for Future Research

The findings of this survey are interesting, but they cannot be said to be representative or 100 percent reliable. The author would encourage other researchers to investigate this area again, more thoroughly, and to consider the following:

- Allow more time to gather responses; at the end of the day, though some circumstances were beyond control, this was rather a rushed investigation and it is likely that a bigger sample size could have been obtained if more time had been allowed.
- It was assumed that respondents to this survey, having a personal interest in the topic, would have a working knowledge of what the various identity categories meant; as it turned out, this was mistaken. This author would advise anyone interested in creating a similar survey in future to include brief descriptions of what each category actually means, if they have the space to do it.
- This survey was focused purely on gender identity, and thus it does not account for other possible factors to audience receptions of a media franchise, such as race, economic class, sexuality, marital status, religion or political affiliation. If any of the results gathered here seem strange, their oddity might be due to one or more of these unexamined factors.
- Future researchers interested in this topic may wish to link their sampling to particular geographic areas, language communities or ethnic groups.

Conclusion

In the end, most of the respondents who filled in the free-response text box expressed dissatisfaction with allegory and metaphor in place of actual inclusion. "I understand that [allegory] is easier," said one, "but I would prefer someone who's experience is closer than mine showing up in the cast." "I'm still waiting for that perfectly actualized character," said another. More forthrightly, another respondent stated, "Metaphors are not representation. They do not help in explaining issues to cisgender folks—instead, they just give excuses to them to view characters as not actually trans." Representation and inclusion are not merely matters of box-ticking or quota-filling. "What sucks most about being trans," one respondent said, "is how other people don't even believe you really exist. *Star Trek*, as far as I can tell, doesn't ever really touch on this subject. In fact, I can't think of a single transgender character in *Star Trek* whatsoever. Transgender people are not represented in *Star Trek*." Another respondent reinforced this point: "For all functional purposes, there are no trans people in *Star Trek*. There are aliens whose experiences might be metaphorically similar to trans people [...] characters impersonating another gender for ulterior purposes [...] and references largely played as jokes." One respondent who professed a sincere love for the franchise signed off with this poignant note:

I'm hopeful that the new series will address trans issues in a direct fashion without resorting to shapeshifting or other metaphors to skirt around an explicitly trans narrative. I'd love to see stories involving actual trans characters, I'd love to see a future where being trans didn't have to be a big narrative, where it could just be treated as a normal part of life. I hope to see that the future I grew up with has a place for people like me in it too.

Notes

1. The title of this essay comes from a precept of Vulcan philosophy, sometimes abbreviated "IDIC"; infinite diversity in infinite combinations is held by the Vulcans to be the basis of all truth and beauty (as opposed to the simplistic Earth precept that "truth *is* beauty," and vice versa). The concept was introduced in the *Star Trek* (Original Series) episode "Is There No Truth in Beauty?" (season 3, episode 7; 1968), and referenced again in almost every iteration of the franchise. In the Vulcan language, the precept is summed up as "kol-ut-shan" (*Voyager* season 5, episode 13).

2. As two respondents pointed out, Jonathan Frakes actually insisted that a male actor should be cast as Soren, but was overruled.

Works Cited

Balarajan, Meera, Michelle Gray and Martin Mitchell. "Monitoring Equality: Developing a Gender Identity Question." *Research Report 75*. Manchester: Equality and Human Rights Commission, 2011.

Drushel, Bruce E. "A Utopia Denied: *Star Trek* and Its Queer Fans." Bruce E. Drushel, ed. *Star Trek* (IB Fan Phenomena). Bristol: Intellect Books, 2013.

"The Outcast." *Star Trek: The Next Generation*. Paramount Domestic Television; CBS Television Distribution. 16 March 1992. Television broadcast.

"Turnabout Intruder." *Star Trek*. NBC. 3 June 1969. Television broadcast.

Zubernis, Lynn, and Katherine Larsen. *Fandom at the Crossroads: Celebration, Shame and Fan/Producer Relationships*. Newcastle Upon Tyne: Cambridge Scholars Publishing, 2012.

Deep Space Gender

Miles O'Brien, Julian Bashir and Masculinity

Andrew Howe

One of the more interesting character pairings in *Star Trek: Deep Space Nine* (*DS9*) is the relationship between medical doctor Julian Bashir (Alexander Siddig) and chief engineer Miles O'Brien (Colm Meaney). This friendship works conceptually due to their extreme differences. Julian is a talented genius embarking upon his career; he excels at everything, although not to his full potential. He is also a bit of a playboy. Conversely, Miles is a middle-aged family man and Average Joe with a tireless work ethic. Despite their differences, these two characters have just enough similarity to bond them together not only as colleagues but also friends: both are hard working, dedicated to Starfleet, and derive from former British colonies (India and Ireland), a distinction that comes into sharper focus as the Federation comes into conflict with several other empires throughout *DS9*'s run. An aspect of this relationship that has largely been ignored is the show's depiction of the issues they face that intersect with gender. Most of the episodes that focus upon Miles or Julian concentrate more on their friendship than on relationships with their wife (Keiko O'Brien) and girlfriends (Jadzia, Leeta, and others). More importantly gender-wise in the *Star Trek* universe, however, are the travails these men experience, the impact that these experiences have upon their masculinity, and how they help each other through these crises. Throughout the series, one of the most common storylines employed was—in the parlance of the show-runners—"let's torture O'Brien." Possibly more than any other permanent character in all of the various *Star Trek* iterations, Miles is subjected to all manner of affronts to his masculinity, suffering physical degradation, mental anguish, and spiritual and moral crises. Equally, Julian, who on the surface seems to live a life of excitement and virility, is plagued by family secrets, a reputation of arrogance, and fears involving not living up to his full potential. This study examines the show's treatment of masculinity in a time of uncertainty and upheaval for the Federation through these two characters, and will consider episodes such as "Whispers," "Time's Orphan," and "Hard Time" for Miles O'Brien and "Distant Voices" and "Dr. Bashir, I Presume" for Julian Bashir.

Star Trek *and Gender*

The genius of *Star Trek* is its universal appeal, driven by characters and storylines that go through problems and grapple with identity issues that can apply to all members of an audience. Thus, the aspects of gender intersecting these two characters—romance, settling down, parenting—fall under the aegis of masculinity only so far as these two characters are male. True, there may be specific brushstrokes that apply to men only, but by and large the depictions of gender are true to Gene Roddenberry's broad vision of a universal narrative. Julian and Miles are relatable to both male and female viewers. On the surface, *DS9* is the series perhaps the least focused upon gender. The fact that Benjamin Sisko is black has attracted much of the attention; when not zeroed in on Sisko, the focus of the show's identity politics have usually been accorded to Dax (as a joined species), Odo (as a changeling), or Kira (as a former terrorist). As a narrative about establishing a frontier outpost between several expansionist empires, *DS9* is in essence a colonial text. As Jon Wagner states:

> The *DS9* station is a postcolonial place, an abandoned concentration camp with an ominous look, in a rough neighborhood where cultural diversity has its menacing side, where it is not easy to tell right from wrong, and where transients do things our heroes would rather not know about [Wagner 187].

Although more a frontier town (replete with a sheriff, bar, and promenade) than a concentration camp, Wagner has a point. The series features more than its fair share of aliens, many of which are coded as racial minorities. However, despite the focus on race, gender is still a critical part of this liminal space, with characters acting in roles that challenge traditional expectations of role and behavior, perhaps made less threatening due to the use of aliens as proxies. Very little of the gender criticism accorded to *DS9* has involved Miles, Julian, or their relationship with each other. Despite the fact that Sisko is the only captain in *Star Trek* depicted through a full arc of parenting decisions (Kirk has a son, but they do not meet until David Marcus is an adult), very little criticism has been dedicated to his relationship with Jake, or with his own father. In his introduction to his book *Gender and Sexuality in* Star Trek, David Greven states: "I freely admit that I'm not a follower of *Deep*

Space Nine" (Greven 1). True to his word, his critical work includes substantial analysis of every live-action *Star Trek* series except *DS9*, of which there are only three references, equally as many as he grants to Marilyn Monroe, *The Iliad*, and the Book of Genesis, and far fewer than he does to William Shakespeare, *Moby Dick*, and *Buffy the Vampire Slayer* (the analysis of which receives more than half of one of the book's nine chapters). The only Julian mentioned in this work is Julian of Norwich![1] Wagner's *Deep Space and Space Time* does focus heavily upon *DS9* and discuss Julian and Miles in detail, but only in regards to storytelling, memory, doubling, holographs, family, and friendship. There are some aspects of gender that work into the analyses of Wagner's and Lundeen's last two themes, but none that are substantive. However, there is much to say about these two characters and the ways they interact with each other. Greven notes *Star Trek*'s allegorical power in framing gender: "Allegory emerges as a politically powerful mode in *Trek* for exploring the human experience of gendered identity and sexuality" (Greven 1). Although he does not focus upon *DS9*, there are plenty of episodes in the series that uncover profound truths about gendered identity, on both allegorical and visceral levels.

Chief Engineer Miles O'Brien

Throughout the series, no character is subjected to more forms of trauma than Miles O'Brien. The appeal of this character, and the reason he was elevated from recurring guest star in *The Next Generation* (*TNG*) to series regular in *DS9*, is that he is an Average Joe, an everyman with whom most audience members can relate. Miles is not a Starfleet officer, giving him a working class credibility that combines talent, experience, and work ethic. When compared to previous men from the *Star Trek* canon, Miles lacks the bravado of Commander Riker and the polish of Lieutenant LaForge, the brute strength of Lieutenant Worf and the calm rationality of Captain Picard. He is even further removed from the charismatic swagger of Captain Kirk and the unemotional logic of Commander Spock. Miles is thus interesting in that he lacks many of the key aspects of masculinity that typify many of his colleagues. Simply put, there is no other character quite like him. Even though he shares a certain crankiness with Doctor McCoy and a mechanical aptitude with Chief Engineer Scott, not to mention an "I'll do it my way, thank you very much" sense of craft with both these characters, he lacks a veneer of Starfleet respectability that these other two share. In addition to being consistently depicted as working class, Miles' marriage is another interesting feature of his masculinity. As Daniel Bernardi notes, the O'Briens are: "the first interracial human relationship consistently represented in the Trek mega-text.... In many episodes,

O'Brien and Keiko's differences—and how they overcome those differences—are explored and narrativized. Their relationship is depicted as both conflicted and loving" (Bernardi 130). The contrasts between Miles and his wife are pronounced, making for much narrative fodder. In addition to their race (Keiko is Asian) and gender differences, the issue of class is also key: Keiko O'Brien is a teacher, Miles an engineer who spends his days not designing but instead repairing the station. The divergence of their goals as the series progresses and the conflict with the Dominion intensifies serves to exacerbate their differences. Miles wants to do his duty, stay on the front lines, and help his friends fight against the enemy. Keiko wants to take their two children and retreat to a place far behind the battle lines, valuing safety over duty.

The Season 2 episode "Whispers" serves as a sort of mid-life crisis episode for Miles, although in the end the crisis is not as it is first presented to the viewer. After returning to the station from an extended trip, Miles notices that everyone around him is acting strangely. His daughter, Molly, refuses to kiss him. Later, Molly is sent away to stay with another family, but not so that Miles and his wife can be intimate as he assumes, as Keiko summarily rebuffs his amorous advances. At work, things are equally as disquieting, as he discovers that Captain Sisko has assigned critical tasks usually performed by Miles to other workers, and furthermore has ordered the Chief Engineer to get a physical before returning to work. At every turn, Miles' status as husband, father, and professional is being undermined. For the latter, his paranoia increases as his station access is restricted and the chain of command at Starfleet will not listen to him. For the former, the root of his stability in facing threats to the station—his family—suddenly becomes a source of anxiety. As Wagner points out, this is why family is so rare in the *Star Trek* universe: "Domestic and personal comforts are, at least until the quest is completed, dangerous distractions and temptations. It should not come as a surprise, then, if the central characters in *Star Trek* do not enjoy secure, comforting intimate relationships" (Wagner 100). This is what makes Miles so unique. Family is often a concept of reformulation in *Star Trek*, e.g., Captain Picard forming close-knit bonds on the *Enterprise* while his only remaining blood family dies on earth, or Captain Janeway bonding with Seven of Nine, who in turn forms a surrogate family with the Borg Children. There are other characters who are married, and others with children. However, Miles is the only main character with both, even if they often exist largely in the background. In the end, "Whispers" employs a *deus ex machina* that allows the audience to see Miles in full-on, mid-life crisis mode without the character having to experience any permanent consequences. In this regard, it is unrealistic when it comes to masculinity, as mid-life crises often leave in their wake relationships that have undergone lasting changes, and often not in positive ways. As it turns out, the Miles the audience has been following is a replicant unwittingly tasked with murdering a dignitary visiting Deep Space Nine. The real Miles is only brought out in the penultimate scene to establish the ruse, which is sold to the audience in that the replicant appears in every scene, making "Whispers" a rare example of a Trek episode with no B or C storylines. According to show-runner Ira Stephen Behr: "In a way, it's *Invasion of the Body Snatchers* from the body snatcher's point of view. That's what ultimately makes the show tragic and interesting, that the body snatcher doesn't know it." (Erdmann 117). The paranoia angle is interesting vis-à-vis masculinity with the possibility of a mid-life crisis, but the episode's focus upon "programming" is even more critical. The Miles replicant had been programmed to kill. The fact that a seemingly normal family man has an act of violence hardwired into his coding brings to mind issues of gendered violence. Even though what Keiko and Molly really fear is the replicant, the metaphor for fearing the male head of household is easy to identify. As Julian says to a stunned, real Miles: "There was no way to prove he wasn't you. He passed a physical exam with flying colors. And he sure knew his way around the station." The implied message is that seemingly normal family men can harbor deep secrets and commit horrible acts of violence due to societal programming. This episode allows viewers a glimpse into the mid-life crisis of a beloved character while maintaining a narrative mechanism for making things whole in the end.

The Season 4 episode "Hard Time" introduces a psychological feature most well known for occurring in returning veterans of war: Post Traumatic Stress Disorder (PTSD). Although members of all genders experience PTSD, and the phenomenon attends all sorts of traumas above and beyond warfare, it is in this arena and with returning male veterans that much of society's focus has been placed. Robert Hewitt Wolfe, who wrote the episode, consulted his psychotherapist wife in constructing a realistic portrayal of Miles' PTSD (Erdmann 326). Colm Meaney, who plays Miles, noted about the episode: "The fact that it was so emotional made me have to go to the top of my range" (Erdmann 327). The set-up for the episode involves Miles being falsely accused of espionage and receiving the punishment of 20 years worth of memories of difficult jail time. The episode subsequently oscillates between his memories of these years and his difficulty in adjusting to life on the station. Miles has to re-learn everything; he is not very good at darts, and Jake has to remind him about the names and functions of basic tools. He begins to act strangely, hoarding food as he did in prison. More troubling is that he becomes increasingly irritable with his family and friends. He is physically abusive to Quark when the latter annoys him, and snarls at Julian: "If there's one thing I haven't missed in the last twenty years it's your smug, superior attitude." He forgets that his wife is pregnant and yells at his daughter when she seeks his attention. The scene cuts to Miles knocking over plastic barrels in a cargo bay. He opens a weapons locker, sets a phaser to its highest setting, and is going to kill himself when Julian intercedes. He tells the doctor: "You don't understand at all. I'm not doing this for me. I'm doing it to protect Keiko and Molly and everyone else on the station… from me!" He continues: "I nearly hit Molly today. All she wanted was a little attention. And I nearly hit her." Miles begins crying and Julian slowly draws out the story behind his friend's PTSD. Even though they are implanted memories, they are very real to Miles. The only reason he was able to survive for 20 years in prison was due to a fellow inmate, Ee'char, who became his mentor, spiritual guide, and friend. Shortly before he was released, Miles beat Ee'char to death for food hoarding when in actuality his friend was saving food for them to share. The guilt over this act lies at the core of Miles' difficulty in re-adjusting. Dealing with the impact of stress on his personal life and in the workplace mirrors that of returning veterans of war. Throughout the episode, he becomes angrier and angrier when people ask him how he's doing. He loses himself in work, avoiding counseling sessions and snapping at those who try and help him, telling Julian: "I don't want your help, I don't want your friendship. I just want to be left alone!" He bottles up his rage until it explodes, a stereotypical response to pain. For Miles, it's about more than masculine pride or about failing to serve as the husband and father he needs to be. The problem cuts to the very core of his identity as a human: "When we were growing up, they used to tell us that humanity had evolved. That mankind had outgrown hate and rage. But when it came down to it, and I had the chance to show that no matter what anyone did to me I was still an evolved human being, I failed. I repaid kindness with blood. I was no better than an animal." A loyal and quick-thinking friend, Julian comes up with the perfect response, noting that the fact that Miles feels guilt suggests that he is indeed a human instead of an animal. The specter of Ee'char, who appears throughout the episode and often triggers one of Miles' PTSD episodes, smiles and says "Be well, Miles," evidence that the Chief Engineer is able to forgive himself and begin to find positive ways of addressing his pain. In the last scene, what could be an awkward moment is not when Molly runs up to her father and hugs him, saying "Daddy's home, daddy's home." He says, "That's right, daddy's home," shoots a knowing look at this wife and hugs his daughter as the music swells. The family unit has been put back together. Miles will always have terrible memories of his prison sentence and the horrific act that punctuated it, but he has begun to put it all behind him.

The Season 6 episode "Time's Orphan" further explores Miles' role as father and husband. A futuristic take on *The Emerald Forest* (1985), the episode sees Molly sucked into a temporal vortex and returned to Miles and Keiko a few minutes later, but as a wild teenager who grew up on an unpopulated planet. The O'Briens are forced to come to grips with the needs of their daughter, the dictates of Starfleet, and their own desires, all of which are in conflict. As Wagner notes, in most cases in the *Star Trek* canon, familial duty is largely sublimated to duty: "Doctor Crusher and *DS9*'s Commander Sisko and Chief O'Brien are faced with the delicate task of reconciling parental responsibility with the knowledge that their communal responsibilities must come first" (Wagner 100). However, Miles' situation is different. Unlike Crusher and Sisko (and Worf, occasionally), Miles has a spouse, is co-parenting, and has anxieties of relationship that go above and beyond the others, who may date but are largely free to focus upon their children. It is interesting to note that, for once, Miles puts his family before Starfleet, disobeying a direct order in doing so. As the episode begins, Molly and Keiko have just returned to the station during a lull in the war with the Dominion. They picnic on an uninhabited planet and talk about Molly getting older. She announces that she wants to be an exo-biologist when she grows up, and her parents watch approvingly as she does a cartwheel. Miles says "Life doesn't get any better than this" and promises to put in for a transfer if the war heats up again. For the first time in the series, his dedication to family trumps responsibility to Starfleet. Right as Miles makes this vow to fully commit as a father and husband, Molly is seen going into a cave in the background. Her scream a short time later suggests that, no matter how fully invested a father might be, there are things above and beyond what a parent can control. As it turns out, Molly has fallen into a temporal rift that transports her back to the same cave, but at a much earlier time in history. Miles attempts to stay positive for his wife: "We're going to get her back. Everything's going to be all right." They are able to recover her using a transporter, but Molly returns as a feral 18-year-old who bites Miles and tries to hit Keiko before she is rendered unconscious. The rest of the episode involves Miles and Keiko trying to help Molly reacclimatize. As Michele Barrett notes: "She has been disculturated to a shocking degree; in fact, she acts out the behavior of a 'feral child' entirely raised outside human company" (Barrett 104). This story brings to mind the Enlightenment notion of *tabula rasa*, with Miles and Keiko learning something about their own humanity by observing their daughter stripped of all civilizing influence. It also calls to mind feral children of note, whether they be fictional (Mowgli in Rudyard Kipling's *The Jungle Book* and Tarzan in Edgar Rice Burroughs' *Tarzan of the Apes*) or actual (Victor of Aveyron, Marcos Pantoja, and Oxana Malaya).[2] The difference is that in this case, the father is re-introduced and, along with his wife, leads the effort in re-programming their daughter. They teach her positive interaction by rolling a ball back and forth, using the words please and thank you. Ethical dilemmas are considered, including using the transporter to get back Molly as a younger girl, even though it would mean the death of the 18-year-old Molly.

An interesting aspect of this episode is that Miles must learn to let go of his desire to do it all. He is an everyman, not a superman, and must rely upon the *DS9* community, who rally around him in order to help. Worf volunteers to take care of baby Yoshi and finds himself totally outmatched as a surrogate parent. In a comic insight into his masculinity, Worf tells his wife: "I am a Klingon warrior and a Starfleet officer. I have piloted starships through Dominion minefields. I have stood in battle against Kelvans twice my size. I courted and won the heart of the magnificent Jadzia Dax. If I can do these things I can make this child go to sleep!" He then announces "I have work to do," sets his jaw, and grimly marches into the next room. This B story introduces humor into the narrative in order to cut the tension that only gets more pronounced as the O'Briens continue to deal with Molly. She is only happy in the holosuite approximation of her planet, becoming wild and violent otherwise. Miles does not push his daughter too hard but is there for her when she needs him. He is not embarrassed by her actions, defending Molly when he feels as if Starfleet's decisions regarding her future are not in her best interest. Here is where his growth as a father within the episode is most noticeable. Miles has learned that giving up control is sometimes necessary, and he and Keiko decide that they must give up their happiness in order to ensure their daughter's. They resolve to steal a runabout and return Molly to the planet, and then to send her through the rift and seal it. They do just this, although once again the help of community is established when Odo catches them stealing the runabout, nevertheless allowing them to leave. Miles is willing to give up his career, perhaps even face jail time, and worst of all give up his daughter, all in order to keep Molly safe from Starfleet bureaucracy. He makes the ultimate sacrifice as a parent, telling his 18-year-old daughter: "When you look up at the stars, that's where we'll be, watching you." After watching her walk through the portal, Miles takes a few moments to console his wife. Luckily, that delays him from closing the time rift for a few moments, as on the other side teen Molly discovers young Molly and encourages her to walk through the portal. The family reunites happily, Molly having returned from her adventure and her parents having learned a truth about the nature of parental sacrifice. It is interesting to note that this plot was originally conceived as an episode involving Worf/Alexander for *TNG*, but over the years Michael Piller, Ira Stephen Behr, and Hans Beimler[3]—all fathers—nixed the story (Erdmann 577–578). Much as with "Hard Time," the writers sought professional counsel, consulting with a number of psychologists and clinical social workers in working on the script (Erdmann 579). The result is a marvelous episode exploring the difficulty of parenting, specifically in coming to terms with the fact that many things lie outside the control of a parent.

Throughout the series, Miles grows as a family man and member of the station's micro-society. Gender is performative and, in his professional and personal life, Miles plays the role of colleague, husband, and father. He is depicted as a put upon head of household, but the conservative gender politics end there. He's a blue-collar worker and tinkerer, having a work ethic unmatched in the series. It's interesting to note that, in *DS9*'s alternate universe episodes ("Crossover," "Through the Looking Glass," "Shattered Mirror," "Resurrection," and "The Emperor's New Cloak"), where just about every character is an inverse image of him or herself, Miles is pretty much the same. After years as a warrior, and then as an engineer first on an exploratory vessel and now on a station—albeit one on the frontlines of an inter-galactic war—Miles makes the decision at the end of *DS9* to return to earth, more for his family and conception of what he should be as a husband and father than for any other reason. In the process, he leaves behind his best friend and the character against whom he is most often contrasted: Dr. Julian Bashir.

Medical Doctor Julian Bashir

Julian shares a few similarities with Miles. Both are scrupulous, hard working, and dedicated to Starfleet. Both have ties to former colonies of the British Empire (Julian is a Londoner of Indian descent, Miles is Irish), perhaps purposeful in a series focused upon the problems of imperial expansion. When discussing the Other in *Star Trek*, Kirk Junker notes that their "origins in the British Isles are very much a part of their characters. They hang out together in Quark's, drink 'pints,' play darts; in short they conform to the American view of how someone from the British Isles behaves" (Junker 140). Although he is correct in surmising that these characters are British, Junker misses the point that they are not so much from the British Isles as having ties to British colonies that faced historic oppression. Thus, in addition to the element of gender performance one adds colonial mimicry when it comes to hanging out in pubs, throwing back pints, and competitions of skill such as darts, all activities linked to masculinity. Despite all of their similarities, in most ways these two characters could not be more dissimilar, however. Miles and Julian exist as one of many "opposites attract" pairings that populate the *Star Trek* canon.[4] Whereas Miles is morose, world weary, middle-aged, and married, Julian is charming, energetic, young, and single. From his introduction as a character, he is portrayed as brash and arrogant, running afoul of Major Kira the minute he sets foot on the station. He is in many ways reminiscent of the young men who flocked first to the new world, and later to the western frontier, in order to find fortune and adventure.[5] Julian privileges experience over existence and certainly has come to the right time and place for that pursuit. He is highly intelligent and skilled, yet throughout the first five seasons struggles with the knowledge that he is not living up to his potential. All of these elements impact his gender performance, but it is in his relationships with women that Julian is reduced to a stereotype. Although it would be a stretch to denote him as a lothario, he is certainly linked romantically to numerous women on the station, dating both colleagues and visitors to *DS9*. He has a long-term relationship with the Dabo girl Leeta before she finally settles down with Rom, and does not shy away from charged quips or innuendo. One out of numerous such examples is his reaction during the time travel episode "Trials and Tribble-ations" when he sees the skimpy uniform worn by Jadzia Dax and says, admiringly: "I'm going to like history!" Further evidence that, for Julian, everything revolves around sex comes later in that same episode, when he ends up flirting with a woman he subsequently believes could be an ancestor. In a panic, he tells Miles: "This could be a predestination paradox. I could be destined to fall in love with that woman and become my own great-grandfather.... If I don't meet with her tomorrow I may never be born! ... I can't wait to get back to Deep Space Nine and see your face when you find out that I never existed!" John Putnam notes that this is a variation of the grandfather paradox (Putnam 165),[6] although in Julian's world the focus is about sex rather than violence, switching the inciting action from one of killing the grandfather to failing to be seduced by the grandmother!

As Wagner points out, Julian's choice of holosuite program in the episode "Our Man Bashir" indicates his obsession with sex: "Bashir is a James Bond-style secret agent with a voluptuous 'valet' named Mona Luvsitt, who is everything that a would-be ladies' man like Bashir could want" (Wagner 102). Julian is depicted as highly sexed throughout the series. However, despite his obsession with the opposite sex, there is a gentleness and kindness about Julian. He clearly develops feelings for Ensign Melora Pazler in the Season 2 episode "Melora." Due to her inability to exist easily in the gravity of the station (she is used to much lower levels of gravity on her home planet), Melora has a difficult time discharging her Starfleet duties. Ultimately, she is Julian's patient, and despite their mutual attraction he sublimates his desire for her in order to help her succeed at her job. By this point in the series Julian has learned to, when necessary, tone down his excess of masculine charm and personal desire for the greater good. There's also a touch of pathos to Julian's journey as a young man seeking love, as it never seems to work out. During the Season 2 episode "Armageddon Game," he confides in Miles that he was once in love with a Parisian ballerina named Palis Delon but instead chose Starfleet. By the beginning of the final season, two of his ex-girlfriends have moved on to marry other men: Leeta marries Rom, and Jadzia marries Worf. It is interesting to note, however, that despite his many relationships with women the person with whom Julian connects most deeply is Miles. As Greven notes, this is not the first time that the formula of the buddy film featured in *Star*

Trek[7]: "Never shown to be married, Kirk and Spock (as well as McCoy) share their most intense emotional bond with each other" (Greven 6). Miles is married, and Julian constantly in a relationship or pursuing some women or another, but their most profound connection is with each other. Part of what drives this relationship is that they are constantly learning from one another, despite the bickering and because of their innate differences. In "Armageddon Game," the two bond while being hunted by a joint T'Lani/Kellerun coalition, talking about women and marriage and defending their own personal philosophies as they await rescue. Julian suggests that family and duty can interfere with one another: "It's no secret that your assignment to this station hasn't been conducive to your marriage." Julian continues by noting that his life holds more excitement: "Talani women are quite attractive.... For me, tonight's celebrations would have been an adventure. The most you could have hoped for was a good meal." Miles counters by stating that: "Marriage is the greatest adventure of them all. It's filled with pitfalls and setbacks and mistakes ... but it's a journey worth taking because you take it together." Coming early in the series, Miles' logic in this episode doesn't convince Bashir, although his feelings on the matter evolve over time. Julian's maturity when it comes to moving from one-night stands to an implied long-term relationship with Ezri Dax in the series finale is not localized to any episodes per se, but instead consists of discrete moments in B or C storylines spread across numerous episodes. There are two other aspects of his journey that intersect with his masculine identity and fear of commitment, however, that feature heavily in numerous episodes: his fear of failure and complex relationship with his past.

The Season 3 episode "Distant Voices" is a testament to Julian's self doubt upon the occasion of his 30th birthday. Throughout much of this episode, he lies in a coma and dreams a narrative where he grows older progressively, becoming more and more infirm in the process. Wagner notes the elements of Freudian psychology in what is essentially an early mid-life crisis: "In dreams, Bashir encounters various aspects of his own personality in the visage of his *DS9* crewmates, and he must use these parts of himself in concert, in order to complete repairs on the dead *DS9* station (which represents his own mind), if he is to recover from the coma" (Wagner 73). It is more than just self-healing, however, as the specter of aging and not having measured up dominate this episode. After being attacked by an alien who sends pulsing energy through his brain, Julian wakes up in the infirmary. Inexplicably, his hair has begun to gray, with Garak quipping: "I guess you had reason to feel worried about turning 30, after all. Either that or your job is more stressful than I thought." Almost immediately, Julian begins to hear whispering voices in the background. In reality, these are his friends trying to resuscitate him, but they also serve as whispers of self-doubt. At first, Julian attempts to use logic in order to explain what is happening to him, considering viruses, parasites, and subspace anomalies as potential culprits. Of course, metaphorically it is the process of aging he is attempting to understand, to no avail. Eventually, Julian realizes that he is in a coma, and also the reason why the characters in the play he has created are acting so strangely. Each of his colleagues in this dream represents a single aspect of his humanity: Miles is his doubt and disbelief, Kira his aggression, and Odo his suspicion and fear. As he tells Jadzia: "Dax, to me you've always represented confidence and sense of adventure." Although not identified as such, Sisko represents his professionalism and Quark, who cowers in a corner of the bar, his fear. Julian is stalked through the station by the Letheon alien who attacked him, who at first represents a spooky presence in the background, then an actual physical threat, and finally the voice of self doubt, a move from more corporeal to metaphysical concerns that in one sense mirror anxiety over aging (although at one point toward the end of the episode, Julian does break his hip, a reminder that not all end-of-life concerns about mortality are abstract in nature). The Letheon robs him of his confidence, strength, and intelligence, noting that Julian was a good enough tennis player to turn professional but gave up due to his parent's lack of approval. He also notes that, during his final year at Starfleet Academy, Julian purposefully missed a question on the final exam: "You purposefully answered the question wrong.... You didn't want to be first in your class. You couldn't take the pressure." Julian realizes that in order to overcome his affliction and wake up, he has to fix the station, which in essence is coming to grips with the process of aging. He does this and manages to awaken, presumably with help from his medical staff. However, just because he succeeds in this episode and comes to a new awareness about aging on his 30th birthday, that does not mean that he has rid himself of his self doubt. As the Letheon reminds him:

> You're not going anywhere, doctor. You're staying right here, trapped on this station, watching while I destroy you piece by piece. And when all the best parts of you are gone, when there's nothing left but the withered shell, then and only then, will I put you out of your misery. You can't escape, doctor. You can run if you want to, but you can't outrun death.

The Letheon who said these words may have been in Julian's imagination and the crisis averted, but the truth remains: Julian is getting older and, for the first time, has come to grips with the process of aging and eventual mortality.

Another Season 3 episode, "Explorers," brings together Julian's fears about measuring up both professionally and personally. In the beginning of this episode, in what will constitute the B story, Julian responds in kind when a Dabo girl at Quark's begins to flirt with him, pretending to cough in order to attract his attention. Never the one to pass up an opportunity when it comes to a beautiful woman, he recommends a hot toddy for her cough, ordering a second because he himself "feels a bit of a cough coming on." A few moments later, however, Julian's day is ruined when Jadzia brings word that Dr. Elizabeth Lense has arrived on the station. As the joke runs throughout the seven seasons of *DS9*, Julian "mistook a preganglionic fiber for a postganglionic nerve," allowing Lense to pass him and graduate valedictorian in their class at Starfleet Academy. The fact that Dr. Lense is a young and beautiful woman who seems just as popular as Julian may add to his anxiety. The fact that she does not even recognize him after arriving at the station sends him into a tailspin during which he gets drunk with Miles. Of course, by the end of the episode we find out that Dr. Lense didn't really rebuff Julian, she simply had thought that he was an Andorian. She confesses to him that she both envies his assignment on Deep Space Nine and is impressed with his research, and the two head of to the infirmary to talk shop. Coming just a few episodes after "Distant Voices," Julian is able to put a few of his anxieties to rest. Several others, most notably those involving his parents and a secret past, are dealt with at a later time.

The Season 5 episode "Dr. Bashir, I Presume" finally introduces Julian's parents—Richard and Amsha—as well as the secret the family has been hiding for decades. As Michele Barrett points out, as a character Julian was always a bit too good to be true, noting that he "has an extraordinarily high order of reasoning, perfect hand-eye coordination, the ability to compartmentalize his own brain, and mathematical computational abilities that are far above the plausible. These abilities make him rather 'inhuman'" (Barrett 87). As it turns out, the doctor was genetically enhanced as a child, which is revealed when his parents are invited to the station by Dr. Lewis Zimmerman in order to provide context on their son, who has been chosen as the model for the new Emergency Medical Hologram (EMH). The whole episode hinges upon relationships, both when it comes to a B story romance (Zimmerman and Rom are both in love with Leeta) and, in particular, parental sacrifice. Toward the beginning of the episode, Miles states a familiar refrain when it comes to his advice to Julian about settling down and starting a family: "You should give it a try sometime." A short time later, the doctor's hesitance in starting a family is properly contextualized with the arrival of his parents on the station. Amsha is unconditionally loving and supportive, but Richard is a bit of a con man, telling Julian's colleagues that his son is "my gift to succeeding generations" and "we knew he was destined for greatness." Of course, behind closed doors we find out that everything is an act. Richard is not who he appears, instead a sort of charismatic drifter who moves from job to job because the grandiosity of his plans never match his abilities. As Julian reminds him: "You always have good prospects, and they're always just OVER that horizon." Richard comes from a lower class background that he has worked hard to hide from others. As Barrett notes: "On Deep Space Nine, however, the question of social class is much closer to home—it is a part of the great melting pot that the station represents.... Doctor Bashir's father is depicted as a downmarket Londoner" (Barrett 70). Due to Julian's suave and sophisticated bearing and his lofty education, it is easy to forget that he came from humble origins.

Well meaning but clueless, the Bashirs reaffirm their commitment to keep his genetic enhancement secret when they find him in the infirmary. Of course, it is not Julian they find but his holographic facsimile, and their confession is overheard by both Miles and Dr. Zimmerman. Julian resolves to resign from Starfleet, commiserating with Miles and telling him a story not of minor enhancement, but of a holistic change: "I was six, small for my age, a bit awkward physically, not very bright. In the first grade, when the other children were learning how to read and write and use the computer, I was still trying to tell a dog from a cat and a tree from a house." After getting genetic treatment, Julian notes that he was improved in every way, both mentally and physically. He became the star pupil of a different school, noting that: "In the end, every thing but my name was altered in some way." It is interesting how Julian frames this discussion, focusing upon parental and societal expectations, making statements such as "all I knew is that I was a great disappointment to my parents" and "there's no stigma attached to success." Always a supportive friend with the right thing to say, Miles notes the intangibles that cannot be modified by genetic reprogramming: "I don't care how many enhancements your parents had done. Genetic recoding can't give you ambition or a personality or compassion or any of the things that make a person truly human." Julian's confrontation with his parents does not go as well, and he indicts his father for not taking responsibility, telling him: "Your gift is about to be revealed as a fraud, just like you." In the end, although his son is now in his mid–30s, for the first time Richard takes responsibility. The Bashirs confess to Starfleet and negotiate a deal. Blameless in the decision to genetically enhance, Julian will be allowed to stay in Starfleet. Richard, however, will spend two years in a minimum-security prison, a sacrifice that will ensure that his son does not follow him down that path of never living up to his potential. Julian is finally free to move forward with his life, freed from his past. A great burden has been lifted from his shoulders, and he is finally able to commit to a woman, who turns out to be Ezri Dax in the last episode of the series ("What you Leave Behind").

DS9 played with gender roles unlike any *Star Trek* series before or after. Much of this was through the character of Jadzia Dax, a joined species consisting of a bipedal host (Jadzia) and another entity (Dax) with a much longer lifespan. Sisko refers to this character throughout the series as "old man" due to the fact that the former host of the Dax symbient was male, a narrative device introducing numerous plotlines of confused gender identity. Finally, Jadzia Dax featured in the first overtly gay storyline to take place in any of the *Star Trek* films or television series. Often lost in the focus upon gender in the series, much of it directed toward Jadzia, is a focus upon the male characters, their relationships, and the issues that arise such as parenting (Benjamin and Jake Sisko), romance (Benjamin and Kasidy Yates, Miles and Keiko, Odo and Kira, Worf and Jadzia), and friendship (Miles and Julian, Ben and Jadzia, Odo and Quark). Of the latter, the friendship between Miles and Julian is the most sustained and the most fascinating. They each experience their own, very different challenges, but never alone as they support and aid each other as they grow in parallel. Although their issues invested in gender are more general to the field than necessarily specific to masculinity, such is the universalizing appeal of *Star Trek*, where it is acceptable for Kira to be the aggressive character and Julian to be a bit vain about his appearance. Normative, gender-based stereotypes are, to a large degree, overthrown in this fictional world, with characters freed to become who they want to be. That is not to say, however, that Miles and Julian are completely free from the orbit of human gender politics. No matter how much it aspires to be a text about a somewhat idealized future, *Star Trek* is a product of its time and place, and as a result reflects many of the gender concerns of its era built upon the mistakes of the past. As Alice George notes, the frontier setting in *Star Trek* provides the perfect opportunity to re-negotiate some of these issues: "*Star Trek* also was able to rework an imperfect American past by using a mythic Old West to promise a brighter and greater future. The series thus offered viewers the stability found in the familiarity of a nostalgic past, even as they faced the uncertainty of the future" (George 20). Although George specifically references *TOS* in this quote, the same applies for the series that followed, including *DS9* and its outpost space station on a colonial frontier. Miles O'Brien faces personal and professional anguish, which come together in his concern over raising a family in the midst of a terrible war with millions of casualties. Julian Bashir faces personal and professional uncertainty, stoked by fears of failure and an inability to commit. However, with the optimism that typifies the *Star Trek* canon, plus the help of each other as loyal friends, Miles and Julian are able to confront their demons, deal with these challenges to their masculinity, and become better men for it.

Notes

1. Julian of Norwich was an English Christian mystic during the late 14th and early 15th centuries. She is noted as the author of *Revelations of Divine Love*, the first book known to be authored by a woman in English.
2. Pre-teen Victor was found in the woods of southern France during the late 18th cen-

tury. Pantoja was discovered with wolves as a late teen in the Sierra Morena mountains of Spain during the 1960s. Seven-year-old Malaya was found in the Ukraine, having largely grown up in the company of a pack of dogs after being neglected by her parents.

3. Piller and Behr were the show-runners for *Deep Space Nine* during its seven-year run, and Beimler the supervising producer.

4. The quintessential such pairing is Kirk/Spock in *The Original Series* (*TOS*), although Odo/Quark in *DS9*, and Tuvok/Neelix in *Voyager* are also successful pairings.

5. See Steven Sarson's *British America* for a study of the New World and its draw for Europeans seeking opportunity, and Frederick Jackson Turner's *History, Frontier, and Section* for an exploration of the western frontier and the people who populated it.

6. In this temporal paradox, a time traveler creates conditions in the past that make his/her presence in the present untenable, and therefore unable to return to the past and create the initial disturbance (e.g., a time traveler killing his own grandfather, making his own birth at a later time impossible). The entire *Terminator* franchise has been built around this theoretical time travel scenario.

7. Buddy films involve a male/male pairing and feature action, adventure, and plenty of bickering. They were made famous in the late 1960s and early 1970s, with films such as *Butch Cassidy and the Sundance Kid* (Dir. George Roy Hill, 1969), *The Sting* (Dir. George Roy Hill, 1973), and *The Man Who Would be King* (Dir. John Huston, 1975), although they owe a debt of gratitude to Abbott and Costello and the road movies of Bob Hope and Bing Crosby.

Works Cited

Barrett, Michele, and Duncan Barrett. *Star Trek: The Human Frontier*. New York: Routledge, 2001.

Bernardi, Daniel Leonard. *"Star Trek" and History: Race-ing Toward a White Future*. New Brunswick: Rutgers University Press, 1998.

Erdmann, Terry J., and Paula M. Block. *Star Trek: Deep Space Nine Companion*. New York: Pocket Books, 2000.

George, Alice L. "Riding Posse on the Final Frontier: James T. Kirk, Hero of the Old West." *"Star Trek" and History*. Ed. Nancy R. Reagin. Hoboken: John Wiley, 2013. 7–21.

Greven, David. *Gender and Sexuality in* Star Trek: *Allegories of Desire in the Television Series and Films*. Jefferson, NC: McFarland, 2009.

Junker, Kirk W., and Robert Duffy. "Saying 'Yours' and 'Mine' in *Deep Space Nine*." *Aliens R Us: The Other in Science Fiction Cinema*. Ed. Ziauddin Sardar and Sean Cubitt. London: Pluto Press, 2002. 134–148.

Putnam, John. "Terrorizing Space: *Star Trek*, Terrorism, and History." *"Star Trek" and History*. Ed. Nancy R. Reagin. Hoboken: John Wiley, 2013. 143–157.

Sarson, Steven. *British America*. London: Hodder Arnold, 2005.

Turner, Frederick Jackson. *History, Frontier, and Section*. Albuquerque: University Press of New Mexico, 1993.

Wagner, Jon, and Jan Lundeen. *Deep Space and Sacred Time: "Star Trek" in the American Mythos*. Westport, CT: Praeger, 1998.

From Supercrip to Assimilant

Normalcy, Bioculture and Disability in the Star Trek *Universe*

Ken Monteith

> And just as *Star Trek* has inspired technological inventions, it can also provide a path to inclusion, acceptance, and the ability to see past individual differences to the humanity we all share. In the future we see on Star Trek, disability is a non-issue. Geordi can see just fine with his VISOR, thank you.
>
> —Ilana Lehmann, *All You Need to Know About Disability Is on* Star Trek, 337

> "Infinite diversity in infinite combination"—Vulcan proverb (*TOS*: "Is There in Truth No Beauty?")

When he relaunched the *Star Trek* franchise as *The Next Generation* (*TNG)* for television, Gene Roddenberry created a character that paid tribute to one of the original series's fans: George La Forge. Several fan sites describe La Forge as a convention regular who stood out because of his muscular dystrophy, while *TNG* biographer Larry Nemek describes La Forge as a "quadrapalegic" who "endeared himself to Gene Roddenberry and much of fandom" (15).[1] La Forge's enthusiasm and friendship with Roddenberry became the inspiration for Geordi La Forge, the blind con officer on *Enterpise-D*, eventually promoted to chief engineer and described by Roddenberry as "an away-mission regular" (Roddenberry 1987). From its inception, *Star Trek* (*TOS*) included disability as part of its infinite diversity, providing characters who overcame impairments and who were often more in touch with their humanity because of these impairments. And yet, disability plays a more active role in *Star Trek* than providing catalysts for teachable moments, or, walk on characters as plot points—disability is integral to *Star Trek*'s worldview. Despite technological advances, individuals in the *Star Trek* universe still inhabit vulnerable bodies. Geordi La Forge's VISOR enables him to see wavelengths beyond human perception, yet the VISOR itself causes him pain. Melora Pazlar's experience allows her to navigate low gravity environments with a grace and and agility unfamiliar to other Federation species, yet her exoskeleton enabling her to navigate in full Federation standard gravity also causes her pain. Seven of Nine has superior strength, astounding regenerative abilities, and access to the collective memories and cultural archives of countless thousands of assimilated species, yet her experience as a Borg drone causes mental pain if not a sci-fi form of autism.

To assimilate, or to accommodate one's body so that it fits into the Federation, is to experience pain; and yet, the greatest personal failing of a member of the federation is to avoid pain and become an assimilant. This study uses the term assimilant as a partial nod to the Borg, the cybernetic villians of later series; but for the purpose of this examination, I identify two types of assimilant: the person who can pass as normate[2] without raising the suspicion of others, and, the person who gives in and stops fighting for his or her individuality. When it comes to disability, *Star Trek* makes sure the audience knows that the character embodies difference, either through prosthetic devices that visually highlight the disability, or (and including) a requirement that the character explains his/her disability to the audience.

Despite the Federation's hierarchical power structure, autonomy (in the face of some adversity) is the currency of the *Star Trek* universe. Characters (disabled as well as fully abled) are intended to inspire the audience. As Roddenberry comments in his writer's guide for *TNG*, "They [The Crew] have been selected for this mission because of their ability to transcend [sic] their human failings. We should see in them the kind of people we aspire to be ourselves" (9). Such characters create an example for the audience to follow: we too can overcome our limitations, become better people, and become autonomous individuals. In doing so, *Star Trek* casts disability not as a bodily affliction, but as an affliction of free will. The sense of autonomy I invoke here is more in line with individuality of spirit; yet at the same time, this is an individual spirit that follows orders and acts in accord with Starfleet regulations. Grappling with a disability leads a character to regaining of "the humanity we all share" (to quote Lehmann, above) and serves as an example (337). Disabled individuals must fight for autonomy all the while being marked as different because of that same disability. These differences are not without their advantages, since such differences often save the day and serve as a turning point during a *Star Trek* episode, allowing the disabled character to become the hero of that episode. *Star Trek* provides the viewer with any number of supercrips who adapt and overcome through their own force of will and individual ego, individuals who embrace their difference and in the end, celebrate their uniqueness. Their personal histories are celebrated as cultural achievements. In *Star Trek*, disability is a socially constructed anchor holding utopian ideals in place.

Enabling/Disabling Utopia

Before examining individual characters, I would first like to discuss *Star Trek*'s worldview (or universe view?) in relation to disability studies. In his work *The End of Normal: Identity in a Biocultural Era*, Davis investigates how disability fits into a neoliberal (if not utopian) philosophy. As Davis describes it, utopian conceptions of disability are inherently problematic. Such a world-view would appear to celebrate diversity, acknowledging that each individual is unique, and as such, each individual is *as unique as* any other individual in society. In a sense, uniqueness becomes the very thing everyone has in common. *Star Trek* celebrates uniqueness and diversity, suggesting that the Federation becomes stronger when all diverse elements work together for a common goal—or as the Vulcans proverb goes, Infinite Diversity in Infinite Combination—and yet as Davis comments, diversity itself as an ideology creates a dilemma. Davis writes: "The problem with diversity is that it really needs two things to survive as a concept. It needs to imagine a utopia in which difference will disappear, while living in a present that is obsessed with difference" (13). The mission of the *Enterprise* is to "seek out strange new worlds,"—the opening voice-overs by Captains Kirk and Picard already cast difference as strange and new. In seeking out new sentient species, *Star Trek* is already obsessed with difference, and yet at the same time, these species mirror an aspect of humanity, and ultimately, are cured because of humanity. But as a utopia obsessed with diversity, the *Star Trek* universe ignores many of the social problems experienced by its viewing audience in order to argue for a diversity that unites rather than divides. Davis comments that such utopian visions overlook or ignore real social difference in order to celebrate this kind of diversity. Davis continues:

> And it [utopian idealogy] needs to suppress everything that confounds that vision. What is suppressed from the imaginary of diversity, a suppression that actually puts neoliberal diversity into play, are various forms of inequality, notably economic inequality, as well as the question of poverty [13].

There are no rich or poor in the *Star Trek* future: money and property are not markers of social accomplishment or cultural status.[3] And unless it is a topic for a special episode, race settles comfortably in the background. Instead, each individual is judged on actions and merit. As such, the problems to be solved in *Star Trek* are individual problems, or, problems of individuality. Giordi La Forge's race is superseded by his disability, for example, even though race is very much an issue for *TNG*'s viewing audience.

If the Federation has (apparently) solved social problems like poverty and racism in the 23rd and 24th centuries, then what issues do the writers have to explore episode to episode? Disability provides a dramatic venue for *Star Trek* writers, where social questions can be introduced without explicitly naming an issue. As Davis suggests, disability is ideal for such an introduction:

> Impairments are commonly seen as abnormal, medically determined, and certainly not socially constructed. This may be because disability is not seen as an identity in the same way as many see race, gender, and other embodied identities. And the reason for that is that disability is largely perceived as a medical problem and not a way of life involving choice [7].

Disabled individuals are sentimentalized, valorized, and marked as problems to be solved because such individual focus hints at larger social issues without having to meet them head on, keeping the utopia from descending into a dystopian vision of the future. Seven of Nine (for example) has been raised as Borg, but rather than examine the social implications of living in a collective society, she is diagnosed as medically abnormal. The big social issues have been solved in the 23rd and 24th centuries, so it seems, and only the smaller (episodic) issues remain. In an episodic television series, disability is the shorthand of character development and accomplishment. The audience quickly understands the visual markers employed to denote disability, and can quickly join in the sentimentalization of the disabled character, and can rejoice in the resolution presented at episode's end. In other words, disability provides a pre-packaged identity an audience can recognize. *Star Trek*'s audience is already culturally hardwired to recognize a number of disability stereotypes even if these stereotypes can not be identified by name—in her work "The Politics of Staring," Garland-Thomson presents a classification of how viewers see and culturally recognize disability. While Garland-Thomson presents four categories, I want to examine two: the wondrous and the sentimental. As Garland-Thomson explains, the wondrous "are the monsters of antiquity, who inspired awe, foretold the future, or bore divine signs" and otherwise appeared to be extraordinary because of their difference (59). Contemporary wonders, Garland-Thomson argues, have become transformed into a supercrip stereotype, a figure "who amazes and inspires the viewer by performing feats that the nondisabled viewer cannot imagine doing" (60–61). The supercrip characters of *Star Trek* are often the ones who save-the-day during their episode, relying upon their unique talents that come as a result of their disability. While an audience may marvel at a supercrip's abilities, the sentimental invites the audience to feel bad for, or to feel that they need to protect, a disabled individual. Or as Garland-Thomson writes: "Whereas the wondrous elevates and enlarges, the sentimental diminishes" (63). While invoking either the sentimental or supercrip stereotype for a *Star Trek* audience, the writers ask their viewers to rely upon a ready-made identity already circulating in the culture; but in effect, this reliance brings the values of contemporary society to bear rather than to propose utopian or inclusive solutions.

From Sentiment to Supercrip

In the original series, one of the most memorable disabled characters introduced to *Star Trek*'s audience may be Captain Christopher Pike. A central figure in the two-part episode "The Menagerie," Pike is the former captain of the *Enterprise* and was one of Mr. Spock's previous commanding officers.[4] The episode presents the audience with a Federation anomaly: The only crime punishable by death is to visit the planet Talos IV, and, Mr. Spock has committed treason by hijacking the *Enterprise* so that he may return Captain Pike to this same planet. Both seem out of character for the Federation's utopian ideals, but makes for good television.

The anomalies of the episode continue. Spock seeks to return Pike to Talos IV yet Pike was not disabled as a result of his previous visit to this planet. The episode glosses over exactly how Pike became disabled, yet Captain Pike's disabilities are so profound that his body is fully enclosed in a mobile life-support metal box on casters. This full-body enclosure resembles a square-ish iron-lung, with Captain Pike's head and shoulders visible, sticking out the top. The box is controlled by Pike's brainwaves, yet despite the fantastic technology that this box must possess to keep Pike alive and respond to his brain waves to initiate movement, the only way Pike can communicate is through a beeping light: one light-beep for yes; two light-beeps for no. While the light-beeps may add to the drama of the episode, the technology itself seems out of step with imagined 23rd century technological advances. Universal translators allow Vulcans, Klingons, Romulans, Humans, and the like to communicate, and yet a disabled starship captain has to light-beep his way through a conversation using yes or no answers. The life support box on wheels provides Pike with autonomous movement, but denies him a voice. As Kathryn Allen comments, the disabled Captain Pike serves as a foil to Captain Kirk, a reminder to Kirk of what has come before in the command chair, and a contrast to Kirk as embodied (or disembodied) masculinity (9–10). Kirk feels both pity for Pike and recoils at Pike's vulnerability. We discover that the Federation also pities Captain Pike: despite the disability, Pike's rank and status as a commanding officer is still intact. Commodore Mendez explains to Kirk that Starfleet "just couldn't take that away from him" ("The Menagerie"). As a disabled character, Captain Pike resides squarely in Garland-Thomson's category of the sentimental; he elicits pity from Captain Kirk, from Starfleet, and even from the Vulcan (and supposedly emotion free) Mr. Spock. Spock is arrested and given a court-marshal hearing because he attempts to return Captain Pike back to Talos IV. And again, as we are reminded in the episode, Talos IV is not only off limits to Starfleet personnel, but it is also the only death penalty enforced law in the Federation. The Talosians have the ability to enter an individual's mind and create illusions so profound that the individual is no longer in contact with reality. In a sense, the Talosian's remove autonomy and replace it with fantasy. But why does Spock risk his career and life to return Pike to Talos IV? Pike did not receive his injuries as a result of his previous visit to the planet. His loyalty and supressed emotions not withstanding, Spock sees the Talosians as a kind of cure for the locked-in Pike. Talosian psy ability becomes the prosthesis that the Federation cannot provide. Once returned to Talos IV, Pike appears on the view screen as his younger self, in full health, walking hand in hand with Vina, a disabled woman the Talosians saved from a starship wreckage. Spock succeeds in returning Captain Pike to Talos IV, where Pike can live out his life under the illusion of perfect health.

The real crime of the episode is not that Mr. Spock stole a starship, or, that the Federation health plan only provides disabled veterans with beeping mobility boxes: the real crime of the episode is that a disabled individual would rather live in an induced reality in which he experiences full health rather than continue to suffer and serve as either an example or an object of pity. Not only can the Talosians serve as a kind of prosthesis, providing Pike with a fully bodied existence, Talosian abilities are so strong that all other individuals who meet Pike will also experience Pike as a fully abled body. Talosian-Pike will not be seen as disabled; and in fact, he will be able to communicate and interact with other people on an equal footing. Without the mobility box, Pike will not invoke pity, he will not be sentimentalized, and he will not appear to be less than those he encounters. The prosthetic relationship is not always one between technology and biology, as McReynolds argues:

> A prosthetic relationship requires cooperation; both bodies must consciously work together. When two agents engage as prosthesis, functionality necessitates a rapport—an emotional, physical, psychological, and mental connection between the bodies—that is not possible in cases where an inanimate object is affixed to one's body [116].

McReynolds' definition describes something more like a symbiotic relationship rather than one group accommodating or providing an imagined access for another. In the case of Captain Pike, the prosthetic relationship with the Talosians is more than a collusion with the enemy: it is a rejection of Federation ideals and the Federation as cure. In order for a Federation prosthetic relationship to fully work, Christopher Pike must buy into the idea that he is disabled, and must hold up his end of this unspoken social contract. Pike must be seen as disabled so that he can then be pitied and serve as a warning for his fellow Federation compatriots. In their work *Narrative Prosthesis* Mitchell and Snyder argue that disabled characters challenge the fixity and perception of a continually healthy body, commenting:

> The terror of the challenge to the self's boundaries, which are believed to be more or less absolute, suggest that the spectacle of extraordinary bodily difference upsets the viewer's faith in his/her own biological integrity. The viewer of the freakish spectacle does not experience a feeling of superiority in his or her closer proximity to the normal ideal, but rather sense his or her own body to be at risk [37].

The Federation cannot fix Captain Pike so he must be placed in a box and become a fixture: Pike must become a spectacle that inspires a kind of terror in the spectator. Seeing Captain Pike, Captain Kirk may then realize that his actions have consequence, that his body—for all its health and vitality—is also vulnerable. Instead of serving as a warning and as an example, Pike becomes assimilated into Talosian society, rejecting humanity, choosing to live in what appears to be captivity, and yet at the same time free, rather then exist in a Federation box.

If *TOS* Captain Pike is intended as a partial foil for Captain Kirk, later iterations of the character serve as a mentor and father figure to J.J. Abram's rebooted Kirk. As Katherine Allen argues, In the 2009 J.J. Abram's re-boot Captain Pike's injuries are either less severe, or more easily cured: injured Pike rests in a standard wheel chair and has control of his upper body as well as his voice. Reboot Pike wears his injuries and can narrate how he came by them. His injuries are a badge of honor as well as a warning that bodies, even in 23rd century reboots, are vulnerable. And, Reboot Pike has the potential to be rehabilitated. Allen writes:

> Technology is often the "fix-all" for whatever ails or deforms the body.... In utopian visions, when integrated into the able body, technology makes the human body better—an idealized version of itself. When technology is applied to the disabled body, however, all too often it is in an attempt to cure or normalize what is deemed "wrong" with the body. Take the technology away and the disabled body's supposed lack remains [10].

Reboot Pike is not a cyborg but a patient, a patient who apparently lacks the full-bodied ability to command a starship. It could be argued that one could still captain a starship from a wheelchair, but instead, Pike is promoted to admiral and given a desk job, allowing Reboot Kirk to remain *Enterprise* captain even though he gained the captain's chair through a series of misadventures.

"Pity is the worst of all"

In the original series, we are also introduced to Dr. Jones, a blind and telepathic human assigned to the Medusan Ambassador, Kollos. Medusans, like their Greek mythological namesake, are so disturbing to look at that, instead of being turned to stone, humans who look at them are driven insane. Dr. Jones uses her telepathic abilities in negotiations, representing the ambassador and keeping Federation dignitaries from losing their minds (and, we can argue, losing their autonomy). But of greater interest, Dr. Jones wears a sensor net over her clothing, a prosthetic net that enables Jones a type of vision. As she tells Captain Kirk,

> Do you think you can gather more information with your eyes than I can with my sensors? I could play tennis with you, Captain Kirk. I might even beat you. I am standing exactly one meter, four centimeters from the door. Can you judge distance that accurately? I can even tell you how fast your heart is beating ["Is There in Truth No Beauty"].

While her sensor net allows Dr. Jones to experience her environment, the net itself appears to be part of her garment, allowing Jones to pass as sighted. The net does not call attention to itself as a prosthetic but rather appears as a fashion statement from the future. Building upon Allen's comments above, I would argue that Dr. Jones's sensor net "cures and normalizes" her, and normalizes her so well that Captain Kirk assumes that Jones is yet one more potential female conquest. Since Jones does not immediately fall for Kirk's attempts at flirtation, Kirk assumes she is playing hard to get, making Dr. Jones all that more attractive. Kirk's male pride becomes bruised throughout the episode with each apparent rejection, suggesting that he does not have the autonomy to pursue Jones. The 23rd-century starship still operates under the expectations of its 1960s audience, so as a woman, Jones is applauded by the senior staff for her beauty and not her doctorate; yet when it is revealed she is a blind woman, the senior staff act paternalistic, sentimentalizing her and discounting her abilities. Dr. McCoy is suspicious of Jones early in the episode, when, after a dinner in her honor, McCoy admits to Kirk that there is something "vulnerable" and "disturbing" about her. This comment comes after Jones diplomatically negotiates her way past the attentions of all the main original series characters: Kirk gives her a rose, Spock wears a Vulcan medal to honor her time on Vulcan, Dr. McCoy kisses her hand as she leaves, but not before the men perform several awkward toasts commemorating her beauty. After Dr. Jones leaves the dining room—and after rebuffing attempts to be escorted by one of the male senior staff back to her quarters—Dr. McCoy tells Kirk that there is something "vulnerable" and "unsettling" about Dr. Jones, foreshadowing the episode's big reveal: Dr. Jones can pass as a sighted person. Ilana Lehmann points out that Kirk learns of Dr. Jones's blindness only after Dr. McCoy outs her (2). McCoy exclaims, "I realize that you can do almost anything a sighted person can do, by you can't pilot a starship" ("Is There in Truth No Beauty").

Blindness might explain why Dr. Jones is indifferent to the 23rd century's advanced flirting techniques. Before McCoy outs Dr. Jones, Kirk continues with his flower and roses pursuit, bringing Jones to the ship's botanical area, where he lectures her about loneliness and love, and how Jones will miss out on finding a connection with someone of her own species, someone who looks like her, if she continues to work with the Medusians. Kirk even becomes aggressive with Jones, tossing her around when she volunteers to mind-meld with Kollos so that the *Enterprise* can be navigated out of uncharted space, as Kirk apparently would do with any sighted woman on his ship to whom he was attracted. But once Jones's status as a blind woman is revealed, the pieces seem to fall in place for Kirk. Or, to use Katherine Allen's phrasing "Take the technology away and the disabled body's supposed lack remains" (10). As a strong and independent woman who is not impressed by the male crew, Dr. Jones becomes a problem that must be solved: she appears immune to the captain's advances and her disability explains (at least to Kirk) why she is uninterested in Kirk's company. When Dr. McCoy outs Dr. Jones as blind, Kirk comments, "Yes, of course. It is the only reasonable explanation. You can't see and Kollos can't hurt you" ("Is There in Truth No Beauty"). But with this revelation, Dr. Jones is also immediately sentimentalized. Spock asks her, "I fail to understand why you apparently try to conceal you blindness, Dr. Jones," prompting Kirk to step in and answer for her, "I think I understand," the captain comments, pre-empting Dr. Jones's response, "You [referring to Dr. Jones] said it. Pity is the worst of all" ("Is there in Truth"). When Dr. Jones does respond, she explains that she hides her disability because of how she is treated differently by society as a blind woman, even though her sensor net gives her superior abilities. "Pity is the worst of all" because it marginalizes her abilities as a professional as well as a person.

The crises of the episode comes when the *Enterprise* is thrown into uncharted space, and only Kollos the Medusian ambassador, whose abilities in navigation far outweighs the abilities of star fleet officers and computers, can safely navigate the ship back. Although Dr. Jones has experience communicating telepathically with Kollos, Spock mind-melds with the ambassador and serves as the Medusian's proxy. Spock is little more than an automaton responding to Kollos's commands, but more trust is placed in Spock because he is an able-bodied male. And why wouldn't Jones's sensor net allow her to pilot the *Enterprise*, with or without a mental link to Kollos? The problem with Dr. Jones flying the ship is not necessarily that she is blind, but that she was not honest with the fully sighted crew. If Jones prefers to hide her disability, and therefore not provide herself as an example of a disabled individual who can then inspire the crew, then how can she be trusted with an entire starship? It is not made clear in the episode if Kollos has use of Spock's eyes when the ambassador has control of Spock's body, but it must have calmed Dr. McCoy to know that an untrustworthy blind person would not be flying a starship.

The Next Generation: Geordi as Supercrip

We might wonder how Dr. McCoy would have reacted to Geordi La Forge at the helm of the *Enterprise D*, for as Gene Roddenberry himself comments, "Yes, the *Enterprise* is being driven by a blind man." (*TNG Writer's Guide* 16). And yet, La Forge is not just any blind man: his prosthetic VISOR[5] enables him to function above and beyond human capabilities. Roddenberry describes the character as follows:

> An away mission regular who is racially black and birth-defect blind—although with prosthetic super-high tech artificial "eyes" which can detect electromagnetic waves from all the way from raw heat to high frequency ultra-violet, making other crewpersons seem "blind" by comparison.... Because of his "eyes," Geordi can also perform some of the functions of a tricorder [7].

La Forge's VISOR does more than cure his blindness: it makes him a walking tricorder ideal for away missions, and yet we often see Geordi *use* an actual tricorder when assigned on away missions, so we may well assume his VISOR is supplemental. Roddenberry's description casts La Forge as both a cyborg and a supercrip. On the one hand, La Forge can accomplish tasks with his VISOR that unassisted crewmen can only marvel at—Giordi can see the heat signatures of hidden aliens, he can perform spectra analysis and comment on the chemical composition of substances, he can report on situations at a distance by focusing or zooming in on the action. As Roddenberry comments, other crew members are "blind by comparison" (7). But the VISOR raises a number of questions: why is it tuned to frequencies outside the organic capabilities of a human eye? Is the human range of vision so refined that even 24th century technology cannot replicate it? And why does the VISOR look like a hair band worn like a pair of glasses? Could a prosthetic not be fashioned that looks more like actual glasses? The answer may be that if La Forge looked too normal, the audience (and other characters) would not be able to identify him as disabled, and as such, the audience would not be amazed at

Geordi's visual abilities. The VISOR becomes a sci-fi short hand for blindness: Geordi is always marked as different. Beginning with the film *Star Trek: First Contact*, we see Geordi fitted with artificial eyes, eyes that sit in the character's own eye sockets. In one scene, Geordi is part of a team looking for Zefram Cochrane, the inventor of the warp drive who has gone missing after hearing that his experiment will change the future. The audience experiences Geordi's frame of reference as he zooms in on Cochrane's heat signature from a distance, easily locating the scientist and saving valuable time. However, even though he is fitted with ocular implants for the films, Geordi La Forge is not allowed to pass as fully normate. A close-up of his new eyes show the audience that the pupils have rotating elements that appear to be more like focusing lenses. And, for a character whose racial background is intended to be "racially black" (Rodennberry 7) his irises are a brilliant techno-blue. While blue eyes are not unheard of for individuals of African descent, this particular shade of techno-blue sets Geordi apart as an extraordinary individual, reinforcing his identity as disabled.

From the onset of the character's creation, Geordi La Forge was set up to be a supercrip who fully buys into his role as a disabled example. Roddenberry initially described Geordi as an educator, working with the "starship school for children," and he anticipates that in this role, Giordi will encounter students who "feel jealousy at his having vision abilities so marvelously beyond their own." (31) As previously mentioned, one of the conditions Rosemarie Garland-Thomson sets in her description of the supercrip is that the spectator cannot imagine performing the same extraordinary tasks with his or her own body. In other words, the '"normal" body is confronted with a limit and ironically is found to be lacking ("Politics of Staring" 60–63). Jealousy, of course, would naturally follow. Geordi would have to be called upon to diffuse the situation, make the "injured" fully bodied parties feel better about themselves while reasserting his own difference. From the first episode of season one, the audience is told that the VISOR causes Geordi pain, so his abilities came with a trade-off ("Encounter at Far Point"). Despite causing him pain, Geordi is not ready to give up his VISOR for an alternate form of vision. The VISOR grants La Forge abilities and even perhaps an autonomy not accessible to his fellow officers. While his android friend Lt. Commander Data seeks to understand and become more human, Geordi La Forge chooses being a supercrip over being normal. In the *TNG* writer's guide, it was already planned that Geordi would visit a planet where he would receive "equivalent of 'human eyes,'—and their limitations lead to the major disappointment of his young life" (Roddenberry 31). Instead of this scenario playing out in an episode, La Forge regains the use of his eyes in one of the films—in *Star Trek: Insurrection* the planet has regenerative powers and La Forge becomes normalized, yet once beyond the influence of the planet, Geordi again becomes blind. La Forge is not offered a cure but has a cure thrust upon him by circumstance—the cure does not come as a result of a choice.

Accommodation Comes to DS9

While Geordi La Forge has a cure thrust upon him in the film only to have it taken away, Melora Pazlar consciously chooses to forgo a cure offered by *DS9*'s Dr. Bashir. On her home world, Melora is a fully bodied and accomplished individual, but because Elaysians evolved in a lower gravity than most other sentient species, Pazlar experiences standard Federation gravity as a crushing weight, necessitating an exoskeleton and mobility chair to get around. Rather than being treated with pity (as Dr. Jones), Melora is treated as a novelty: Dr. Bashir especially, wants to see Melora Pazlar perform in her native low-g environment. Pazlar's quarters have been refurbished so that she can reduce the power of the gravity plating and experience a more normal environment, and Bashir hopes to be invited in to see some zero-g gymnastics after he has escorted her to her accommodations. Pazlar quite literally shuts him out, and shuts down Bashir's flirtation. Bashir later confronts Pazlar, insisting that her attitude needs to change if she is going to be a successful member of the station's crew. Mansplaining the 24th century, Bashir comments: "here in space, we need to rely upon each other" ("Melora"). Pazlar's exoskeleton and mobile chair provide a partial autonomy so that she can contribute and interact with other Star Fleet personnel. And yet, Bashir wants to make her over so that Pazlar is autonomous in a Star Fleet way. Bashir confronts what Pazlar calls "the Melora Problem" (rather than calling it, the Elaysian problem), pointing out that even though 24th century humanoids claim acceptance and diversity, she is still treated as a delicate novelty rather than as an officer in her own right. Pazlar is understandably defensive, having been cast as "a problem" that needs to be fixed or solved. Federation norms suggest that she must be the disabled example for other members of the Federation, but Pazlar has no reason to think of herself as disabled since she is normal according to her own cultural and species-specific guidelines. And yet, her mantra becomes "I will adapt,"[6] seeking the autonomy and independence championed in Star Fleet. Much to Bashir's dismay, adapting does not necessarily mean becoming the poster child for Elaysian difference. Pazlar wants to do everything herself to prove that she is just as capable as any other member of the Federation. Bashir attempts to cure what he sees as Pazlar's antisocial behaviour, her anger at being treated differently than other crewmembers, by suggesting that "here in space" each person acts as a kind of prosthesis for one another.

Instead of a "Melora Problem," I would argue that the episode highlights a prosthesis problem—accommodation is a process by which both the disabled and able-bodied are required to adapt in order for true cooperation to happen. Although she is a fully functioning individual, Melora Pazlar's exoskeleton sets her apart and requires that she continually prove herself as equal. The issue Pazlar raises is that while prosthesis and accommodations are seen as a cure, the exoskeleton and access ramps are only partial solutions. The *DS9* staff and crew may feel that they have made the appropriate structural changes to the space station to accommodate Pazlar: the audience hears that Chief O'Brien and his staff have installed ramps over raised door thresholds and adapted Pazlar's quarters. However, parts of the station, including Commander Sisko's office, are still inaccessible to Pazlar, suggesting that since Pazlar is not physically able to attend meetings in the command center, she works for the command staff rather than working with them. But what if the crew were to meet Pazlar half-way? What if the station's gravity was reduced to make it easier for Pazlar to navigate the shared environment? Or, if Chief O'Brien created a device that reduced gravity in Pazlar's immediate vicinity as she moved through the station? Such a trade-off would recognize differences between Melora and the other crewmembers, and require that the crew seek out and explore living in a changing environment. To meet Pazlar half way in this manner would suggest that Federation normal is not a universally normalized experience. Bashir sees Pazlar as a patient, and as a woman he can win over with his medical prowess. And a romance does develop between the two as Bashir attempts to adapt Melora's body so that it can function in full Federation gravity without the assistance of her exoskeleton. Instead of offering objects or prostheses to supplement her body, Bashir offers to remake her biology—cortical stimulators and futuristic medical sounding explanations are invoked to cure what is essentially a healthy woman. Bashir applies the Federation standard of autonomy to Pazlar and finds her lacking, assuming that Federation standard is a universal standard, and therefore, the correct and proper standard that all healthy members of the Federation must follow. What Dr. Bashir offers is a fully bodied Federation ideal, and yet Pazlar turns him down since completing the doctor's procedure would mean that she might not be able to return to her home world, or, fully feel herself to be Elaysian. While Melora Pazlar appears as a plot line to help develop and advance the Bashir character on *DS9*, the *Star Trek* fanbase has embraced the character, casting her in several non-canon book series, including the series *Star Trek: Titan*.[7]

Star Trek: Titan: *Enforcing Autonomy*

Accommodation and diversity are the driving forces behind the *Star Trek: Titan* series.[8] Even though the *Titan* is of a new design, the crew retrofits individual crew quarters to meet the needs of its diverse members—the ship is designed to accommodate Federation normate officers, not non-humanoids. When Pazlar meets Captain Riker about the position of stellar cartographer, Riker addresses her accommodations. "We've got a pretty radical structural idea for your quarters" explains Riker, commenting that Pazlar is one of "several members of the crew who have special environmental requirements" (*Taking Wing* 30). Pazlar's quarters are vertically oriented, "the only vertically oriented crew quarters every built into a Federation starship" Pazlar reflects, and yet she also ponders, "that 'built' was probably the wrong term; Ledrah [chief engineer] and her staff had actually retrofitted a narrow space spanning three decks in order to fashion living quarters suitable for an Elaysian" (33). What Riker describes as radical, Pazlar describes as a coincidence of ship design: there just happened to be a narrow space that could be accommodated for her lower gravity requirements. Like on *DS9*, accommodation is something of a trade-off. Pazlar gets temporary relief from full Federation gravity, but at all other times, she is expected to adapt. Additionally, Pazlar's cabin has a sort of air lock, or gravity lock, that acclimates visitors from Federation standard gravity to Elaysian standard, ensuring the other crew members are not made uncomfortable by an abrupt shift in gravity. As the head of *Titan*'s stellar cartography section, Pazlar does have a degree of independence and is allowed to celebrate her uniqueness, but when that independence is deemed inappropriate, Federation officials act to bring Pazlar back into step. Pazlar often reduces the gravity levels in the stellar cartography section to better suit her needs. Floating among the holographic projections, Pazlar experiences space as a direct experience, giving her greater insight into her work as a cartographer.

> She [Pazlar] routinely left the gravity off completely, the better to soar among the simulated stars. In the holographic realm, the walls and the ship could be forgotten, and Melora could drift unencumbered through the heavens, dancing gavottes with planets, bathing in nebular mist, cradling newborn T Tauri stars in her hands, communing with the eloquent silence of space [*Orion's Hounds*, loc 295 of 5313].

Pazlar's experience as an Elaysian enables her to explore and chart the universe in a visceral and direct manner; abstract ideas become more real and tactile. Stellar cartography allows Pazlar a professional and personal space; however, this space is still regulated by Star Fleet codes of conduct. As described in the first novel of the series, *Taking Wing*, "Because of its variable-gravity capabilities, the delicate Elaysian had come to regard the lab, with its unique, low-g window on the universe, almost as her own private domain" (82). The key words here are almost and delicate. Stellar cartography is very much a public space, and even though Pazlar is section head, she must be protected from that same space for her own good—or at least that is the reasoning of the counselling staff on board *Titan*. As the book series progresses, the stellar cartography section becomes more like a holodeck, and much like the EMH Doctor from *Star Trek: Voyager*, Pazlar can use the technology to project a holo-image of herself throughout *Titan*. Projecting an image of herself allows Pazlar to interact with the crew and attend staff meetings without leaving Elaysian levels of gravity, yet the counselling staff become concerned, suggesting that Pazlar's virtual isolation is a symptom of a social disability.

As a "delicate Elaysian," Pazlar is seen as someone who must be protected from herself; the visual presence of her exoskeleton is a constant reminder of her delicate nature, reminding the full-g characters of their own full-g status. Living in reduced gravity becomes diagnosed as an obsessive disorder, rather than everyday existence for the Elaysian. In using the holo-projection system to broadcast a version of herself to interact with the crew, Pazlar can present an image of herself without her exoskeleton. She appears to be fully abled, and excepting that she is using a hologram image of herself, she could pass as normate. In many ways, what Pazlar performs here is similar to the service the Talosians provide *TOS* Captain Pike—individuals interacting with Pazlar, and Pike, are unaware of those characters' disabilities. Again, medical personnel insist that a Federation standard is the norm: socialization must take place face-to-face and in a specific gravity, with all tokens of disability on display. Anything less is a threat to the Federation definition of autonomy.

The Borg: Disease or Disability?

One of the greatest threats to Federation autonomy is the Borg, a cybernetic collective introduced in season two of *Star Trek: TNG* ("Q Who?"). The Borg are an ideal villain for the *Star Trek* universe, since assimilation into the collective removes all autonomy and individuality from the assimilated individual. Assimilated individuals, or drones, have no free will and many have body parts replaced with prosthetic devices. In a sense, the assimilant is made over using a new set of standards for what is normate: a contributing piece to a larger whole. In terms of disability, the Borg expose a double standard within the *Star Trek* universe—there is a sliding scale of autonomy, and those Federation individuals who are regarded as more autonomous are more easily saved and rehabilitated than those who are more likely to follow orders without questions. Star ship captains are the most autonomous of all: Jean-Luc Picard may be transformed into Locutus of Borg ("The Best of Both Worlds"), but his Borg implants turn out to be cosmetic—Picard does not lose any limbs in the process and can be returned to a fully abled body by episode's end. Other assimilated characters are shot and killed rather than be given the chance for rehabilitation[9] (*Star Trek: First Contact*). For Jean-Luc Picard, his Borg time appears to be more like an infection or an affliction easily cured; for a character like Seven of Nine, being Borg is a lifetime condition that must be managed and constantly monitored. Picard's autonomy as captain seems to have inoculated him, downgrading assimilation to a disease, while Seven of Nine's lived experience makes assimilation a disability.

Autonomy as an underlying core value of the Federation may be best seen in the interactions between *Star Trek: Voyager*'s Captain Kathryn Janeway and mid-series addition Seven of Nine. A drone who was assimilated at the age of six, Seven of Nine becomes Janeway's personal project—Janeway is determined to return Seven of Nine to autonomy, a task far more difficult than merely removing Borg technology. Where Jean-Luc can be cured and rehabilitated, Seven of Nine must be socially reconditioned to fit Federation norms; in other words, Seven of Nine is socially disabled.

Physically, Seven of Nine reads as a supercrip. Her enhanced strength, mental agility, and the collective knowledge of countless assimilated species save the day throughout the remainder of *Voyager*'s series run. Excepting for a hand brace and some techno-looking accessories adhered to the actor's face, Seven of Nine appears to inhabit a fully abled body. The mystery of Seven of Nine is her unseen technology; her struggle is not immediately apparent as visible prosthesis, but as an internal reckoning with her place in society. Ilana Lehmann diagnoses Seven of Nine as exhibiting behaviours associated with autism, as Lehmann writes:

> Initially, Seven's difficulty in fitting in with the rest of the *Voyager* crew is mutual because the crew isn't sure they want her on board. Seven did, after all, try to betray them to the Borg. Much like children with autism, Seven's efforts to fit in with the crew aren't consistent; at times she appears not to value the outcome [266].

That she should not value the outcome, to become an individual, is consistent with the character's storyline. Assimilated as a child, Seven of Nine knows no other social existence except that of being a member of a collective—she has never had to set personal goals and then achieve them. Achieving autonomy is not a core value of the society in which she was raised, so like Melora Pazlar, Seven of Nine does not consider herself disabled. But since Seven of Nine has no personal desire to become autonomous, she falls outside of Federation standards and can be diagnosed as disabled. Once Seven of Nine is diagnosed as disabled, she becomes a ward of the state, or, a ward of Captain Janeway. She is not allowed to make her own decisions, "You lost the capacity to make a rational choice the moment you were assimilated," Janeway tells Seven of Nine, "They [the Borg] took that away from you, and until I'm convinced you've gotten it back I'm making the choice for you" ("The Gift").

Because Seven of Nine is biologically human, *Star Trek* mandates that she follow Federation norms, and others take steps to act in her best interest. As a character without choice, Seven of Nine stands out among the *Voyager* crew: since she is not a member of the Federation, she is not allowed to wear a Star Fleet uniform. Instead, the character wears a form fitting jumpsuit, highlighting her "humanity" and supermodel figure. If we follow Lehmann's diagnosis of autism, then we could argue that Seven of Nine's jumpsuit provides full body pressure and reassurance, a treatment often prescribed to autistic individuals (Grandin). This full body pressure may also substitute for the constant presence of the collective. However, I would suggest that Seven of Nine's outfit is a subtle (or not so subtle) form of resistance—she presents herself to the crew as hyper-feminine and as an ultimate example of health. Seven of Nine physically challenges the *Voyager* crew as to what it means to be disabled in ways that Melora Pazlar and Dr. Jones could not, and challenges the *Star Trek* audience to reconsider what it means to be human. Seven of Nine embodies the unsettling and vulnerable qualities that so disturbed Dr. McCoy when he had to interact with Dr. Jones; but paradoxically, it is not her techno-bits or prosthetics that are the vulnerable and unsettling elements of her person. Seven of Nine's wardrobe choice exudes individuality; the crew must make a conscious effort to treat her as one of their own, a potential equal, while ignoring her potentially inappropriate workplace attire. Instead of having a prosthetic limb or VISOR that sets her apart and marks her as disabled, Seven of Nine's entire body as highlighted by her bodysuit acts as prosthesis. As Mia Consalvo comments, "As a drone, Seven of Nine was not constructed as a gendered creature, and so was not required to 'perform' a gender or engage in gendered activity" (185). Seven of Nine's behavior is incongruous with her appearance. For this study, I would argue that the body suit enacts a prosthetic relationship on *Voyager*; it serves as a constant reminder that Seven of Nine is being made over into a human, and even though she may appear to by hyper-feminine, the woman herself is not responsible for, or aware of, that social performance. While a body suit would seem to be an ideal garment on a star ship—there are no flaps or pockets to catch or snag when moving around the ship or crawling through Jeffries tubes—most of the female crew wear standard uniforms and there is very little room for self expression. "In addition to highlighting fears about loss of individuality," writes Consalvo, "the way the Borg assimilate a person also speaks to another great fear, the loss of bodily integrity" (195). Seven of Nine's suit accentuates her gender, but more importantly the garment reveals that Seven of Nine inhabits a complete and integral body. Because she is socially unaware of how her outfit deploys both gender and an apparent fully abled body, the other members of the *Voyager* crew must negotiate and resituate themselves in accordance to this new dynamic.[10]

A Question of Aspiration

I want to return to Roddenberry's comment that the characters in *Star Trek* are "the kind of people we aspire to be ourselves" (9). As a character introduced mid-series, Seven of Nine may have been added as a ratings boost, but her struggle with autonomy may reflect concerns within the viewing audience. Mia Consalvo comments, "Just as the Borg present a complete loss of individuality they also point out a limitation in contemporary society, where individuality is not as individual or particular as American beliefs would suggest" (194). While a neo-liberal mindset suggests that each person is a unique individual, actual lived experience demonstrates that individuals are asked to conform and limit their autonomy in numerous ways, and on a daily basis. For an American audience, ideas of self-reliance give way to realities of social interdependency. As Garland-Thomson illustrates, disability as an affront to the American ideals of self-governance and self-reliance, commenting:

> The disabled body stands for the self gone out of control, individualism run rampant: it mocks the notion of the body as compliant instrument of the limitless will and appears in the cultural imagination as ungovernable, recalcitrant, flaunting its difference as if to refute the fantasy of sameness implicit in the notion of equality [*Extraordinary Bodies* 43].

The disabled body then is something that must be controlled, since it exists outside parameters of what passes as normal. Instead of disabled individuals fighting to prove their humanity and individual uniqueness, the Borg homogenize experience, suggesting that any individual can be exchanged for any other. Uniqueness is overrated when individuals are innately fungible. But in a moment of dramatic irony, Seven of Nine exposes the sameness and ubiquity among the *Voyager* crew. Seven of Nine's body is not governed by her will; she is a recalcitrant individual not responsible for her actions. If the audience is to take Seven of Nine as a model for aspiration, then would it not suggest that the character encourages the viewer to gain control of the self, to not stand out, and to grapple with the realities of his/her own uniqueness?

Star Trek does something incredibly valuable when it comes to disability. The films and series may highlight the individual conditions and struggles of disabled individuals, but more importantly, the *Star Trek* universe shows individuals attempt to create an identity that is true to his/her unique characteristics in the face of an existential realization—uniqueness is overrated even though it is held up as an essential quality. We are all unique: we are all disabled. As Andy Clark explains in his book *Natural-Born Cyborgs*, we assume that the future will celebrate our unique qualities, but in reality, we are confronted with "an ancient western prejudice—the tendency to think of the mind as so deeply special as to be distinct from the rest of the natural order" (26). Clark argues that as we become more connected and dependent on technology, and as social media and the internet expose us to more of the world, we begin to fear that there is not, "something absolutely special about the cognitive machinery that happens to be housed within the primitive bioinsulation (nature's own duct-tape!) of skin and skull" (26). *Star Trek* suggests that there is nothing deeply special about any one of us and rather, we are all vulnerable and disturbing. While disability creates an instant identity for a character appearing on the television or movie screen, *Star Trek*'s use of disabled characters encourages the audience to question the very idea of an individual essence. For a show that celebrates diversity, *Star Trek* instead suggests that there is no real diversity even in a utopian future.

Notes

1. Nemek's word choice here illustrates an underlying bias regarding disability: Rather than being an endearing and enthusiastic fan, La Forge is seen as "endearing himself" to Roddenberry and other fans, suggesting an agenda on La Forge's part, or, that La Forge must push for acceptance.

2. Coined by Rosemarie Garland-Thomson, the term represents individuals who are not members of a minority group representing a culturally idealized everyman.

3. Excepting the Next Generation's Ferengi, who are often portrayed as cultural throwbacks to an age when capitalism mattered, but even individual Ferengi (*DS9*) are given storylines where they overcome greed to embrace a Federation humanity.

4. Pike was also captain of the *Enterprise* in the pilot episode "The Cage," scenes of which became material for the flashbacks of "The Menagerie."

5. According to the *Star Trek Encyclopedia*, VISOR is an acronym (or perhaps a backronym) for "Visual Instrument and Sensory Organ Replacement" (546). The acronym does not appear in Roddenberry's Writers Guide for *TNG* so most likely was created after the fact once the character became more fully developed.

6. A phrase we often hear repeated by *Voyager* cast member Seven of Nine.

7. While this book series might be considered non-canonical, the inclusion of Troi and Riker's wedding, and the mention of the star ship *Titan* in the film aligns this book series with the "official" timeline—the inclusion of Melora Pazlar in this series as a member of the senior staff and as a series regular illustrates the character's attraction with the fan base.

8. At the start of the *Star Trek: Nemesis* film, we learn that not only have Dianna Troi and William Riker married, but Riker is to captain the starship *Titan*, a ship made up of the most diverse crew ever commissioned in fleet history. The *Titan* crew is made up of a variety of sentient species with differing abilities and bodies. Pazlar is recruited as the head of stellar cartography; the con officer is an amphibian who must wear a full-body water-breathing suit; the ship's doctor and chief of medicine looks like a velociraptor, but with longer arms. Many of the crew members are not humanoid, but have features resembling birds, insects, and one even is described as resembling a potted plant.

9. This issue is a major point of character development in the *Star Trek: Titan* book series. It is revealed that *Titan*'s head of security was the life-partner of Sean Hawk, the con officer turned Borg in the course of the film *Star Trek: First Contact*. In the film, Lt. Worf shoots Hawk rather than try to rehabilitate him: Keru (*Titan*'s security chief) tries to rationalize why Hawk would be killed while it is common knowledge that Picard and Seven of Nine were de-assimilated. "Both Picard and the woman *Voyager*'s crew had repatriated had been nanoprobe-infected for far longer than Sean had" (*Taking Wing* 150).

10. Ironically, the ex–Borg woman is one of the few individuals on *Voyager* to express an individual style, which perhaps subtly reminds the crew that Seven of Nine is not the only

crewmember for whom Captain Janeway makes decisions. In the opening episodes of the series, Janeway makes the decision that strands *Voyager* in the Delta quadrant. During the first few seasons, individual crewmembers confront their own sense of autonomy in the face of that decision, either rebelling against the captain and her mission, or, reconciling themselves to going along for the ride.

Works Cited

Allen, Kathryn. *Disability in Science Fiction: Representations of Technology as Cure.* Palgrave, 2013.

Baird, Stuart. *Star Trek: Nemesis.* Paramount, 2002.

Bennet, Christopher. *Star Trek Titan: Orion's Hounds.* Pocket Books, 2006.

Clark, Andy. *Natural Born Cyborgs: Minds, Technologies, and the Future of Human Intelligence.* Oxford University Press, 2003.

Consalvo, Mia. "Borg Babes, Drones, and the Collective: Reading Gender and the Body in *Star Trek*." *Women's Studies in Communication*, Vol. 27, No. 2, 2004, pp. 177–203.

Davis, Lennard J. *The End of Normal: Identity in a Biocultural Era.* University of Michigan Press, 2013.

"Encounter at Farpoint." *Star Trek: The Next Generation,* Season 1, episode 1, 28 Sept. 1987.

Frakes, Jonathan. *Star Trek: First Contact.* Paramount, 1996.

_____. *Star Trek: Insurrection.* Paramount, 1998.

Garland-Thomson, Rosemaire. *Extraordinary Bodies: Figuring Physical Disability in American Culture and Literature.* Columbia University Press, 1997.

_____. "The Politics of Staring: Visual Rhetorics of Disability in Popular Photography." *Disability Studies: Enabling the Humanities.* Edited by Sharon L. Snyder, Brenda Jo Brueggemann, and Rosemarie Garland-Thomson. Modern Language Association of America, 2002, pp. 56–75.

"The Gift." *Star Trek: Voyager*, Season 4, episode 2, UPN, 10 Sept. 1997.

Grandin, Temple. "Calming Effects of Deep Touch Pressure in Patients with Autistic Disorder, College Students, and Animals." *Journal of Child and Adolescent Psychopharmacology*, Vol. 2, No. 1, 1992.

"Is There in Truth No Beauty?" *Star Trek,* Season 3, episode 5, NBC, 18 Oct. 1968.

Lehmann, Ilana. *All You Need to Know About Disability Is on* Star Trek. Mind Meld Media, 2014.

Martin, Michael A., and Andy Mangels. *Star Trek Titan: Taking Wing.* Pocket Books, 2005.

McReynolds, Leigha. "Animal and Alien Bodies as Prosthesis: Reframing Disability in *Avatar* and *How to Train Your Dragon*." Ed. Kathryn Allen, *Disability in Science Fiction: Representations of Technology as Cure.* Palgrave, 2013.

"Melora." *Star Trek: Deep Space Nine,* Season 2, episode 6, 31 Oct. 1993.

"The Menagerie, Part I." *Star Trek,* Season 1, episode 11, NBC, 17 Nov. 1966.

"The Menagerie, Part II." *Star Trek,* Season 1, episode 12, NBC, 24 Nov. 1966.

Mitchell, David T., and Sharon L. Snyder. *Narrative Prosthesis: Disability and the Dependency of Discourse.* University of Michigan Press, 2000.

Okuda, Mike, and Denis Okuda. *The Star Trek Encyclopedia.* Second edition. Pocket Books. 1997.

"QWho." *Star Trek: The Next Generation,* Season 2, episode 16, 8 May 1989.

Roddenberry, Gene. *Star Trek Writers/Director's Guide.* Third Revision, Paramount/Norway Productions, 1967.

_____. *Star Trek: The Next Generation Writer/Director's Guide.* Paramount Pictures, 1992.

Mothering the Universe on *Star Trek*

ERICKA HOAGLAND

As the opening sequence of the second installment of the *Star Trek* franchise, the critically praised *Star Trek: The Next Generation*, builds to its dramatic crescendo, the iconic opening speech, now delivered by Captain Jean-Luc Picard, comes to a pointed close: "To boldly go where no one has gone before." Debuting on September 28, 1987, *The Next Generation* (hereafter *TNG*) was equally indebted to its groundbreaking predecessor and to the cultural landscape of 1980s America for shaping its journeys into the "final frontier." This involved not only eschewing the cowboy ethos of Captain James T. Kirk in favor of the "cosmopolitan diplomacy" of Picard (Geraghty 147), but also the androcentric language of that ethos by replacing the "man" with "one" in the final sentence of the USS *Enterprise*'s mission statement.[1] As it turns out, the inclusive potential signified by "one" is misleading, as it cannot fully excise the mission statement from its heteronormative roots, just as the exciting promise of going places yet undiscovered is rarely fulfilled. This is especially the case in the focus of this study: the narratives regarding femininity, and by extension, motherhood, in *Star Trek* are noteworthy for their conventionality, rather than their liberality, and this tension, between maintaining an ideological status quo and challenging or subverting it, is a common feature of science fiction in general. Working out of Helen Merrick's observation that gender generates and represents "problematic spaces [that] are crucial to sf imaginings" (241), and that one such problematic space is that occupied by mothers, this paper examines the "absent presence" of mothers in the *Star Trek* universe. The presentation of mothers/motherhood in the franchise, then, reflects its "ambivalence and equivocation over women's place" that Lynne Joyrich discusses in her study of femininity on *TNG* (64).

This ambivalence and equivocation has by no means been resolved since

TNG; in fact, its attempts to work against those positions in later series and films has only further entrenched the franchise within them, or worse, disguised the franchise's New Traditionalism as postfeminism. As such, this study also works out of Lee E. Heller's observation that "the sincere acknowledgement of gender equality is riddled with conservative contradictions" (242). Though Heller argues this point in relation to *TNG*, it can be sustained beyond that show; more specifically, this study explores the articulations of this tension as it manifests in *TNG*, *VOY*, and in the most successful pre–Abrams *Star Trek* film, *First Contact*. Through an examination of actual and symbolic mothers, including Beverly Crusher, Deanna and Lwaxana Troi, Kathryn Janeway, B'Elanna Torres, and the most dangerous "mother" on *Star Trek*, the Borg Queen, this study intends to demonstrate that the utopic promises extended by the Federation are not, ultimately, extended to mothers. Indeed, the absence of mothers (and wives, for that matter) in the original *Star Trek* series suggests that the vastness of space cannot accommodate such bodies, which are better left at home or, at least, wrapped in stereotypes about maternity. This speaks to the ways in which the *Star Trek* universe has been shaped by and responded (not always successfully) to social forces, particularly those impacting women.

Finally, this study is a continuation and expansion of previous scholarship that has acknowledged both the "progressive *and* restrictive" constructions of female characters in the franchise (Consalvo 180; my emphasis). This scholarship is rich and deep, and has done important work in thinking through the franchise's representations of and relationship to women, femininity, and feminism. Just as mothers have been an "absent presence" in the franchise, however, so, too, has the scholarship often consigned questions about maternity, motherhood, and the mother to secondary analyses or passing observations.[2] As Andrea L. Press observes, "we live in a paradoxical cultural moment characterized by only a partial incorporation of feminist gains" (109). The same can be said of *Star Trek*: in reaching for the stars, it has left some behind. The question is, then, was this by necessity or design?

Postfeminism and the Code of Motherhood

Demi Moore's naked pregnant body on the cover of the August 1991 issue of *Vanity Fair*, was, in the words of George Lois, "an instant culture buster"; for many, including *Vanity Fair*'s then-editor Tina Brown, the image was a "startlingly dramatic symbol of female empowerment" ("Flashback"). The image of Moore photographed by Annie Liebowitz would prove to be iconic in more ways than one: from formal images of pregnant celebrities like those of Moore that would increasingly grace the covers of magazines, to informal selfies of "baby bumps" posted on social media, the pregnant body has been demystified and commodified at the same time, signaling the limits of Lois' "culture buster" argument. Anxiety over pregnant, and lactating, bodies persists, as the uproar over another magazine cover, this one from the May 10, 2012, *Time* issue that shows a young mother breastfeeding her three-year old son, demonstrates. Criticism of this cover was roughly split between those who found the image distasteful, and those who felt *Time* was monopolizing and "whipping up the mommy wars" through the cover's title, "Are You Mom Enough" ("Jamie Lynne Grumet").

Perhaps letting the image of Moore cradling her pregnant belly speak for itself, the actual article in that *Vanity Fair* issue spends just a few paragraphs on Moore's pregnancy and her thoughts on motherhood, focusing instead on her relationship with then-husband Bruce Willis, her past romances, and her status in Hollywood. Shifting its focus away from Moore as mother was paradoxical (perhaps even hypocritical), given both the commodification of her pregnant body on the magazine cover as well as the image's implied progressive gender politics, but it was not surprising. Rather, it reflected American culture's ongoing and increasingly visible struggle to reconcile its two selves: the one that celebrated "traditional values" (Moore as expectant mother), and the other that aspired to a more emancipated and humanist ideal (Moore's unabashed and empowered nakedness). By comparison, the *Time* magazine cover relies on a challenge—its aggressive title—that reinscribes the traditional values of family and motherhood as a set of expectations meant to separate "true" mothers from mere poseurs. The racial and class implications of the cover are in turn reinforced by the image of Jamie Lynne Grumet—a trim, attractive, twenty-six-year-old white woman who runs a non-profit—staring back at the viewer, as if to reinforce the challenge posed by the title. This cover in particular reflects Mary Douglas Varvus' sharp observation about the "inordinately important role" media representations play in "constructing the definition of motherhood, both prescribing and proscribing behaviors for 'good' mothers" (48), most forcefully presented in "*Good Housekeeping*'s 'New Traditionalism' campaign of the 1980s" (49).

Indeed, the 1980s saw the emergence of two campaigns—postfeminism and New Traditionalism—that fought for the "souls" of American women. Varvus refers to postfeminism as a "de-politicizing ideology" whose dangerous logic insists that femininism is no longer necessary (49). Or as Zsófia Kulcsár points out, mainstream representations of women, like the magazine covers above, "tend to imply that feminism has only a past but not a future because in contemporary societies there is no need for it anymore." The slipperiness of "post"—implying both "after" as well as "beyond"—has played a key role in creating a false notion of the project's actual identity. More a "media friendly version of feminism," postfeminism has played a key role in the "undoing of (academic) feminism" (Kulcsár). Part of this undoing has to do with how postfeminism takes particular aim at second-wave feminism, in some instances degrading its achievements, and in others, arguing that its aims have yet to be met. As such, postfeminism has been seen as both a productive assessment of feminism as well as a backlash against it. Likewise, its neoliberal ethos is underscored in its emphasis on women's "individual choices and practices [through which they] empower (and disempower) themselves, building identities linked to individualistic and consumerist culture" (Boyd 104). Rosalind Gill's definition of postfeminism that Boyd outlines also highlights the "key paradox" embedded within the project, which is that "women's perceived empowerment often resembles stereotypical behaviors and beliefs that have been ascribed as 'appropriately' feminine" (Boyd 104). For some, however, postfeminism at its best "celebrates female transgression, independence and power," and significantly, "categorically rejects the orthodoxies and identity politics of academic feminism" (Bartlett 27). It looks beyond "oppression as a point of contact among women," and focuses instead upon "a celebration of female agency and sexuality" (27). This particular view of postfeminism highlights its liberating and even utopic potential.

That potential is what *Star Trek* aspires to, but as a product of mainstream postfeminism influenced by New Traditionalism, the post-original series installments of the franchise have made minimal inroads with respect to imagining more expansive and empowered roles for women. In the case of mothers in particular, the franchise has always been bound by certain particularities of this identity. As Lindal Buchanan observes in *Rhetorics of Motherhood*, "the code of motherhood" has proven to be exceedingly durable in American public discourse. Motherhood's "Janus-like capacity to generate compelling persuasive means while buttressing restrictive gender roles" is tied to the way in which the "Mother" inspires trust and also "discourages critical distance," thus shutting down productive analysis of the gender system (18; 7). This was the seemingly inevitable result of a steady process in the 18th and 19th centuries that firmly separated the male and female sexes, and tied female sexuality to passivity, maternity, and domesticity. By prioritizing reproduction and childbearing as the central functions of the female sex, and in turn, viewing childrearing as an important "civic function," by the Victorian era motherhood was understood to be the "pinnacle of feminine accomplishment" (17; 18).

Patrice DiQuinzio points out that "assumptions about women's mothering are [...] deeply embedded in U.S. society and culture and are [...] complexly intertwined with other fundamental beliefs and values" (qtd. in Buchanan 115). For *Star Trek*, those assumptions, which idealize the "good mother" as selfless, compassionate, and patient, are contingent on a denial of selfhood, thus "transforming a complex, multifaceted woman into a familiar, reassuring character" (Buchanan 118). Rather than viewing motherhood as a "moving plurality of potential behaviors, always undergoing supervision, revision, and contest, constructed in particularity" (Bowers qtd in Buchanan 123), motherhood in *Star Trek* consequently undergoes what Buchanan calls a "flattening effect" (118). This flattening effect manifests in two ways: one, by casting female characters in roles that are easily coded within the matrix of motherhood, and two, by generally diminishing the presence and significance of mothers through a reliance on stereotypes and outright expulsion. In turn, *Star Trek* finds itself at odds with "two kinds of maternal nurture: the instinctual and biological [and] conscious, chosen, cultural motherhood" (Bundtzen 123). This begins with the heavily ambivalent treatment of mothers and motherhood that can be seen in *Star Trek: The Next Generation*, to which this study now turns.

"What about a family?" Motherhood on Star Trek: The Next Generation

The original *Star Trek* series "is renowned for imagining an egalitarian Earth—absent of racism, sexism, and capitalism—that exists in a hostile galaxy overcrowded with uncivilized and violent alien worlds" (Bernardi 211). As Bernardi notes, the series' attempt to eke out a liberal-humanist vision—one which was highly responsive to, and influenced by, the Civil Rights movement and Cold War anxieties—was compromised by both network interference, such as rejecting Roddenberry's pitch for a female second-in-command, as well as the tendency to relegate the integrated supporting cast to "the margins of most of the stories" (217). The erasure of otherness on a series ostensibly celebrating difference is disappointing, but hardly surprising: the racial stereotypes from which the series failed to extricate itself proved to be far too entrenched and familiar. Bernardi clearly demonstrates this in his readings of the Japanese-American helmsman Sulu and the communications officer, Uhura. In the case of the latter, her black femininity is contained via comfortable tropes about the female black body that highlights and objectifies its desirable otherness, while the limits of her gender are underscored by her role on the *Enterprise* as that of an inter-galactic phone operator. Indeed, the original series was awash in what Karin Blair calls "disposable female[s]," characters, typically aliens, "fantastic, erotic, and exotic" in appearance, whose sole function (aside from providing Kirk with an extraterrestrial sexual conquest), was to aid in the resolution of the episode's dramatic problem (292). At the end of the episode, the disposable female would sacrifice her own interests, or even her life, thus fulfilling her purpose and saving Kirk from making any long-term romantic commitments.

While the disposable female archetype was still periodically used in the next television incarnation of the franchise, *Star Trek: The Next Generation*, she had been notably replaced by variations of the caregiver/mother archetype, which expanded the role of female characters in the *Star Trek* universe but also set clear and often restrictive boundaries for these characters. This would have telling consequences for both storylines and character arcs for the two most central female characters in *TNG*, chief medical officer Dr. Beverly Crusher and the *Enterprise*'s counselor, the Betazoid empath Deanna Troi. Most obviously is Troi's role as the ship's counselor, whose very profession emphasizes the "feminine" qualities of nurturing and compassion. Her empathic capabilities were frequently useful, especially in detecting deception or hostile intent, and paired well with Captain Picard's diplomatic approach to interactions with other races. Likewise, she often helped crew members with various problems, typically romantic or familial in nature, further strengthening Troi's association not just with the caregiver archetype, but with more "feminine" or "soft" storylines and conflicts. Her regular presence on the bridge is reminiscent of Lt. Uhura's limited role on the original *Enterprise* bridge: if she talks at all, it is to inform Picard of something she "senses" or "feels," in much the same way that Uhura lets Kirk know that "hailing frequencies are now open." Essentially the function of both women is to contribute to productive communication between their male superiors and the alien races with whom they dialogue. One could argue, of course, that this is a crucial function, and it is, but it is nonetheless a function that assumes a supporting role, rather than a generative or determinant one. The episodes that feature the Troi character in a central role are typically either variations on another archetype, the damsel in distress, explorations of Troi's romantic relationships, or presentations of Troi's loving but conflicted relationship with her overbearing mother, Lwaxana Troi. All three types inform the narrative of motherhood that the show weaves around Troi: despite her clear focus on her career, she is the mother-in-training. In fact, her career is preparing her for her maternal future, just as the physical presentation of this character insists upon it.

Like Deanna Troi, Beverly Crusher "combines both her professional duties and a certain toughness with the traditional 'feminine virtues' of nurturance, constancy, and maternal care" (Joyrich 66). As the *Enterprise*'s chief medical officer, she is the highest ranking female on the ship, and her medical expertise is crucial to saving the *Enterprise* crew on several occasions, including saving the assimilated Picard and the ship from the Borg in the two-part episode "The Best of Both Worlds." While female doctors are certainly not anomalous (though rather hard to find in *Star Trek*), medicine is nonetheless coded as a masculine profession, linked as it is to the larger field of science. The introduction of Crusher's character ushered in at least one prominent female science officer throughout the remainder of the franchise's television history, from Jadzia Dax in *Deep Space Nine* and B'Elanna Torres in *Voyager*, to T'Pol in *Enterprise*, who occupied the roles of science officer, subcommander, and attaché, respectively. Attaching a masculine profession to a female character made her by default more valuable, her contributions to the ship more quantifiable. As Joyrich's observation above makes clear, however, Crusher's masculine profession is interpreted through a feminine lens, which underscores what appears to be her primary maternal identification. In turn, this identification is problematized by the irregularity with which the show engages in Beverly Crusher *as mother*; despite the presence of her son Wesley on the *Enterprise*, mother and son are only sporadically shown interacting with one another, albeit with great affection. Instead, the surrogate father-son relationship with Picard is stressed, sending the clear message that a boy clearly needs a father, and only occasionally his mother. Stripped of her motherhood and yet bound by her maternal role, Crusher is also, like Deanna, portrayed as routinely seeking, but never finding, personal romantic fulfillment. Of course, this is especially problematic for a mother-in-training like Deanna, but the double bind in which Crusher is situated, and which I discuss below, is especially helpful in illustrating the series' "ambivalence and equivocation" regarding mothers.

Simply put, *Star Trek: The Next Generation* routinely struggles, and regularly fails, to accord selfhood to the mothers it presents. This is in keeping with the larger failure of Western culture to recognize mothers and mothering outside of the traditional heterosexual familial paradigm, as well as to accord women selfhood in general. In America in particular, legislation like the Equal Rights Amendment of 1972 sought to legally recognize the selfhood of the nation's women, but despite a promising start—ratification by thirty states in a year—the initiative would experience five rescinded ratifications and not meet its extended 1982 deadline. Opposition to the Equal Rights Amendment in the decade preceding the series' premiere in 1987 relied heavily on appeals to traditional gender roles, which the proposed amendment would allegedly upend. The ERA's failure was symptomatic of a growing backlash against women and the feminist project, so clearly articulated by Susan Faludi and others; the rise of social and political conservatism in Reagan-era America; the emergence of the Religious Right; and the deepening fractures between pro-choice and pro-life America. *TNG*'s inability to reconcile its utopic ideals with its conservative gender politics is intricately bound to that charged context. Likewise, it is both victim and contributor to the popularized and generalized discourse on postfeminism outlined above that argues against the continued relevance of the feminist project in a purportedly more gender equal society, despite abundant evidence to the contrary. Emerging as it did in the decade that brought us the "power dressing" woman, the woman who could "bring home the bacon, [and] fry it up in a pan," and a First Lady described as both a strident anti-feminist and a feminist icon, perhaps it is not surprising that *TNG* appears to be so confused about women in the 24th century.

The most striking manifestation of this "confusion"—which, as it turns out, is nothing of the sort—is the separation of women and their relationship to motherhood into two distinct spheres. In order to achieve selfhood, women in *TNG* are encouraged to deny their "private/personal maternal selves," that self that bears and raises children within a recognizable familial arrangement. For *TNG* that arrangement has already been established as a heterosexual one, but this study speaks here, too, of other familial arrangements that have been or are still today labeled as "perverse" within the discourse of heteronormativity, including, but not limited to, single-heterosexual and homosexual mother/father families, and families headed by lesbian, gay, or transgender couples. Thus, Beverly Crusher's primary identification in the series is as *Dr.* Beverly Crusher, and her secondary identification is as a mother to the largely and conveniently absent Wesley Crusher. In other words, her selfhood is contingent upon separating her from her identity as a mother. But *that* selfhood is paradoxically contingent upon her public performance of maternal care. Thus, the "public/professional (maternal) self" on *TNG* lays bare the lie of the "power dressing" female Federation officer so clearly invoked through the character of Beverly Crusher: she cannot "have it all," and her professional self cannot be separated from her maternal identity, despite the fact that that identity is constantly diminished or dismissed. In turn, selfhood becomes almost impossible to achieve.

Admittedly, there is one character in *TNG* who does not easily fit within the schematic just proposed: the female security chief, Tasha Yar. Unlike Deanna Troi and Beverly Crusher, Yar is more heavily associated with the masculine, militaristic identity of the Federation, an identity that the show spectacularly fails to separate itself from, despite the presence of the great diplomat, Jean-Luc Picard. Yar eschews more feminine pursuits, preferring martial arts, and her boyish haircut sharply contrasts the feminine hairstyles of Troi and Crusher. For Yar, there is no tension between the two selves described above in large part because her character was written off the show before the end of the first season at the request of the actress who portrayed her, Denise Crosby. Crosby was dissatisfied with the lack of character development for Yar, a problem that may have something to do with the uncertainty and anxiety invoked by a powerful female occupying a traditionally male occupation. More specifically, her character may have tapped into the long-simmering debate over women in the military; very rarely are women shown as part of security teams in the franchise, suggesting that the militaristic and violent necessities of space travel are best handled by men. The show's mishandling of the character and the replacement of Crosby's character with the male Klingon Worf effectively killed one of the clearest opportunities for the series to enact its egalitarian mission, and to look outside of the circumscribed maternal roles for women upon which it insisted. Nonetheless, Yar is a reminder of the destabilizing and productive potential of *truly* post-feminist figures, while her own ambivalent relationship to motherhood—influenced by her violent childhood as an orphan in a rape culture—speaks to those alienated by New Traditionalist rhetoric.

As it turns out, the most visible mother on *TNG* is not Beverly Crusher, or even Troi's colorful mother, Lwaxana, but Guinan, Ten-Forward's bartender, portrayed by Whoopi Goldberg. A civilian living and working on the *Enterprise*, Guinan is firmly positioned outside of the Federation regulations that bind Troi and Crusher, one of several factors which marks Guinan as different, not just from the other women and mothers on the *Enterprise*, but from all those who call the ship home. As Rhonda V. Wilcox points out about Guinan, she is "purposefully mysterious" (23); little about her is known, aside from her great age—she is at least 500 years old—and her race, the El-Aurians (or "Listeners"), who are known not only for their great lifespans, but for their quasi-empathic capabilities and "an awareness that superseded the normal flow of time and space ("El-Aurian"). It is Guinan, not Troi, nor for that matter, a ranking Starfleet officer, who counsels Commander Riker when he must decide how to address Picard's assimilation by the Borg. She even helps Wesley Crusher realize that his true place is on the *Enterprise*, and not with his mother on Earth when Beverly Crusher is appointed the head of Starfleet Medical Academy. In essence, she "represent[s] the incomprehensibly powerful mother figure," the "magic mother," who is defined primarily by her extraordinary virtue and wisdom (26; 27).

The prominent role that the series assigns to Guinan's symbolic mothering reflects its ambivalence towards the *actual* mothers on *TNG*, whose maternal identities are either deemphasized (Beverly Crusher), parodied (Lwaxana Troi), or as the season two Deanna Troi episode "The Child" demonstrates, erased altogether. All of this is in keeping with the defensive strategies enacted by a patriarchy anxious to maintain its power. In the case of Lwaxana Troi, one such strategy is parody: episodes featuring Deanna's mother delight in how Lwaxana embarrasses her daughter through her brazen sexuality and straight talk, and frequently spotlight Lwaxana's search for a husband (both for herself and Deanna) and her admonishing Deanna regarding starting a family. Her arrival on the *Enterprise* typically leaves its "father," Jean-Luc Picard, comically trying to keep his distance from Lwaxana, who has made it clear she finds him very attractive. Her femininity painted in the broadest and stereotypical of strokes, paradoxically it is through her maternal self that the Lwaxana character is afforded the most depth, though this self, too, is also stereotyped. This is most notable in the episode "Dark Page": so guilt-ridden by the accidental death of her oldest daughter, Lwaxana has erased her daughter from her memory. Those suppressed memories resurface during a visit to the *Enterprise*, and the psychic break is so severe that Deanna must enter her mother's mind in order to save her. It is her failure *as a mother* to watch over her child that causes Lwaxana shame and grief; not once in her tearful exchange with Deanna is her husband, Ian, implicated as also having "failed" as a father, even though he too was present at the drowning accident that took their daughter's life. Although the episode sensitively portrays the most tragic experience for a parent—the loss of a child—it is troubling that in one of the few episodes where Lwaxana is not the misbehaving woman, she is instead portrayed as the failed, guilt-ridden mother.

The episode "The Child" is also troubling. First, it depicts one of two rapes that the Deanna Troi character would experience over the course of the series' seven-year run (Beverly Crusher, too, would be "raped" in the seventh season episode "Sub Rosa" by an entity that engaged in mental manipulation and abuse, effectively forcing her into a sexual relationship with him). Next, in the only episode depicting Troi as an actual, rather than symbolic, mother, the child she has is a child of rape. It is what happens after the rape (an entity curious about humanity impregnates her while she is sleeping, which cancels out the question of consent) that the series brings viewers back to its unease with mothers. After revealing her pregnancy to Picard, he convenes a meeting of the *Enterprise*'s senior staff—comprised almost entirely of men—to discuss "what is to be done about this." The conversation that follows is a thinly veiled metaphor for the male-dominated discourse on reproductive rights in the United States. Riker's inquiry regarding the identity of the father has the tone of accusation; his incredulity is not just informed by his ongoing romantic interest in Troi, but by a latent patriarchal privilege that views unmarried pregnant women as unacceptably transgressive. Read slightly differently, his reaction is decidedly protective: if he knows who "did this" to Troi, he can punish the offender, and in so doing symbolically assert both his romantic and patriarchal rights over Troi. Lt. Worf, the *Enterprise*'s Klingon chief of security, urges the pregnancy to be terminated, "for the safety of the ship and the crew." Neither Deanna's desires nor the life of the child she is carrying are relevant. The pro-life arguments that insist on the priority of the fetus, regardless of its own health, the health of its mother, or the manner of its conception, are inverted in Worf's statement to prioritize the concerns of the many against the choice of one mother. Not surprisingly, the science officer, the android Data, views Troi's predicament as an opportunity for study, and argues that the pregnancy should be carried to term.

This scene reflects Barbara Katz Rothman's observation that "it is women's motherhood that men must control to maintain patriarchy" (141). Having failed to prevent the pregnancy—Picard declares the discussion "over" when Troi states, in no uncertain terms, that "I am going to have this baby"—the same men who were arguing over her baby's fate surround Deanna in the delivery room. The difference between this scene and the earlier scene is that only Worf maintains his previous position. Riker and Data, on the other hand, join Deanna in welcoming the baby. It would appear, then, that Deanna's intrinsic rights over her own body have been respected, and that perhaps patriarchy has not "won." But just as quickly as she becomes a mother, her child is taken from her. Like the pregnancy, the child, Ian, grows at an accelerated rate, and that causes the dangerous cargo the ship is carrying to reach critical levels. This time the child is, in fact, responsible for putting the ship at risk. The entity departs/dies in order to save the ship from disaster, thanking a tearful Deanna before disappearing. The next scene shows a smiling Deanna on the bridge as Riker and Picard tease Wesley Crusher, who is apparently the only child allowed to be on the *Enterprise*. Critics of this episode have commented not only on how quickly Deanna recovers from the loss of her child, but how her son is never mentioned again by anyone, including his own mother. This is how Deanna is rendered an "absent present" mother, just as Beverly Crusher is consistently rendered one by subordinating her maternal claim on her son to the claim on Wesley made by the paternal Federation.

In its regulation of the maternal identities of its two most prominent female characters, and its conservative gender politics masked as enlightenment, *Star Trek: The Next Generation* finds itself adrift. One senses the series *wants* more for its female characters, but cannot extricate itself from the same old narratives, ones which, for mothers at least, prefer them so neatly tucked away on the *Enterprise* they might as well be back on Earth. The arrival of a female captain on a ship seventy-five years away from Earth, then, would reinvigorate this problem that had been largely put aside in the franchise during the run of *Star Trek: Deep Space Nine*, and do so specifically by pitting two "mothers" against one another.

Mothering in the Delta Quadrant

Alien mothers are regularly presented as "exaggerated and *overdetermined* figures" (Heidkamp 340; emphasis original), a particularly apt description of *Star Trek*'s most (in)famous mother, the Borg Queen. Before she was introduced in the second installment of the *TNG* film franchise, *Star Trek: First Contact* (1996), the Borg was an apparently leaderless collective linked by a shared hive mind, resembling both in structure and in practice the rhizome. The absence of a clear hierarchy alone made the Borg unique, both within the franchise and outside of it, as did its status as a pseudo-species of cybernetic humanoids. What made the Borg truly terrifying was its willful erasure of individuality through an act—assimilation—akin to rape and equivalent to genocide. The Borg's unique character was, for fans and critics alike, undone by the Borg Queen's introduction in *First Contact*, which brought the Borg more in line with the traditional sf rendering of aliens as hive cultures ruled by a queen. The Borg Queen's ostensible purpose was to bring "order to chaos" within the Borg Collective and throughout the universe via assimilation. Her sexually suggestive behavior towards Data in *First Contact* was that of cybernetic sexpot, a "techno-bodied femme fatale" (Consalvo 179), which added a layer of sexual menace to the genderless and sexless Borg. More importantly, her implied identification as the "mother" of the Borg reinterpreted the Borg menace as a maternal one; despite her posthuman signification, she was a continuation of an all-too familiar theme. What had changed was the horrifying size of that theme/threat.

Mia Consalvo correctly observes that the Borg Queen in *First Contact* is a "throwback to the original series' depiction of women," who uses her sexuality to achieve her goals; because her femininity is the source of her power, Consalvo argues, the Borg Queen's strategies are limited to the level of receptiveness others display to her overtures (184). This is a crucial point for what it can reveal regarding how the Borg Queen interacts with both Jean-Luc Picard and Data, and how that strategy must be abandoned when she faces off against Janeway in *Voyager*. Viewers learn that Picard, renamed "Locutus" when he is assimilated by the Borg in the *TNG* episode "The Best of Both Worlds," was the Borg Queen's longed for consort; when they reunite in *First Contact*, she points out to Picard that he can still hear "our song." The Borg Queen romanticizes the Collective's hive mind by referring to it as a "song," one which the still traumatized Picard has struggled for years to forget. Later, the passionate kiss she shares with Data is part of a seduction process in which she promises Data pleasures he cannot experience as an android, or for that matter, as the human he longs to become. Compare these examples to the Borg Queen's interaction with Janeway in the series finale "Endgame": the two antagonists make a deal—one that will enable *Voyager* to safely return to the Alpha Quadrant while giving the Borg advanced weaponry and shield technology—in an exchange that is charged, but stripped of sexual tension. The Borg Queen clearly perceives Janeway as an equal; in a neat reversal of her exchange with Data, it is the Borg Queen who is tempted, as she naturally would be, by the technology that Janeway offers.

Consalvo contends that the Borg Queen "does not engage in activity," rather, she is an "organizer of experience," but this statement does not entirely hold. As the Borg Queen adopts a more maternal presence to counter and threaten Janeway's "children" and her identification as the *Voyager*'s "mother," the Borg Queen is, in fact, a "primary actor" (189). This is especially true regarding the battle between these two mothers over Seven of Nine, the "daughter" they would both claim as their own. David Greven points out that when the Borg Queen "places her gloved hand on Seven's face" in "Dark Frontier," she "is a tender mother figure," who appeals to Seven's desire for kinship and family (181). This is a striking shift from Alice Krige's sexualized portrayal of the Borg Queen in *First Contact.* In "Dark Frontier," the Borg Queen is played by Susanna Thompson, whose portrayal Greven describes as "cerebral and precisely modulated"; consequently, Thompson's Borg Queen is more Machiavellian than sexpot (179). While the "unsexing" of the Borg Queen is not complete in *Voyager*, it has been substantially diminished, not only, as Greven points out, in Thompson's interpretation of the character, but also in her physical presence. Her breasts are small, her round hips downplayed by technological embellishments, in effect "flattening" her femininity, which is further accomplished when she is reunited with Seven, whose voluptuous body loudly announces her retrieved female body and "conventional femininity" (182). This "repression of sexuality [so typically] associated with motherhood" (Wilcox 25) is important in the construction of the "warring matriarchies" that Michelle Erica Greene describes in her analysis of "Dark Frontier" (qtd. in Greven 183). By repressing the sexuality of both characters, the Borg Queen and Janeway can more comfortably maintain both their "maternal warmth and autocratic masculinity" (Greven 183), and for Janeway in particular, to occupy the role of both mother *and* father to her crew, as Aviva Dove-Viebahn observes (605).

What separates the two is that Janeway "sees her daughter not as a continuous other but as an autonomous and separate self" (Bassin et al. 8). In this way, Janeway's mothering is aligned with neoliberalism, and presented as superior to the Borg Queen's suffocating motherhood. At the same time, Janeway embodies even more fully the collapsing of the professional self with the maternal identity even as she escapes from that bind by assuming an "autocratic masculinity." This hybridity (Dove-Viebahn) and gender liminality (Greven) hints at a way for selfhood to be maintained or recovered, particularly for symbolic mothers like Janeway, but it does not account for the displacement of actual mothers like Samantha Wildman, who is cast within the role of the neglectful working mother. Where Janeway's symbolic mothering is key to guiding her "family" back to the Alpha Quadrant, and thus takes center stage, it is curious that the one biological mother-daughter bond is almost completely pushed aside.

Samantha Wildman is, literally, the absent mother, appearing in only eight of the 172 episodes in the series.[3] She has been both displaced and *re*placed by Naomi's godfather, Neelix, in a variation on the replacement of the maternal Beverly Crusher with the paternal Federation. In presenting both an absent actual mother, and an ever-present symbolic mother who also happens to be the captain, *Voyager* repeats, with a twist, its predecessor's "sins," while attempting to ameliorate them by giving equal weight to the domestic and the militaristic through Janeway's hybrid mix of mothering and fathering (Dove-Viebahn 605). This "improvement" is muted by the decision to replace Naomi's mother with the "Male Mother" Neelix, which David Greven argues is a reflection of the series' queer politics (74). While not being dismissive of the radical potential of such figures, this maneuver nevertheless suggests that mothers like Samantha Wildman (and by extension, Deanna Troi and Beverly Crusher) are expendable, that the work of mothers can be done just as well, if not better, by male figures. This "exclusionary tactic" reinforces the "masculinist nature of sf" while at the same time highlighting the truly "problematic space[s]" occupied by mothers in *Star Trek* (Merrick 241). In turn, this space is additionally problematized by emphasizing symbolic mothers over and against actual mothers.

Furthermore, by domesticating Janeway's leadership,[4] she is rendered a more acceptable powerful female, a strategy that also reinforces the "masculinist nature of sf," as does pitting her against another powerful "mother." Or as Debra Bonita Shaw rightly points out: "a woman may captain a starship only if she is [...] motivated by filial and domestic concerns" (81). Furthermore, collapsing Janeway's leadership into her latent maternal self allows the show to recast her triumphs, and especially her failures, as motherly ones. "Endgame" clearly demonstrates this. The viewer sees now Admiral Janeway racked with guilt over the loss of so many of her "children" and resolved to bring them *all* back home safely, even if that means violating the Temporal Prime Directive and dying in the process. As tempting as it is to read Janeway in this final episode as the hybrid parent Dove-Viebahn describes, Janeway reads more as a mother in search of redemption, which is underscored by her willingness to sacrifice herself. It is sacrifice that defines Janeway as woman, as captain, and as symbolic mother, and thus aligns her with traditional notions of femininity and motherhood. Likewise, she is inserted into the same pseudo-progressive matrix that has trapped the franchise's mothers, the one which, "make[s] [mothers] seem more significant than they actually are" (Tudor and Meehan 130).

Conclusion

What emerges is a franchise struggling with the "masculinist nature of sf" (Merrick 241) and with its own "misogynistic elements" (Greven 174). In featuring the franchise's first female captain, Kathryn Janeway, *Star Trek:*

Voyager offers a limited redress to what continues to be a perennial problem within the franchise. Indeed, much of what Deborah Tudor and Eileen R. Meehan observe about the Abrams' reboot can be applied to these older installments of the franchise, including most significantly the ongoing contradiction between the franchise's egalitarian ethos and the narratives that frequently consign the female characters to minor or stereotypical roles that emphasize their romantic lives or their roles within the family. These narratives are so prevalent as to be a trope within the franchise itself, and key to defining several of the more major female characters that emerged when the franchise was reimagined in the mid-1980s with *TNG*.

This is striking because, in a very simple sense, mothers are everywhere in the *Star Trek* universe, birthing and raising generation after generation of the Federation's children (and its enemies). They serve on Federation vessels, die on away missions, leave their children at the *Enterprise*'s daycare, and so on, but they are either peripheral figures or their identification as mothers is subjugated to their professional identities. Most of the mothers in *Star Trek*—the human mothers, at least—are back at home, on Earth or one of its established colonies. Viewers *know* they exist, they must, but the physical presence of mothers dispels the fantasy of space exploration by reminding us of the domestic space and maternity. They cannot, however, be dispensed with entirely: thus, their absence becomes a presence unto itself, just as the diminishing of the maternal identity of the women serving on Federation starships makes it all the more present.

Even the most present mother—the Federation starship—cannot escape the franchise's insistence on and reliance upon maternal stereotypes. On one hand, there is the best-known Federation starship, the *Enterprise*, whose name speaks of collective effort, a willingness to take risks, to attempt the impossible—and *Voyager*, whose name reinforces the explorative mission of the Federation, as well as the ship's long journey back to the Alpha Quadrant. On the other hand, both ships embody home and family. The physical and symbolic presence of this "mother" is powerful and inescapable; she is romanticized and idealized. Only if she is treated with respect can her children be safe and find their way home. Multiple times she is threatened by another, monstrous mother, and if necessary, she will be sacrificed to defeat her foe. That she, and all that she represents, triumphs, speaks to the affectionate nostalgia that both binds her to her family and insists on keeping her place carefully circumscribed.

That this is largely the fate of the living, breathing mothers that call the Federation starship home exposes *Star Trek*'s unease and uncertainty with these figures. Or to put it another way: the franchise cannot ignore mothers, but it can, and often does, render mothers ineffectual and irrelevant. This is in keeping with the rhetorical valorizing of motherhood and its concomitant devaluing in virtually every sector of American culture. For "motherhood's place in the cultural matrix," as Lindal Buchanan puts it (117), is a vexed one. The franchise's response to this is to put mothers like Beverly Crusher in limbo, to deny Troi her maternal self, and to erase Samantha Wildman almost completely. Powerful mothers are mystified (Guinan), demonized (the Borg Queen), and haunted by regret (Janeway). In *Star Trek*, the "contested terrain" of motherhood is voided (Glenn 2), rendered a terra nullius, and emerges as a frontier clearly in need of further exploration.

Notes

1. Or as Debra Bonita Shaw nicely puts it: "*TNG*'s postfeminist revision of *TOS*'s opening statement" (69).
2. One of the more notable exceptions is the critical work on Captain Kathryn Janeway, including that of Susan De Gaia, Michele A. Bowring, Aviva Dove-Veibahn, and David Greven. See too Rhonda V. Wilcox's important "Goldberg, Guinan, and the Celestial Mother in *Star Trek: The Next Generation*," *The Mid-Atlantic Almanack* 4 (1995): 18–31.
3. By contrast, Scarlett Pomers, who portrayed Samantha Wildman's daughter, Naomi, appeared in 17 episodes in the series.
4. This phrase is a reworking of Dove-Viebahn's description of Janeway as a "domestic leader" (602).

Works Cited

Bartlett, Anne Clark. "Defining the Terms: Postfeminism as an Ideology of Cool." *Medieval Feminist Forum* 34 (Fall 2002): 25–30. Print.

Bassin, Donna, et al. "Introduction." *Representations of Motherhood*. New Haven: Yale University Press, 1994. 1–28. Print.

Bernardi, Daniel. "*Star Trek* in the 1960s: Liberal-Humanism and the Production of Race." *Science Fiction Studies* 24 (Jul. 1997): 209–25. Print.

Blair, Karin. "Sex and *Star Trek*." *Science Fiction Studies* 10.3 (1983): 292–97. Print.

Boyd, Patricia R. "Paradoxes of Postfeminism: Coercion and Consent in *Fifty Shades of Grey*." *Feminist Theory and Pop Culture*. Ed. Adrienne Trier-Bieniek. Rotterdam: Sense Publishers, 2015. 103–14. Print.

Bundtzen, Lynda K. "Monstrous Mothers: Medusa, Grendel, and Now Alien." *The Gendered Cyborg: A Reader*. Eds. Gill Kirkup, Linda Janes, Kath Woodward, and Fiona Hovenden. Routledge, 1999. 101–09. Print.

"The Child." *Star Trek: The Next Generation*. CBS. 21 Nov. 1988. Television.

Consalvo, Mia. "Borg Babes, Drones, and the Collective: Reading Body and the Gender in *Star Trek*." *Women Studies in Communication* 27.2 (2004): 177–203. Print.

"Dark Frontier." *Star Trek: Voyager*. UPN. 17 Feb. 1999. Television.

"Dark Page." *Star Trek: The Next Generation*. CBS. 1 Nov. 1993. Television.

Dove-Viebahn, Aviva. "Embodying Hybridity, (En)Gendering Community: Captain Janeway and the Enactment of a Feminist Heterotopia on *Star Trek: Voyager*." *Women's Studies* 36 (2007): 597–618. Print.

"El-Aurian." *Memory Alpha*. N.d. 5 Jul. 2016. Web.

"Endgame." *Star Trek: Voyager*. UPN. 23 May 2001. Television.

Geraghty, Lincoln. "Television Before 1980." *The Routledge Companion to Science Fiction*. Eds. Mark Bould, Andrew M. Butler, Adam Roberts, and Sherryl Vint. New York: Routledge, 2009. 141–52. Print.

Glenn, Evelyn Nakano. "Social Constructions of Mothering: A Thematic Overview." *Mothering: Ideology, Experience, and Agency*. Eds. Evelyn Nakano Glenn, Grace Chang, and Linda Rennie Forcey. New York: Routledge, 1994. 1–29. Print.

Greven, David. *Gender and Sexuality in Star Trek*. Jefferson, NC: McFarland, 2009. Print.
Heidkamp, Bernie. "Response to the Alien Mother in Post-Maternal Cultures: C.J. Cherryh and Orson Scott Card." *Science Fiction Studies* 23.3 (1996): 339–54. Print.
Heller, Lee E. "The Persistence of Difference: Postfeminism, Popular Discourse, and Heterosexuality in *Star Trek: The Next Generation*." *Science Fiction Studies* 24 (Jul. 1997): 226–44. Print.
"Jamie Lynne Grumet Breastfeeds on the Cover of *Pathways to Family Wellness* Magazine." *Huffington Post* 11 Sep. 2012. Web. 20 Jun. 2016.
Joyrich, Lynne. "Feminist Enterprise? *Star Trek: The Next Generation* and the Occupation of Femininity." *Cinema Journal* 35.2 (1996): 61–84. Print.
Kulcsár, Zsófia. "Critique of Post-Feminism." *E-Journal of American Studies in Hungary* 7.2, Sep. 2011. Web. 20 Jun. 2016.
Lois, George. "Flashback: Demi Moore." *Vanity Fair: Hive*. Aug. 2011. 7 Jun. 2016. Web.
Merrick, Helen. "Gender in Science Fiction." *The Cambridge Companion to Science Fiction*. Eds. Edward James and Farah Mendlesohn. Cambridge University Press, 2003. 241–52. Print.
Press, Andrea L. "Feminism and Media in the Post-Feminist Era: What to Make of the 'Feminist' in Feminist Media Studies." *Feminist Media Studies* 11.1 (2011): 107–13. Print.
Roberts, Robin. "Rape, Romance, and Consent in *Star Trek: The Next Generation*." *Extrapolation* 40.1 (1999): 21–35. Print.
Rothman, Barbara Katz. "Beyond Mothers and Fathers: Ideology in a Patriarchal Society." *Mothering: Ideology, Experience, and Agency*. Eds. Evelyn Nakano Glenn, Grace Chang, and Linda Rennie Forcey. New York: Routledge, 1994. 139–57. Print.
Shaw, Debra Bonita. "Sex and the Single Starship Captain: Compulsory Heterosexuality and *Star Trek: Voyager*." *FEMSPEC* 7.1 (2006): 66–85. Print.
Tudor, Deborah, and Eileen R. Meehan. "Demoting Women on the Screen and in the Board Room." *Cinema Journal* 53.1 (Fall 2013): 130–36. Print.
Varvus, Mary Douglas. "Opting Out Moms in the News: Selling New Traditionalism in the New Millennium." *Feminist Media Studies* 7.1 (2007): 47–63. Print.
Wilcox, Rhonda V. "Goldberg, Guinan, and the Celestial Mother in *Star Trek: The Next Generation*." *The Mid-Atlantic Almanack* 4 (1995): 18–31. Print.

Photons and Phantoms

Kathryn Janeway as Gothic Heroine

Eleanor Dobson

A Victorian governess stands alone in a candlelit room, a grand setting decked out in wooden paneling and candelabra. Stark flashes of lightning flare, accompanied by rumbling thunder and the white noise of torrential rain. The cup of tea she holds clinks in its china saucer as she tilts her head, taking in the features of her new home, observing the tapestry hanging above the fireplace and the ornate clock on the mantelpiece. But the storm raging outside diverts her attention. As she moves towards the rain-lashed window, it is blown ajar in the gale. She gently pushes it to. A reflection is brought into view: the spectral glow of a human figure. The governess turns to face the intruder, and is met with nothing more than a painted portrait of a beautiful dark-haired woman in an evening dress. She pauses. Surely she herself bears a startling likeness to the lady in the picture…

This is no typical Victorian governess: this is Captain Kathryn Janeway of the Starship *Voyager*, enjoying a rare opportunity "to get away from being a captain for a while" (*Star Trek: Voyager* "Cathexis," 1x12). Janeway (Kate Mulgrew) performs within this "holonovel"—a recreational virtual reality narrative on the holodeck—in three episodes of *Star Trek: Voyager*, all originally airing across the series' first two seasons in 1995: "Cathexis," "Learning Curve," and "Persistence of Vision." These three episodes have different directors and writers, yet through nesting Janeway's holonovel within the broader narrative arc of each installment, each explicitly posits *Voyager*'s captain as a Gothic heroine existing within a cultural tradition extending back to (and beyond) the nineteenth century. After "Persistence of Vision," "Janeway Lambda One" (as the holonovel is designated) is abandoned; perhaps after this episode's traumatic events which see Janeway begin to have hallucinations of the characters and objects from the holonovel elsewhere on the ship, returning to the Gothic thrills of the holonovel might prove all too traumatic. While Janeway originally envisages her participation in this story as a form of escapism, the holonovel repeatedly echoes and indeed, eventually encroaches upon, her experiences at the helm of *Voyager*. The holonovel's setting, characters, and plot mirror a number of celebrated nineteenth- and twentieth-century Gothic texts, including Charlotte Brontë's *Jane Eyre* (1847), Henry James' *The Turn of the Screw* (1898) and Daphne du Maurier's *Rebecca* (1938); there are also, however, significant parallels to be drawn between these literary antecedents and Janeway's daily life as captain of a stranded starship. She might be considered a cousin of the trio of heroines who front these novels: Jane Eyre, the unnamed governess, and the second Mrs. de Winter. Janeway is, in many ways, an isolated woman, often under threat, and yet even in extreme conditions and under enduring pressure she remains tenacious. In much the same way as *Jane Eyre*'s autobiographical pretext, *Rebecca*'s first person perspective and the governess's manuscript in *The Turn of the Screw*, Janeway's "Captain's log" is a personal record of her experience told in her own voice. Like these literary forerunners, Janeway is presented as *Voyager*'s central protagonist: "[u]sually it is from her perspective that the story is told" (Poe 218). Through these episodes, which lend *Voyager* a supernatural aura, Janeway takes up the Gothic mantle, bringing the resolute and empowered Gothic heroine into the twenty-fourth century.

This study first examines the holonovel itself, identifying the Gothic tropes that characterize Janeway's narrative of choice. No doubt, as a cultured woman Janeway would have delighted in the story's unabashed intertextuality, relishing the process of deciphering the copious allusions to the aforementioned novels. Subsequently, this article examines Janeway's anxieties external to the holonovel but brought into focus by its themes, suggesting that her state of childlessness and romantic turmoil in particular connect her to the Gothic heroines that she admires in fiction. Finally, it turns to *Voyager*'s predicament as a stranded ship, a futuristic interpretation of the isolated manor house of nineteenth- and twentieth-century Gothic texts. In doing so, it seeks to establish Janeway's conformity to (and, in some ways, rejection of) the stereotypes of the Gothic heroine: while many of the threats posed to the Gothic heroine become Janeway's, she ultimately rebels against and overcomes many of the Gothic's patriarchal dangers.

Janeway's Cousins

During filming, the crew referred to the set for Janeway's holonovel as "the Jane Eyre set" (Poe 10), and Jeri Taylor described the historical moment in which the events of the narrative take place as the "[e]ighteen-forties to eighteen-fifties" (18), the period which saw the original publication of Brontë's novel. The plot of the holonovel shares a number of parallels with *Jane Eyre*, most notably, the passionate love Lord Burleigh (Michael Cumpsty) feels for his children's governess, Lucille Davenport. This directly mirrors the Byronic Edward Rochester's falling for Jane, who is also in his employment, educating his ward, Adèle Varens. In her study entitled *Hamlet on the Holodeck: The Future of Narrative in Cyberspace* (1997), Janet Horowitz Murray recognizes the wealth of similarities between Janeway's holonovel and *Jane Eyre*, the literary work "which established the governess gothic genre" (16). Like Brontë's text, Janeway's holonovel "takes place in a mysteriously haunted household and emphasizes the perils of the governess's intense social relationships rather than the physical terrors of the situation" (16). Furthermore, Murray sees significance in the similarity between the names of Jane Eyre and Kathryn Janeway, and comments upon the resemblances between their characters more generally: both demonstrate "a strong resistance to being bullied, a willingness to stand on principle, and the courage to face fear and isolation head-on" (16).

The other most telling reference to *Jane Eyre* in Janeway's holonovel is the possibility that Lord Burleigh's first wife is not actually dead as he and his son Henry (Thomas Dekker) claim. Like Jane, who hears the strange "demoniac laugh" of Rochester's deranged wife Bertha Mason, Janeway overhears a piano being played, "several times ... a lovely Mozart sonata" (*Star Trek: Voyager* "Persistence of Vision," 2x8). The sound is that of a piano appears to be a nod to *The Turn of the Screw*, in which the governess learns that "[t]he musical sense in each of the children was of the quickest" (219), the two of them playing "gruesome fancies" (219); the governess even refers to *Jane Eyre* as she speculates: "[w]as there a 'secret' at Bly—a mystery of Udolpho or an insane, an unmentionable relative kept in unsuspected confinement?" (179). Janeway assumes that the musical performer is Lord Burleigh's daughter Beatrice (Lindsey Haun), who, when confronted with this theory in front of her father, gasps and drops the teacup she is holding—her "mother's cup"—which smashes on the floor. The implication here is that it is not Beatrice who plays the piano at all, but her mother, whom Beatrice claims is "not dead! I saw her last night!" (*Star Trek: Voyager* "Learning Curve," 1x16).

Janeway's holonovel's tantalizing appeal is, in part, embodied in the multiple possibilities that might explain these strange goings-on. Perhaps Lady Burleigh is indeed dead, and Beatrice is finding it hard to adapt to her mother's demise, fantasizing that she still exists. Alternatively, Lady Burleigh might have actually passed away, but her ghost is haunting the house and returning to visit her daughter. Lastly, the possibility exists that she might be, like Bertha Mason, installed as a madwoman in the attic. "One thing above all I must demand," declares the dark and brooding Lord Burleigh when he and Janeway first meet, "you are never, under any circumstances, to go onto the fourth floor, is that clear?" ("Cathexis"). Janeway does seek answers from Lord Burleigh: "[w]hy shouldn't I go to the fourth floor? What's up there?" she queries, to which he cryptically replies, "[t]hose are questions you must not ask" ("Persistence of Vision"). Perhaps this floor of the house—tellingly, high up and quite likely the top floor (the "attic")—is reserved for the imprisoned Lady Burleigh.

The portrait of the woman, whose spectral reflection comes into view when Janeway closes the window, is, through these later references to Lord Burleigh's wife, presumably Lady Burleigh herself. This trope refers back to *Rebecca* (a novel which is, in part, based upon *Jane Eyre*), in which the second Mrs. de Winter is manipulated by the sinister housekeeper, Mrs. Danvers, into wearing a costume adopted by Rebecca herself in earlier years. Indeed, Janeway's physical similarity with the portrait suggests this resemblance between her and Lord Burleigh's wife, evoking the Gothic conceit of the *doppelgänger*, just as the second Mrs. de Winter is made to physically evoke the first. While "[j]ealousy and envy of her husband's first wife—the beautiful, upper-class Rebecca—propels the nameless heroine down the dark corridors of Rebecca's past" (Light 7) in du Maurier's novel, these nods to du Maurier's precedent posit that similar events will unfold in Janeway's holonovel. If "the real Rebecca took shape and form before [the second Mrs. de Winter], stepping form her shadow world like a living figure from a picture frame" (du Maurier 327), perhaps the portrait in Janeway's holonovel might function as a similar—if somewhat less metaphorical—gateway between the world of the living and the world of the dead.

The severe housekeeper, Mrs. Templeton, who first appears in a steel grey dress looking sternly over her spectacles (an accessory which mysteriously disappears after "Cathexis"), is clearly a reference to *Rebecca*'s formidable Mrs. Danvers, "tall and gaunt, dressed in deep black" (du Maurier 80) with "prominent cheek-bones and great, hollow eyes" (80), rather than the more amiable Mrs. Fairfax and Mrs. Grose of *Jane Eyre* and *The Turn of the Screw* respectively. Mrs. Templeton's first speech to Janeway establishes her authority:

> Let's make something clear, Mrs. Davenport. My job is to make sure that this household runs smoothly. I have been with Lord Burleigh for nearly twenty years *because* this household runs smoothly. He has come to trust me. And I will not brook any behavior that might jeopardize that trust, so you will be expected to follow the rules that *I* set down ["Cathexis"].

While Janeway responds to this demonstration of power by asserting herself—"I have been hired by Lord Burleigh, and it's his orders I will follow, not yours"—Mrs. Templeton's response—"[y]ou would be wise not to make an enemy of me"—establishes the threat that the housekeeper might come to pose, a gesture towards the "actual malice" (du Maurier 87) that the second Mrs. de Winter reads in Mrs. Danvers' eyes. This threat is realized in "Persistence of Vision," in which Janeway's hallucinations largely consist of characters and objects from the holonovel appearing elsewhere than on the holodeck. Opening the door in a bid to escape her quarters where, until this point, auditory hallucinations of Mark Johnson (Stan Ivar), her fiancé left behind on Earth, have been plaguing her, she finds Mrs. Templeton brandishing a knife. "Everything was fine until you came here," she states, "I took care of him. He trusted me. But when you arrived, all that changed. You've done nothing but cause trouble. We don't want more trouble in our lives." Mrs. Templeton attacks Janeway, cutting her hand. Here, Mrs. Templeton's menace is fulfilled. She functions in a similar way to *Rebecca*'s Mrs. Danvers at this moment, although her attachment is to Lord Burleigh rather than his late wife; indeed, Mrs. Danvers confronts the second Mrs. de Winter in similar language: "[w]hy did you ever come here? ... Nobody wanted you at Manderley. We were all right until you came" (du Maurier 289). While Mrs. Danvers attempts to drive the second Mrs. de Winter to suicide—"[w]hy don't you jump?" (296) she goads—she never poses a direct physical threat, however. Perhaps there is also something of Bertha Mason about her in this moment, specifically in her predilection to direct physical attack. Bertha attempts to kill Rochester by setting the curtains of his bed ablaze (an act she would later repeat with Jane's bed, and one which burns Thornfield Hall to the ground, leaving Rochester blind), and assaults her brother, Richard Mason, first with a knife (Mrs. Templeton's weapon of choice) and then with her teeth, "like a tigress" (Brontë 212).

This host of familiar Gothic tropes and allusions permeates the narrative in which Janeway has chosen to participate, contributing to a sense of psychological oppressiveness which, altogether, might appear to negate the relaxational purpose of performing within the holonovel. Why, might we ask, would Janeway select such a story? While Janeway's holonovel has attracted little critical attention to date, those scholars who do address these episodes, such as Murray, see something particularly Victorian in Janeway herself. James F. Broderick recognizes the literary prowess of the full range of *Star Trek* Captains, but states that, of all of them, "Captain Janeway ... really gets into literature—literally—by entering into novels... portraying characters from Victorian-era fiction" (6), indicating her particularly close affinity with the literary genres she admires. Murray, meanwhile, has succeeded in dissecting and analyzing a variety of characters' literary or cinematic preferences as they are expressed on the holodeck:

> Holonovels provide customized entertainment for a variety of tastes. They reveal unexpected sides of familiar characters. Just as Jean-Luc Picard, the highly cultured captain of *Star Trek: The Next Generation*, enjoys film noir, his android crewman,

> Commander Data, identifies with Sherlock Holmes, and the sensitive Dr. Julian Bashir of *Star Trek: Deep Space Nine* prefers James Bond spy adventures, so the conscientious Captain Janeway turns to gothic fiction in her well-earned leisure hours [15].

Some of these generic partialities are, perhaps, less surprising than others. That Commander Data (Brent Spiner) has a penchant for Sherlock Holmes is not only highly plausible but artistically satisfying, given the android's talent for logical reasoning. Janeway too radiates nineteenth-century propriety and heroic charisma. Perhaps it is no wonder that "Captain Janeway, a person of Victorian integrity" (25) periodically substitutes "her spandex-sleek Starfleet uniform for a hugely crinolined Victorian dress" (13), taking on the role of the fictional Lucille Davenport. The nineteenth-century Gothic novel, however appropriate it may seem as Janeway's favored genre, was not in fact the writers' first choice for her preferred virtual entertainment. As Stephen Edward Poe records:

> When Jeri Taylor wrote the first draft of the teaser, she constructed a scenario in which Janeway was a pioneer woman in a covered wagon, headed out West. She had a husband and children. Day to day living was at a very simple level, often requiring her to do things for which she was quite unprepared and untrained—such as building a campfire. In short, nothing remotely like her job as a starship captain. Taylor thought it was a great metaphor for the captain's predicament in the Delta Quadrant, and would also provide a unique method of developing and enhancing Janeway's character [11].

This concept proved impossible due to financial reasons, along with Mulgrew's reluctance to work with horses, and so Janeway's holonovel metamorphosed into the Gothic tale that graced viewers' television sets during 1995.

These scenarios do, in fact, have a number of features in common: both deal with the loss of a former home, the heroine's adaptation to her new surroundings, and the care she must provide for a man and his children. Of the two scenarios though, only the Gothic novel touches upon one of the tragedies of Janeway's predicament: in the pioneer holonovel, Janeway might have found a recreational outlet in which she could try to exercise and satisfy her maternal desires towards her own holographic children, but in the Gothic holnovel, while she expresses a real fondness for the children in her care, they are unforthcoming and respond to her affection with rudeness. The rebuttal of her attempts to express her maternal nature secures Janeway's position as the Gothic heroine, traditionally a woman who is yet to have children of her own.

Absent Mothers and Maternal Desire

The holonovel's children—Beatrice and Henry—invert the eerily polished politeness of Flora and Miles in *The Turn of the Screw*, while also seemingly standing in for the children that Janeway will never have: they reject her as a maternal substitute for their (supposedly) deceased mother. "I'm not asking that you *replace* their mother," the holographic Lord Burleigh informs her upon their first meeting, "but I think they'll respond to a woman's sensibilities" ("Cathexis"). The children's response, however, leaves much to be desired. Beatrice informs Janeway that she is still in contact with Lady Burleigh, claiming that she no longer has the first sampler that she created under Janeway's tutelage, as she "gave it to mother" ("Learning Curve"). This familiar Gothic trope of the undead mother persists (Anolik 25), and in a hallucination, Beatrice asks Janeway, "[w]hat about my mother's grave? There's no-one inside. The coffin is empty" ("Persistence of Vision"). In a reversal of this notion of Gothic "motherlessness," Janeway is prevented from having her own children. In a later episode, "The Q and the Grey" (1996), the omnipotent Q (John de Lancie) addresses Janeway's childlessness directly:

> You're stuck out here, thousands of light-years from home, and you aren't getting any younger, are you? All your hopes for home, hearth and family grow dimmer every day. Admit it, Kathryn, you're lonely too. And you wonder if you will ever have a child [*Star Trek Voyager* "The Q and the Grey," 3x11].

While Michèle Barrett celebrates Janeway as "post-feminist in the extreme," "a woman who has sacrificed not one iota of her femininity in the accomplishment of her job as, effectively, a military strategist and leader" (49), this is, in fact, far from the case. Janeway sacrifices much: while opportunities for romance present themselves, she resists engaging in satisfying long-term romantic relationships, believing, as Michèle A. Bowring has suggested, that a relationship with a member of her crew "would undermine her authority" (395), and as such, she abandons any chance of having children of her own. A state of romantic turmoil and long-standing childlessness characterizes the situation of the Gothic heroine (Anolik 38), and while sometimes this disorder is resolved—"[r]eader, I married him" (Brontë 448) declares Jane Eyre, revealing that she and Rochester have had a son together since the novel's climax—the heroines remain childless at the end of both *The Turn of the Screw* and *Rebecca*. The second Mrs. de Winter in particular seems to struggle with her childlessness; while she imagines her future children, speculating that the furniture "would know a period of glorious shabbiness and wear when the boys were young—our boys—for I saw them sprawling on the sofa with muddy boots" (du Maurier 83), she never falls pregnant. Over the course of the novel she notices people inspecting her body, "taking in my clothes from top to toe, wondering, with that swift downward glance given to all brides, if I was going to have a baby" (150), and is brusquely questioned by her husband's sister: "you're not by any chance starting an infant, are you? ... I must say I do hope you will provide a son and heir before long. It would be so terribly good for Maxim. I hope you are going nothing to prevent it" (211). This is still a concern at the novel's climax; she assures herself, "[w]e would have children. Surely we would have children" (452), possibly a response to the revelation that her husband's first wife had "a certain malformation of the uterus ... which meant she could never have had a child" (442–43). Of course, Rebecca keeps her condition a secret from her husband, claiming to be pregnant with another man's child in order to provoke him to murder her. While the second Mrs. de Winter, her concerns aside, may well go on to have a baby after the novel's events, the governess in *The Turn of the Screw* dies unmarried, seemingly in love with her master (the children's uncle) whom she barely knows. Furthermore, she is plagued by the notion that the children, who she believes are visited by ghosts (Peter Quint and Miss Jessel), are slipping out of her grasp, a concern which she expresses in the language of ownership: "[t]hey're not mine ... . They're his and they're hers!" (James 237). In the end, the governess does lose the children: Flora rejects her, demanding "take me away from *her!*" (281), and Miles suddenly (and inexplicably) dies. The implication is that even in the holonovel, which presents Janeway with an opportunity to care for surrogate children, the similarities between the holonovel and *The Turn of the Screw* imply that rejection or death may well be plot developments as Janeway's narrative develops.

While Janeway's maternal desires are frustrated on the holodeck, Aris Mousoutzanis reads one of *Voyager*'s central struggles in the "conflict between a monstrous Borg matriarchy and [Janeway's] conservative matriarchy" (69). Janeway certainly operates as a foil to the Borg Queen, whose violent pseudo-maternal mission is to transform billions into her own "children": but she and her progeny are typified by a distinct monstrousness. Janeway's crew, on the other hand, might be read as a (somewhat extensive) family, the only true substitute for Janeway's lack of biological children. The holonovel, then, might be seen to serve as an environment in which Janeway can seek a more traditional maternal role in which, liberated from the confines of her official position as *Voyager*'s captain, she might attempt to live within a tighter nuclear family unit.

Romantic Anxieties

The absence of filial affection on and off the holodeck is accompanied by a corresponding absence of romance. Stranded in the Delta Quadrant, light-years away from Earth and her fiancé, and constrained by her "Victorian integrity" (Dove-Viebahn 604), Janeway resorts to near total romantic abstinence, to which Aviva Dove-Viebahn refers as a "relative asexuality" (604). She is, however, far from an asexual being. Janeway exists within "a trend of tough, smart, and sexually ambiguous heroines on the small screen" (Brown 6), a vogue that also saw the creation of characters such as "Dana Scully on the *X-Files*" (6). Neither a "kick-ass heroine" nor "a campy space-vixen" (Bowring 389), Janeway is a balance of masculine and feminine: "sexy but tough" (Brown 61). She does express desire for and attraction to a handful of individuals (some holograms) over the course of *Voyager*, desire which is inevitably cut short, and either does not or cannot result in the production of children—the one regrettable exception being the hyper-evolved amphibious offspring of herself and Tom Paris (Robert Duncan McNeill) in "Threshold" (1996), commonly considered the worst episode of *Voyager* ever to air (McIntee 97).

The Gothic holonovel provides Janeway with an erotic outlet, although she appears to find this troubling. The title of "Cathexis" is a psychoanalytic term which specifically refers to the investment of libidinal energy, and suggests Janeway's tormented psychological state with regards to her sexuality. In "Persistence of Vision," while wearing her Victorian costume in her quarters before her visit to the holodeck, she takes a moment to look at a photograph of Mark and her Irish setter, Mollie. It is in this installment of the holonovel that Lord Burleigh, tormented and breathless, kisses Janeway (as Lucille), stating "I have fallen in love with you." The next time she looks at the photograph, she will be suffering from visual and auditory hallucinations, a symptom she initially considers to be the result of the psychologically and morally unsettling kiss (Murray 16). This is in contrast to the deep spiritual significance when, in *Jane Eyre*, Rochester calls out to a seemingly telepathically-receptive Jane, sparking her return to him. Janeway's hallucinations instead mirror one interpretation of *The Turn of the Screw*: that the "ghosts" are just an expression of the governess's madness. Indeed, the Gothic heroine often doubts her sanity, particularly in moments of romantic turmoil—as the second Mrs. de Winter relates upon seeing Rebecca's bedroom, "[f]or one desperate moment I thought that something had happened to my brain" (du Maurier 197). Perhaps Janeway too, like her literary predecessors, is suffering from a psychological disturbance, inextricably bound up with her romantic frustration and evoking the hysterical symptoms of the Gothic governess.

In fact, in this episode the hallucinations experienced by a number of crew members are revealed not to be the result of psychological trauma, but the manipulative telepathic abilities of a single alien. For a number of individuals, these visions are amatory in nature: Ensign Harry Kim (Garrett Wang) sees his girlfriend appear before him, Commander Tuvok (Tim Russ) his wife T'Pel (Marva Hicks), and Lieutenant B'Elanna Torres (Roxann Dawson) has a passionate fantasy about Commander Chakotay (Robert Beltran). These hallucinations might be thought to stem from the trauma of separation from a partner, or the anxiety surrounding the development of romantic feelings that are not entirely welcome. In Janeway's case, the alien creates a vision of Mark, a hallucination which, initially at least, she knows to be artificial, stating "I don't know who you are, what you are, but I won't let you touch me" as he tries to embrace her. "What about the man on the holodeck?" he asks,

> You didn't seem to mind him touching you did you? In fact I think you liked it. Now I ask you Kath, was that fair to me? I've stayed faithful to you. I vowed to wait for you no matter how long it takes. Shouldn't you do the same?

Under his questioning her control lapses. The moment in which they kiss, an instance of contact that mirrors that between Janeway and Lord Burleigh earlier in the episode, sees Janeway fall into a trance. This scene encapsulates the threat of seduction that usually poses great risks to the Gothic heroine (Anolik 25). In *Jane Eyre*, Rochester, if not for external intervention, would have married Jane illegally without admitting the existence of his dangerous wife whom he has imprisoned within the house, having already admitted to ill-judged sexual liaisons with a string of lovers earlier in his life. In *Rebecca*, the second Mrs. de Winter supports her husband even after she finds out that he has murdered his first spouse. In both of these narratives, the object of the Gothic heroine's desire behaves dangerously and immorally. Seduction at their hands may well prove to be a perilous thing.

Janeway's romantic (un)availability (both as herself and as Lucille in her holonovel) is complicated further still by her character's marital status. In "Cathexis," the role she plays is immediately established as "Mrs. Davenport," a married woman. With no reference to a "Mr. Davenport" ever made within the holonovel, he becomes yet another of the narrative's mysteries. That he is never mentioned by Janeway or Lord Burleigh as their romantic chemistry intensifies, however, suggests that Lucille may be a widow (the fact that she does not wear Victorian mourning dress might indicate that a considerable amount of time has passed since his death). The absence of her husband within the context of a Gothic novel is troubling: how did he die? And might she herself have been the cause? As most Gothic heroines are unmarried (at least for the majority of their novels), the existence of a Mr. Davenport suggests a lover in Janeway's own past, and may be a reference to the looming shadow of the fiancé she has left behind in the Alpha Quadrant, central to the intense guilt she experiences in this episode.

Conclusion

It is evident, having considered the range of motifs with which Janeway's holonovel plays, and the corresponding concerns in Janeway's existence off the holodeck, that she can be situated as a heroine within her own Gothic narrative, albeit one with a sci-fi foundation. This, then, raises the question: why does Janeway participate in a narrative with an explicitly nineteenth-century setting, and one laced with dead mothers, oppressive housekeepers, and eerie noises in the night? Ruth Bienstock Anolik claims that the original reason for the emergence of these tropes was as a cultural warning to female readers of the dangers that marriage might pose through the loss of their property and independence, her argument crystallizing around certain laws which restricted women's autonomy in the eighteenth and nineteenth centuries (38). Speaking of one particular example of twentieth-century Gothic literature, she asks, "why would [an author] re-construct [these tropes] at a time when women were becoming increasingly liberated and vocal? … By [the twentieth century] … such warning appears belated and superfluous" (38). Anolik suggests that twentieth-century Gothic narratives that perpetuate the threat of patriarchal systems might be interpreted as "solely the product of literary influence … haunted by the nightmares of a haunted literary tradition" (38). This is indeed the case with Janeway's holonovel, which self-consciously adopts the conventions—and clichés—of Gothic literature in order to position itself in the center of a web of chilling (if familiar) motifs.

Yet *Voyager* offers a counter to Anolik's somewhat idealistic claim that total equality between men and women had been reached by the close of the twentieth-century. *Voyager* does depict a female captain constrained within a patriarchal system and judged by the standards of a patriarchal culture. As Phyllis M. Betz records:

> When a female captain was introduced into the Star Trek franchise, Captain Janeway in *Voyager*, many fans responded negatively, stressing, not surprisingly, many of the same arguments offered to justify the unsuitability of women assuming roles as leaders of nations. What is important to note is that this series was televised in the 1990s, so despite the social advancements made by women, their appearance in genre fantasy still causes tensions and criticism from readers [14].

Janeway exists within the patriarchal matrices of both the twentieth and twenty-fourth centuries, yet her enactment of a Gothic narrative seeks to free her from their confinement. Traditionally we might not expect a woman to turn to Gothic genres for liberation, but Janeway demonstrates many of the markers of the Gothic heroine's empowerment and few of her shortcomings and restrictions. Linda Dryden asserts that "[i]n gothic, fantasy and horror the representation of women tends to focus on female sexuality, the female as object of the male gaze, and the female as victim, usually in a sexual or erotic manner" (154). "[T]he science fiction genre," she claims—and she explicitly refers to the *Star Trek* franchise within this bracket—"perpetuates female stereotypes from the Gothic genre" (155). While in many ways Janeway conforms to the long-established notion of the Gothic heroine, there are ways in which she resists total assimilation by this stereotype, all while expressing her femininity in a rare opportunity to don a dress and earrings: she escapes objectification, stands by her decision to suppress her sexuality, and throws off the yoke of victimhood.

While it is unlikely that James had starships and space travel in mind when writing *The Turn of the Screw*, there is one passage in particular which resonates with *Voyager* and Janeway's predicament in particular, in which the governess "had the fancy of our being almost as lost as a handful of passengers in a great drifting ship. Well, I was strangely at the helm!" (James 163–64). Although Janeway's relationship with the tradition of Gothic heroines is made explicit by her holonovel, the situation in which she finds herself, separated from her home by unthinkable distance and "at the helm" of "a great drifting ship" (an updated version of the isolated manor house, perhaps) is Gothic in and of itself. *Star Trek*'s famous mantra—"to boldly go where no *man* has gone before"—is reversed in Janeway; rather than a narrative of male-gendered penetrative exploration, her ultimate mission is one of a feminized "home-coming" (Mousoutzanis 69), an escape from the Gothic expanse of unexplored space and, ultimately, all of the dangers it conceals.

Works Cited

Anolik, Ruth Bienstock. "The Missing Mother: The Meanings of Maternal Absence in the Gothic Mode." *Modern Language Studies* 33.1/2 (2003): 24–43.

Barrett, Michèle. "Post-Feminism." *Understanding Contemporary Society: Theories of the Present*. Ed. Gary Browning, Abigail Halcli and Frank Webster. London: SAGE, 2000. 46–56.

Betz, Phyllis M. *The Lesbian Fantastic: A Critical Study of Science Fiction, Fantasy, Paranormal and Gothic Writings*. Jefferson, NC: McFarland, 2011.

Bowring, Michèle A. "Resistance Is *Not* Futile: Liberating Captain Janeway from the Masculine-Feminine Dualism of Leadership." *Gender, Work and Organization* 11.4 (2004): 381–405.

Brabazon, Tara. *Ladies Who Lunge: Celebrating Difficult Women*. Sydney: UNSW Press, 2002.

Broderick, James F. *The Literary Galaxy of Star Trek: An Analysis of References and Themes in the Television Series and Films*. Jefferson, NC: McFarland, 2006.

Brontë, Charlotte. *Jane Eyre*. Ed. Margaret Smith. Oxford: Oxford University Press, 2008.

Brown, Jeffrey A. *Dangerous Curves: Action Heroines, Gender, Fetishism, and Popular Culture*. Jackson: University Press of Mississippi, 2011.

"Cathexis." *Star Trek: Voyager*. Writ. Brannon Braga. Dir. Kim Friedman. CBS. 1 May. 1995.

Dove-Viebahn, Aviva. "Embodying Hybridity, (En)gendering Community in *Star Trek: Voyager*." *Women's Studies* 36.8 (2007): 597–618.

Dryden, Linda. "*She*: Gothic Reverberations in *Star Trek: First Contact*." *Postfeminist Gothic: Critical Interventions in Contemporary Culture*. Ed. Benjamin A. Brabon and Stéphanie Genz. Basingstoke: Palgrave Macmillan, 2007. 154–169.

du Maurier, Daphne. *Rebecca*. New York: The Modern Library, 1943.

James, Henry. *The Aspern Papers; The Turn of the Screw; The Liar; The Two Faces*. New York: Charles Scribner's Sons, 1908.

"Learning Curve." *Star Trek: Voyager*. Writ. Jean Louise Matthias and Ronald Wilkerson. Dir. David Livingston. CBS. 22 May. 1995.

Light, Alison. "'Returning to Manderley': Romance Fiction, Female Sexuality and Class." *Feminist Review* 16 (1984): 7–25.

McIntee, David. *Delta Quadrant: The Unofficial Guide to Voyager*. London: Virgin, 2000.

Mousoutzanis, Aris. "'Death is irrelevant': Gothic Science Fiction and the Biopolitics of

Empire." *Gothic Science Fiction 1980–2010*. Ed. Sara Wasson and Emily Alder. Liverpool: Liverpool University Press, 2011. 57–72.

Murray, Janet Horowitz. *Hamlet on the Holodeck: The Future of Narrative in Cyberspace*. New York: Free Press, 1997.

"Persistence of Vision." *Star Trek: Voyager*. Writ. Jeri Taylor. Dir. James L. Conway. CBS. 30 October. 1995.

Poe, Stephen Edward. *Star Trek Voyager: A Vision of the Future*. New York: Pocket Books, 1998.

"The Q and the Grey." *Star Trek: Voyager*. Writ. Kenneth Biller. Dir. Cliff Bole. CBS. 27 November. 1996.

"Threshold." *Star Trek: Voyager*. Writ. Brannon Braga. Dir. Alexander Singer. CBS. 29 January. 1996.

Strange New Worlds
Gender Disparity in Star Trek: TOS

MICHAEL PRINGLE

A common-place corrective amongst Trekkies is to deny that Captain Kirk usually handled conflict with a phaser-blast or a punch, and while this is largely true it does not quite explain away all the phaser-blasts, pseudo-judo blows, and battles in that occur in the original series of *Star Trek*. Despite Starfleet's peaceful mission there is clearly a warrior ethos in Kirk's character, and violent, "masculine" action is a staple element of the series. By all accounts, Gene Roddenberry had the character of his Captain for *Star Trek* firmly in mind long before he had solidified the makeup of the rest of the bridge crew.[1] He wanted a different kind of hero who worked and played well with others in a more diverse, progressive future where all genders, races, nationalities, and even species could pull together towards a greater good. The goal was to create a hyper-professional meritocracy where "old" ideas of difference didn't matter anymore. In some ways he succeeded in creating an alternate model for a heroic male lead with a mixed (race, gender, species) crew, but in significant ways his series could not break free of conventional gender stereotypes of the mid–1960s and failed to provide women with the roles their place on the bridge seemed to promise. Despite only a three-year run, James T. Kirk became a heroic icon of masculine leadership for several generations, with Spock, Bones, and Scotty trailing only slightly in popularity. For women on the series, only Uhura comes close to that iconic status, and only because she toughed out the early years before being allowed more substantial roles. By looking at the pilot, early scripts from the first season, and various autobiographies that highlight corporate pressure and the "casting-couch" culture, this essay will trace the successes of *Star Trek: TOS* in creating a fresh take on heroic masculinity (specifically in Kirk, Spock and Bones), but also its failure in reimagining women's roles (specifically in Uhura, Yeoman Rand, and Nurse Chapel). The original series creates interesting male bonds and roles, but largely re-inscribes stereotypical women's roles in spite of Roddenberry's vision of future equality. What was new and fresh in the series largely develops among the male leads, and while some episodes stretch the possibilities for women's roles, it is the later manifestations of the series that would better incorporate women as essential crew members.

"The Cage" (1965) served as the pilot for the series, and the handsome Captain Christopher Pike is the most clearly conceived character on the *Enterprise*. The rest of the bridge crew is quite different from that which would inhabit the series, most notably in the character of "Number One" played by Majel Barret (later "Nurse Chapel" in the series). She is a cool, unemotional professional who is described as "a human computer." Spock is also there, yelling most of his lines, smiling warmly, and inexplicably limping. Apparently, women are new in Starfleet command positions because Captain Pike barks at a young yeoman for entering the bridge (though she was following his orders), then mutters as she leaves: "I still can't get used to women on the bridge." The comment receives a raised eyebrow from the Executive Officer, to which Pike, responds, "Of course, you're different Number One.[2]" The exchange creates an awkward moment on the bridge that highlights the gender shift. It is her character who defeats the Talosians (actually women playing alien, male roles), sees through their illusions, and calls their bluff by overloading phasers to improvise the bombs which force the release of Pike. While leading the rescue mission she delivers crisp orders, to which one crewman responds, "Yes sir … er, yes ma'am." Roddenberry clearly intended to have women in positions of power within Starfleet, but test audiences for "The Cage" (both men and women) rejected a woman executive officer, and studio executives insisted on changes. Her role was cut, Spock moved up to Number One, and her character traits eventually emerge as Vulcan characteristics. Despite her "alien," cool demeanor in the pilot, the Talosians (who can read minds) declare that she harbors sexual fantasies about the Captain. Again, the sublimation of human desires deemed necessary in a woman officer becomes an essential, "alien" characteristic of the iconic Spock, and the most dynamic, interesting roles would generally be assigned to men.

Where No Man Has Gone Before

It seems that *Star Trek: TOS* had greater success in imagining alternative male roles from those prevalent in the 1960s than with female roles; however, taken individually, it can be difficult to distinguish specific differences in the three male leads from other male characters on television in the era—cop, doctor, cowboy, detective, patriarch—because at different times they partake of them all. Science Fiction allows for greater character-deviation from the norm (ranch, hospital, precinct station, family home, etc.) due to the range of settings, situations, and thematic "big questions" which mark the genre. Kirk has often been characterized as a "cowboy" figure, riding into the new frontier and bringing justice and civilization at phaser-point or a quick punch to the chin. Roddenberry had pitched the series as an extension of the western genre, promising the kind of action sequences and shoot-outs that audiences seemed to appreciate. "This newborn proposal for a series downplayed the intergalactic aspects of the show by describing it (as all Trekkers worth their pointed polyvinyl ears know) as *Wagon Train* to the stars" (Shatner 21). Network executives actually held Roddenberry to his promises of action, and those who see Kirk as a shoot-em-up cowboy figure can find plenty of examples to support their claims. It is important to note, however, that Kirk's character is not easy to shoe-horn into the category. He is not a stoic, rugged individualist; rather, he is an impassioned and articulate defender of humanist values, a skilled diplomat, and he is always (ultimately) a team player. Generally he tries for nonviolent solutions and is a firm proponent of the Federation's non-interference policy (unless, of course, he really, *really* thinks they ought to interfere). Captain Kirk is clearly a commanding leader, and some episodes paint him in more militaristic colors than others: for example, a tightly scripted and well-directed episode from season one is "Balance of Terror," where the *Enterprise* responds to a Neutral-Zone infraction by the Romulans and pits Kirk against their newest ship and finest Commander. The tense, cat-and-mouse action between the two ships is patterned after submarine war-movies, and the episode highlights the *Enterprise* as a battleship rather than an exploratory vessel "on a five year mission to seek out, and explore new worlds." The ship has teeth, and Kirk is quite prepared to bite when necessary—and sometimes when it is not.

In sharp contrast, another episode from the first season that shows a different aspect of the Captain's militaristic side is "Errand of Mercy," where Kirk becomes increasingly disgusted by the Arganians, a peaceful people who refuse to fight back against the ruthlessly dictatorial Klingons. Kirk actually comes to resemble Kor, the brutal Klingon Commander, in his disdain for a people who will not fight for their freedom. The Arganians repeatedly tell Kirk they neither want nor need his assistance, but he refuses to believe it and insists on saving them. It turns out that they are an extremely advanced race (Spock assesses them "as far above us … as we are to the amoeba"), and that they truly needed no assistance with the Klingon invaders. Kirk and Kor find themselves arguing for the same "right" to fight each other when the Arganians step in to stop the impending battle, and then leave in a blaze of light saying "beings such as yourselves cause us pain." Unlike "Balance of Terror," which clearly valorizes Kirk's military acumen, "Errand of Mercy" points to the dangers of relying too much on military force and a bellicose attitude. The cold war parallels are clear in the episode, and the entire command crew is chastened at the conclusion, when Kirk summarizes their actions for the ship's log. After he turns off the recorder there is an uneasy pause, which Kirk fills, admitting "I'm embarrassed." As Captain of a starship, Kirk must be an intergalactic warrior, policeman, investigator, diplomat, scientist, damage controller, rescuer, etc. In many situations it is not immediately clear which hat he should be wearing, and he sometimes gets it wrong. Furthermore, this study disagrees with the common criticism that William Shatner was a bad actor; rather, it can be argued that he did a very good job of bringing the character of Kirk to (bigger-than) life. While there are many scenes that could have used another take or two, it is important to remember that they were producing 30 episodes a year on a shoe-string budget. In comparison, a premium, one-hour series today will only film about a third of that number on a much more lavish set and with a more robust budget. Audience expectations are much higher today, particularly in terms of special effects, polished acting, and careful editing, but it is unfair to bring those expectations to a show created under conditions from half a century ago. Even for an avowed fan there is always a certain nostalgic, "campy" fun in watching the excesses of the series (and some of Shatner's more eccentric performances), but in re-watching the first season in chronological order one is struck again by how good and interesting *Star Trek: TOS* manages to be despite its limitations, and much of that interest is generated by the male leads.

The most common formula for framing the success of the combined characters of Kirk, Spock, and McCoy is "chemistry." The term implies bonds and attractions (frequently framed as homoerotic), and without disputing that chemistry played a role, one can assert that the male leads were formally structured in such a way as to enhance and dramatize the difficult decisions Kirk often had to make. As mentioned above, individual episodes force Kirk to quickly assess what role the *Enterprise* should be playing in whatever crisis they encounter. Mr. Spock and Dr. Leonard McCoy ("Bones") are clearly scripted to be nearly opposites, often giving Kirk conflicting advice during tense situations, almost parallel with the classic "good and bad angels on the shoulder" (for example, "The City on the Edge of Forever" or "The Galileo 7"). Of course neither is unequivocally right or wrong—the series was at least as interested in ambiguity as in moral closure—but the pair allowed scriptwriters to clearly outline the basic moral dilemma surrounding some of the tougher decisions Kirk had to make. Dr. McCoy was added to the series a few episodes into season one, most likely as a counter-balance to Spock's logical, utilitarian outlook. "Bones" seems to be a bundle of contradictions: he's a liberal "good-ol-boy"; the best Doctor in Starfleet whose most common diagnosis is "He's dead, Jim"; a sensitive, empathetic nurturer who is a hot-headed bellower; a pacifist on a warship; a careful diagnostician who relies on gut-instinct; and a rule-breaker who constantly forces others to follow medical regulations. Somehow, DeForest Kelly makes the character work, and his romantic insistence on individuality, intuition, and humanism often run into conflict with Spock's utilitarianism, best summed up in his famous line from the film *The Wrath of Khan:* "the needs of the many outweigh the needs of the few, or the one." In the movie Kirk ultimately chooses the one (actually, via *deus ex machina*, he gets both), but in what is often touted as the best episode from season one, "The City on the Edge of Forever" (written by Harlan Ellison) he sides with the many.

While there are many examples of polar attitudes between Bones and Spock, the Edith Keeler incident is one of the most dramatic. In a time-paradox plot, a temporarily deranged Dr. McCoy finds himself transported into Earth's past by "The Guardian of Forever," where he alters the future such that his own future ceases to exist. Kirk and Spock travel back to locate him and to fix the time alteration, where they find that the beautiful, philanthropic, brilliant, charismatic Edith Keeler (played by Joan Collins) is the source of the "time eddy." The paradox is that Dr. McCoy saves her from dying in a traffic accident in 1930, thus permitting Edith to lead a pacifist movement that delays the American entrance into World War II and allows the Germans to develop the atomic bomb first and win the war. Kirk's job is to stop Bones from altering their time-line, but while in the past attempting to do so he falls in love with Edith Keeler. Mentioned earlier in the essay as one of the strong women characters, she is in many ways the most positive human character in the whole series, framed as nearly perfect by "future" standards (her only fault is being too far ahead of her time, in that she champions the Federation's ethos centuries before it becomes possible to maintain). Before he knows her role in the paradox, Kirk begins dating her, and as he finds out she is the problem he reveals to Spock, "I believe I'm in love with Edith Keeler." Spock responds, "Jim, Edith Keeler must die." In the time-paradox she represents the end of the entire Federation's future even as she promotes its values, but as a serious possible partner for Kirk she also represents a dangerous threat to the series itself, in that Kirk must first and foremost remain faithful to his ship and his crew. Face averted, the Captain clings to Bones to prevent him from saving her, and Edith Keeler dutifully falls under a truck. While the doctor did not know about the paradox, McCoy could never have been brought to the conclusion that Edith must die, and in a horrified, accusatory tone he asks Kirk, "Do you know what you've done?" Spock, who insisted repeatedly on the need for her death based on the needs of the many, has to answer for him: "He knows Doctor. He knows."

While Spock is only half Vulcan, it is his human side he chooses to repress. In opposition to Bones he is data-driven, rule-oriented, logical, and definitely not "one of the boys." More than just a foil to the doctor, Spock's "alien-ness" plays a key role in creating a different kind of male interaction in the series. Fifty years later it is difficult to see what is so alien about Spock's character, but in 1966 Roddenberry had to fight hard to keep both Uhura and Spock on the bridge, because they were deemed so different that they might alienate a mostly white, conservative, Neilson-poll audience. After movies such as *Star Wars, Alien, Predator,* and *Avatar*, eccentric eyebrows and pointy ears barely register as different, yet what seems minor to us today was deemed profoundly different then. *Star Trek: TOS* highlights difference in many episodes (certainly a key cultural anxiety of the 1960s) and as Frederic Jameson argues, offers our present to us in a more comprehensible, "defamiliarized" form: "SF does not seriously attempt to imagine the 'real' future of our social system. Rather, its multiple mock futures serve quite a different function of transforming our own present into the determinate past of something yet to come" (565). In "Tomorrow Is Yesterday," Captain Christopher, a near future fighter pilot (late 1960s) is beamed aboard a time-traveling *Enterprise*, where Spock's appearance shocks him so much he cannot speak. Of course this is another kind of defamiliarization, where human attributes are presented in an alien form—it may, in fact, be impossible to imagine the truly alien—but his otherness removes him from the human norm, which tends to highlight "normal" assumptions and call for explanations. Spock's alien status sometimes serves as a plot device, (for example, "The Amok Time" and "Devil in the Dark") but more often it tends to make noticeable certain unspoken assumptions in human interactions. Because he is humorless Spock becomes the butt of some jokes on the bridge, where Kirk and others smile knowingly; however, the joke is sometimes turned on the humans when they discover that Spock's ways are superior. Spock is outsider enough to cast an alien eye on human behavior, but insider enough to establish his credibility as a critic.

The Enemy Within

Number One (Spock's role) was originally assigned to a woman. Clearly, Roddenberry wanted women to take on active and important roles in the series, and some restrictions on his vision came from audience expectations and the exigencies of a weekly TV series: for example, the requirement by NBC executives for action driven plots and the rejection by test audiences of a women Executive Officer in the series pilot. "The Cage," while admired, was deemed too "cerebral," and lacking the simple action formula that drew high ratings. To green-light the series executives wanted to vet the first three scripts (more action/less complexity), insisted on a male Number One, and also wanted to jettison Spock's character, but Roddenberry held his ground on his only alien: "I knew I couldn't keep both, so I gave the stoicism of the female officer to Spock, and married the actress who played Number One. Thank God it wasn't the other way around. I mean, Leonard's cute, but ..." (qtd. in Shatner 68). Roddenberry did not give up on having strong women's roles, but they tended not to be assigned to regular crewmembers in the first season. The only permanently assigned woman officer on the bridge is Uhura, and while she is portrayed as very professional and capable (often "manning" a range of bridge stations when others are pulled away or incapable) she is generally a bit player throughout season one. Women do not serve simply as eye-candy in miniskirts, however, and it is surprising in looking back through the first season with an eye towards gender roles that several times Kirk is saved by a woman. For example, in the third episode, "Where No Man Has Gone Before," Sally Kellerman[3] portrays Dr. Elizabeth Dehner, a psychiatrist with ESP. When the ship passes through a "field" that enhances the powers of those with ESP, Kirk's old friend and crew mate Gary Mitchell quickly becomes drunk on his god-like power and threatens the ship and crew. Dehner, who also gains the powers, joins Mitchell briefly, but comes to Kirk's aid in his battle against Mitchell, allowing the captain to triumph. The two "gods" have a pre-jedi-lightening-bolt-battle, which leads to both their deaths. She resists the temptations of absolute power and saves Kirk and the crew through self-sacrifice. There are other examples of one-time, strong women's roles in the first season such as Dr. Helen Noel, "Dagger of the Mind"; Lenore Karidian (strong, in a crazed-serial-killer sort of way), "The Conscience of the King"; Areel Shaw, "Court Martial"; and Edith Keeler in "The City on the Edge of Forever."

Many critics simply assume sexism in the series, and there are certainly examples to support that position, but (as an admitted fan) I wish to point out that *Star Trek: TOS* at least made an effort to place women in important positions in its proposed future. The recurring women characters on the *Enterprise* (Uhura, Yeoman Rand, Nurse Chapel) tend to be slotted into supporting roles during the first season, though in "What Are Little Girls Made Of?" Nurse Chapel plays a heroic role in defeating her former lover, the mad scientist who wants to rebuild humanity in android form. As *the* female bridge officer, Uhura was the most obvious candidate for more substantial parts, and writers tried to incorporate her more fully into the series. In her autobiography *Beyond Uhura*, Nichelle Nichols tells of strong racist attitudes at the studio lot, recalling racial slurs, withheld fan mail, and the cutting of any scene in which she played a significant part. She went to Gene Roddenberry near the end of season one to quit: "I've put up with the cuts and the racism, but I just can't do it anymore.... Gene, you've been wonderful, but there's too much wrong here, and I can't fix it" (163). She met Dr. Martin Luther King, Jr., at an NAACP fundraiser the next evening, and told him she was quitting the series when he mentioned he was a fan: "'You *cannot*' he replied firmly,' and you *must* not. 'Don't you realize how important your presence, your character is?'" (164). King convinced her to stay (to Roddenberry's delight) and it proved to be a good choice because her role on the show became more significant over time and ultimately led to a lucrative film career. Nichols brought poise and dignity to the role of Uhura, and in retrospect, King seems to have been right: while Uhura's role would not stand up to the scrutiny of later feminist criticism, the positive portrayal of a black women working on an equal footing with white men was an important antidote for the negative racial stereotypes of black women on 1960's American television. In other words, even though she wasn't doing much on the bridge during season one, the simple fact that she was there as part of the command crew matters. Nichols places the blame for her poor treatment at the corporate level of the network, a point on which most of the actors seem to agree. However, there were also some attitudes within the "inner circle" of writers, directors, and producers which limited the scope of women's roles in the series.

Despite some strong parts for women in *Star Trek: TOS,* even the best roles were cast in relationship to a strong male counterpart, while men could have strong roles on their own. Also, men enjoyed a kind of "band of brothers" camaraderie, but the women did not have a corresponding band of sisters. Uhura fits awkwardly into this model (witness her singing scenes in "Chalie X" and "The Conscience of the King"), and while she is not paired with a strong male character (probably due to fears of miscegenation at the corporate level) she seems more of an entertainer than an essential contributor to the ship's mission. Roddenberry's vision of a future meritocracy where talent and hard work count more than race or gender was a strong element of the DNA of *Star Trek: TOS*, but in the more pragmatic world of bringing a weekly series to television there was a strong "casting–couch" culture, where women's roles were cast less on what they could do than on what they were willing to do. Roddenberry had affairs with both Nichelle Nichols and Majel Barrett before the series began, prior to casting them on the show (he later married Barrett after his divorce from his first wife), and the belief was strong on the set that any woman who got a good part had slept with the boss. In her autobiography *The Longest Trek*, Grace Lee Whitney, who played Yeoman Rand in season one, felt the need to deny that she had a "personal relationship" with Roddenberry even 32 years after she had left the show: "Who knows? Maybe if Gene had gotten me in the sack, I might have done all three seasons of *Star Trek* instead of only half a season!" (73). During season one Whitney was raped on the studio lot by a man she only refers to as "The Executive," who lured her away from a cast party by telling her how he planned to push to develop the character of Yeoman Rand more fully in the series. In her autobiography she parallels the assault with "The Enemy Within," an episode where the Captain is split into two beings by a transporter malfunction: "Good Kirk" and "Evil Kirk." The violent, rapacious version of the Captain tries to rape Yeoman Rand, who then accuses "Good Kirk" of the act with the corroboration of other crewmembers. After the two Kirks are reunited, an insinuating Mr. Spock (entirely out of character) say to Rand: "The imposter had some ... uhm ... very interesting qualities, wouldn't you say, Yeoman?" Grace Lee Whitney analyzes the scene:

> I can't imagine a more cruel and insensitive comment a man (or Vulcan) could make to a woman who had just been through a sexual assault! But then, some men really do think women want to be raped. So the writer of the script (ostensibly Richard Matheson—although the line could have been added by Gene Roddenberry or an assistant scribe) gives us a leering Mr. Spock who suggests that Yeoman Rand *enjoyed* being raped and found the evil Kirk attractive. This scene is doubly ironic in view of how wonderfully caring and compassionate the *real* Leonard Nimoy was a few weeks later when the *real* Grace Lee Whitney was sexually assaulted and violated by The Executive [95].

The fact that Whitney believes that Roddenberry, or any writer for the series, might have added that line is indicative of more dangerous and negative gender stereotypes and biases in *Star Trek: TOS*, despite its overtly progressive agenda for gender roles.

Restrictions on female roles would appear to emerge from Roddenberry's difficulty in thinking beyond 1960s gender stereotypes; and though he peoples the *Enterprise* with men and women, early scripts often falter in describing what the women are actually doing there in their revealing miniskirts. Women are frequently framed with men staring appreciatively at their swaying backsides as they sashay by to the brassy rhythms of 1960s "sexy" music (for example, in "Tomorrow Is Yesterday," when the time-traveling Captain Christopher is gob-smacked to find women on the *Enterprise*). The male gaze certainly frames much of their activities, and the miniskirts seem to be exploitive, however, Nichelle Nichols makes an interesting point about them:

> Some thought it demeaning for a woman in the command crew to be dressed so sexily. It always surprised me because I never saw it that way. After all, the show was created in the age of the miniskirt, and the crew women's uniforms were very comfortable. Contrary to what people think today, no one really saw it as demeaning back then. In fact, the miniskirt was a symbol of sexual liberation. More to the point, though, in the twenty-third century, you are respected for your abilities regardless of what you do or do not wear [169].

Part of the great appeal of *Star Trek: TOS*, and much of the reason Nichols didn't quit the series, is precisely that vision of a future where abilities matter more than race or gender. Women are often put on display in the series, but in one of the more nuanced discussions of gender in the series Patricia Vettel-Becker argues its central aesthetic was female beauty, and that "the series may have resonated with female viewers at the time who were renegotiating their own feminine positions within a rapidly changing social and technological landscape" (144). As mentioned above, there are a number of strong women's roles in the first season that seem to support the vision; however, (and here I might also add "alas" as a fan) too often women are portrayed through diminished gender stereotypes that deeply undercut the humanistic vision of equality.

What Are Little Girls Made Of?

The most blatantly stereotyped feminine roles in the series are those of seductresses, surprisingly however, these roles often undercut essentialized notions of gender: for example, the construction of "Nancy" (actually a salt-vampire masquerading as Bones' lover in "The Man-Trap"), or Eve in "Mudd's Women," who proves to be far more substantial than a pretty face. To approach the constructed nature of femininity in the series, a good place to begin is with the machines constructed to be "female." In "What Are Little Girls Made Of?" Dr. Corby, an old flame of Nurse Chapel (who, we discover here, gave up a promising career in bio-research to join Starfleet), turns up alive after being lost for ten years on a hostile planet. It unfolds that Corby employed technology from an ancient civilization to transfer his consciousness into an android—and while at it, he also constructed a sexy, scantily clad android (Andrea) to serve him. Corby's ultimate goal is to use this process to eliminate death, to edit out negative human desires, and to create a galaxy-wide utopia. He holds the away team captive while he tries to convince them of the viability of his scheme, and to escape Kirk is forced to unleash his beastly sexuality on poor Andrea (kissing her), whose android circuitry is simply not up to it. In a scene that may have inspired Mike Meyer's Fembots, Kirk sexually arouses the "Little Girl" who then stalks the hallways looking for someone to kiss/kill. When the Kirk-android spurns her she calmly destroys it with a phaser, then finds the Corby–android and tries to explain her nascent arousal: "To … love … you … to … kiss … you …" She manifests a male fantasy of an ultimate desiring-machine. The painful dialogue is mercifully cut short by a blast from a phaser pressed between the two androids (perhaps a mutual suicide?). Despite being AI, Andrea the android is infantilized, needy, emotionally driven, and hyper-sexualized in a way that is very different to the "male" androids, which reinforces the general division of gender types on the series.

The episode "Tomorrow Is Yesterday" presents another example of created femininity, where the ship's computer has a gender issue. We discover that the *Enterprise* had recently been overhauled on Cygnet 14, a "planet dominated by women," and feeling that the computer lacked in personality, they gave it a female one. The voice oozes sexuality and addresses the Captain as "Dear." In an otherwise tense episode this "malfunction" serves as comic relief, where Kirk's every interaction with the computer sounds as though he's called for phone sex (again highlighting the way depictions of femininity fit into the pattern of male fantasies, though this interaction is very public). At one point, an affronted Mr. Spock lists the computer's symptoms, ending primly with "It also has an unfortunate tendency to giggle." The sultry, sulky, weepy, giggly computer is definitively "feminine," and as a comic device it actually works well in the show. Because the voice is so exaggerated, it may be intended as a parody of such gender stereotypes (it was written by D.C. Fontana, the only woman writer for the series), but it can be difficult to determine tone, as the show is still filmed and directed by men. After all, this is an episode where Kirk and Christopher spend some time ogling the swaying backside of a woman crew member, yet Kirk certainly finds himself uneasy under similar, unwanted sexual attention. The general portrayal of women characters onboard the *Enterprise* do not vary much from the gendered "programs." It is interesting to note how much literal hand-holding occurs during tense situations in the first season of *Star Trek: TOS*, where strong male characters reach out to hold the hands of frightened crew-women. During action sequences men step forward to shield women, who then cower in fear behind them. Rather than add to the strength of an away team, women tend to become liabilities: falling when they run, seeking protection, shrieking at any shock, and weeping. For every Dr. Elizabeth Dehner who boldly puts her life on the line and fights to save others, there are five whimpering, fearful crew-women hiding behind a male counterpart. Even competent professionals like Uhura and Nurse Chapel do a fair amount of peering fearfully around the shoulder of a male protector. This "weaker-vessel" mentality is aligned with frequent images of women submitting to male domination.

The dominant/submissive pattern is evident throughout season one, where fawning women coo over Kirk's power. The most blatant example, however, does not involve Kirk. In "Space Seed" the ship's historian, Lieutenant Marla McGivers, becomes enslaved to Khan Noonien Singh's sexual magnetism. Khan (played by Ricardo Montalbán) is a superman from "the Eugenics Wars of the 1990s," who managed to escape earth and survive on a "sleeper ship" with his fellow uber-mensch. Called aboard to render her opinion of the dormant dominants, Lt. McGivers kneels before Khan's sleeping pod and purrs "Magnificent." Once awakened he quickly seizes power over the Lieutenant, undoing her hair and warning her that Caesars such as himself "dare take what they want." He humiliates her by making her beg to remain in his presence, physically abuses her by twisting her arm until she writhes at his feet, then "forces" her to join him in taking over the *Enterprise.* Their relationship moves quickly from one of dominance and submission to sado-masochistic. As Grace Lee Whitney put it, "Some men really do think women want to be raped." There would be nothing wrong with the series exploring a popular sexual fantasy if it recognized it as fantasy and offered alternate possible roles, but one can argue that the "normal" mode of sexual representation on *Star Trek* only slightly varies, and that even women characters who seem to be strong on their own are brought back under submission, usually by attraction to Kirk (Edith Keeler in "The City on the Edge of Forever," Helen Noel in "Dagger of the Mind," and Areel Shaw in "Court Martial," for some examples). A look back at the actual military bases, science labs, and space programs of the 1960s reveals an almost universally male population (witness the famous footage of mission control during the first moon landing), so as with the case of Uhura's character, I think it matters that women were at least present in Starfleet. The professed ethos of the Federation (and, implicitly of *Star Trek: TOS*) is equality, and the series makes gestures towards gender equality even as some rather dangerous and stifling gender stereotypes undercut that goal and make at least part of the "future" look disturbingly like the 1960s network-lot from which the series emerges. The Captain's relationship to men certainly overshadows his connections to women, and it is important to note that his flings (with the possible exception of Edith Keeler) are framed as a kind of infidelity to the *Enterprise* (always a "she"), and several episodes sum up the relationship between Captain and ship as a marriage.

James T. Kirk, Mr. Spock, and Dr. Leonard McCoy created a fresh take on heroic masculinity in the mid–60s, and while it was not appreciated by the network which cancelled it after three seasons, the trio became iconic for several generations of viewers. While some of that appeal was "chemistry" between the lead actors who brought the roles vividly to life, much of it also arose from structural tensions between the opposing world-views of Bones and Spock, as well as to the wider possibilities of setting, theme, and action available within the Science Fiction genre. While those possibilities were there for the women characters as well, they were rarely allowed to fully exploit them, and despite some successes, the series failed to live up to the values of equality for women that the Federation was ostensibly spreading across the universe. At its best, *Star Trek: TOS* points to a bright future that achieves racial, gender, and class equality, while at its worst, it espouses those values even as it undercuts them with some tired stereotypes. While some critics have dismissed the series as sexist, racist, and jingoistic, it is important to step back to the time period and see what else was available on network television. If the series failed to live up to the expectations of the next generation of feminists, post-structuralists, and post-humanists, it should still get some credit for offering alternative models in its day. Audiences understand what is best about the series, and every time the franchise powers up for another voyage there are legions of them ready to ship out again.

Notes

1. I draw from Roddenberry's discussion of the genesis of *Star Trek* in selected, excerpted clips of interviews that can be found throughout Paramount's digitally remastered collection of the original series (2009) by selecting the "Additional Data" heading in the main menu of each disc.

2. All direct quotes from episodes, and specific references to scenes, are drawn from *Star Trek the Original Series*. Season 1. Paramount Pictures, 2009. Blue-Ray disc.

3. Most famous for her role as "Hot Lips" O'Houlihan in *M*A*S*H*.

Works Cited

Jameson, Frederic. "Progress Verus Utopia; or, Can We Imagine the Future?" 1982. *Science Fiction: Stories and Contexts*. Compact ed. Ed. Heather Masri. Bedford St. Martins, 2015, pp. 557–72.

Nichols, Nichelle. *Beyond Uhura:* Star Trek *and Other Memories*. Boulevard Books, 1994.

Shatner, William, and Chris Kreski. *Star Trek Memories*. HarperCollins, 1993.

Star Trek: The Original Series. Season one. CBS, 1966. Remastered with additional commentary by Paramount Pictures, 2009. Blue-Ray disc.

Vettel-Becker, Patricia. "*Star Trek*, Aesthetics, and 1960s Femininity." *Frontiers: A Journal of Women's Studies*, Vol. 35, No. 2, 2014, pp. 143–178.

Whitney, Grace Lee, and Jim Denney. *The Longest Trek: My Tour of the Galaxy*. Quill Driver Books, 1998.

Female Leadership, Sacrifice and Technological Mastery on *Star Trek: Voyager*

Lorrie Palmer

At its (warp) core, *Star Trek* has always been grounded not just in scientific humanism but in the cultural, physical, and discursive depiction of technology. The appearance and functionality of flip-phones, laptop computers, and touch-screen interfaces have their antecedents in the hand-held tricorders of the series, beginning with the 1966–1969 run of the first TV *Star Trek* (*TOS*), and in the desktop devices and workstations used by the captains and crews in *The Next Generation* (*TNG*), *Voyager* (*VOY*), *Deep Space Nine* (*DS9*) and *Enterprise* (*ENT*), from 1987 through to 2005. There is a scene in *Star Trek: Voyager* (1995–2001), during the episode "Flesh and Blood" (7.9, 7.10), when three women confer together on the technical challenge of disrupting the holo-emitters of another starship. Their expertise drives the narrative logic of the scene as they disrupt traditional portrayals of women and technology (including those embedded within the *Trek* canon). *Voyager* crystallizes a critical nexus in which gender and science fiction conventions meet and diverge, particularly around interlocking articulations of leadership, sacrifice, and technological mastery. Because these traditions have been predominantly embodied by male protagonists, particularly starship captains and their chief engineers across 50 years of *Star Trek* in television and in cinema, *Voyager* emerges as a significant factor in how we understand the gendering of technology in science fiction, in this specific franchise, and in expanding real-world implications. The series positions its three central female characters Captain Kathryn Janeway (Kate Mulgrew), Seven of Nine (Jeri Ryan), and Chief Engineer B'Elanna Torres (Roxann Dawson) in roles of command and authority as they navigate their professional identities over the course of *Voyager*'s long journey through unknown space.

This study will draw out these identities through an overview of *Voyager*'s reception by academics, critics, and fans, particularly as character studies of the three Starfleet women. Textual analysis will frame several notable episodes, including "Dreadnought" (2.17), "Deadlock" (2.21), "Year of Hell" (4.8, 4.9), "Dark Frontier" (5.15, 5.16) and "Endgame" (7.25, 7.26) along with relevant scenes from additional film and television depictions across the franchise. Throughout this discussion, the contrasts between other *Trek* narratives and *Voyager* will show the ways in which leadership is driven by the willingness to sacrifice oneself to save others and that this sacrifice necessitates deep mastery of technological systems. In varying combinations, these narrative themes define *Voyager*. This tech-heavy science fiction series characterizes Janeway, Seven, and B'Elanna as strategic, stable leaders (against contrasting representation of male leaders), while demonstrating what the absence of gender-based power dynamics in outer space can look like (thanks to the series' recurring villain, the Borg Queen). Finally, alongside gendered expressions of trust and control between characters, this study will also highlight several striking parallels in education and mentorship experienced by women and girls that effectively bind together the show's narrative, its active circle of fandom, and society's evolving negotiation of gender roles (and rules).

Origins and Reboots: Men, Women and Starships

Ian Grey has called for a reconsideration of *Star Trek: Voyager* ("Now, 'Voyager': In Praise of the Trekkiest 'Trek' of All," 2013) by pointing to the series' significant representation of women in space. Grey writes: "On *Voyager*, female authority was assumed and unquestioned; women conveyed sexual power without shame and anger without guilt. Even more so than *Buffy*, which debuted two years later, it was the most feminist show in American TV history" (Grey, 2013). Gone, he says, were the militarism and machismo born in *TOS* and later embraced by writer-director J.J. Abrams in his rebooted *Star Trek* (2009). The opening salvo of the new cinematic franchise conflates leadership and fatherhood as James T. Kirk's father George (Chris Hemsworth) sacrifices his life for his ship, his crew, and his wife, Winona (Jennifer Morrison)—at that moment giving birth to their son in an escape pod—by setting the U.S.S. *Kelvin* on a collision course with the hostile Romulan vessel, *Narada*. The ensuing crash is spectacular as a CGI debris storm, a blinding fireball of mutual incineration, and as a classic evocation of the male leadership traditions of *Star Trek*. Starfleet officers will repurpose vital shipboard technologies toward self-sacrifice, the most noble and masculine marker of Federation heroism. As Spock (Leonard Nimoy) dies in the deadly blue glow of radiation while restoring the warp drive in *Star Trek II: Wrath of Khan* (1982), as the new James Tiberius Kirk (Chris Pine) re-enacts (and reverses) this sacrificial act of brotherhood in Abrams' first sequel, *Star Trek Into Darkness* (2013), and as the android Data (Brent Spiner)[1] perishes while deliberately igniting a thaleron weapon onboard a Reman warship to save his captain, Jean-Luc Picard (Patrick Stewart), and his ship, the USS *Enterprise-E* in *Star Trek: Nemesis* (2002), this tradition affixes heroic masculinity to technology. That the men of the Federation would willingly die as an imperative of their leadership, that they would immolate themselves—in radiation, fire, or the shattered fuselage of an exploding starship—by redirecting powerful technological forces to self-destruct, has defined the iconic *Star Trek* brand as masculine. It requires autonomy and agency, as well as expertise in mechanical and computerized systems, to make this sacrifice, to set such machines into motion. However, these characteristics are likewise central to the women of *Star Trek: Voyager* more so than in Gene Roddenberry's original series or even in the more recent iterations of the franchise.

For example, Abrams does not alter the relative agency of the only significant female character on the *Enterprise* bridge, Nyota Uhura (Zoe Saldana), for the new millennium. Whoopi Goldberg (Guinan, *TNG*) has recounted the moment in 1966 when she shouted for her family to come from another room to see *Star Trek*'s original Uhura (Nichelle Nichols), the first African American woman she had ever seen on TV *not* being a maid (Asher-Perrin, 2013). The communications officer of the *Enterprise* was skilled at verbal and electronic languages but was conceived largely as a shipboard receptionist tasked with conveying messages to the captain. The contemporary Uhura occupies a similarly narrow characterization, identified predominantly as Spock's love interest (and former student). She is assigned to the bridge by Captain Pike (Bruce Greenwood) but leaves her post four times to run after (and, when necessary, comfort) her boyfriend as he exits the room in response to an unfolding crisis. Despite Abrams' previous television projects featuring strong female protagonists—*Felicity* (1998–2002), *Alias* (2001–2006), and *Fringe* (2008–2013)—it is not clear in *Star Trek* that he has any equally substantive direction for the new Uhura. Saldana (of Puerto Rican and Dominican heritage) is a proven action actor (*Avatar*, 2009; *The Losers*, 2010; *Columbiana*, 2011; *Guardians of the Galaxy*, 2014), however, is offered only slightly more active agency in *Star Trek Into Darkness*, as her character uses her linguistic training in Klingon to take part in an away mission to capture John Harrison/Khan (Benedict Cumberbatch). This Uhura, like her 1960s predecessor, never approaches the threshold set by the women of TV's *Voyager*.

Gender in Space: Critical and Popular Perspectives of Janeway, Seven and B'Elanna

Having been flung 70,000 light years from home into the uncharted and frequently hostile Delta Quadrant, *Voyager* is cut off from Starfleet support and must instead rely on innovative engineering and navigation, skillful alliance-building with alien species ("Bliss" 5.14, "The Void" 7.15), and a nuanced adherence to protocols. All of these operational adaptations are guided by the specialized leadership skills of Janeway, Seven, and B'Elanna who together comprise the preeminent scientific and technological expertise on the ship. The pilot episode, "Caretaker" (1.1), establishes *Voyager*'s driving ethical premise: the Captain refuses to endanger another species in order to save herself and her crew, electing to accept their stranding in the far flung Delta Quadrant and to face a 75-year journey to get back to Earth. Captain Janeway merges her own crew with that of the Maquis vessel that *Voyager* was pursuing in the Alpha Quadrant and which was caught up in the same interstellar dragnet as her own ship.

There is disagreement on Janeway (and indeed on all three of the female characters under discussion here) in academic analyses. On the one hand, Aviva Dove-Viebahn attributes this captain's successful leadership to the dissolution of boundaries between "the military and the domestic, Starfleet and the Maquis, machine/alien and human" (598). Janeway, she says, creates a feminist heterotopia of hybridity and community, in which the "juxtaposition of contrasting or opposing elements" is a source of strength and survival (599). Michèle A. Bowring has a different perspective as she frames the captain through a strict either/or gender binary, essentializing Janeway as only able to occupy one of two positions: the "treacherous female" or the "obsessed masculine warrior" (395) based on the storylines in "Counterpoint" (5.10), "Equinox" (5.26, 6.1), and in the series finale, "Endgame." Bowring asserts that Janeway is trapped in the rigid hegemonic dualism in which a "weaker feminine side" ultimately proves to be her undoing as it subsumes her more effective "ruthless masculine side" (394). Unfortunately, this latter view perpetuates the binaries of male/masculine/active and female/feminine/passive by yoking human traits and abilities to biology alone.

Interestingly, in contrast to *TNG*'s "The Best of Both Worlds" (3.26, 4.1) and to the 1996 film, *Star Trek: First Contact*, the most seductive technologized female leader in all of *Star Trek*, the Borg Queen, subverts this trend in *VOY*. In the Season Five episode, "Dark Frontier" (5.15, 5.16), the Queen tells Seven that her compassion and empathy make her weak, not because they are feminine but because they are "human qualities." The present study notes that, because both characters are women, there is no gender-based power disparity between them. Despite Bowring's essentialist reading, strength and weakness are not gendered in *Voyager*. Mia Consalvo illuminates this type of conceptual bind in much of feminist research, whereby "typically 'feminine' traits such as nurturing behavior" results in the rejection of such a character as a "throwback" whereas, if a female shuns these behaviors "and acts in a more typically 'masculine' fashion, we instead claim the character is dismissing feminine traits that are always devalued, and instead valorizing the primacy of male traits" (198). This is a recurring conundrum for cultural and media critics dealing with portrayals of gender, the body, and technologized power.

To wit, critiques of Seven of Nine have revealed the conflict manifested in how the character is costumed, in how Jeri Ryan performs the role, and in the polysemous possibilities for fans and critics in their interpretations of the former Borg drone. Her spandex uniform, high-heeled shoes, sleek blonde French twist, and pin-up curves co-exist incongruously with the "often hilarious extreme hauteur" (Grey) and the unsentimental confidence that Ryan brings to Seven of Nine. Simply based upon how the Borg are personified within the franchise—as a species embodying the technologies, identities, and histories of those they "assimilate" by force—Seven is an intrinsically hybrid character. Some scholars have reduced her to a heterosexual male fantasy. Anne Cranny-Francis foregrounds Seven's "tight-fitting silver suit that emphasizes her womanly body" (158) but simultaneously reads her as infantilized, based upon events in the character's first appearance ("Scorpion" [3.26, 4.1]) where she claims that Seven is made legible as merely "the daughter of her father" (159), yet not of her mother (also a scientist), who is also present in the sequence Cranny-Francis discusses. In contrast, Consalvo observes that "the physical dimensions of the character are hardly transgressive" while considering this a particularly exceptional fact when taken alongside "the way Seven of Nine is given intelligence, boldness, rationality and a remarkable lack of interest in the opposite sex," thereby complicating traditional heterosexual gender expectations. These expectations, entwining the goals of *Voyager*'s production team (Rick Berman, Brannon Braga, Michael Piller, and Jeri Taylor) with the heterosexual male demographic their creation of Seven would seem to favor, have since been further complicated by subsequent and ongoing resistant readings, made especially relevant as syndication, DVDs, and online video streaming make the show available for sustained analysis by a diverse spectatorship far beyond its initial network broadcast. For example, survivors of child abuse and other traumas have been inspired by the ways in which Seven overcomes the emotional and physical violence of her assimilation at the age of six, a challenge that is central to her re-humanization process aboard *Voyager* ("The Raven"4.6).[2] And, similarly, not all male fans have responded the way the producers intended. "Zalzidrax" posts online about the introduction of Seven, noting that he "was a (mostly) hetero teenage boy and the blatantness of the 7 of 9 pandering still felt kind of insulting" (2013). However, female fans often push back against this reductive response to Seven's physical appearance. "Sarah Highnote" writes that she "LOVED 7of 9. Yes they oversexualized her, but frankly, she was essentially sex-less when they rescued her. Sexuality meant nothing to her. It was interesting to watch her rediscover her humanity, and yes, her sexuality" (2013). Seven's independence, signaled by her lack of deference to her male colleagues on *Voyager*, is a departure from the portrayal of female characters in *Star Trek*. Her body—a synthesis of the organic and the technological—makes this departure culturally resonant and one which is further refined and made explicit by Chief Engineer, B'Elanna Torres.

A frequent contributor of *Trek* scholarship, Robin A. Roberts describes B'Elanna "as a scientist, a title I think she has earned, though others might dismiss her as a mere engineer, like Scotty in classic *Trek*" (2000, 210). While Roberts makes the point that B'Elanna, along with Janeway and Seven, demonstrates "how to practice science without being constrained by a white, male-dominated hierarchy such as Starfleet" (2000, 204), her own dismissal of engineering as a vital profession overlooks its gendered history as well as B'Elanna's specific technological skills and her self-identification. In *Making Technology Masculine: Men, Women and Modern Machines in America 1870–1945*, Ruth Oldenziel recounts the 19th-20th century exclusionary practices of engineering in which the profession ensured that "with few exceptions women and African Americans were kept on separate educational and employment tracks" (54). This institutional segregation based on race, class, and gender—across all engineering fields (mechanical, civil, electrical)—revealed the anxious male certainty that relinquishing any ground

> to women would have endangered the delicate balance of mastery and middle-class manliness that was increasingly under attack in the growing federal and corporate bureaucracies. The exclusion of women from the production floor sealed a tacit pact between the fraternity of elite engineers and the rank-and-file engineers [Oldenziel 89].

This connection between engineers and the resulting reification of white masculinity offers a cultural and historical context to B'Elanna Torres' position on *Voyager*. It also more effectively relates her specialized knowledge to technology than does Roberts' broadly generic "scientist" label. B'Elanna repeatedly and pointedly references her own identity in these terms: "It may be the warriors who get the glory, but it's the engineers who build societies. Don't forget that" ("Flesh and Blood" 7.9, 7.10). In episodes such as "Barge of the Dead" (6.3) and "Prototype" (2.13), she announces, "I'm an engineer," and, in the latter, adds, "I'm responsible for repairing and maintaining all the systems on the ship." While "scientist" is indeed a critical discursive category through which to emphasize Janeway's educational and professional background as captain of *Voyager*, it is technology that unites her leadership and mastery with the equally visible skillsets of Seven and B'Elanna. Roberts touches on this relationship when she notes that unlike "other *Star Trek* series, *Star Trek: Voyager* depicts the struggle with technology as a female struggle" (2000, 214). It is through mastery over the mechanical and computer systems of the ship that the three dominant female characters in *Voyager* rewrite the technological basis of heroic sacrifice as not an exclusively male expression of leadership.

Navigating the Episodes: Leadership, Sacrifice and Technological Mastery

Voyager made an initial splash in popular culture by placing one of its first female captains on a Federation starship[3] and, more notably, for presenting the first one ever to sit in the big chair of a *Star Trek* television series. A 1995 *Entertainment Weekly* cover story pictured Mulgrew as Janeway with the subtitle, "Boldly Going Where Only Men Have Gone Before." The concept of the woman leader—in *Star Trek* and in science fiction more generally—is traditionally linked to tropes of the out-of-control female body (often alien), the femme fatale (seductive), or the monstrous mother (reproductive). These leaders preside over dystopian realms that ultimately reveal the baseline colonialist truth that male "aggressiveness and action are needed to reinvigorate the society and bring technological advances" (Roberts 1999, 46). However, *Voyager* shifts these trends to instead valorize female leaders and their mastery over complex shipboard technologies, most notably in relation to heroic sacrifice (both the act itself and the willingness to commit the act).

As an organization steeped in nautical rhetoric and ritual, Starfleet embeds its leadership cadre with this maritime tradition. In "Dark Frontier" (5.15, 5.16) young Naomi Wildman (Scarlett Pomers)—the first child to be born on *Voyager* and soon designated as the official "Captain's Assistant"—proposes to Janeway a plan for rescuing Seven from the Borg. The captain assures her that there are three things to remember about being a Starfleet captain: "Keep your shirt tucked in, go down with the ship, and never abandon a member of your crew." The Season Two episodes "Dreadnought" (2.17) and "Deadlock" (2.21) confirm *Voyager*'s intention to position its female characters within this traditionally male narrative. Captain Janeway and B'Elanna Torres individually negotiate ethical and technological realities and conclude that their death will save their ship and crew (as well as innocent millions). When she was still with the rebel group, the Maquis, B'Elanna reprogrammed a Cardassian missile (designed as a small starship, given artificial intelligence, and christened "Dreadnought") to work for the resistance. She also integrated the human with the technological by changing the male "voice" of the ship from Cardassian to her own, thus rewriting its pre-engineered gender identity and setting up a parallel between herself and a machine.[4] *Voyager* finds this weapon malfunctioning in the Delta Quadrant and speeding toward a heavily populated planet that it "thinks" is the enemy. B'Elanna transports over to the vessel to repair it and divert it from its deadly course. With eleven minutes to target, B'Elanna crawls into the core of the weapon then reports back to Janeway that she intends to detonate the warhead even as Dreadnought cuts off life support in retaliation. Fighting for oxygen, B'Elanna turns down Janeway's offer to return to *Voyager*, her last chance to do so. It is B'Elanna's willingness to die that prompts the weapon to reconsider its targeting. While this internalizing struggle plays out onboard Dreadnought, Janeway has evacuated *Voyager* and advised the First Minister of the planet that, should B'Elanna fail, she will "use this ship to detonate the warhead before the missile reaches you" as she sets her ship to self-destruct. Janeway dismisses the bridge crew and takes the helm, ready to pilot the vessel into the path of Dreadnought. With B'Elanna embodying a technological hybridity through her identification with the missile-ship and Captain Janeway commanding *Voyager* (just as George Kirk does with the USS *Kelvin*), both women reveal and rewrite the role that technological mastery plays in leadership and sacrifice in the *Trek* franchise.

The captain's strategic logic—and her "down with the ship" ethos—is likewise foregrounded in "Deadlock" (2.21), as a spatial rift creates two *Voyagers*, two captains, and two crews. The rift causes widespread destruction on one ship while the other ship is unaffected. B'Elanna leads a team to reinforce the warp core while Janeway instructs her crew to magnetize the ship's hull to cushion it from the proton bursts coming from the spatial rift. However, systems continue to fail, so Janeway (with a bloody gash on her face) orders everyone off the bridge and works alone to seal the breach. On the other *Voyager*—clean and undamaged—Captain Janeway sees a ghostly image of herself on the bridge, looking "like hell." With now two members of her *Voyager* family dead (Harry Kim and Ensign Wildman's newborn daughter), the Janeway on the damaged ship solves the technological puzzle, realizing that the other ship has caused the proton bursts. From this point, the two Janeways and the two B'Elannas confer via onscreen communications at a workstation in main Engineering. The technological debate on both ships is isolated to these two women (and their doubles), as potential solutions are exchanged, discussed, and rejected. Later, both Janeways are framed in a two-shot in front of the warp core as the battle-scarred Janeway advises her counterpart to return to her ship to run a metallurgical analysis. The other Janeway assesses the situation: "You're going to sacrifice your ship." She knows this, she says, because it is what she would do. In a last-minute twist, it is the pristine *Voyager* that self-destructs, as Vidiians board it to harvest the crew's organs while being unaware of the duplicate *Voyager*. The Janeway on the undamaged ship meets the raiders with a friendly greeting as she detonates the vessel around them all.

This dissolution of shipboard structure and systems unfolds across a significantly extended scenario in Season Four's "Year of Hell" (4.8, 4.9). The Krenim Imperium is using a timeship to repeatedly trigger temporal incursions in order to gain an advantage over their enemies, the Zahl. Months pass as *Voyager* tries to continue through Krenim space, as ship and crew gradually deteriorate. To strengthen her position, Janeway forges an alliance with two other species and their ships, coordinating the attack against the timeship and its obsessed captain, Annorax (Kurtwood Smith). Piloting her ship alone on the bridge, as an ally's crippled vessel drags across *Voyager*'s bow, Janeway looks out through a force field (all that's left of her forward section) and advises the rest of the fleet, "Torpedo launchers are down. I'm setting a collision course." The camera pushes in to her gaunt, grimy face when, just before impact, she passes final judgment on Annorax: "Time's *up*." *Voyager* rips through the Krenim vessel, destroying them both and restoring the original timeline as it was before the "year" began. Janeway refuses to cede control of time and space to a male captain who has destroyed lives and entire planets just to save one person, his wife (who died as a result of one of his first temporal incursions). This contrast between the two captains diverges from the message in the *TNG* episode, "Angel One" (1.13), described by Robin Roberts as one which presents the "disorder of women rulers" and characterizes their leadership as "unnatural" (1999, 59). *VOY* therefore reverses the *Trek* (and sci-fi) convention of a female leader as dystopian.[5] "Year of Hell" (4.8, 4.9) instead puts an out-of-control irrational male leader in that role. Annorax's mastery of technology here is positioned as cataclysmic while Janeway's is depicted as both tactical and sacrificial. *Voyager*'s diverse expressions of gender continue as men, women, and starships interact in space.

Starship Technology: Male Containment and Female Trust

Another timeship episode, "Relativity" (5.24), reinforces the show's previous depiction of a male captain's instability, likewise contrasting it against the female leadership of both Janeway and Seven. The juxtaposition is further characterized as a conflict between control or containment (male) and trust (female). Using her enhanced Borg vision, Seven of Nine locates an explosive device hidden behind one of *Voyager*'s access panels, which we see through her point-of-view, rendering the camera itself as both female and technological. She has been recruited by Capt. Braxton (Bruce McGill) from the 29th-century timeship, *Relativity*, to go back to the starship's maiden voyage in the 24th century and stop the unknown saboteur, each time telling her to avoid Janeway whom he considers erratic and unpredictable. Seven uses straightforward Borg logic and reminds Braxton that "Captain Janeway is quite resourceful. Has it occurred to you that she may be helpful?" He rejects this, dismissing Janeway as "reckless." However, during her final attempt to stop the bomb from being planted on *Voyager*, Seven is discovered by Janeway and Tuvok (Tim Russ) years before they actually meet her. Although she assures them that she is there to save the ship, Janeway insists on knowing the whole story. Upon hearing her own (future) words to Seven that part of being human is learning to trust, Janeway joins her. The two women enter a Jefferies tube to find a future version of Braxton about to plant the device. His motive is revenge against Janeway for stranding him on Earth in the 20th century ("Future's End" 3.8, 3.9). So, as in "Year of Hell" (4.8, 4.9) male control over temporal technologies is portrayed as having those characteristics traditionally associated with female leadership in science fiction: irrationality and disorder. The trust between Seven and Janeway—crystallized by the advanced technological knowledge and canny leadership qualities they share—suggests that the male imperative to control and contain the "unruly" female produces a negative force on a massive scale.

When this drive to control and contain the half–Klingon engineer, B'Elanna Torres, unfolds in "Juggernaut" (5.21), it reflects the series' complex portrait of female leadership, along with women's mastery of (and analogous link to) technological systems. The episode opens with Tuvok attempting to train B'Elanna to control her emotions, particularly her temper and her anger, through meditation. A mixed-race actor herself, Roxann Dawson effectively plays a half–Klingon/half-human character here who relates a childhood memory of schoolyard (and racialized) bullying by a boy who made fun of her cranial ridges. Tuvok advises B'Elanna that she must learn to control her anger, a sentiment later echoed by her boyfriend and ship's pilot, Tom Paris (Robert Duncan McNeill). Meanwhile, a nearby Malon freighter is carrying toxic radioactive waste and experiencing a containment failure that is threatening to set off an explosion that will contaminate everything within a radius of three light-years. As the episode proceeds, a distinct parallel between the potentially explosive freighter and B'Elanna is made clear. However, through her leadership role and her engineering expertise, she effectively merges both her anger and her professionalism; her control is self-motivated rather than imposed externally. After the away team's leader, Chakotay (Robert Beltran), is wounded, Tuvok suggests to Janeway that he assume that role as B'Elanna's "volatile nature" could jeopardize the mission. The captain responds that, were she to do this, it would send the message that she does not trust B'Elanna, adding simply, "But I do."

So, as an engineer, a Klingon, and the new leader of the away mission, B'Elanna orders a rerouting of the containment grid as well as critical repairs to the ship's environmental systems. In the process, she confronts a Malon core laborer, disfigured by theta radiation; he has been sabotaging the ship to get revenge against his employers for his fatal exposure. At first, B'Elanna attempts to find common ground with him through their anger ("I know how you feel. You're so angry you want to pay them back.") but when he resumes his attack, she beats him to the ground with a metal pipe, then helps an injured Neelix (Ethan Phillips) and a Malon crew member to exit the chamber. Janeway's trust in B'Elanna's leadership as well as in her engineering skills stands in contrast here to the perspective of the male members of *Voyager* who, although they love and respect B'Elanna, consider containment a necessary counterbalance to her natural tendencies. *Voyager*'s female engineer harnesses the power of her emotion (a valued aspect of her Klingon identity more than it is a stereotypically feminine trait) to the trust her captain has in her ability to think rationally and lead wisely in a crisis.

Connecting Narrative, Fandom and Real-World Experience

These differing perspectives of men and women within the show's narrative, and their potentially gendered implications, likewise emerge in some fan commentary. From RogerEbert.com, site of Grey's *Voyager* article, a poster called "MrBlackguard" (assumed to be a male based on the username) writes, "The half–Klingon engineer comes off as having perpetual PMS rather than an alien mindset" (2013). Elsewhere, at MetaFilter.com, "not that girl" comments: "I remember, early in *Voyager*'s run, getting really excited when Janeway and Torres get all caught up in trying to solve a scientific problem together. Two women, talking to each other about something that is not men but is instead something important that they are both very capable in and passionate about" (2013). This fan's reference to the Bechdel Test[6] is noteworthy as this simple benchmark has helped illuminate the surprisingly small number of female-centered film and television texts that meet it, although *Voyager* does so consistently. And, as "not that girl" points out, it frequently does so by associating its female characters with technology.

This association is uniquely generative among the females on *Voyager*, with mentorship and cross-training a necessity for a 75-year journey. The practices depicted onscreen offer a positive counterpoint to the real-world pedagogy of science and technology. We see women passing specialized knowledge to the next generation in the interactions between Seven of Nine or Captain Janeway and young Naomi Wildman, all of which function to further the girl's scientific and technological education. In "Dark Frontier" (5.16, 5.16) when instructing Naomi on the three rules for starship captains, Janeway also encourages her to look at the computer's recent transpectral analysis. Naomi recognizes the data on the screen as sensor logs as they agree that it was an embedded Borg signal targeting Seven's alcove, a clear factor in Seven's subsequent decision to return to the collective. Seven similarly collaborates with Naomi in "Bliss" (5.14) as they work together to save *Voyager* from the mind-control inflicted on the entire crew by a hostile entity that has "swallowed" the ship and left only the two of them unaffected.[7] Seven's domain onboard the vessel is the Astrometrics lab (stellar cartography and navigation) from where she now refines her computer scans of the suspicious entity. This prompts three subsequent scenes in which male crewmembers begin to confine her to smaller and smaller technological actions: Tuvok blocks her from the lab, Tom prevents her from activating the Emergency Medical Hologram (Robert Picardo)—a crewman who also would not have been swayed by the entity's mind control—and, finally, Chakotay informs her she will be placed in stasis, ostensibly to prevent any nearby Borg from detecting her.[8] Each successive encounter constricts Seven's ability to move freely within the spaces of the ship, eventually threatening her with total immobility. Having instructed Naomi to remain hidden in the cargo bay, Seven retreats to that location, erects a force field, and teaches the girl how to enter a series of commands on the Borg interface. They both ignore Chakotay's order to cease their action; containment is not an option when the ship is at risk. The trust between Seven and Naomi (who was once fearful of the "Borg lady" ["Once Upon a Time" 5.5]) is expressed here through their shared technological engagement, each one activating a direct interface with the ship. *Voyager*'s focus on this positive relationship between female characters and starship technologies is, in fact, the pivot point around which the series concludes.

Trek *and Beyond: The Interface of the Feminine and the Technological*

The series finale, "Endgame," opens 33 years in the future as Starfleet celebrates the 10th anniversary of *Voyager*'s return to Earth after 23[9] years in the Delta Quadrant. Captain Janeway has risen to the rank of admiral and occasionally drops by to lecture Starfleet cadets on the Borg, as she is now that organization's foremost authority, having "developed technology and tactics that could defeat" them. This episode closely associates Janeway with technologies crucial to the narrative. She acquires a chrono-deflector (for time travel) from a Klingon trader and collects schematics on the tactical hardware that she has mastered (transphasic torpedos and adaptive hull armor) to take back through time to *Voyager*. Her goal is to persuade her younger self, Captain Janeway, to pass through a nearby Borg transwarp hub and use one of its corridors to fly her ship directly back to the Alpha Quadrant (thus preventing several tragic outcomes for her crew). The Admiral has a synaptic transceiver implant that allows her "to pilot a vessel equipped with a neural interface," linking her with a machine, much like B'Elanna with Dreadnought and Seven with the Borg collective. The stage is set for two female leaders, Admiral Janeway and the Borg Queen (Alice Krige), to face off.

This episode represents Starfleet's last encounter with the Borg in the *Trek* film and television canon and offers us the chance to draw a comparison between discourses of science fiction females—whether captains, cyborgs, or engineers—and the technologies that defy or define them. Aviva Dove-Viebahn and Mia Consalvo emphasize that the Borg were originally characterized (and commonly viewed) as masculine because "their collective voice is always male, most Borg appear male, and the hive mind is given primacy over the Borg body" (Dove-Vieban 611). Consalvo notes that the Borg, although seemingly presented as genderless when introduced in *TNG* ("Q Who" 2.15, "I, Borg" 5.23) ultimately "defaulted to masculine stereotypes," such as being "cold and logical" as well as "highly skilled in dealing with technology" (183), noting too that only male actors portrayed them (at that point).[10] On the other hand, Robin A. Roberts characterizes them as a "feminine collective consciousness" (2000, 215) and posits that the "Borg ship evokes a womb and the alien from *Aliens*—the interior is dark, womblike, as each Borg nestles into a crevice in a wall" (1999, 94). While this critique effectively extends Barbara Creed's 1993 analysis of the Queen in the *Alien* film franchise (1979–1997) as an example of Freud's "vagina dentata" (*The Monstrous-Feminine*, 22), it does not accurately account for the mise-en-scène we see inside Borg vessels (and its clear contrast to the set design from *Aliens* [1986]). Borg ships are heavily industrial spaces, with metal beams and catwalks, starkly geometric construction, and are punctuated with sophisticated touch-screen consoles. The "crevice" enclosures mentioned by Roberts are referred to in *Trek* as "alcoves"; these act as individual vertical sleeping quarters in which drones regenerate. When the insectile species in the *Alien* films invades a space, it becomes warmly humid and dripping with moisture, fluids abound (corrosive acid as blood), all evoking the Queen's primordial, oozing egg chamber. However, this emphasis on biology is markedly different from the dry industrial interiors and high-tech communication and navigational displays that characterize Borg vessels.

The monstrous femininity of the Borg Queen is largely associated with *Star Trek: First Contact*, in which she attempts to seduce Data with promises of becoming more fully human, when "properly stimulated." In this film, Picard has memories of her caressing his face during his forced transformation into Locutus (*TNG* "The Best of Both Worlds" 3.26, 4.1), a gesture she repeats in the present. However, because the key players in *Voyager*'s pivotal encounters with the Borg are the Queen, Janeway, and Seven, all women, the standard tropes are disrupted. Consalvo considers that the

> Queen is a throwback to the original series' depiction of women—as limited to using their bodies to achieve their goals (which are many times to find a man). [...] But ultimately she is reduced to a sexual being relying on her techno-femme fatale body to achieve her ends. Her power is shown as lying in her femininity, and when others resist her wiles, her strategies collapse [184].

Consalvo also points out that Seven is a strong contrast to the Queen, providing "an alternative view to the gendering of women in *Star Trek*" by being both sexy and a "tomboy," and by possessing "knowledge of technology" that is unparalleled (184). This study suggests instead that the Queen's techno-femme portrayal undergoes a fundamental transformation in *Voyager*, one that reflects the female homosociality of her encounters with Janeway and Seven. The Queen's strategies do not "collapse," rather they adapt. Her guise of femininity, steeped in the mandatory heterosexuality common to *Trek*—and central to her encounters with Picard and Data—is exposed as purely performative. With female characters in these storylines,[11] the writers are able to move them beyond stereotypes to instead depict the intersection of women and technology in terms of leadership, sacrifice, and mastery.

Therefore, it is significant that Janeway's first encounter with the Queen (originally played by Susannah Thompson) is in "Dark Frontier" (5.15, 5.16) because that episode is driven by the willingness of Seven of Nine to sacrifice herself to save *Voyager*. The Queen wishes to persuade her former drone to relinquish her restored humanity and return to the collective to report valuable intel on Janeway's vessel. The final struggle between the two leaders is both technological (for control of the tactically crucial transwarp hub) and personal. The Queen tells Admiral Janeway, "You wish to ensure the well-being of your collective. I can appreciate that." As they barter for their respective futures, the Queen demands that Janeway trade her the Federation database along with the hull-armoring technology from the future in exchange for the Queen tractoring *Voyager* out of the Delta Quadrant and back through the transwarp corridor to Earth. This negotiation takes place through the admiral's use of a "synaptic interface" to project her image into the Borg cube while remaining safely hidden on her nearby shuttle. When the Queen seems to gain a strategic advantage by suddenly beaming Janeway aboard and inserting nanoprobe tubules into her neck, activating the assimilation process, the admiral's ploy appears to have failed. However, Janeway has redirected the deadly interface by dosing herself with a neurolytic pathogen that infects the Queen and, rapidly, the machine collective of the Borg, initiating a cascade of explosions across the entire hub. As the Queen disintegrates, the dying admiral whispers in her ear that this will "bring chaos to order."

Unlike the dystopian storms unleashed by unethical male captains (Braxton, Annorax) "chaos" here, when set off by a woman leader, is a positive force. It permits *Voyager* to escape back to Earth, releasing transphasic torpedos in its wake, and destroying the Unicomplex that is the core of the Borg empire. The conventions of women leaders as alien, threateningly seductive, unnatural, and disorderly are shifted. When the formerly seductive alien Queen is in conflict with another female leader, the component of "femininity" is rendered irrelevant to their respective exercise of power. She loses her battle with Starfleet fair and square through the superior strategies and tactics of an opponent who masters complex technologies of transportation, communication, and weaponry. Janeway's deliberate collision course with the Borg closes out the series with a distinctively female heroic sacrifice. Ian Grey writes that *Star Trek: Voyager*

> offered American audiences something never seen before or since: a series whose lead female characters' agency and authority *were* the show. It was a rare heavy-hardware science fiction fantasy *not* built around a strong man, and more audaciously, it didn't seem to trouble itself over how fans would receive this [2013].

This reception, of the series and of its female characters, is perhaps most keenly articulated in the conflict between Janeway and the Borg Queen, an apocalyptic showdown that has prompted at least one fan, "dRaderman," to celebrate it with a YouTube compilation titled, "How *Voyager* Raped the Borg"[12] (13 June 2007).

While this fan's choice of words[13] is ill-conceived at best, the ten-minute video he/she has produced is visualized not through faces or bodies but through starships and their spectacular technologies. The video cuts together explosive visual effects sequences that depict all of *Voyager*'s kinetic space battles with multiple Borg cubes and spheres. Unseen in the video, but always present, is Captain Janeway in command of her ship and crew. A propulsive orchestral score lends dramatic emphasis to the visuals.[14] In the often-brutal world of the YouTube comments section, there is a post by "Judy Young" that reacts to the video and to the series itself: "This was great. Really how *Voyager*'s crippled one of the most iconic villainous races in Sci-fi history. And it was done under the auspices of a woman" (2015). To which "RoMa Gra" adds, "Three, actually: Admiral Janeway, Captain Janeway AND 7 of 9!" (2015). The narrative arcs of *Star Trek: Voyager* under discussion here, alongside the show's evolving fandom, frames a similar rewriting of gender and technology occurring in contemporary society. Collectively, these examples illustrate how this series both directly and indirectly reflects these social changes.

Women and Girls: To Boldly Go

When all five *Star Trek* (TV) captains appeared at the Destination Star Trek London event in 2012, Kate Mulgrew got a standing ovation second only in enthusiasm and duration to William Shatner's. She has publicly discussed her awareness that Captain Janeway is a role model to women and girls, particularly in the field of science.[15] One fan who attended later wrote in his blog: "You can tell that she is incredibly proud of her inspirational role. She knows she is not a scientist, she does not pretend to be but she knows how she is regarded. She knows that young girls may watch *Voyager* and dream of sitting in the big chair and she wants them to know that they can" (Gallagher, 2012). Mulgrew's Kathryn Janeway, along with the characters of Seven of Nine and B'Elanna Torres, help us imagine technological mastery independent of traditional gender roles in *Star Trek*, science fiction more broadly, and in the real world. We see the roles that society has yet to challenge, as well as those that evoke the narrative of *Voyager*, in everything from primary and secondary education to changing business practices. When Seven and Captain Janeway mentor young Naomi Wildman, their interactions provide a model toward which real-world science and technology education can aspire. Studies show that, despite there being no difference in the *abilities* between boys and girls in STEM (Science-Technology-Engineering-Mathematics) education, there arises a gender-biased perception of competence in these areas as early as age five (Chang 2013). Further, that perception is distinctly gendered.

> Connecting STEM and girls presents a unique challenge because even at a young age, girls are socialized on what it means to be a girl. Being a scientist, getting dirty, working with technology, and taking things apart are too often associated with boys [Gerstein 2015].

This gendered socialization finds its material expression in how businesses manufacture and market toys. In 2013, Debbie Sterling, CEO of the GoldieBlox toy company (interactive engineering and construction toys for girls) released a tart and fizzy commercial depicting a trio of racially diverse girls building a large-scale, imaginative Rube Goldberg machine set to a reworked Beastie Boys song ("Girls" 1987). The new lyrics, sung in a chorus of determined young voices, reject the narrow options the toy aisle (and the world) gives to non-male children: "Girls, to build a spaceship/Girls, to code a new app/To grow up knowing/That they can engineer that." Breaking free from similar containment, a young girl in Ontario fought back in 2015 against her local library's "boys only" policy for a summer class in robotics, protesting gendered access to technological knowledge, collecting over 31,000 signatures, and gaining the support of her town's mayor and of "female robotics engineers" (Lodi). She won and the library opened enrollment to all students. As a Stanford-trained engineer, GoldiBlox founder Sterling has expressed dismay at the under-representation of females in STEM fields; the *New York Times* reports that only 11 percent of the world's engineers are women (Waldman 2013) and fewer still are women of color. *Forbes* reports some good news, however: thanks to Sterling's efforts, the mega-chain Toys 'R' Us now carries Goldiblox engineering kits for girls (Guglielmo, 2013).

From the ripple effect that is made possible by small changes, we see that the line of female succession from *Voyager*'s fictional characters to fans, students, and to our increasingly technologized world matters. While the nostalgia of *Star Trek*'s masculine heroism and its genesis glow of sacrificial brotherhood is canonized in J.J. Abrams' cinematic reboot, it is the warped core of the Federation starship *Voyager* that burns significantly brighter.

Notes

1. Portrayed by male actor, Brent Spiner, the android is depicted as a heterosexual male, notably demonstrated in the *TNG* episode, "The Naked Now" (1.3), as he remarks that he is "fully functional" before initiating a sexual encounter with fellow bridge officer, Tasha Yar (Denise Crosby).

2. *Voyager*'s real-world impact is made visible through the character of Seven of Nine, whose narrative arc is "a thinly veiled, story of child abuse survival, and one that's proving to be a great inspiration to survivors now, in the real world" (Grey 2013).

3. Janeway is not the first female captain of a Starfleet vessel. The first, an unnamed captain, appears in *Star Trek IV: The Voyage Home* (1986) in command of the USS *Saratoga*. In the *TNG* episode: "Yesterday's *Enterprise*" (1990) is Capt. Rachel Garrett (Trisha O'Neil) and, in "Conspiracy" (1988), is the African American Capt. Tryla Scott (Ursaline Bryant). In the franchise's last television series, *Enterprise* (2001–2005), we see Capt. Erika Hernandez (Ada Maris) of the USS *Columbia* in "Home," "Affliction," and "Divergence" (all in 2005).

4. Although Gene Roddenberry wanted Capt. Kirk to have a female "Number One" in the original series—and cast his future wife, Majel Barrett, in that role for the pilot episode, both Paramount and NBC felt that the American television-viewing public was not ready to see a woman that far up the chain of command, especially in the scientific-military hierarchy of Starfleet. Barrett's voice, however, has lived on—as the omnipresent computer voice of both the *Enterprise* and *Voyager*, making an overt identification between the female and the technological.

5. *Voyager* is not immune to these narrative conventions. In the 1997 episode, "Favorite Son," the predominantly female planet, Taresia, uses DNA manipulation to implant the males of passing species with Taresian genes in order to reproduce their own kind, a process that kills the male victim.

6. The Bechdel Test was developed by graphic artist Alison Bechdel in 1985 and poses three simple criteria by which to examine any media narrative: (1) it has to have at least two women, who (2) who talk to each other, about (3) something besides a man. Assessment of a text through this lens is helpful in raising cultural awareness about the under-

representation of complex, independent female characters in film, television, and other media forms.

7. The entity infects everyone with individualized visions of home, but Seven and Naomi have never seen Earth or the Alpha Quadrant and are not susceptible to this form of coercion.

8. Under the control of the sentient spatial entity, Janeway also blocks Seven's attempts to free *Voyager* from its influence when she sends an EM surge to the console in main Engineering where Seven works to shut down the impulse drive. It is the young girl, Naomi Wildman, who rouses Seven from the resulting unconsciousness so that they may continue to fight the alien's influence over *Voyager* and her crew.

9. Although the starship *Voyager* and her crew were flung into the Delta Quadrant at a distance that would normally take 75 years to traverse back to the Alpha Quadrant, they encountered several shortcuts along the way, either through temporary technological fixes, spatial anomalies, or with the assistance of advanced alien races. These encounters enabled Janeway to trim decades from their journey.

10. In the *VOY* episode, "Survival Instinct" (6.2), we see a female Borg drone (designation Three of Nine) who is separated from the collective along with two other (male) drones. She remembers her Bajoran identity and her real name, Marika Willkarah (played by Bertila Damas). Also, in a continuing storyline in Seasons Six and Seven, four Borg children are taken onboard, one of whom is a female named Mezoti (played by Marley McClean) in episodes, "Collective" (6.16), "Ashes to Ashes (6.18), "Child's Play" (6.19), The Haunting of Deck Twelve (6.25), and "Imperfection" (7.2).

11. This is not to discount queer or lesbian readings. There is a substantive body of fan-produced slash fiction pairing Janeway/Seven (J/7) as well as scholarly works addressing the same relationship. (See Michele A. Bowring, 2004; Julie Levin Russo, 2002; David Greven, 2009; and collections of online fanfic at http://archiveofourown.org/tags/Kathryn percent20 Janeway*s*Seven percent20of percent20Nine/works and at http://slashyvoyager.livejournal.com/).

12. Unfortunately, this video has since been removed from the website.

13. dRaderman apologized for the title after other commenters understandably objected to the word "raped."

14. The music is "Molossus" by Hans Zimmer and James Newton Howard.

15. The connection between female education in STEM fields and *Star Trek: Voyager* is visible in Kate Mulgrew's participation in the PBS radio series, *Audio Portraits of Women in STEM: Her-Story, Then and Now*, as narrator (production date: Jan. 1, 2008). The series explores "women pioneers in science and technology" and what they are doing "to encourage the next generation" (*United States. National Science Foundation*).

Works Cited

Asher-Perrin, Emily. "The Endurance of Lieutenant Uhura Means We're Changing for the Better." Tor-Com. 30 April 2013. Web. 26 August 2016. http://www.tor.com/2013/04/30/endurance-of-uhura-better-society/

Bowring, Michèle A. "Resistance Is *Not* Futile: Liberating Captain Janeway from the Masculine-Feminine Dualism of Leadership." *Gender, Work and Organization* 11.4 (July 2004): 381–405.

Chang, Alicia. "Bridging the Gender Gap: Encouraging Girls in STEM Starts at Home." *The Huffington Post*. 27 December 2013. Web. 18 August 2016. http://www.huffingtonpost.com/alicia-chang/bridging-the-gender-gap-encouraging-girls-in-stem_b_4508787.html.

Consalvo, Mia. "Borg Babes, Drones, and The Collective: Reading Gender and the Body in *Star Trek*." *Women's Studies in Communication* 27.2 (2004): 177–203.

Cranny-Francis, Anne. "The Erotics of the (cy)Borg: Authority and Gender in the Sociocultural Imaginary." *Future Females, the Next Generation: New Voices and Velocities in Feminist Science Fiction Criticism*. Ed. Marlene S. Barr. Lanham, MD: Rowman and Littlefield Publishers, 2000.

Creed, Barbara. *The Monstrous-Feminine: Film, Feminism, Psychoanalysis*. London: Routledge, 1993.

Dove-Viebahn, Aviva. "Embodying Hybridity, (En)gendering Community: Captain Janeway and the Enactment of a Feminist Heterotopia on *Star Trek: Voyager*." *Women's Studies: An Interdisciplinary Journal* 36.8 (14 November 2007): 597–618.

Gallagher, Jamie. "Kate Mulgrew-Captain Janeway-Science Grrl." Jamiebgall.co.uk. 13 October 2012. Web. http://www.jamiebgall.co.uk/captain-janeway-sci-grrl/4575935299. 17 June 2015.

Gerstein, Jackie (Dr.). "STEM for Elementary School Students—How to Instill a Lifelong Love of Science." *Education Insider*, 13 August 2015. Web. http://blog.iat.com/2015/08/13/stem-for-elementary-school-students-how-to-instill-a- lifelong-love-of-science/. 2 September 2016.

Greven, David. *Gender and Sexuality in* Star Trek*: Allegories of Desire in the Television Series and Films*. Jefferson, NC: McFarland, 2009.

Grey, Ian. "Now, 'Voyager': In Praise of the Trekkiest 'Trek' of All." RogerEbert.com. 11 June 2013. Web. http://www.rogerebert.com/balder-and-dash/now-voyager-the-least-beloved-star-trek-offered-some-of-the-franchises-strongest-feminist-messages. 29 May 2015.

Guglielmo, Connie. "GoldieBlox Wins Toys 'R' Us in Quest to Redecorate 'Pink Aisle' with Engineering Kits for Girls." *Forbes*. 3 July 2013. Web. http://www.forbes.com/sites/connieguglielmo/2013/07/03/goldieblox-wins-toys-r-us-in-quest-to-redecorate-pink-aisle-with-engineering-kits-for-girls/#19f7cfc249c4. 3 September 2016.

Highnote, Sarah. "Now, 'Voyager': In Praise of the Trekkiest 'Trek' of All." Web. 2013. RogerEbert.com. http://www.rogerebert.com/balder-and-dash/now-voyager-the-least-beloved-star-trek-offered-some-of-the-franchises-strongest-feminist-messages. 9 June 2015.

HX-1138. "Jeri Ryan Talks Seven's Arc and Corset 'Breast Mounds.'" Online posting 12 April 2012. TrekMovie.com. http://trekmovie.com/2012/04/11/jeri-ryan-talks-sevens-arc-and-corset-breast-mounds/. 15 Jun. 2015.

Judy Young. "How *Voyager* Raped the Borg." Online video clip. YouTubewww. Google, 2015. Web. 16 June 2015.

Lodi, Marie. "Girl Fights Library's Boys-Only Robotics Program." *Jezebel*. 4 July 2015. Web. http://jezebel.com/girl-fights-library-s-boys-only-robotics-program-1715777611. 7 July 2016.

MrBlackguard. "Now, 'Voyager': In Praise of the Trekkiest 'Trek' of All." Online posting. 2013. RogerEbert.com. http://www.rogerebert.com/balder-and-dash/now-voyager-the-least-beloved-star-trek-offered-some-of-the-franchises-strongest-feminist-messages. 9 June 2015.

Not that girl. "The Series Is an Anti-Action, Existential Feminist Family Drama." Online posting. 20 June 2013. MetaFilter.com. http://www.metafilter.com/129268/The-series-is-an-antiaction-existential-feminist-family-drama. 9 June 2015.

Oldenziel, Ruth. *Making Technology Masculine: Men, Women and Modern Machines in America 1870–1945*. Amsterdam: Amsterdam University Press, 1999.

Roberts, Robin A. "Science Race, and Gender in *Star Trek: Voyager*." *Fantasy Girls: Gender in the New Universe of Science Fiction and Fantasy Television*. Ed. by Elyce Rae Helford. Lanham, MD: Rowman and Littlefield, 2000.

Roberts, Robin A. *Sexual Generations:* Star Trek: The Next Generation *and Gender*. Urbana: University of Illinois Press, 1999.

RoMa Gra. "How Voyager Raped the Borg." Online video clip. YouTube. Google, 2015. Web. 16 June 2015.

Russo, Julia Levin. "NEW VOY 'cyborg sex' J/7 [NC-17] 1/1: New Methodologies, New Fantasies." 2002. Web. 4 July 2016. http://j-l-r.org/asmic/fanfic/print/jlr-cyborgsex.pdf.

Star Trek. Desilu Productions. 1966–1969. Television.

Star Trek. Dir. J.J. Abrams. Perf. Chris Pine, Bruce Greenwood, Zoe Saldana, Zachary Quinto, and Leonard Nimoy. Paramount Pictures, 2009. Film

Star Trek: First Contact. Dir. Jonathan Frakes. Perf. Patrick Stewart, Brent Spiner, Gates MacFadden, Jonathan Frakes, Marina Sirtis, LeVar Burton, Michael Dorn, James Cromwell, Alfre Woodard, and Alice Krige. Paramount Pictures, 1996. Film.

Star Trek into Darkness. Dir. J.J. Abrams. Perf. Chris Pine, Zachary Quinto, Zoe Saldana, Karl Urban, and Benedict Cumberbatch. Paramount Pictures, 2013. Film.
Star Trek: Nemesis. Dir. Stuart Baird. Perf. Patrick Stewart, Tom Hardy, Jonathan Frakes, and Brent Spiner. Paramount Pictures, 2002. Film.
Star Trek II: The Wrath of Khan. Dir. Nicholas Meyer. Perf. William Shatner, Leonard Nimoy, Nichelle Nichols, James Doohan, Ricardo Montalban. Paramount Picture, 1982. Film.
Star Trek: Voyager. United Paramount Network (UPN). 1995–2001. Television.
United States. National Science Foundation. Education and Human Resources Directorate. Division for Human Resources Development. Program for Gender Diversity in Science, Technology, Engineering, and Mathematics Education. *New Tools for America's Workforce: Girls in Science and Technology*. 2006. Web. http://www.nsf.gov/pubs/2006/nsf0659/nsf0659.pdf. 2 Sept. 2016.
Waldman, Katy. "This Awesome Ad, Set to the Beastie Boys, Is How to Get Girls to Become Engineers." Slate.com. 19 November 2013. Web. http://www.slate.com/blogs/xx_factor/2013/11/19/goldieblox_commercial_rewrites_the_beastie_boys_urges_young_girls_to_pursue.html. 18 June 2015.
Zalzidrax. "The Series Is an Anti-Action, Existential Feminist Family Drama." Online posting. 20 June 2013. MetaFilter.com. http://www.metafilter.com/129268/The-series-is-an-anti-action-existential-feminist-family-drama. 9 June 2015.

"This is me cargo"
The Commodification and Hyperreality of Women in "Mudd's Women"

HALEY M. FEDOR *and* DEREK FRASURE

This study attempts to plot two different courses through an episode of the original *Star Trek* series and its relationship to women both in the historical time of readers and in its own fictional time of "space, the final frontier." First, we will consider an analysis of the episode on its own terms, and with the insight that feminist, political, and anthropological thinkers can provide. This section attempts to understand the episode "Mudd's Women" in terms of the commodification of women. The second section will define some basic concepts in postmodernism and linguistics to propose a theory of femaleness that "Mudd's Women" offers. This section attempts to evaluate the meaning of specific themes developed in the first section. The two should be read as a syncretic exploration of a complex episode and set of social relations. These are not offered as a definitive or exclusionary way that fans should understand "Mudd's Women," but are offered as inducements to thought, understanding, and conversation surrounding a series that produced innumerable opportunities to consider the human condition, possibility, and the place of both in the arts.

Harry Mudd and His Enterprise *of Trafficking Women*

When one thinks of gender and gender issues in *Star Trek,* images of Kirk paired with exotic, swooning, alien women come to mind. This is the image that pop culture has fashioned. In reality, Kirk and fellow captains in the original series prize equality and fairness. Occasionally Kirk breaks the rules, particularly the Prime Directive, which prohibits interference with the development of any alien civilizations. When Kirk and the *Enterprise* do interfere in alien civilizations, Kirk cites compassion for the lives that would be affected by dispassionate distance.

But what about interference with the arrangements between other humans? Kirk consistently interferes in the affairs of other humans, whether they are within the Federation or not. In the first season of the original series, the episode "Mudd's Women" deals with exactly this concern. The *Enterprise* pursues a ship, one that refuses to answer repeated hails, into an asteroid field, with disastrous consequences. The ship is destroyed, but not before the *Enterprise* has broken three lithium crystals in an attempt to shield the occupants and safely beam them aboard. They recover all four passengers: a man named Harry Mudd (who initially uses the alias "Leo Walsh") and three voluptuous women.

Mudd's character wears clothes befitting a futuristic bordello pimp, complete with one large, dangling earring. Each of the women with him is adorned with makeup and glitzy, revealing attire to accentuate their irresistible beauty. When Spock, and later Kirk, ask if these women are part of Mudd's crew, he says matter-of-factly: "This is me cargo." Mudd defends his refusal to answer the *Enterprise*'s hails by implying that with such precious cargo of "young lovelies" he couldn't be sure of their intentions. Kirk vows to get to the bottom of this, but immediately notes the attractive and captivating qualities all three women have. Concerned by the mysterious and "magnetic" effect these women have on the male crewmembers, Kirk is obviously troubled by the "almost hypnotic" power they seem to possess. Their mystery is heightened by Mudd's refusal to allow McCoy to conduct medical exams on any of the women.

Mudd is charming, playful, and is in essence a con man with a lengthy criminal record. Upon making a joke at Spock's expense, one woman apologizes, telling Spock: "He's used to buying and selling people," but she is immediately silenced by Mudd. He dictates how they should behave and answers all the questions. This line carries connotations of sexual slavery, given that the only "cargo" Mudd has are beautiful women. In effect, Mudd perpetrates a form of gender oppression. Luce Irigaray expands upon this sort of gender oppression in *This Sex Which Is Not One* (69). Building off of Simone de Beauvoir's theory of woman viewed as the Other (that is one who is not "one of us," an outsider, deviant, or non-idealized subject) socially and culturally, Irigaray suggests that women—and thus femininity—are always defined against masculinity, and thus seen as deficient or atrophied in comparison. Women, and their femininity, thus only have value in that they serve or foster relationships between men. By themselves, women have no value, like any other commodity. But in the dealings and exchanges between men, women come to have an immense value. This proves to be absolutely true for Mudd's women. Eventually Mudd tells Kirk that he recruits "wives" for settlers, and calls it "a difficult, yet satisfying task." Viewers have no insight into how exactly these women, all from different colonies, were recruited and at one point Mudd explains: "Just as I told you, three lovely ladies, destined for frontier planets, to be the companions of lonely men, to supply that warmth of a human touch that's so desperately needed—a wife, a home, a family. I look upon this work as a sacred public trust." Mudd insists that the women come voluntarily, from planets with no eligible men for husbands. The pathos-laden appeal (a rhetorical device aimed at evoking an emotional response in the audience) suggests that the women are all suitable for domestic labor and sexual gratification, and not much else. One of the women, who is named Eve, confirms Mudd's speech, revealing a backstory with only automated machines and brothers for company. Consequently, Eve and the other women, who have similar backgrounds, are somehow unable to find husbands for themselves. This arrangement is quite convenient for Harry Mudd, who will profit greatly off of this exchange.

The notion of marriage being an exchange between two men is not a new one, given Claude Lévi-Strauss' theory of kinship, and Luce Irigaray's theories on the value and traffic of women. Lévi-Strauss' *The Elementary Structures of Kinship* is an attempt to understand the concept of marriage and the structural principles of kinship. Kinship being an organization that retains and gives power, Lévi-Strauss builds upon Marcel Mauss' theory of gift exchange, suggesting that women are the most profound gift of all, to be exchanged between men (Lévi-Strauss 65). There is a clear distinction between the gift and the giver. Women are the gifts, and the men are the ones who conduct the exchange; women cannot give themselves away. Accordingly, Irigaray sees women as being treated as commodities. Karl Marx defines the concept of a commodity in his magnum opus of political-economy, *Capital Vol. 1*, as "an external object, a thing which satisfies human needs of whatever kind. The nature of these needs, whether they arise, for example, from the stomach, or the imagination, makes no difference" (Marx 125). In this way, we can understand women as commodities because of the ways in which they satisfy male needs for companionship, sex, homemaking, and child-rearing. These are what feminists working later in the Marxist tradition call domestic and emotional labor, often undervalued and underpaid/unpaid compared to men's traditional roles in agricultural, industrial, managerial, and creative labor. One cannot exist without the other. The lack of recognition of women's work as labor in the same sense comes from a fundamental misconception of how value is created. Marx identifies two basic forms of value: use value and exchange value. Anything with value is in some way useful to satisfy needs, which again can be imaginary or for basic sustenance. So, to have value a commodity must first be useful. Secondly, it acquires a different value through exchange. A house has use value because it's a place to live; but a house can also have value expressed in market relations of the money commodity (dollars) and be traded independently of any use (house flipping, for example). The usual story we're told about exchange value is that supply and demand determine the value of commodities. However, Marx tempers this insight by noting that if supply and demand are in equilibrium they cease to have an explanatory function about why items have a given value relative to other commodities. The proposed resolution to this problem is what Marx calls the labor theory of value. This theory states that objects have a given value because they have a certain quantity of congealed human labor in them. Value is relative depending on given technology and worker skill level as a social average. Differences in the speed and skill of individual workers represent losses and gain on individual scales, but do not change the average value of the commodity produced. Thus, the value of a commodity is a socially determined thing. The introduction of the social into the production and consumption of commodities is Marx's great insight. Marx argues that exchange values dominate in capitalism, but since commodities are supposed to serve human needs a return to emphasis on use value might generate a different type of society. The notion that buying and producing represent asocial acts is what Marx calls the commodity fetish: "It is nothing but the definite social relations between men [and we might note that the exclusion of women from this statement is significant] themselves which assumes here, for them, the fantastic form of a relation between things" (op. cit. 165). Meaning that market relations conceal human relations; making exploitation through economic activity more palatable to people than in interpersonal interactions, even when the result is the same. This is more true of women's status as laborers being concealed by ideologies that fix women as helpers to capital accumulation, rather than having an active and vital part in keeping the system running. Women are mothers and wives whose labor is expected to be unpaid. Marx was not overly specific about the gendered quality of labor, the ways in which women's domestic and emotional labor has been viewed as non-productive and is hyper-exploited; so subsequent critics like Silvia Federici have needed to flesh out this history of exploitation. Irigaray thinks in this manner, building off of Marx's theories of value, and as such the exploitation of women has become a foundation of patriarchal and capitalist societies. "The production of women, signs, and commodities is always referred back to men (when a man buys a girl, he "pays" the father or the brother, not the mother…), and they always pass from one man to another, from one group of men to another" (Irigaray 173). This is in reference to dowry traditions, where men pay a "bride price" of some sort, be it currency or goods, in exchange for the hand of the woman in marriage. Because the work force is assumed to be masculine, the "products" that are maintained and exchanged are women.

According to Gayle Rubin, women are not in any position to realize the benefits of their own circulation. "As long as the relations specify that men exchange women, it is men who are the beneficiaries of the product of such exchanges—social organization" (Rubin 44). It is this kind of social organization that Mudd is creating. Originally intending to take Eve and the others to the planet Ophiuchus-3 for settlers, Mudd is happy to create an exchange and social contract with the lithium miners on Rigel-12 when the *Enterprise* arrives there to replace the broken lithium crystals. For Lévi-Strauss, the exchange of women is a fundamental principle of kinship, inferring that the subordination of women is a product of these relationships. Eve's confirmation that they must rely on Mudd as a go-between reveals that she and the other women have no ability to exchange themselves and find a husband. They need Mudd to fashion them into a commodity capable of circulating among other goods and services, and worthy of men in the marriage market.

When the *Enterprise* goes to the planet Rigel-12, Mudd employs the women to use their beguiling charms upon key officers in order to obtain information about their destination and to communicate directly with the miners, striking a deal to exchange the women for lithium crystals. "Lithium crystals, my dear, are worth three-hundred times their weight in diamonds, thousands of times their weight in gold," Mudd tells the women. It is no mere matchmaking as an end unto itself, for there is a profit to be made off of the bodies of these women. Of course, Mudd's dreams of riches go unfulfilled, as Kirk arrests Mudd for illegal activity and promises to haul him back to Earth for a trial, offering jokingly to appear as a character witness in Mudd's defense.

Kirk questions the nature of this effect that allows Mudd's women to manipulate the men of his ship—himself almost included, following a private scene with Eve:

> KIRK: "What is it? Is it that we're tired, and they're beautiful? And they are incredibly beautiful."
> MCCOY: "Is it that they just act beautiful?"

McCoy is correct, as it is later revealed that the women are consuming the "Venus Pill" in order to enhance their beauty. So dangerous is the Venus Pill that it is considered illegal; here, beauty is such an important commodity that it has been banned from use. In Mudd's cabin when the effects of the pill wear off, we see the women in age makeup with mottled skin, their hair frazzled and unkempt. After the next dose takes effect, the women are seen caressing themselves, running their hands over their bodies in narcissistic delight, their beauty restored. The Venus Pill is a sort of counterfeiting. It is dangerous insofar as it sells a different commodity than what buyers appear to be getting. The Venus Pill defetishizes commodities by revealing the nature of one commodity as implicated in a network of deception. The Venus Pill harkens back to a capitalist Earth, and so too the entire exchange between Mudd and the miners seems primitive for this reason. If we feel uncomfortable with this kind of exploitation it is because we are seeing beyond the commodity fetish to the utopia Gene Roddenberry imagined, and dare I say shared in some measure with Karl Marx. The idea of the pill's immorality plays out explicitly within the episode under more conventional guises.

This scene contains a crucial conversation between Eve and Mudd, where Eve calls the pills "a cheat," and implies it would be different if there was genuine affection instead. Having been sent to seduce Kirk, Mudd informs her that ship captains are already married—to their ships: "You'd find out the first time you came between him and the ship," he says. This proves to be true, as Kirk's displaced sexual desire onto the ship itself is a consistent theme throughout the series, and in this episode in particular. Indeed, Eve does get between Kirk and his precious *Enterprise*, and he is willing to barter her for lithium crystals in order to keep the *Enterprise* functioning.

When meeting with the miners, they inform Kirk that the lithium crystals aren't for sale, but that they would "prefer a swap." They ask to see Mudd's women, demanding that Kirk "trot them out" like livestock or champion racehorses, to gauge whether or not they're even worthy of a trade. The miners assure Kirk that he has no choice in this matter.

Following this exchange is a scene involving the miners and the women dancing, although Eve declines. The head miner, Ben Childress, (whose name seems to be a pun on a lack of children—and thus a lineage) chooses to take another woman from her current partner, starting a fight in the process. This causes jealousy, leading Eve to run out into a sandstorm, after yelling: "Why don't you just run a raffle and the loser gets me?" In a moment of cavemanesque triumph, Ben Childress rescues Eve from the storm and brings her unconscious form to his living quarters. When Eve awakens, she cooks Childress a meal, but he's upset by it:

> CHILDRESS: "I had things where I wanted 'em. And I do my own cooking. I've not laid a hand on you. Remember that!
>
> EVE: "Oh, the sound of the male ego. You travel halfway across the galaxy, and it's still the same song."
>
> CHILDRESS: "I guess I'm supposed to sit, roll my eyes. 'Ooh, female cooking again.' I've tasted better. By my own hand."

This exchange is followed by an argument on how to properly clean cookware, and Childress demanding to know what happened to her looks. Eve replies solidly that she tired of him and "slumped." This prompts a violent outburst from Childress, who rushes to tower over her, gripping her by both arms. "You're homely," he tells her, "I've got enough in crystals to buy queens ... by the gross!" Instead of hitting her, Childress strikes playing cards that sit on the table.

When Kirk and Mudd finally arrive, the first thing that Childress says is: "I didn't touch her." While this is true in regards to sexual assault, Childress did grab her physically. His actions and subsequent denial to Kirk and Mudd, reveals his aggressively masculine mindset about what constitutes inappropriate physical behavior, and how little threatening violence seems to matter. Kirk and Mudd's intrusion could very well have prevented something worse from happening. Kirk forces Harry Mudd to reveal that Eve and the other women have been regularly consuming the Venus Pill, which he says, "give[s] you more of whatever you have." Men are supposedly more muscular under its regimen, and women become "rounder." What is so shocking to Childress is that their beauty is a fraud—to him, it is the worst crime, and one he fully intends to blame, and take out, upon the women—particularly Eve. Following a rant about his toil and labor in order to secure wives, Eve cuts him off and declares that the miners never wanted wives.

> EVE: "This is what you want, Mr. Childress. And I hope you remember it and dream about it, because you can't have it! It's not real!"

Eve grabs several of the Venus Pills, swallowing them before anyone can take them from her. Almost instantaneously, she is transformed and beautiful once more. "Is this the kind of wife you want, Ben?" Eve asks, "Not someone to help you? Not a wife to cook, and sew, and cry, and need, but this kind? Selfish, vain, useless." Sauntering over to Childress, he is captivated once more.

Kirk reveals that what Eve actually ate was colored gelatin, not the real drug. What this beauty comes down to, he posits, is confidence. "You either believe in yourself, or you don't," he tells Eve. Childress is very happy to have Eve stay now that he knows she has not committed any type of fraud; the commodity of beauty is inherent to her, not obtained through illegal methods. Kirk gets his crystals, after asking Eve if she wants to stay on the planet, "You've got someone up there called the *Enterprise*," she tells him. This exchange not only suggests that Eve would go with them if Kirk were a "free" man, but also that Kirk will gladly take the crystals in exchange for Eve and the other women, profiting off the exchange of their bodies in return for valuable goods. The women's bodies have value as commodities, but seemingly only when they possess beauty or confidence—or both.

There is another way we might understand the Venus Pill and its implications in a more abstractly theoretical way to gain insight into how femininity as a concept operates both today and in the 24th Century. The following section attempts to historicize a certain movement in artistic and intellectual life preceding, during, and after the episode "Mudd's Women" and how it affects our understanding of what the episode conveys and how we evaluate the success or failure of that attempt.

Venus Pill, Baudrillard, Hyperreal Femininity

Postmodernists are mortified by violence and oppression and deeply ethically committed to finding ways of subverting the thought processes that lead to those ends. As such, we will employ the late 20th century postmodern French philosopher Jean Baudrillard's concept of hyperreality to help us understand the Venus Pill's desirable effect on femininity and its underlying oppressive violence.

Jean Baudrillard, often called the "high priest of Postmodernism," defined a schema of four stages of the sign that will help us understand reality and hyperreality, but first we must understand what a sign is. A sign is what linguist Ferdinand Saussure defined as the relationship of the signifier and the signified. What this means is that something in the real world is signified—a tree, an emotion, a person, a geographic location—and it is represented by a signifier made up of a sound or series of sounds, ie. a word. The sign is the symbiotic combination of both signified and signifier, as both are meaningless independent of the other. A signifier must have a relationship to the signified to be intelligible; thus a sign requires both parts. The famous *Next Generation* episode "Darmok" is an example of these problems of signification, language acquisition, and (un)intelligibility seated within the larger *Star Trek* universe, with Picard's struggle to grasp a language that operates on metaphor and a context that is alien to him.

Baudrillard takes Saussure's conventional schematization of the sign and points out the ways in which signs are not as simple as the conventional understanding would suggest because there are many ways in which a sign might mislead us about the real world and our firm grasp of it. In typical Postmodern fashion, Baudrillard identifies four stages of a sign that deeply trouble the representational character of words and images:

1. It is the reflection of a basic reality.
2. It masks and perverts a basic reality.
3. It masks the *absence* of a basic reality.
4. It bears no relation to any reality whatever: it is its own pure simulacrum (170).

The third order is often the most difficult to grasp. To take one example, this one from Baudrillard himself:

> Disneyland is there to conceal the fact that it is the "real" country, all of "real" America, which is Disneyland (just as prisons are there to conceal the fact that it is the social in its entirety, in its banal omnipresence, which is carceral). Disneyland is presented as imaginary in order to make us believe that the rest is real [op. cit. 172].

The idea is that Disneyland presents an idealized Main Street USA, which not only does not exist as it is depicted, but does not exist at all. Not only is there simply no such place, but the representation is ideological insofar as it asks us to believe that it is the real America to which we're all failing to live up to when we conduct our real lives. Similarly, Baudrillard argues that prisons by existing as a concrete place of incarceration and observation conceal the fact that U.S. society is broadly carceral with its omnipresent surveillance cameras, neighborhood watches, NSA listening programs, background and social media checks, and confessional style of reality tv and tabloid that always function together to discipline us into obedient, (re)formed citizens. These orders of the sign allow us to understand the underlying hyperreality of Mudd's Venus Pill and its idealized presentation of femininity.

While *Star Trek* is not a postmodern series, we can use Baudrillard's schema to analyze the representation of women in "Mudd's Women" through the insights that Postmodernism provides. The first stage of femininity would be the female qua female, that is women as they actually exist. This stage of the sign is gender that only exists outside the influence of the Venus Pill when Eve speaks for herself. This is the mode of representation that feminism seeks for women—the ability of women to narrativize their own lives, desires, experiences, thoughts, and bodies. This agency is typically denied through masculinized forms of speaking for a woman (more recently and colloquially called "mansplaining"). The second stage of femininity as a sign would be that of a distorted but still present reality of gender. Cosmetic surgery, makeup, and the entire beauty industry would likely fit into this category, as they present real women, but not as nature would offer them. This stage of the sign offers a contested territory where women can lose their reality when unrealistic standards of beauty supplant natural bodies; meanwhile it can also be an area for counter-signification wherein women can co-opt discourses of femininity to choose their own gender presentations and destroy sexist nature discourses (childbearing and rearing as women's natural duty). The third stage of femininity as a sign is where the representation of gender masks the absence of a basic reality of gender. Extreme photo editing for an idealized female form impossible in nature and certain kinds of dehumanizing pornography could both exemplify this stage. Both the examples present a certain idea of gender that goes beyond distorting reality into the realm of creating an artificial reality that supersedes the lives and bodies of real women. The standard set by editing a model's photo to have bodily proportions that cannot be physically achieved creates a situation in which women attempt to live up to its ideal and end up failing, causing either psychological or physical harm. Images consumed and idealized by men set up these unrealistic standards on the covers of magazines, and in a different way through pornography. While someone might want to engage in dehumanizing practices as part of a consensual BDSM relationship, this does not occlude the reality that women are often dehumanized through pornography in ways that create non-consensual violence. Pornography often presents women as hypersexualized and its close-up camera angles rhetorically reduce the performers to scarcely personified orifices. A habit of seeing women in this way teaches male viewers that women should always be ready and available as objects for sex, rather than fully fleshed out persons. The meme of an angel in the streets and a devil in the bedroom is illustrative of the contradictions that women are expected to live. Thinking in this manner masks the absence of these ideals in the basic reality of women's actual bodies and lives. Finally, the fourth stage of femininity as a sign is that of gender presentation bearing no relation to reality. This is the stage of Harry Mudd's Venus Pill. Women are given a pill that makes their bodies appear entirely different, not only younger and healthier, but also morphologically different. The Venus Pill presents women as entirely something (and "thing" is the appropriate use here given their treatment by Mudd and the miners) other than what they are. There is no reality to the presentation of the Venus Pill other than their sex, species, and race. The Venus Pill is desirable, despite, or rather because of, its hyperreality. Why is hyperreality seductive where reality is not?

The Venus Pill's hyperreal femininity unveils a constitutive part of gender—its utilitarian fictitiousness. The Venus Pill exists for both men and women, but its gendered name and deployment within the episode point to the ways in which women are marked as Other,[1] that which is different from the universal masculine.[2] Women are othered and thereby subject to the trafficking discussed above. The fiction of what women should look like or be like functions much like advertising that keeps the whole system of exchange moving by producing desire. Desire exists from a position of relative lack—you want what you do not have but someone else does. If women bring happiness, beauty, and companionship to a miner's life, then these are the things we can assume they lack. It is not hard to imagine those qualities lacking for a planet of fewer than ten people in which harsh environmental conditions dominate. Women are idealized as possessing exactly the qualities these miners should desire. However, women are people, the same as the miners. The gendered essence of femininity is a fiction; men in other circumstances are just as likely to possess the qualities that the miners lack. However, that fiction helps Harry Mudd use the Venus Pill to sell the miners what they already think the women should possess. The pill is not the trick; it is the miners' ideas about women. This is why Ben Childress decides to keep his wife after discovering the deception. He still believes in the fundamental idea that Eve will provide for him the qualities that he desires. "Mudd's Women" creates a certain amount of dissatisfaction for this reason, because the traffic in women is not fully resolved. Everyone's ideas about gender are still left relatively undisturbed by the end of the adventure. We've seen through the fourth stage of the sign, but are unwilling to admit that there is no more truth to the third stage and to inquire into the basic reality of who women are.

Conclusion

These two different takes on "Mudd's Women" illustrate the complex status of gender in an episode where there is still more to say. We could discuss the very ideology of women needing a savior, as Kirk inevitably had to save them, rather than the women being capable of saving themselves. This no doubt perpetuates a tradition of storytelling in which women are objects, even when we are supposedly learning their value. However, we chose to focus more on the merits of this episode and the interesting ways in which it intersects with broader traditions of feminism and critical theory. The problem of "Mudd's Women" is the same one that persists in our interpretation of it. We are only given the story of Mudd's women through the male lenses of Mudd and Kirk, never on their own terms. When the women are allowed to speak it is only in response to discussions initiated by, and centered upon, the men around them. Problems like this run deep within attempts to recover women's voices in both sympathetic and unsympathetic art works and history more broadly. Nonetheless, we can learn from what scraps we are given, and moreover take instruction from the way Mudd's women are treated. Overall, this episode can be seen as reactive storytelling set within the larger framework of a series that makes a conscious effort at depicting a progressive future for the human race where prejudices like racism are not tolerated. Yet, despite overt condemnations of racism, the traffic of women, within the original series is still present.

Notes

1. Venus was a goddess of love who was too proud of her own beauty.
2. That is to say the way in which the masculine is universally assumed unless otherwise specified. For example, the way most people automatically say "he" if someone references anything from a doctor to a dog in conversation.

Works Cited

Baudrillard, Jean. *Selected Writings*. 2nd edition. Stanford University Press, 2002.
Irigaray, Luce. *This Sex Which Is Not One*. Cornell University Press, 1985.
Levi-Strauss, Claude. 1969. *The Elementary Structures of Kinship*. Revised edition. Beacon Press, 1969.
Marx, Karl, and Ernest Mandel. *Capital: Volume 1: A Critique of Political Economy*. Translated by Ben Fowkes. Reprint edition. Penguin Classics, 1992.
Roddenberry, Gene. "Mudd's Women." *Star Trek*. Directed by Harvey Hart. Desilu Studios, 1966. Streaming.
Rubin, Gayle S. *Deviations: A Gayle Rubin Reader*. Duke University Press, 2011.

Hybrids

Interspecies Intercourse and Biracial Identity in Star Trek

KEVIN J. WETMORE, JR.

From its very inception, *Star Trek* has presented sexual interaction between different species and the offspring of those couplings: hybrid, multi-species characters such as fan favorite Mr. Spock, the product of a human mother and Vulcan father. Since this origin, the various incarnations have seen a number of hybrids, cross-species and other impossible combinations of DNA: Deanna Troi (*TNG*, Human/Betazed), K'Ehleyr (*TNG*, Human/Klingon), Alexander son of Worf (*TNG*, quarter human, three quarters Klingon), Sela (*TNG*, Human/Romulan), Ba'el (*TNG*, Klingon/Romulan), Tora Ziyal (*DS9*, Bajoran/Cardassian), and B'Elanna Torres (*VOY*, Human/Klingon, etc.). This is not to mention the possible progeny from numerous interspecies relationships from Kirk and his numerous conquests, to various pleasure planets and temptresses and tempters, to the more stable pairings of Kes and Neelix and B'Elanna Torres and Tom Paris of *Voyager*. The *TNG* episode "The Perfect Mate" even features a class of women within a species whose role is seemingly to imprint and bond with males of any species. *Memory Alpha* lists forty-one characters in the *Star Trek* canon that are hybrids ("Hybrids"). *Star Trek* offers a future in which all alien species can and do enjoy sexual relations with one another and the collective series love characters that are the product of these inter-species relationships. In fairness to *Star Trek, The Next Generation* offers an explanation for how this might be biologically possible. The episode "The Chase" (*TNG*) argues that a common ancestor throughout the Alpha quadrant, seeded by an ancient humanoid race that found the Alpha and Beta quadrants free of humanoid species, means the humanoids can interbreed safely (Vulcans, Humans, Klingons, Romulans, Betazeds, Bajorans, Cardassians and presumably any humanoid species), with some help from technology to address differences in specific species.

The problem, of course, is that none of these couplings and offspring is biologically possible. Athena Andreadis argues, correctly, that the "rule of chromosomal pairing [that] dictates that reproduction is possible only when the chromosomes of the two prospective parents can completely and exactly align" indicates that the hybrid characters of *Star Trek*, while often the most interesting characters, are biologically impossible and could not exist (26). She further notes that not only are such beings impossible in reality, they are "impossible even if we accept the premises of the show" (Andreadis 29). Her examples include the problem of different hemoglobin, different organs, different life spans and the rules of biology. In the case of hemoglobin, for example, Human blood is red, Vulcan blood is green, and Klingon purple because the hemoglobin in each species bonds oxygen to different molecules: iron, copper and manganese, respectively. These bloods cannot blend. Spock has green blood, but his mother has red blood—this should not and could not work (Andreatis 29–30). Likewise, Klingons have redundant organs, which would indicate that DNA would not allow a Klingon to reproduce with a human, thus allowing for K'Ehleyr, Alexander and B'Elanna, as the genes for organs would not match. Vulcans have an extra eyelid, require less sleep and live longer as they come from a planet with a far brighter star than most other species in the Federation. Thus, their circadian rhythms and life spans make it impossible for humans to reproduce with them, making Spock nothing short of an impossibility (Andreatis 28–33). This begs the question of what we are to do with biological impossibilities that exist in the world of *Star Trek*, to which the answer is that species is a metaphor for ethnicity in all incarnations of *Star Trek*. *Star Trek* hybrids are not inter-species, they are biracial. The biology of *Star Trek*'s hybrids is actually a cultural construct, not a genetic one. After all, "there are no genetic markers for race" in the way there are for gender or species (Zack xvi). Hybrid characters on *Star Trek* are either biracial or multiracial, and their behavior and identity is modeled after biracial and multiethnic identity in the real world.

Star Trek is an American cultural product, often reflective of American attitudes and concerns. The Federation and especially Starfleet are presented as a future variation of the United States: egalitarian pluralism within an agreed-upon framework (but dominated by white males, if we are honest). Accommodations are made for individual identity and group cultures, but ultimately assimilation within that framework is expected. Individuals have self-determination of that identity within that framework. Worf may wear his father's sash; Spock can accessorize with an IDIC necklace, but they both start with their respective Starfleet uniforms. Indeed, when Worf kills Duras his defense to Captain Picard is one of his culture: "Sir, I have acted within the boundaries of Klingon law and tradition" ("Reunion," *Star Trek: The Next Generation*). Picard, however, responds:

> Mr. Worf, the Enterprise crew currently includes representatives from thirteen planets. They each have their own individual beliefs and values and I respect them all. But they have all chosen to serve Starfleet. If anyone cannot perform his or her duty because of the demands of their society, they should resign. Do you wish to resign? ["Reunion," *Star Trek: The Next Generation*].

Picard obviously posits that one must place one's identity as a member of Starfleet over and above one's identity as a particular species or ethnicity. *Trek* stages identity conflict within the larger frame of ethnicity and American notions of race. One must be a member of the collective first, and only then may one assert identity from one's heritage. Just as *Star Trek* was the site of the first televised interracial kiss, the joining of different alien species also carries with it implications for real world understanding of interracial relationships and multi-ethnic identity. Single-species characters on *Star Trek* have a firm sense of self (think of all of Kirk and Picard's pronouncements about what it means to be human), whereas bi-species characters are almost always presented as deeply conflicted about identity, from Spock's rejection of his human side to Worf's fundamental essentialism in regards to Klingon identity and behavior to biracial Klingon females rejecting and hating their Klingon heritage (most notably K'Ehlyr and B'Elanna Torres). This essay concludes that hybrid characters in the various iterations of *Star Trek* reflect our culture's own tension over mixed race identity. With an eventual focus on Spock, Worf (not a biological hybrid, but a Klingon raised by humans and thus a cultural one), and B'Elanna Torres, the essay considers hybrid not as biological construct but rather a cultural construct, one with implications for one's own self-understanding and identity.

American Racial Identity and Star Trek

The last laws against miscegenation were repealed in 1967, followed by "a bi-racial baby boom" (Root 3). This fact means that the much-celebrated first interracial kiss in "Plato's Stepchildren" was airing as a new attitude towards multiracial identity was forming in the United States, which explains the shift in attitude (at least on the surface) towards multi-species characters in *Star Trek*'s various incarnations. Yet *Trek* emerged out of a period of monolithic assumptions about racial realities and identities. Elaine Pinderhughes outlines the history of the "doctrine of hypodescent" also known as the "one drop rule"—anyone of mixed race ancestry is to be categorized with the non-white group (76). This rule applies in *Star Trek*: Spock is Vulcan, not human, even to himself. He might, in the occasional instance, admit to his human heritage, but the series often identifies him not as a multi-species individual or a Vulcan-Human but solely as a Vulcan. The legacy of hypodescent continues in later incarnations of Trek, despite the advances in society and in the series themselves concerning ethnic identity. For all the advanced thinking their series displays, B'Elanna, Alexander and K'Ehleyr are Klingons, not humans, despite mixed race heritage. Yet the later series can be perceived as demonstrating a shift in ethnic understanding, particularly because of the social context in which they were created. Spock existed for audiences who still accepted the "one drop rule" of identity; whereas the "biracial baby boom" generation came of age as *The Next Generation*, *Deep Space Nine* and *Voyager* were initially airing.[1] Daniel G. Reginald notes that the 1990s was the period of the development of "multiracial consciousness," reflected in this case, in the latter incarnations of *Trek* (334). Spock was a Vulcan because he was part Vulcan. Only those of sole human ancestry are considered human, the original series' version of whiteness. Picard's crew, on the other hand, are much more accepting of biracial characters having both halves of their identity affirmed. Counselor Troi is half human, half Betazed, and while she is valued for her abilities as a Betazed, she and those around her celebrate and embrace her human identity as well.

Individual identity is never sui generis but rises from context and the perception of others as much as one's own actual ethnic heritage and self-identification. As in contemporary America, biracial characters on *Star Trek* can also self-select with which culture and group they identify. For example, Sela identifies as Romulan, despite the physical evidence of her human heritage, and loathes any implication of a possible human identity. Spock never denies his human ancestry, but obviously self-identifies as Vulcan. What's more, the rest of the crew frequently identify him as Vulcan and not human, from McCoy's comments on his being "green-blooded" and "pointy-eared" to the assertion that he does not understand the humans around him according to those humans when Spock is in command of the ship. Elaine Pinderhughes argues that:

> Biracial identity is a dynamic, changing phenomenon shaped not only by the parents' racial identity and their attitudes about it, but by the child's interaction with a variety of persons in the systems with which he or she must interact, including peers, extended family and his or her community [75].

This idea extends further into Starfleet. Each character's sense of identity is both shaped by belonging to the multi-ethnic collective that is Starfleet, but within the Fleet, characters of multi-species origin face some of the same challenges as their real-world counterparts. For example, the idea that identity is monolithic, and thus one must pick one heritage or the other. "Which are you?" is the first question frequently aimed at biracial individuals (Miller 24). This question is asked because biracial individuals threaten the stability of pure racial identity. Yet, as Maria P.P. Root observes, multiracial individuals can self-identify as multiracial or as monoracial, selecting one of their heritages to be their identity (5). They are free to claim one heritage (Spock) or both (Troi). Interestingly, later incarnations of *Trek* confirm the idea that multiple researchers have repeatedly demonstrated and confirmed "having both parts of their racial heritage accepted and confirmed" is vital to the formation of a healthy biracial identity" (Pinderhughes 79). This self-identification, however, does not take place in a vacuum, as noted above. Spock, raised as a Vulcan on Vulcan in the face of anti-human prejudice repeatedly denies the human part of his identity. Deanna Troi, on the other hand, has embraced both sides of her heritage and is presented as a well-balanced, self-aware individual.

Miri Song argues that ethnicity is always fluid and situational (17). For example, Worf is the only Klingon on the *Enterprise*, but when the Dominion War begins, he is the only Klingon raised by humans on a Klingon vessel. It is in fact the social context that matters more than the actual traits that define one's species (pointed ears, forehead ridges, etc.) Kerry Ann Rockquemore and David L. Brunsman observe that "social factors override physical traits in the process of racial identity construction" (27). It is not his ears that set Spock apart, it is the fact that he is the only Vulcan on a ship of mostly humans.

Case Study One: Spock

From almost its inception, *Star Trek* has been interested in Mr. Spock's conflicted self-identity. Although his ears and persona separate him from the other characters and mark him as Other, the tension in Spock's hybrid nature serves as a focal point. As noted above, given the period and context of the series, Spock as a bi-species character could be read through the idea of the one-drop rule. He is Vulcan in the eyes of virtually everyone on the *Enterprise*, including himself, despite being half-human. Spock is Vulcan not only because of his appearance, but because of his logic and his rejection of emotion. McCoy only refers to Spock as "pointy eared" when Spock is being logical in the face of McCoy's emotional response. In other words, McCoy's casual racism rises not in response to appearance, which is constant, but to behavior. It is through the racial qualities that McCoy attacks Spock. While he might ask, "Must you always be so damn logical?" (as he frequently does), the knee-jerk reaction is to attack Spock's physical traits: "Why you pointy-eared, green-blooded...," because that is what separates Spock from humans on the surface. Yet early in the series, Spock's human heritage is explored when a virus that brings all emotion to the surface infects him. We learn Spock's great regret is being unable to show love to his human mother:

> CHAPEL: You hide it, but you do have feelings.
> SPOCK: I'm in control of my emotions ["The Naked Time," *Star Trek*].

As he begins to break down his emotions come to the surface: "My mother, I could never tell her I loved her. An Earth woman, living on a planet where love, emotion, is bad taste.... I respected my father, our customs. I was ashamed of my Earth blood." Spock notes that his response to being half human is shame, a statement similar to the experience of a number of biracial Americans, encouraged by society to feel shame for not being fully one or the other: "People of color who have internalized the vehicle of oppression in turn apply rigid rules of belonging or establishing 'legitimate' membership," which privileges those closest to an imagined "purity" (Root 5). Spock must be more Vulcan than other Vulcans in order to overcome being part human. Later in the series we meet his parents in "Journey to Babel." Amanda tells Kirk: "It hasn't been easy on Spock. Neither human nor Vulcan, at home nowhere except Starfleet" ("Journey to Babel" *Star Trek*). Spock's own mother offers a remarkable assessment: Spock is "neither" Vulcan nor human instead of both. In doing so, she asserts that purity defines someone's ethnicity, which is strange for a woman with biracial children.

Second, we might note her appraisal of Starfleet, constructed as a place where those of multi ethnic origin can feel "home." This statement also reflects the reality of the sixties, in which institutions, such as the military, desegregated before the rest of the nation, and (in theory at least) offered the potential for a meritocracy. Only in such a context could Spock, who isn't either of his heritages, according to his own mother, find a place to belong. But in order to do so, he must subsume his humanity. In private, Sarek chastens Amanda for "embarrassing Spock," itself a contradiction, since embarrassment is an emotion. "He is a Vulcan," he tells his wife. "He's also human," Amanda responds, in direct contradiction of her earlier assertion that he is "neither." Sarek finds the whole situation distasteful, and would prefer to keep distance from his son, who joined Starfleet over his father's objections. But when Sarek falls ill, Amanda and Spock fight over his prioritizing captaining the ship over saving his father. Amanda tells Spock that "human ... is not a dirty word." Spock is fascinated, as his own rejection of his human side is not the issue. Furthermore, as a self-identifying Vulcan, conveying his Vulcan father to a peace conference, he is behaving exactly as a Vulcan would. The need to be as Vulcan as possible drives Spock to not display any humanity at all. Spock asks, "Mother, how can you have lived on Vulcan so long, married a Vulcan, raised a son on Vulcan without understanding what it means to be a Vulcan?"

Spock defines being a Vulcan: "It means to adopt a philosophy, a way of life which is logical and beneficial. We cannot disregard that philosophy merely for personal gain, no matter how important that gain may be." Note: logic is not biologically Vulcan, it is a cultural choice. It is something Vulcans must work at, which is demonstrated in *Star Trek: The Motion Picture*, in which Spock works to attain the Kolinahr, a Vulcan ritual designed to purge all vestigial emotion, which Spock fails to do when he is concerned for his human friends, and in *Star Trek V: The Final Frontier*, in which Spock's half-brother Sybok rejects logic in favor of a life full of emotion, and finally in the *Star Trek* reboot, in which Sarek admits Vulcans are biologically more emotional than humans but have adopted logic as a survival strategy. In other words, logic, the defining personality trait of Vulcans is neither biological nor inherited. It is cultural and must be learned. In order to prove how Vulcan he is, Spock must be the most logical of all.

At heart, Spock eventually comes to terms with his own multi-ethnic identity. When Sybok attempts to gain control of Spock by showing him their father's disgust at Spock's birth that his second son is "so human," Spock responds instead, "I am not that outcast boy. I have found my place and I know who I am" (*Star Trek V: The Final Frontier*). Indeed, his later appearances in episodes of *The Next Generation* confirm this. In "Unification Part II" Spock and Data work together on equipment while conversing about their own experiences as outsiders in Starfleet.

> DATA: You are half human.
> SPOCK: Yes.
> DATA: Yet you have chosen a Vulcan way of life.
> SPOCK: I have.
> DATA: In effect, you have abandoned what I have sought all my life ["Unification, Part II," *Star Trek: The Next Generation*].

Spock responds that the opposite is also true—Data has been given by design what every Vulcan seeks all their lives—emotionless logic. Data also acknowledges that Spock had a choice in terms of how he identified culturally, and *chose* to be Vulcan. Spock does not disagree. This older Spock knows who he is and is comfortable with his choices and his identity. This is not the conflicted Spock of "The Naked Time." Yet, at the conclusion of the exchange, it is revealed that while Spock may be at peace with whom and what he is, the human is still there:

> DATA: As you examine your life do you find that you have missed your humanity?
> SPOCK: I have no regrets.
> DATA: "No regrets"? That is a human expression.
> SPOCK: Yes. Fascinating ["Unification, Part II," *Star Trek: The Next Generation*].

Perhaps Spock is so Vulcan because he has lived so long among humans that he distinguishes himself from them, and yet their influence is still present in him as a person and a cultural being. He defines himself in opposition to humans, needing to out-Vulcan other Vulcans to prove his own identity as a Vulcan, even as his own human side lurks beneath the surface, let out at opportune moments. In "Journey to Babel," McCoy asks Amanda if Spock might not be more human than he seems. The irony is, while this is true, Spock is also more Vulcan than he seems.

J.J. Abrams' *Star Trek* reboot also reframes Spock's multi-ethnic heritage. As a child, Spock is confronted by three older bullies at school:

> BULLY 1: Spock
> SPOCK: I presume you've prepared new insults for today.
> BULLY 1: Affirmative.
> SPOCK: This is your thirty-fifth attempt to elicit an emotional response from me.
> BULLY 1: You're neither Vulcan nor human and therefore have no place in the universe.
> BULLY 2: Look! He has human eyes. They look sad, don't they?
> BULLY 3: Perhaps an emotional response requires physical stimuli. [Pushes Spock]
> BULLY 1: He's a traitor, you know—your father. For marrying her. That human whore [*Star Trek* (2009)].

With this last taunt, Spock begins to fight the first bully, eventually climbing on top of the larger boy and mercilessly punching his face in the emotional response the bully indeed sought. (As Spock once told another young Vulcan male, "you may find that having is not so pleasing a thing after all as wanting. It is not logical, but it is often true" ["Amok Time," *Star Trek*]).

From this exchange we may surmise some important aspects of Spock's identity formation. As Amanda asserted in the original series, Spock is neither/nor, here according to the Vulcan bullies and therefore belongs nowhere (apparently Vulcans are also capable of racism and prejudice). Second, according to Vulcans, emotion is the indicator of humanity (we never hear Spock nor any other Vulcan refer to humans as "round-eared" or "red-blooded"—the physical attributes do not matter, it is the psychology of humans that is their identity). Third, Spock's push button is his mother; insult him, call him half- breed, he is fine. Insult mom and he goes nuts. Spock is clearly deeply conflicted about his human mother, and it is the human part that conflicts him. Spock's father arrives to deal with his son after the incident with the bullies. He tells Spock that Vulcans are, in fact, the much more emotional race:

> SAREK: Emotions run deep in our race. In many ways more deeply than in humans. Logic offers a serenity humans seldom experience. The control of feelings so that they do not control you.
> SPOCK: You suggest that I should be completely Vulcan, and yet you married a human.
> SAREK: As ambassador to Earth it is my duty to observe and understand human behavior. Marrying your mother was logical [*Star Trek*].

Again, Vulcans are emotional—logic and emotional suppression are cultural, not biological. They define themselves through this cultural aspect and then use it to Other humans. Humans have emotions, Vulcans do not (except, of course, they do, but humans don't suppress theirs). Sarek later reveals, after her death, that he married Amanda because he loved her. In times of personal crises, Vulcans can and do admit to emotions. Lastly, we might note, as in all other cases, Spock's solution to the problem of being half human is to be more Vulcan than the Vulcans. And yet, later, when he is admitted into the Vulcan Science Academy, the Minister refers to his human mother as "a disadvantage," suggesting Spock is special since he had to overcome his biracial heritage. Spock's response is to refuse the offer and join Starfleet. When informed no Vulcan has ever refused admission, he responds, "Then as I am half human your record remains untarnished," throwing logic in the face of prejudice. Spock uses his heritage and his logic as weapons and shields. It is only in Starfleet that Spock finds a welcoming home.

Indeed, the narrative arc of J.J. Abrams's reboot concerns Spock coming to terms with his own dual nature. Future Spock (or Spock Prime) encourages Kirk to push Spock until he displays emotion, just as the bullies in his childhood did. Kirk, however, does it not to show Spock's supposed ethnic inferiority but so that Spock will come to terms with the fact that he is emotionally compromised and needs to embrace and learn to deal with his human side (It doesn't hurt that such behavior will also put Kirk in charge of the *Enterprise*, but Kirk's journey is the opposite one—to learn the kind of discipline that Spock embodies.)

Spock is *Star Trek*'s first multiracial character. He denies his human heritage, but it always lurks. It is in the perceived tension between Vulcan and human that Spock finds his true identity, as part of the "talented tenth"—a self-identifying Vulcan who must exceed in order to prove himself as good as the others on Vulcan, despite his heritage, and who then, when the only Vulcan among humans, finds himself subjected to prejudice in the opposite direction. Spock is a problem for them because of his Vulcan heritage. Spock finds a home in Starfleet, yes, but he is neither human nor Vulcan after all. Or, more accurately, he is too human on Vulcan and too Vulcan when with humans. Context determines identity.

Case Study Two: Worf

Worf is biologically of sole Klingon descent. Both of his parents were Klingons. He was, however, raised by humans, which makes his identity as much a hybrid's as Spock's. Worf spent his early formative years with his biological parents on the Klingon homeworld. He survived the Khitomer

Massacre and was adopted by Sergey and Helena Rhozenko and subsequently raised on Earth. In other words, he is a Klingon raised by human foster parents in a virtually all-human environment. Miri Song states that "an individual's ethnic identity is also fundamentally shaped by interactions with one's co-ethnics," but also that individual identity is also shaped by "dominant representations and stereotypes" encountered from those who are different (Song 41). Worf's answer, like Spock, is to fully embrace his Klingon identity, even though it is primarily shaped by childhood memories and second-hand accounts of Klingons. Worf had to learn how to be Klingon on a planet full of humans who did not particularly have a high opinion of Klingons. His identity as a Klingon is somewhat compromised by his foster parents. He is embarrassed when they come to visit the *Enterprise*, as he believes they will not understand him or his work.

> SERGEY: He never wanted any human food growing up. Everything had to be Klingon.
> HELENA: I learned to cook *rokeg* blood pie.
> SERGEY: Somehow we never quite learned how to eat it ["Family," *Star Trek: The Next Generation*].

As a Klingon among humans, Worf insisted on being as Klingon as possible (just as child Spock attempted to be as Vulcan as possible). His foster parents knew it would not be easy for Worf to grow up without other Klingons as models and to offer guidance. "We had to let him discover and experience his heritage by himself. Let him find his own path," Sergey explains ("Family," *Star Trek: The Next Generation*). As a result, Worf's identity as a Klingon developed around what he believes Klingons do and are, rather than the experience of actual Klingons. Worf frequently ascribes behavior to Klingons that reflects his ideas of what Klingons are, rather than the reality of Klingon culture. For example,

> WORF: Klingons do not laugh!
> GUINAN: Oh yes they do. Absolutely they do. *You* don't. But I've heard Klingon belly laughs that'll curl your hair ["Redemption," *Star Trek: The Next Generation*].

In other words, Worf might also be backforming his Klingon identity through his own behavior. I do not laugh, he reasons, therefore Klingons do not laugh. He then ascribes such behavior to his identity as a Klingon.

Worf's narrative arc through two series, much like Spock's, concerns his coming to terms with what it means to be a Klingon. He accepts discommendation to preserve the Empire, but then embraces every opportunity to join Klingons when possible. He takes Klingon culture very seriously, offering to marry K'Ehlyr after a one night stand, as it is the honorable thing to do. Indeed, Worf's own struggles with identity are shaped by his encounters with other Klingon hybrids: K'Ehlyr (and then and thus Alexander) and especially the Klingon/Romulan hybrid children, most notably Ba'el, who represent the first non-human hybrid pairing in the series. K'Ehlyr is presented as a foil for Worf, as well as a mate. She is half human, half Klingon who grew up resenting her Klingon half, but it now makes her the ideal emissary between the two peoples. She works for the Empire when it comes to matters human. Her unique history makes her especially well-suited to work between identities and worlds. K'Ehlyr and Troi bond over their own unique heritages which make them special in and useful to Starfleet. The difference is in their attitudes towards their mixed heritages:

K'EHLYR: You must have grown up like I did, trapped between cultures.
TROI: I never felt trapped. I tried to experience the richness and diversity of the two worlds.
K'EHLYR: Perhaps you got the best of each. Myself, I think I got the worst of each.
TROI: Oh, I doubt that.
K'EHLYR: Oh, no. Having my mother's sense of humor is bad enough. It's gotten me into plenty of trouble.
TROI: And your Klingon side?
K'EHLYR: That I keep under tight control. It's like a terrible temper. It's not something I want people to see ["The Emissary," *Star Trek: The Next Generation*].

She later calls her Klingon heritage, "a monster inside me," and confesses to Troi, "My Klingon side can be terrifying, even to me…" Troi, ever the counselor, attempts to assert a positive side to her Klingon inheritance, telling her, "It gives you strength. It is a part of you." To which K'Ehlyr responds, "That doesn't mean I have to like it." Indeed, she does not, and identifies more strongly with her human heritage than her Klingon one, which also makes her a model for *Voyager*'s B'Elanna Torres.

The Klingon raised by humans who must prove his Klingon-ness to himself every day meets and mates with the self-disliking half–Klingon, half-Human who serves as emissary between her two peoples. Although they mate after working out to one of Worf's holodeck combat calisthenics in a raw display of Klingon aggressive sexuality, the next morning, their attitudes towards the event are very different. Worf begins the formal Klingon oath of marriage. She refuses.

WORF: You dishonor our sacred traditions!
K'EHLYR: It was what it was.
WORF: That is a human attitude!
K'EHLYR: I AM human!
WORF: You are also Klingon.
K'EHLYR: So that means we should bond for life?
WORF: It is our way.
K'EHLYR: Yours, not mine! ["The Emissary," *Star Trek: The Next Generation*].

K'Ehlyr is a foil for Worf not just dramatically but in terms of identity. He includes her in Klingon identity ("our sacred traditions," "our way"), but she rejects such inclusion ("yours, not mine"). Worf as a Klingon alone among humans seeks a "we"; K'Ehlyr, who interacts with both, refuses to be just Klingon and asserts the primacy of her human heritage ("I am human"). She is free to choose her identity, but as a cultural hybrid, Worf can only assert his Klingon identity. He takes the social role of Klingon seriously. She does not. For example, Worf is obsessed with his notion of Klingon honor. It is because he did not grow up around it that it has become so important to him. K'Ehlyr calls him on it, saying that he would have "gone through with the oath ... regardless of the consequences to our careers, to our lives." He responds, "Honor demanded no less." She asks him if honor is all he cares about, "Don't you *feel* anything else?" Worf subsumes everything else about himself to honor.

These arguments will be repeated and enhanced when K'Ehlyr returns to the *Enterprise* a few years later with their son, the product of that earlier mating. Worf speaks to Alexander about what it is to be a Klingon and sees in his son what he must have feared growing up: a Klingon who knows nothing of Klingon ways but rather prefers to behave like a human:

> WORF: He knows nothing of our ways!
> K'EHLYR: Our ways? You mean Klingon ways, don't you?
> WORF: He IS a Klingon!
> K'EHLYR: He is also my son and I am half human. He will find his own way ["Reunion," *Star Trek: The Next Generation*].

Again, she serves as identity foil for Worf. K'Ehlyr is a biracial Klingon who favors her human half but has learned to move between cultures effectively. Worf is a "pure" Klingon who knows less about Klingon ways than the mother of his son. Alexander is biologically three quarters Klingon, one quarter human, but has been raised by his mother without being fully contextualized in either culture. As with her own identity, K'Ehlyr seeks to allow her son to find "his own way." Worf invests in group identity; K'Ehlyr in individual identity. Both are the products of their upbringing and their contexts as much as their genetics. Perhaps this is most interesting is when Worf must confront his own prejudices about hybrids. While his own son is of mixed-race descent, he is infuriated to discover bi-species children in the former prison camp on Carraya IV, where he had been told his father was held prisoner. Instead he finds Klingons and Romulans living together. Becoming enamored of Ba'el, he goes to kiss her and learns her Klingon hair hides her Romulan ears. He then learns while her mother is Klingon, her father is Tokath, the former Romulan commander of the camp. Worf tells her he cannot accept her existence, as Romulans are treacherous and cowardly and no Klingon would ever mate with one ("Birthright, Part II," *Star Trek: The Next Generation*). Overcoming his initial shock and racism, Worf then attempts to teach the children of Carraya IV, all Klingon-Romulan hybrids, the ways of a Klingon, taking one on a hunt with him, teaching others a game involving spears that they had been using to grow vegetables. The older generation objects, but the younger generation, having grown up within a mostly Romulan culture, are curious about both their Klingon heritage and the rest of the galaxy. In an inversion of his dialogue with K'Ehlyr, he sees the children of Carraya IV knowing only Romulan ways and he wants them to learn "our ways," finally recognizing them as part Klingon as well. Eventually Worf is allowed to bring the ones who wish to leave for a safe outpost from which they might make their own way. The irony is that Worf's own racism against Romulans initially blinds him to their own unique identity and how he might introduce them to aspects of Klingon culture to which they had never been exposed. Worf does not initially accept these hybrids and he cannot understand why the adult Klingons or the hybrid children are not ashamed of the Romulan heritage. As with the logic of Vulcans, there are aspects of Klingon identity that are cultural, not biological. If Worf were half-Romulan, he'd be ashamed, and thus he cannot understand why Ba'el and the others are not. Once he comes to terms with the fact that they are biologically half–Klingon but culturally mostly Romulan, he finds a path to connect with them, by providing them with the example of Klingon culture he never had.

The hybrid children, per Pinderhughs above, have a very healthy sense of identity, as both Klingons and Romulans have been present for their entire lives with mutual respect and love (even if the Romulans dominate and work to suppress some of the Klingon instincts). However, they are curious about the part of their heritage they do not know about. They have a healthy sense of self and identity, they share none of Worf's sense of outrage or offense, but they recognize that some part of their identity is missing and must be engaged in order to feel complete. They teach Worf to overcoming his own prejudices by teaching them to embrace their Klingon heritage as well.

Case Study Three: B'Elanna Torres

The series bible for *Voyager* opens its character profile of B'Elanna Torres by focusing on how her multi-ethnic heritage both defines her and causes her to be in perpetual crisis:

> The Chief Engineer has a façade that's worked well for her: tough, knowledgeable, able to take care of herself, bothered by nothing, In fact, beneath the surface, there dwells a person confused and at war with herself. B'Elanna has a mixed heritage—Klingon and human—that she deplores. Her Klingon side is disturbing to her; she makes every effort to suppress it, preferring to develop her human side [Ruditis 4].

The series bible further states she was raised by her Klingon mother (Miral) in a predominantly human colony (later identified in the series as Kessik IV), and "inevitably grew up feeling like the 'other'" (Ruditis 4). She is both Klingon and human, with the implication of Mexican/Hispanic origins on the human side. She tells Paris that being one of two Klingons in the colony was alienating in every sense of the word: "Nobody ever said anything but we were different and I didn't like that feeling. Then my father left when I was ten years old.... I finally decided he left because I looked like a Klingon, and so I tried to look human" ("Faces," *Voyager*). Split into her Klingon half and human half by the Vidiians, human B'Elanna is terrified and unable to function. Klingon B'Elanna, missing the mitigating effect of her human half, is unable to effect rescue either. "So you need me?" the Klingon half asks the human B'Elanna, who concludes she is imperfect without both halves of her identity.

Different than Spock or Worf, B'Elanna must also deal with the challenges of gender as well as hybridity. Robin A. Roberts sees echoes of "the tragic mulatta," a woman of mixed black/white descent who could belong to both of her heritages, but instead belongs to neither in B'Elanna:

> Customarily represented as a white/black mix, the mulatta could feasibly exist in either world, but rather than seeing this flexibility as a positive, realist writers and critics have depicted this hybridity as a psychological tragedy based on life in a racist American society [206].

B'Elanna (and Seven of Nine as well, according to Roberts) has the potential to be a tragic mulatta as she is psychologically trapped in being half–Klingon. She is "sexually desirable," and has the potential to be sexually exploited, betrayed and abused by the men in her life. Yet Roberts also acknowledges that both characters are powerful, assertive and even "masculine," which means their "identities are both bi-racial and bi-gendered" (207).

Indeed, B'Elanna has experienced prejudice, and has responded to it aggressively. Chakotay orders B'Elanna to study meditation with Tuvok, since she cannot control her temper or aggressive outbursts. She is contemptuous of both the practice and Tuvok at first, telling him, "I'm not a Vulcan." He asks her to recall her earliest memory of a violent outburst.

> B'ELANNA: Daniel Bird.
> TUVOK: I beg your pardon.
> B'ELANNA: Well, he was one of my classmates in grammar school. He was always terrorizing me. He used to point at my cranial ridges and tease me about being half–Klingon. He called me "Miss Turtlehead."
> TUVOK: That angered you.
> B'ELANNA: Of course it did. So I attacked him once, during recess on the gyroswing. I disengaged the centrifugal governor. He was spinning so fast he almost flew apart. Then I yanked him off the swing and started pounding his little face. If Miss Malvin hadn't shown up I probably would have...

TUVOK: Describe the anger you felt at that moment.
B'ELANNA: I wanted to hurt him ["Juggernaut," *Voyager*].

This exchange reveals that some of the root of B'Elanna's rage is found in the racism she experienced as a child. Tuvok then calls her "Miss Turtlehead." "What did you say to me?" she responds with fury. His point being that she still responds to the insult, even when she knows it is neither intended nor real. Her own adult identity has been shaped by rejection by all who know her for being half–Klingon.

She begins a relationship with blonde-haired, blue-eyed Tom Paris, eventually marrying and deciding to have a child together. B'Elanna remains, however, the product of her own upbringing in which, "being Klingon was equated with alienation and loss, and being human represented everything that was desirable" (Ruditis 4). This statement echoes nearly everything written about biracial experience in the United States, substituting any racial minority for "Klingon" and "white" for "human." Because of the privileging of whiteness in American culture, being of color is equated with alienation, Othering and loss, and being white represents everything desirable. B'Elanna does not want to be biracial. She wants to be solely human. Indeed, she fears her offspring will be subject to the same sense of split identity and not belonging. In "Lineage" (*Voyager*), B'Elanna attempts to genetically remove all Klingon aspects of her unborn daughter so that she will not have to endure the challenges B'Elanna faced as a bi-species person. The episode features a number of flashbacks in which B'Elanna is shown on a camping trip with her father and (human) cousins, Elizabeth, Dean and Michael. "They don't like me," she tells him, although it is clear from the behavior of the other children she is not singled out for her Klingon heritage at all and the older children make efforts to include her and thus implying that at least some of her perceived "Otherness" is just that—her perception and not the actual situation. She is further terrified when the Doctor tells her that Klingon characteristics continue for several generations, even if all her descendants reproduce with pure humans, an Alpha Quadrant variant on the "one drop rule." This pushes her to reprogram the doctor to remove all Klingon characteristics from the child growing in her womb. Paris finally asserts his own view of their offspring: "Our daughter is going to have a mixed heritage, just like her mother. It's something you have in common. Something you should be proud of" ("Lineage," *Voyager*). He gives voice to the need for her to be healthy and embrace both heritages.

Roberts further argues that B'Elanna, being dual Klingon and Hispanic heritage is constructed as ethnic even as a human. "With her dark hair swept severely back and her large bushy eyebrows, B'Elanna's racial mix is physically emphasized" (207). She is, in fact, "both Klingon and Latina" (207). Geraldine

Harris sees B'Elanna's "narrative arc is indeed one of a traumatically divided self implicitly measured against a wholeness and unity of (human) identity (123). Her narrative may end happily, finding a home with Paris and their daughter in Starfleet upon the return to Federation space at the end of the series. However, her divided nature is always apparent next to the unified and singular presence of Paris. His humanity and calming presence always ensures that she is still in some ways an outsider fighting for acceptance.

A Brief Side Note Concerning Tora Ziyal

Deep Space Nine offers an interesting hybrid character with a further complication than those faced by Spock, Worf, and B'Elanna. Tora Ziyal is the offspring of Gul Dukat, the Cardassian Prefect of Bajor, ruling the conquered colony from the space station Terok Nor (which became Deep Space Nine), and Tora Naprem, a Bajoran woman who conceived Ziyal during an affair with Dukat.

When the Cardassian occupation of Bajor was ending, Gul Dukat sent Naprem and Ziyal away to Lissepia as he believed (correctly) that they would not be accepted either on Cardassia or Bajor. When their ship crashed on Dozaria after being attacked by Breen warships, Naprem died and Ziyal was enslaved by the Breen, later to be rescued by Kira Nerys and Gul Dukat. While Dukat planned to kill Ziyal if found, as his political career would suffer if it were discovered he had a half–Bajoran child, he instead brought her back to Cardassia, where he lost his family and position as a result of his child ("Indiscretion"; "Return to Grace," *Deep Space Nine*). Ziyal then returned to Deep Space Nine, her father reasoning that she might find more acceptance there. She eventually went to Bajor to study art, but did not feel welcome there as her father was not only the former Prefect during the occupation but was currently at war against the prophets ("Sons and Daughters," *Deep Space Nine*). She returned again to Deep Space Nine where she helped Federation prisoners of the Cardassians escape during the Dominion War, sabotaged the station's weapons, and thus was shot and killed by Gul Damar as a traitor to the Cardassians ("Sacrifice of Angels," *Deep Space Nine*).

What all of this indicates about Ziyal is that like Spock, she is never welcome or belongs anywhere—not Cardassia Prime, Bajor, or even Deep Space Nine/Terok Nor. Not being in Starfleet, she can find no home that will accept both parts of her identity. We might also compare Gul Dukat's change in fortune with American politicians revealed to have biracial children. Dukat loses everything because of his "half-breed" child, whose very existence is a reminder of the occupation and the state of relations between the two peoples, not to mention the prejudice against Bajorans on Cardassia, the opposite of which will guarantee she cannot live on Bajor either. Given the history of *Deep Space Nine*, Ziyal also contains echoes of occupation and war—other American "half-breeds" from Japan, Korea, and Vietnam—children accepted by neither culture. Soldiers returning from Europe with brides and children found few problems with the children being accepted into American contexts. Children from the wars in Asia, however, presented a problematic situation for both America and their other nation by their very existence. David Lamb describes the plight of the biracial children of the Vietnam War:

> They grew up as the leftovers of an unpopular war, straddling two worlds but belonging to neither. Most never knew their fathers. Many were abandoned by their mothers at the gates of orphanages.... But neither America nor Vietnam wanted the kids known as Amerasians and commonly dismissed by the Vietnamese as "children of the dust"—as insignificant as a speck to be brushed aside [Lamb].

Tora Ziyal is *Star Trek*'s Amerasian child, a "leftover of an unpopular war" wanted by neither side afterwards. Her death is a tragedy made all the more tragic by her own acceptance of her identity in a quadrant in which no one else could.

Conclusion

The Federation rejects racism (at least in theory, ask Spock about exceptions such as Dr. McCoy's continual assertions that he is a "green-blooded, pointy-eared hobgoblin"), but it embraces essentialism. Each species in the *Star Trek* universe has traits which are said to be essential to that species and cannot be overcome by any individual of that species with the exception of humans. Yet Starfleet, as Captain Picard noted, above, requires each of these species to subsume their identity into the larger identity of Starfleet. As has been argued in this essay, *Star Trek* uses species identity to comment on, to critique and sometimes to reinforce contemporary American discourses on race and ethnicity. We can track the sixties incarnation with Spock's anti-assimilationist tendencies and choice to out-Vulcan Vulcans while ignoring his human heritage, since humans would never accept him as human anyway. In *The Next Generation*, *Deep Space Nine* and *Voyager*, a more nuanced approach reflected the times. As Daniel G. Reginald observes, binary thinking of "either/or" was being replaced in the nineties with "both/and" (332). Worf, K'Ehlyr, B'Elanna and Ziyal all had to learn how to negotiate identity in contexts in which they were Other and not part of the mainstream ethnicity. Each had different strategies, tactics and approaches to the development of ethnic identity. Worf became, for lack of a better term, a Klingon nationalist, embracing his Klingon identity in the center of humanity without benefit of any other Klingons. Like Spock, he had to be more Klingon than the other Klingons to prove himself. K'Ehlyr and B'Elanna are both deeply conflicted about identity, and prefer their human heritage to their Klingon, but learn how to negotiate within the larger context of Starfleet and the Empire. Ziyal, interestingly, is revealed to be healthy in terms of her understanding of her own identity, and embraces herself as multi-racial. She is challenged, however, by cultures that would prefer she does not exist. In all, *Star Trek* reveals a great deal about how Americans think about racial identity of multiracial people diachronically from the sixties through the millennia, revealing both change and continuity in racial attitudes. As with the first interracial kiss on television, *Trek* has proven that science fiction allows for effective distancing to allow audiences to think about such things as racial identity without being threatened by it.

Note

1. Interestingly, *Enterprise*, the last series as of this writing, had very few hybrid characters. None of the main characters were multiracial and the show boasted the fewest number of hybrid characters in the entire canon: only four, all half human, half other race (Denobulan, Ikkaran, Skagaran, and Terrellian).

Works Cited

Andreadis, Athena. *To Seek Out New Life: The Biology of* Star Trek. New York: Crown Publishing, 1998.
Harris, Geraldine. *Beyond Representation: Television Drama and the Politics and Aesthetics of Identity*. Manchester: Manchester University Press, 2006.
"Hybrids." *Memory Alpha*. April 15, 2016. http://memory-alpha.wikia.com/wiki/Category:Hybrids.
Jenkins, Susan, and Robert Jenkins. *Life Signs: The Biology of* Star Trek. New York: Harper Collins, 1998.
Lamb, David. "Children of the Vietnam War." Smithsonian.com (June 2009). http://www.smithsonianmag.com/people-places/children-of-the-vietnam-war-131207347/?no-ist. Accessed July 7, 2016.
Miller, Robin. "The Human Ecology of Multiracial Identity." *Racially Mixed People in America*. Ed. Maria P.P. Root. Newbury Park: SAGE Publications, 1992. 24–36.
Pinderhughes, Elaine. "Biracial Identity: Asset or Handicap?" *Racial and Ethnic Identity: Psychological Development and Creative Expression*. Eds. Herbert W. Harris, Howard C. Blue and Ezra E.H. Griffith. New York: Routledge, 1995. 73–94.
Roberts, Robin A. "Science, Race and Gender in *Star Trek: Voyager*." *Fantasy Girls: Gender in the New Universe of Science Fiction and Fantasy Television*. Ed. Elyce Rae Helford. Lanham, MD: Rowman and Littlefield, 2000. 203–222.
Rockquemore, Kerry Ann and David L. Brunsman. *Beyond Black: Biracial in America*. 2d ed. Lanham, MD: Rowan and Littlefield, 2008.
Root, Maria P.P. *Racially Mixed People in America*. Newbury Park: SAGE Publications, 1992.
Ruditis, Paul. *Star Trek: Voyager Companion*. NewYork: Pocket Books, 2003.
Song, Miri. *Choosing Ethnic Identity*. Cambridge: Polity, 2003.
Zack, Naomi. "Introduction." *American Mixed Race: The Culture of Microdiversity*. Ed. Naomi Zack. Lanham, MD: Rowan and Littlefield, 1995, xv–xxv.

Where No Girl Has Gone Before?

Teenage Girls in Star Trek*'s Strong Female Future*

Zara T. Wilkinson

Jan Johnson-Smith describes science fiction television in the United States as "the quintessential American Dream" (2), ascribing to the medium a list of qualities that include individualistic, progressive, humanist, and egalitarian. No television franchise embodies these characteristics more wholeheartedly than *Star Trek*, which began in 1966 and now encompasses five live action television series, one animated television series, ten films in the original continuity, and three films in the "rebooted" timeline. The *Star Trek* series are regularly recognized for their attempts to depict a utopian future (Geraghty, "Eight") in which the social problems of the present-day United States have largely become obsolete. A vital component of this utopian future is inclusivity, and each series has increased the number of people who can see themselves in *Star Trek*'s cast and crew:

> The crew of the original series was created to symbolize America in the 1960s—encompassing different races and ethnicities.... On board *TNG* there were female doctors, a blind pilot, and children in command positions, later on *DS9* we were introduced to an African-American single parent ... and in *Voyager* a female played the captain for the first time in a series [Geraghty, "Telling Tales"].

In keeping with this relentless inclusivity, the future depicted by *Star Trek* has always included women of all types. Throughout its rich and varied history, the franchise has provided its audience with female role models, heroes, and anti-heroes. Space is the final frontier, and *Star Trek* shows its viewers that this brave new world is one in which women of all races (human and alien) are starship captains, scientists, warriors, and religious leaders. The original *Star Trek* had one female lead and two recurring characters, and *Star Trek: The Next Generation* featured a larger and more diverse group of women on the *Enterprise*. These were, among others, Dr. Beverly Crusher, Counselor Deanna Troi, Lieutenant Tasha Yar, Guinan, Dr. Katherine Pulaski, and Ensign Ro Laren. Following in its footsteps, later series *Deep Space Nine* and *Voyager* have been lauded for creating a variety of prominent female characters and then giving them interesting storylines and internal conflicts not limited to the stereotypically feminine. The women of *Deep Space Nine* (Jadzia Dax, Kira Nerys, Keiko O'Brien, Kai Winn and Tora Ziyal) and *Voyager* (Kathryn Janeway, B'Elenna Torres, Kes, Seven of Nine, and Samantha Wildman) exhibit a breadth of backgrounds, job duties and personality types that other *Star Trek* series, despite their strong female characters, cannot rival.

Strong women, in real life as well as in television series and films like *Star Trek*, offer adolescent girls powerful role models when they need them most. Adolescence is a difficult life stage for girls, who are beginning to negotiate their place in adult society. The female characters of *Star Trek* provide many potential role models for girls and young women to emulate, but despite these successes *Star Trek* has thus far failed to offer viewers a satisfying depiction of female adolescence itself. The viewers who love *Star Trek* and see themselves and their daughters in its strong, capable, complex women are left without depictions of how girls grow into and become those same women. This lack is particularly striking because male adolescent viewers are invited to identify with multiple characters in *The Next Generation* and *Deep Space Nine*. This essay will explore the *Star Trek* television series' depiction of women and their clear shift in focus from single officers to families and familial relationships. This shift created opportunities to showcase the experiences of the adolescents aboard the series' spaceships and space stations. In all *Star Trek* series to date, however, the adolescents have been exclusively male. During the course of these series, Wesley Crusher, Jake Sisko, Nog, and Alexander Rozhenko grow and mature, develop career paths, and explore how they, as young adults, have changed since they were children. This essay will also examine in some depth the storylines related to these male adolescents in order to determine exactly what adolescent girls have been denied through their lack of representation in *Star Trek*.

Women on Star Trek

When it comes to the depiction of women, *Star Trek* is not without controversy. All of the female regulars on the original *Star Trek* conform to fairly traditional feminine roles: "one embodies a secretary…, one a nurse, and another telephone operator" (Hark 93). Despite their stereotypically feminine occupations, however, Lt. Uhura, Nurse Christine Chapel, and Yeoman Janice Rand are three professional, career-oriented women, and Uhura is all of those as well as a woman of color (O'Keeffe). Patricia Vettel-Becker stresses that it is important for television shows such as *Star Trek* to show single women with careers "who also delight in their femininity" (145). At times, however, the original *Star Trek* seems to value its female characters as women first and capable, professional crewmembers second. In "Who Mourns for Adonais?" McCoy describes Lt. Carolyn Palamas, a fellow officer, as "all woman." In "The Conscience of the King," when Lenore expresses concern that the *Enterprise* has turned its female crewmembers into "just people instead of women," Kirk counters her concern by asserting, "A woman always remains a woman." Anne Cranny-Francis has concluded that "almost all attempts to find liberating fantasy images for women in *Star Trek* seem doomed to failure" (282). Similarly, Jon Wagner and Jan Lundeen criticize the show for its fairly conservative approach to gender: "The original Enterprise not only carries Western gender roles to the far reaches of the galaxy, but it discovers them wherever it goes" (83). While the original *Star Trek*'s female characters, particularly Uhura, are well-loved by many fans, there is also room for both criticism and improvement.

When all *Star Trek* series are taken as a whole, however, the franchise has been lauded for its inclusion of professional, well-rounded female characters who, especially in *Voyager* and *Deep Space Nine*, occupy positions of power. Sherry Ginn argues that "for the most part the *Star Trek* universe shows us myriad examples of ways in which women can envision future space" (124). In particular, Ginn lauds *The Next Generation*'s Dr. Beverly Crusher for demonstrating that in the future a woman could successfully fill many roles simultaneously: mother, Starfleet officer, and Chief Medical Officer. The series finale ("All Good Things...") adds another role: Dr. Crusher (now humorously styled "Captain Picard") is captain of the USS *Pasteur*, establishing that even a (female) physician could be elevated into a command role. Similarly, Robin Roberts ("Science, Race, and Gender") commends *Voyager* for its nuanced depictions of female scientists, specifically Captain Janeway and Lt. B'Elenna Torres, and for what she describes as a corresponding feminist approach to science. In these later *Star Trek* series, as Wagner and Lundeen (1998) quip, "it's hard to find people anywhere in the galaxy who have not discovered the virtues of gender equality" (90). Indeed, over and over the series show that even the enemies of the Federation, such as the Romulans, Klingons, and Borg, have female leaders, soldiers, and scientists. In a particularly noteworthy example, *Deep Space Nine* reveals that the deeply-ingrained sexism in Ferengi society hides women like Ishka, Quark and Rom's mother, who wears clothes, conducts business, and eventually wields considerable political power, paving the way for gender reform on Ferenginar.

A Developing Focus on the Family

In addition to increased visibility and higher status roles for women, the later *Star Trek* series provided viewers with increasingly detailed looks at the family lives of the series regulars. Family is almost entirely absent from the original *Star Trek;* no character on the original *Enterprise* has a successful marriage or a family (Wagner and Lundeen 98). While the ship functions much as a familial unit, actual biological family ties are not privileged:

> Family members are virtually nonexistent in the original series, or family members and their surrogates actually die off. Some representative examples include Kirk's loss of his brother and sister-in-law in "Operation Annihilate" (1967), a wife and unborn child in "The Paradise Syndrome" (1968), and a son in *ST III: The Search for Spock* [Bick 47].

On the *Enterprise,* the familial ties represented by spouses, siblings, and parents are at odds with a Starfleet officer's duty to his or her ship and Captain, as well as professional friendships with crew-mates (Lawrence and Jewett 241). This absence of family ties extends most notably to the attainment of romantic relationships and marriage. Series creator Gene Roddenberry imagined *Star Trek* as a triumph of the platonic ideal over the "mutual possession" of marriage; in an interview about the series, he declared, "Marriage in the form that it is now cannot possibly continue into the future. That's why we have so little of it in *Star Trek*" (Fern 100). The *Enterprise* crewmembers do not have long-term romantic relationships, and they certainly do not have them with each other. Wagner and Lundeen describe the women on the crew of the original *Enterprise* as part of an "extended family" (82). As they appear to their male shipmates as sisters or daughters, their "essentially incestuous guise" (Bick 48) renders them thoroughly off-limits. Yeoman Janice Rand and Nurse Christine Chapel, for example, have particularly unsatisfying romantic lives because of the romantic feelings they have for their male coworkers. Nurse Chapel's unrequited love for Spock is the source of much emotional turmoil for her over the course of the original series, and the growing chemistry between Yeoman Rand and Captain Kirk has been cited as one of the reasons why Rand was written out of the series by the end of the first season (Vettel-Becker 159).

Perhaps as a side-effect of downplaying romantic attachments between crew-mates, the original *Star Trek* is particularly unclear regarding how marriage works in Starfleet. "Balance of Terror" begins with Captain Kirk officiating at a wedding between two crewmembers, Angela Martine and Robert Tomlinson. Kirk delights in this duty, describing it as a "happy privilege." However, while the *Enterprise* crew seems similarly pleased by the wedding ceremony, the episode devotes little attention to what happens when and if the newlyweds decide to start a family. Indeed, this issue is neatly sidestepped when Robert Tomlinson dies before the end of the episode. In "Who Mourns for Adonais?" Kirk and McCoy discuss Scotty's apparent attraction to Lt. Carolyn Palamas in a way that suggests that female officers often leave Starfleet service when they marry:

> McCoy: One day she'll find the right man and off she'll go, out of the service.
> Kirk: I like to think of it not so much losing an officer as gaining—
> Scotty: [to Palamas] Come along.
> Kirk: Actually, I'm losing an officer.

The implication here is clear: a female officer will find it difficult, if not impossible, to maintain a romantic relationship and a professional appointment in Starfleet. Kirk and McCoy assume that Palamas, who is a trained and highly-educated anthropologist, will trade in a successful career for romance. Since McCoy also assumes that Palamas will not end up in a relationship with Scotty, he may intend to insinuate that she will meet someone outside of the crew of the *Enterprise* and choose to remain with them. However, no such statements are ever made about men, and presumably many male Starfleet officers marry without resigning. The episodes "Court Martial" and "The Menagerie Part 1" take place on Starbase 11, a station under Starfleet control. Outposts like this, or on Earth or other planets, could easily offer Starfleet officers the opportunity to maintain both a personal life and a career, as they do in later *Star Trek* series. Overall, the original series raises many questions about the family lives of the *Enterprise* crew but provides few answers.

The Next Generation and *Deep Space Nine* address these same questions somewhat more satisfyingly. While the original *Star Trek* featured only adult professionals, these series show Starfleet officers bringing their families along to their posts (Ginn). Although extended family, such as Deanna Troi's mother Lwaxana, are rarely welcomed on board the *Enterprise* (Richards 76) and visiting family members on *Deep Space Nine* tend to cause hijinks and embarrassment, these series go out of their way to show that starships and space stations are functional communities that include familial living arrangements. With over a thousand people on the *Enterprise* ("Remember Me") and two thousand on Deep Space Nine ("Meridian"), these vessels would need to operate like small towns, with all the trappings of social and civilian life in such places. This is emphasized in "Data's Day," when Data recounts information about an average day on the *Enterprise*, including four birthdays, a school play, four promotions, and a birth. *The Next Generation* and *Deep*

Space Nine are clear that a life in Starfleet is a *life* in Starfleet, with room for romantic relationships, children, and a variety of off-duty pastimes.

Whereas the original *Star Trek* depicts the *Enterprise* as a military vessel akin to a submarine, the later series showcase many more spaces that are clearly delineated for off-duty functions or civilian life, including Ten Forward on the *Enterprise* and the Promenade shops on Deep Space Nine. As a result as their series' focus on family life, the *Enterprise* and Deep Space Nine both include schools. Mark Wildermuth notes that *The Next Generation* features "daycare provided by the Federation" and wryly observes that "[f]eminists who have been arguing for state-supported daycare since the late 1960s would no doubt have felt quite comfortable on this ship" (106). Indeed, the school and childcare facilities allow the crew of the *Enterprise* to balance professional obligations and family life with seemingly few tensions. The *Enterprise* is presented as a family-focused, community-minded ship with an "it takes a village" approach to child-rearing; this can be seen taken to an extreme in the second season, when the teenage Wesley Crusher remains on board after his mother accepts a post at Starfleet Medical on Earth. The school on Deep Space Nine was opened during the series, as the station was newly under Starfleet command at the time of the series premiere. Keiko O'Brien served as schoolteacher, and she eventually had over ten students at one time ("A Man Alone," "Dramatis Personae," "In the Hands of the Prophets"). As it did not originally have any children onboard, *Voyager* seems to lack a formal school. Naomi Wildman is often seen in the care of whoever has the time and the ability to watch or educate her; often, this is Neelix, but at other times Seven of Nine, The Doctor, and Commander Chakotay fulfill this role. Later, when *Voyager* takes aboard several Borg children ("Collective"), Seven of Nine is put in charge of their schooling, developing scheduled lessons and even a science fair ("Child's Play").

Despite establishing family life as integral to the functioning of a starship or space station, even *The Next Generation* and *Deep Space Nine* fall short in the depiction of the impact of communal military living on nuclear families. Almost all of the *Star Trek* characters with children are single parents. Dr. Beverly Crusher and Captain Benjamin Sisko are both shown raising teenage sons after the death of their respective spouses. Worf's son Alexander is born without his knowledge, and Worf gains custody only after K'Ehleyr, Alexander's mother, is murdered. Rom's wife left him and their son Nog for a richer Ferengi, although he later marries professional Dabo girl Leeta. Ensign Samantha Wildman did not realize she was pregnant with Naomi until after *Voyager* had embarked on its first mission, and she spends the next seven years as a single mother while she is separated from her husband. In *Deep Space Nine*, two additional couples attempt to have children, but both situations end in tragedy: Lt. Jadzia Dax is murdered immediately after Dr. Bashir announces that she and Worf should be able to have a child ("Tears of the Prophets"), and one episode after Kassidy Sisko discovers she is pregnant Captain Sisko sacrifices himself and loses corporal form ("The Dogs of War," "What You Leave Behind"). Ultimately, in all *Star Trek* series, the only two-parent household is that of Chief Miles O'Brien and Keiko O'Brien, although they are joined by Lt. Tom Paris and Lt. B'Elanna Torres when Torres gives birth to their daughter as *Voyager* returns to the Alpha Quadrant in the series finale ("Endgame").

The marriage of Miles and Keiko O'Brien has been called "the only successful long-term relationship" in the *Star Trek* universe (Johnson-Smith 112). The O'Briens, first seen on *The Next Generation* and then given more prominence on *Deep Space Nine*, are very functional as both a romantic couple and as parents. They get married in the fourth season of *The Next Generation* ("Data's Day") and have two children: Molly, born in *The Next Generation* episode "Disaster," and Yoshi, born in the *Deep Space Nine* episode "The Begotten." The strength of the O'Briens' relationship is exemplified in the honest depiction of the difficulties of having two parents with individual lives, goals, and careers. The latter is especially difficult on a remote space station with few opportunities outside of Starfleet. Even after marrying and having a child, Keiko, a botanist, is shown working in both the arboretum and the biology lab on the *Enterprise*, as well as on away missions. When the O'Briens are transferred to *Deep Space Nine*, Keiko finds that the station has no need for a botanist and opens the station's first primary school instead. Wagner and Lundeen (1998) describe Keiko somewhat unfavorably as "mostly hanging around [the O'Brien's] quarters in a traditional wife/mother role" (112), noting that when she does work outside the home it is in the traditionally-feminine role as teacher. However, after Keiko is forced to close the school in "The House of Quark," she leaves the station for a six-month expedition to Bajor, serving as the mission's chief botanist. She also takes their daughter Molly, but her departure is not depicted as a situation in which she is leaving her husband or prizing her own career above her family's best interests. Although it is difficult for all of them, Miles O'Brien encourages his wife to have a rewarding career and is still just as much a loving husband when she returns. Through Miles and Keiko O'Brien, *Deep Space Nine* provides a rich and nuanced look at the impact of Starfleet service on the families of the crew, as well as a relationship to emulate.

Adolescents in Space: No Girls Allowed?

Star Trek's changing focus on crewmembers' families and domestic lives allowed the casts to expand to include children and adolescents. *The Next*

Generation and *Deep Space Nine* both feature storylines related to growing up and adjusting to changing societal expectations. These plotlines provide adolescent viewers with positive role models and show viewers of all ages what to expect from adolescence. When *The Next Generation* was still in the early stages of production, series creator Gene Roddenberry was reportedly nearly convinced to include a female teenager named Leslie Crusher. Although Robert Justman argued for the inclusion of Leslie, Roddenberry ultimately decided that a male adolescent made the most narrative sense:

> I thought, Jeez, anybody and everybody has had boy teenagers; let's do a girl.... Let's explore the problems that female adolescents go through, because that's never done.... Then Gene switched it back to Wesley because he felt there would be a wider range of stories available dealing with the character if were a male instead of a female [Nemecek 14].

When it aired, *The Next Generation* featured Wesley Crusher, the son of Chief Medical Officer Beverly Crusher. As a teenage boy genius, Wesley followed in the footsteps of child geniuses depicted in other series and films, such as Will Robinson on *Lost in Space*, Alex Rogan in *The Last Starfighter,* and David Lightman in *War Games*. Despite being a character that was sometimes unpopular with fans, Wesley showed adolescent boys that there was indeed a place for them in the world of *Star Trek*. In their discussions of interviews with MIT students, Henry Jenkins and Greg Dancer have even suggested that the some of the dislike of Wesley Crusher in such audiences may spring from the fact that they identify with the character and "he suggests the gaps between their idealized self-images and their day-to-day interactions" (235). Because Wesley was male, the *Star Trek* audience was never able to learn about the "the problems that female adolescents go through," nor were adolescent girls able to find a home on the *Enterprise*.

These *Star Trek* series foreground the experiences of their male adolescent characters and chronicle their development. *The Next Generation* embraces every opportunity to follow Wesley's development from the child seen in "Encounter at Fairpoint" into a young man. Although initially not allowed on the bridge of the *Enterprise*, and therefore entirely separated from adult life on the ship, Wesley is promoted to acting ensign in "Where No Man Has Gone Before," and as a result he takes over as helmsman. Later, he is seen accompanying an away team in "Justice" and leading one in "Pen Pals." In "When the Bough Breaks," Wesley is kidnapped along with many other children on the *Enterprise*; however, he is regarded as their leader, reflecting his in-between status as an adolescent. What distinguishes Wesley from the other youth in this episode is his ability to take action; when sentenced to death in the earlier episode "Justice," Wesley lacked agency, but in "When the Bough Breaks" he organizes a hunger strike that eventually leads the way for the children's return to the *Enterprise*. Wesley demonstrates social development in many episodes as well. He develops his first crush and has his first relationship in "The Dauphin," when he meets a royal girl who is escorted on the *Enterprise* by a strict chaperone; she eventually is revealed to be a shape-shifter and leaves the ship. Wesley again experiences romance a few years later when he meets Ensign Robin Lefler in "The Game." Compared to his actions "The Dauphin," including asking Geordi and Riker for advice on girls, the Wesley seen in "The Game" is much more confident. He takes Robin on a dinner date, and the two kiss—but not before they save the day.

Perhaps the most significant way that Wesley develops over the course of the series can be seen through his relationship with Starfleet and Starfleet Academy. At first Wesley wishes to follow in the footsteps of both his parents as well as Captain Picard, who acts as his surrogate father. Wesley takes the Starfleet Academy entrance exam in the aptly-named "Coming of Age" and fails. In "Ménage à Troi," he misses the ship scheduled to take him to Earth for his second attempt. Because he does so in order to assist his shipmates, Captain Picard gives him a field promotion to full Ensign. Just before delivering the news, he pauses, and says, "I'm just thinking that I'm saying goodbye to you as you are today." His focus on impending change echoes an earlier conversation Wesley had with Geordi and Data:

> DATA: There is no guarantee that Wesley will be reassigned to the *Enterprise*. Ninety one per cent of Starfleet graduates are not posted to Galaxy class starships on their first assignment.
>
> WESLEY: I never thought of that. I always assumed I'd be coming back to the *Enterprise*.
>
> LAFORGE: I'm sure Captain Picard will request you. That is, if he's still commanding the *Enterprise* when you graduate.
>
> WESLEY: I never thought of that, either. I never thought I'd feel this way about leaving you guys and the *Enterprise*.
>
> DATA: Is that not a part of the human experience? Growth and change?

When Wesley does finally get accepted to Starfleet Academy, however, he does not find it as easy or as satisfying as he had expected. In "The Game," he tells Data, "I thought after being on the Enterprise, it would be a breeze, but there's a lot more to learn than just starship operations." Data assumes that Wesley is talking about the same sorts of social difficulties that Data himself had, including practical jokes and the annual Starfleet academy Sadie Hawkins Dance. A few episodes later, in "The First Duty," Wesley's difficulties seem much more serious; he has been wounded and a fellow cadet killed performing a banned flight maneuver. In "Journey's End," Dr. Crusher tells Picard that Wesley's grades are slipping and that he is in danger of failing out of the Academy.

"Journey's End" is Wesley's last appearance in the *Star Trek* franchise, apart from a deleted scene in the film *Star Trek: Nemesis*. In this episode, Wesley returns to the *Enterprise* for a vacation and finds it difficult to adjust to his childhood home. Dr. Crusher and Captain Picard can also feel the change:

> CRUSHER: I just don't know what to do, Jean-Luc. It's as if somebody took my son away and left this stranger in his place.
> PICARD: But in a sense, that's exactly what happened. When Wesley left the Enterprise three years ago he was a boy, and now he's returned a young man.

At a diplomatic party in Ten Forward, Wesley meets a Native American man named Lakanta, who later guides him on a journey of spiritual discovery. Wesley sees a vision of his father, Jack Crusher, and realizes that he has been following his father's path at the expense of his own desires and identity:

> JACK: You've reached the end, Wesley.
> WESLEY: The end of what?
> JACK: This journey. The one you started a long time ago, when I left you and your mother.
> WESLEY: You mean when you died.
> JACK: You set out on a journey that wasn't your own. Now it's time to find a path that is truly yours. Don't follow me any further.

This vision prompts Wesley to accept what he knew and could not face: that he did not want to be a Starfleet officer like his parents. When Lakanta is revealed to be "The Traveler," an alien who had taken an interest in Wesley in "Where No One Has Gone Before," Wesley leaves with him to seek "another plane of existence, another way of thinking." Donald (1993) describes the *Enterprise* as a "mother ship" with its "apron strings… tied too tightly," and locates Wesley's inability to leave the *Enterprise* (or Starfleet) in his desire to delay the final step of the transition from child to adult (125). Wesley's departure with the Traveler is his long-delayed ascent into adulthood.

Like its parent series, *Deep Space Nine* also featured adolescent male characters. However, instead of the genius Wesley Crusher who often saved the *Enterprise*, the adolescents on *Deep Space Nine* were in some ways more ordinary: Jake Sisko is the son of Commander and later Captain Benjamin Sisko and Nog is the nephew of the Ferengi businessman Quark. Jake and Nog meet and become friends in "A Man Alone." The boys are about the same age and, as Jake says, there are "not exactly a lot of friends to choose from" on the station. Commander Sisko initially feels that Nog is a bad influence on Jake and forbids them from spending time together, as does Nog's father Rom. In "The Nagus," when Rom pulls Nog out of school, it is revealed that Nog cannot read or write. When Sisko realizes that Jake has begun to give up his free time to tutor Nog, he realizes that the boys are good influences on each other and accepts that the two are developing a worthwhile friendship. The two become inseparable and later become roommates, moving into shared quarters on the station. Jake and Nog grow with the series, and by the finale they have become adults with fully realized adult personalities, storylines, and occupations. Like Wesley, much of their growth over the course of the series is represented by their preparations for eventual careers.

Unlike his father, Jake is not interested in joining Starfleet. In "Shadowplay," when Jake admits this to Chief O'Brien and then to his father, his words echo what the Traveler told Wesley Crusher. "Starfleet is too much like you," Jake says. "I need to find what's me." Jake seems to know almost right away that he wants to be a writer, and he explores both poetry and prose writing before discovering a love of journalism. In "Nor the Battle to the Strong," Jake is preparing to write his first article, a profile of Dr. Julian Bashir. When they divert their course due to an attack on a Federation colony, Jake learns firsthand about the horrors of war and ends up with something real to write about. In "Call to Arms," Jake receives a position as "an official correspondent for the Starfleet News Service" and writes his first piece about his father. At the end of the episode, when Starfleet allows Deep Space Nine to be taken by the Dominion, Jake chooses to stay behind as a wartime correspondent. Captain Sisko is not pleased with Jake's decision, but he accepts it. As he later tells Jake's grandfather, "He's not a child anymore. He's responsible for his own actions." In "A Time for War," Weyoun mocks Jake's belief in the freedom of the press and tells Jake that his reports are not being sent to the Federation. Although it is unclear if *any* of his reports are received by the Starfleet News Service during the war, in "You Are Cordially Invited" Jake announces that a collection of his news stories are going to be published as a book. Along with his professional successes, Jake experiences personal growth during his time on the Dominion-occupied station. By the end of the war, he is no longer the scared and overwhelmed boy of "Nor the Battle to the Strong"—he even becomes an active member of the New Resistance and is pivotal to Starfleet's return to Deep Space Nine.

Nog too defies his family's expectations. Rom and Quark both expect that Nog will become a businessman as is appropriate for a young male Ferengi. After a harrowing experience in "The Jem'Hadar," however, Nog decides that he would like to become the first Ferengi in Starfleet. In "Heart of Stone," Nog tells Sisko that he has completed his "Ferengi Attainment Ceremony," which means he is now legally an adult. As he explains, as a new adult he "must purchase an apprenticeship from a suitable role model" and he has chosen Captain Sisko. Both Sisko and Jake are confused by this request, and at first both believe he is joking. Eventually, Nog reveals that he is serious and that he has made this decision because he feels unsuited to a life of acquiring profit:

> Because I don't want to end up like my father.... He's been chasing profit his whole life, and what has it gotten him? Nothing.... He could've been Chief Engineer of a starship if he'd had the opportunity. But he went into business, like a good Ferengi. The only thing is, he's not a good Ferengi, not when it comes to acquiring profit. ... Well, I'm not going to make the same mistake. I want to do something with my life. Something worthwhile.

Nog goes off to Starfleet Academy in "Little Green Men" and is first seen as a cadet in "Homefront." In the latter, he tells Jake, "Jake, they call it the Academy, but what it really is is school." Despite these minor complaints, Nog takes to Starfleet quite well; he receives a field placement on Deep Space Nine and in "For the Uniform" he serves on the USS *Defiant* for the first time. His field promotion to Ensign during the Dominion occupation of Deep Space Nine is further evidence of his success. In the seventh season episode "The Siege of AR-558," however, Nog is injured during a reconnaissance mission and has to have part of one leg amputated. Although he receives a synthetic leg, he is affected greatly by the event and struggles to return to work. Nog overcomes this setback, though, and in the series finale "What You Leave Behind" he skillfully pilots the *Defiant* in one of the last battles of the Dominion War and receives a promotion to Lieutenant. Throughout the series, Nog undergoes a dramatic transformation greater than perhaps any other character in *Star Trek*—an illiterate child who has frequent run-ins with station security becomes a decorated war hero.

Although Jake and Nog are the two main adolescent characters on *Deep Space Nine*, one additional character deserves a mention: Alexander Rozhenko, Worf's son. First seen on *The Next Generation* as a very young child, Alexander reappears on *Deep Space Nine* as a young man. Although Alexander lived on the *Enterprise* with Worf for a while, he was eventually sent back to Earth to live with Worf's adoptive parents. In "The Way of the Warrior," Worf tells Chief O'Brien, "Alexander is much happier living with his grandparents on Earth than he ever was staying with me." In the *Deep Space Nine* episode "Sons and Daughters," Alexander Rozhenko appears as a young officer in the Klingon Defense Forces, serving under General Martok. Worf did not know of his decision to join the military, and indeed it turns out that Alexander did so because he felt abandoned by his father:

> ALEXANDER: All you've ever done my whole life is send me away.
>
> WORF: I am a Klingon warrior. I lead a warrior's life. That is not the path for you. You told me this yourself. And I have come to accept it.
>
> ALEXANDER: You call yourself my father but you haven't tried to see me or talk to me in five years. I wasn't the kind of son you wanted so you pretended that you had no son. You never accepted me. You abandoned me.

When Worf sees that Alexander is performing far behind his peers, he realizes that they each have something to teach the other, declaring, "I will teach you what you need to know to be a warrior, and you will teach me what I need to know to be a father." They reconcile and Alexander joins the House of Martok ("Sons and Daughters") and serves as his father's best man during Worf's wedding to Jadzia Dax ('You are Cordially Invited"). Alexander, who jokes that he "can barely say [his] name in Klingon" ("You Are Cordially Invited") spends his time on *Deep Space Nine* trying to understand and come to terms with his mixed cultural heritage. His father, after all, is a Klingon Starfleet officer who was raised by humans, and his mother was half-human and half–Klingon. After growing up on among humans, Alexander seeks to understand what it means to be Klingon, eventually finding his place in his father's life, in the House of Martok, and as weapons office on the Klingon ship *Ya'Vang*. As with the other adolescent male characters discussed in this essay, Alexander's social and occupational development plays out on screen, ending with him as a young adult who is beginning a new stage of life.

Where No Girl Has Gone Before?

Despite Star *Trek*'s track record of strong and interesting female characters, and the richness with which individual series have depicted the changing roles and priorities of male adolescents, thus far Wesley, Jake, Nog, and Alexander have never had a female counterpart. *Star Trek* has failed to examine female adolescence, to show how adolescent girls grow, change, and find their place in *Star Trek*'s female-friendly future. In fact, the *Star Trek* franchise has featured only two female children as recurring characters, and neither was part of the main cast or named in the opening credits. Molly O'Brien, daughter of Miles and Keiko O'Brien, was born during *The Next Generation* episode "Disaster" and made several appearances in later episodes. Molly was then seen more often in *Deep Space Nine*, which focused more heavily on the O'Briens' family life. Much like Molly, Naomi Wildman made her debut onscreen, during the *Voyager* episode "Deadlock." The half-human daughter of Ensign Samantha Wildman, Naomi was born during the second season. Molly and Naomi both remain children for the duration of their respective series (and, in Molly's case, two series) and do not even begin to undergo puberty. Even Naomi, who initially grows very quickly due to her mixed-species heritage, does not grow so much as to suggest adolescence may be imminent.

Both Molly and Naomi are seen as adults in single episodes, not due to undergoing the normal biological processes of maturation but due to plot devices typical of science fiction shows. An adult Naomi, a Lieutenant still serving aboard *Voyager*, is seen briefly in an altered timeline in the episode "Shattered." She is also mentioned in the future timeline seen in the series finale "Endgame," in which she has a daughter of her own. While these two episodes remind viewers that Naomi will one day be an adult woman with a job and a family, they also emphasize the chasm that *Star Trek* cannot bridge—the contrast between the adult Naomi and her child self in the normal timeline. This chasm is emphasized even moreso in the *Deep Space Nine* episode "Time's Orphan," when Molly is accidentally aged ten years after falling into a time portal. Due to this accident, Molly becomes an eighteen-year-old who has undergone puberty off-screen, during a ten-year period without human contact. The lack of human socialization causes the adult Molly to be completely feral, with little ability to communicate with her parents and no "normal" adult priorities. The physical and emotional changes that Molly has undergone have turned the adorable girl child of *Deep Space Nine* into an unrecognizable, uncontainable adult. Molly's transition is entirely negative, as well as heartbreaking for Miles and Keiko. While this storyline had the potential to explore female adolescence and the transition from girlhood to womanhood, the episode ultimately reduces female puberty to a baffling, off-screen process in which girls turn into uncontrollable wild animals rather than teenagers or adult women.

While Wesley, Jake, and Nog explore such aspects of adolescence as the development of social and romantic relationships, a changing relationship with one's family, and the pursuit of schooling or an occupation, Molly and Naomi are categorically denied the opportunity. Brian Attebery notes that science fiction often demonstrates an inability to follow female characters, especially those with superhuman attributes, through adolescence and into adulthood:

> Super girl can only grow up by disappearing from view. Male writers seem to be able to follow daughter characters just over the line into adolescence.... Beyond the point at which Daddy's little girl becomes her own woman, she vanishes into mystery [90].

A literal example of "vanishing into mystery" can be seen in *The Next Generation* episode "True Q," in which a Starfleet Academy student named Amanda Rogers secures an internship on the *Enterprise*. Amanda is just 18, and the episode emphasizes that she is at a transitional stage of her life. When she discovers that she is actually the child of two Q, Amanda must come to terms with her new powers and identity. Q gives her the choice of joining the Continuum or giving up her powers, and Amanda must decide all too quickly whether to stay as she is or develop into something new. The comparison to adolescence is undeniable, as Roberts points out:

> On the edge of adulthood, she represents femininity at its most seductive and powerful. ... Amanda's transformation depicts the move from girlhood into womanhood. It is surely significant that as she moves into womanhood—she is just eighteen—that "her powers have begun to emerge," as Q explains. Amanda herself finds the changes

> she is going through bewildering and explains, "I thought I was going crazy," a normal response to adolescence ["Sexual Generations" 32].

"True Q," then, depicts womanhood as a state of unknown power. When Dr. Crusher tells Amanda at the close at the episode, "Amanda, you're a Q. You can do anything you want," she may as well be affirming Amanda's agency as she moves into adulthood. In fact, she sounds like Captain Sisko reminding his father that Jake can make his own decisions. "True Q" emphasizes the promise of showing adolescence girls in the *Star Trek* universe, but also the difficulty: Amanda, whose Q background makes her an unquestionable super girl, vanishes "into mystery" with Q just after realizing her own potential.

Future Girls, Future Selves

Real girls do not vanish when they become adolescents. As they grow older, they must forge their own paths, establishing their own identities and finding themselves a place in the world. As they do, they look to the media, especially television, for role models to emulate. Television contributes to young adults' understanding of gender roles and other social expectations:

> The teen years are a key, crucial stage in the development and construction of both individual and collective values and identities. During this sensitive and complex process, individuals usually turn to role models and examples of people important to them, i.e., the so-called socialising agents, like family, peers' group or school. But, besides models, patterns or real stereotypes, young people turn to others that are to be found in media [Garcia-Munoz and Fedele 138].

Jane Brown and Carol Pardun argue that "race and gender are basic motivators for choice of television content, and that adolescents may, indeed, be seeking models with whom they can identify as they develop a sense of themselves in the larger culture" (275). Children and young adults are both more likely to identify with a character who is of the same gender and who they perceive as being similar or as having values similar to their own (Hoffner; Hoffner and Buchanan). Focusing on career decisions, Marilee Long et al. note that television can be especially powerful for girls: "socializing agents like television can help shape girls' identities and visions of future possible selves" (2). Here they draw upon Hazel Markus and Paula Nurius' concept of "possible selves" as imagined future identities. Markus and Nurius argue that people develop possible solves by drawing on their own experiences as well as images from the media: "the pool of possible selves derives from the categories made salient by the individual's particular sociocultural and historical context and from the models, images, and symbols provided by the media and by the individual's immediate social experiences" (954). Thus, television, and particular the televisual depiction of characters with whom they can identity, can have a powerful impact on adolescent girls.

Over the last fifty years, women have assumed more important and more powerful roles in *Star Trek*, and the later series have become well-known for presenting a variety of female characters with compelling storylines. Along the way, girls and young women have watched each of the *Star Trek* series and wondered about their place in the *Star Trek* universe. Even as a developing focus on showing the show's starships and space stations as communities allowed for the inclusion of adolescent boys in multiple episodes, adolescent girls feature as minor characters or love interests or, largely, go completely unseen. Wesley has not been allowed to make way for Leslie. As a result, although *Star Trek* has spent much time exploring how boys develop and mature into adults, the similar experiences of adolescent girls remain a mystery. Scholars have argued that *Star Trek* "represents a future that we would like to make real" (Gerrold 228) as well as a "way of expressing one's dreams and how they can be fulfilled" (Geraghty, "Living" 24). With this in mind, girls deserve to see a future that includes them, one that *they* would like to see become real. Hopefully future *Star Trek* series will correct this oversight, providing adolescent girls with the chance to see characters like themselves on starships and space stations.

After all, where better to see "future possible selves" than in the future?

Works Cited

Attebery, Brian. *Decoding Gender in Science Fiction*. New York: Routledge, 2002. Print.

Bick, Ilsa J. "Boys in Space: 'Star Trek,' Latency, and the Neverending Story." *Cinema Journal* (1996): 43–60. Web.

Brown, Jane D., and Carol J. Pardun. "Little in Common: Racial and Gender Differences in Adolescents' Television Diets." *Journal of Broadcasting & Electronic Media* 48.2 (2004): 266–78. Web.

Cranny-Francis, Anne. "Sexuality and Sex-Role Stereotyping in Star Trek." *Science Fiction Studies* 12.3 (1985): 274–84. Web.

Donald, Ralph R. "The Mary Ann, the Ruptured Duck and the Enterprise: Character Relationships and Air and Space Craft as Metaphors for Human Affinities." *Beyond the Stars III: The Material World in American Popular Film*. Eds. Paul Loukides and Linda K. Fuller. Bowling Green, OH: Popular Press, 1993. 123–133. Print.

Fern, Yvonne, and Gene Roddenberry. *Gene Roddenberry: The Last Conversation: A Dialogue with the Creator of Star Trek*. London: Pocket Books, 1996. Print.

García-Muñoz, Núria, and Maddalena Fedele. "Television Fiction Series Targeted at Young Audience: Plots and Conflicts Portrayed in a Teen Series." *Revista Comunicar* 19.37 (2011): 133–40. Web.

Geraghty, Lincoln. "Eight Days That Changed American Television: Kirk's Opening Narration." *The Influence of Star Trek on Television, Film and Culture*. Ed. Lincoln Geraghty. Jefferson, NC: McFarland, 2007. 11–21. Print.

_____. *Living with Star Trek: American Culture and the Star Trek Universe*. IB Tauris, 2007. Print.

_____. "Telling Tales of the Future: Science Fiction and Star Trek's Exemplary Narratives." *Reconstruction: Studies in Contemporary Culture* 3.2 (2003): n.pag. Web.

Gerrold, David. *The World of Star Trek: The Inside Story of TV's Most Popular Series*. London: Virgin, 1996. Print.
Ginn, Sherry. *Our Space, Our Place: Women in the Worlds of Science Fiction Television*. Lanham: University Press of America, 2005. Print.
Hark, Ina Rae. "Moviegoing, 'Home-Leaving,'and the Problematic Girl Protagonist of the Wizard of Oz." *Sugar, Spice, and Everything Nice: Cinemas of Girlhood*. Wayne State University Press, 2002. 25–38. Print.
Henderson, Mary. "Professional Women in Star Trek, 1964 to 1969." *Film & History (03603695)* 24.1 (1994): 47–59. Web.
Hoffner, Cynthia. "Children's Wishful Identification and Parasocial Interaction with Favorite Television Characters." *Journal of Broadcasting & Electronic Media* 40.3 (1996): 389–402. Web.
Hoffner, Cynthia, and Martha Buchanan. "'Young Adults' Wishful Identification with Television Characters: The Role of Perceived Similarity and Character Attributes." *Media Psychology* 7.4 (2005): 325–51. Web.
Jenkins, Henry, and Greg Dancer. "How Many Starfleet Officers Does It Take to Change a Lightbulb? Star Trek at MIT." *Science Fiction Audiences: Watching Doctor Who and Star Trek*. Eds. John Tulloch and Henry Jenkins. New York: Routledge, 1995. 213–236. Print.
Johnson-Smith, Jan. *American Science Fiction TV: Star Trek, Stargate and Beyond*. New York: IB Tauris, 2005. Print.
Lawrence, John Shelton, and Robert Jewett. *The Myth of the American Superhero*. Wm. B. Eerdmans Publishing, 2002. Print.
Long, Marilee, et al. "Portrayals of Male and Female Scientists in Television Programs Popular Among Middle School-Age Children." *Science Communication* 32.3 (2010): 356–82. Web.
Markus, Hazel, and Paula Nurius. "Possible Selves." *American Psychologist* 41.9 (1986): 954–969. Web.
Nemecek, Larry. *The Star Trek: The Next Generation Companion: Revised Edition*. Simon & Schuster, 2003. Print.
O'Keeffe, Moira. "Lieutenant Uhura and the Drench Hypothesis: Diversity and the Representation of STEM Careers." *International Journal of Gender, Science and Technology* 5.1 (2013): 4–24. Web.
Richards, Thomas. *The Meaning of Star Trek*. Doubleday Books, 1997. Print.
Roberts, Robin. "Science, Race, and Gender in *Star Trek: Voyager*." *Fantasy Girls: Gender in the New Universe of Science Fiction and Fantasy Television*. Ed. Elyce Rae Helford. Lanham, MD: Rowman and Littlefield, 2000. 203–221. Print.
_____. *Sexual Generations: "Star Trek, The Next Generation" and Gender*. Urbana: University of Illinois Press, 1999. Print.
Vettel-Becker, Patricia. "Space and the Single Girl." *Frontiers: A Journal of Women Studies* 35.2 (2014): 143–78. Web.
Wagner, Jon G., and Jan Lundeen. *Deep Space and Sacred Time: Star Trek in the American Mythos*. Praeger Publishers, 1998. Print.
Wildermuth, Mark E. *Gender, Science Fiction Television, and the American Security State*. New York: Palgrave Macmillan, 2014. Print.

To Boldly Go Where No Undead Have Gone Before

Comparisons Between Gene Roddenberry's Star Trek *and Bram Stoker's* Dracula

Simon Bacon

Make It So

At first glance correlating Gene Roddenberry's long running space saga set in the future and Bram Stoker's tale of an undead Transylvanian Count causing havoc on the streets of Victorian England would seem something of a mismatch, not least in that the former encompasses many films, TV series and books, while the latter, at least as considered here, is just a single novel.[1] However, as this study will argue, there are some significant points of comparison, or similarity of intent, that make such an endeavor worthwhile. Both works are centered around the idea of travel and displacement, charting the continuing odyssey of their respective main characters: for *Dracula* it is the vampire Count, and for *Star Trek* it is the film's/series' particular Captain/Commander that is also ideologically representative of the larger Federation. As they begin and continue on their journeys into the unknown, one should always be aware of the colonial aspect of such adventures as the unknown explored in both works is already very well known to those that already live there—the unknown "land beyond the forest" in Dracula may be such for a representative of the British Empire but is home to the vampire and the Romanians that live there. Alongside this, each work is conveyed as though it is part of an ongoing diary/written/recorded memoir: for *Dracula* this is in the form of diary entries, letters and transcripts from other forms of recorded material, and for *Star Trek* it is dictated entries into the Captain's log—though it should be mentioned that Count Dracula's adventures are recorded by others than by himself, while in *Star Trek*, and some of its spin-offs, it is generally the Captain or Commander of the Federation ship/facility who makes his own report. Though perhaps what creates the biggest correlation between the two narratives, and indeed what is the main focus of this study, is their ideological intent, for the vampire and the Federation are driven by the impulse to share their respective visions of life, and un-life; and to bring peace by replicating their ideals or, as one could possibly describe it, by infecting everyone with their ideological contagion. But before explaining this more fully one needs to return to the start of the respective odyssey's when the journeys began.

To Boldly Go

As mentioned above both *Dracula* and *Star Trek* are about travel and the incursion of the unknown into a previously secure or closed system. *Dracula* sees the vampire traveling from the superstitious Old World of Eastern Europe, as represented by his home in Transylvania, and entering London itself, the heart of modernity and the British Empire and destabilizing the New World of late Victorian England. *Star Trek* sees the forces of the Federation, which actually or nominally are identified with the planet Earth and/America, via the SS *Enterprise*, SS *Voyager* or whichever vessel is constructed as the focus of the narrative entering into a new solar system, or planetary orbit, and destabilizing the order that was previously there. In this way, both texts can be seen to conform to descriptions of both the monster and the gothic texts they are traditionally seen to inhabit. Jeffrey Jerome Cohen, in his theory of monsters, sees the monster as "difference made flesh, come to dwell among us. In its function as dialectical Other, of third-term supplement, the monster is an incorporation of the Outside, the Beyond—of all the loci that are theoretically placed as distant and distinct but originate within." (Cohen 7) This more obviously applies to the vampire, but can equally be seen to be valid for the crew of the SS *Enterprise*, for example, who are invariably very different to the beings/entities they encounter—are "monsters" in comparison to the "normalized" aliens—but often echo a quality that the alien society contains but ordinarily suppresses. Further, when viewed this way, the usual story arc for an episode of the science fiction series sees the Federation's representatives arrive into a system; create some sort of event or conflict; and then after some time achieve some form of resolution and then leave. This oddly corresponds to Christopher Craft's definition of the gothic text which, as he describes, "First invites or admits a monster, then entertains and is entertained by monstrosity for some extended duration, until in its closing pages it expels or repudiates the monster and all the disruption that he/she/it brings." (Craft 107) Reading *Star Trek,* the series, with this in mind allows for a reconfiguring of the Federation as being the monster, the outsider, rather than victims/experiencers of monstrosity, and puts the Federatio's continuing "explorations" into outer space more in line with other darker views of human exploration, for instance as seen in Robert A. Heinlein's *Starship Troopers* from 1959 and even The Culture Series by Iain M. Banks, which is comprised of 10 books beginning with *Consider Phlebus* and ending with *The Hydrogen Sonata* in 2012. *Starship Troopers* sees supposed alien aggression as the instigator of planetary colonization and The Culture Series, while somewhat ambivalent about the overall results of intergalactic colonisation, explicitly constructs it as something that is not desired by many.

Curiously, while each narrative can be seen as the continuing explorations of the "monster," these adventures were originally initiated by the incursion (invitation) of an outside force into the home-world of the main protagonist. In *Dracula* the vampire does not just leave his home in Transylvania; he initiates a visit from a young solicitor from a large empire that already "owns" or controls much of the known world. This is seen in the figure of Jonathan Harker, who leaves his normal routes of travel in the capital of the British Empire to go to the "land beyond the forest" (Stoker 266), after the Count had been brought to the attention of his firm. This then opens the doors or routes of communication to the vampire, allowing him to enter into not only England but its capital London as well. Similarly, in *Star Trek* the humans space adventure begins when they bring themselves to the attention of another, far more advanced species/Empire, as seen in the film *Star Trek: First Contact* (Frakes 1996). As explained by Commander William Riker from the SS *Enterprise* from the future to Ephraim Cochrane from the past, and possibly the originator of the Federation:

> Doctor, tomorrow morning when they [the Vulcans] detect the warp signature from your ship and realize that humans have discovered how to travel faster than light, they decide to alter their course and make first contact with Earth, right here.... You get to make first contact with an alien race! And after you do... everything begins to change.

The nameless Vulcan commander then mirrors the similarly unsuspecting Harker, when he lands on the formerly unnoticed world, and unwittingly invites the occupants back into their own world, thus starting the "change" which will also ultimately see them "integrated" in to the Federation. These initial, or first, contacts for the main protagonists of each narrative also forms the basis of their respective "mission statements," which sees them launch themselves into new worlds and new adventures. For *Star Trek* it is the now almost infamous lines which started every episode of the original series,

"Space: the final frontier. These are the voyages of the starship Enterprise. Its five-year mission: to explore strange new worlds, to seek out new life and new civilizations, to boldly go where no man has gone before." Although Count Dracula does not speak in such lofty tones he shares a similar thirst for adventure and the desire to go to new lands and meet new people. This is seen as he tells the following to his newly arrived visitor, Jonathan Harker, near the start of the novel, "I long to go through the crowded streets of your mighty London, to be in the midst of the whirl and rush of humanity, to share its life, its change, its death, and all that makes it what it is." (Stoker 22) The historical context of each statement is worth considering in more depth as while they were written in very different times, they have something of a shared vision.

Written in 1960s America, *Star Trek* came out of the continuing Cold War tensions with the Soviet Union, which had seen the Science Fiction film as the ideal media for expressing anxieties around ideological invasion with films, such as *The Thing from Another World* (Nyby 1951) and *Invasion of the Body Snatchers* (Siegel 1956), expressing the horror of an enemy that is other and yet exactly the same as the self. This change in the form of monstrous invasion signaled a sense of irrelevance in regard to traditional monsters, as explained by Thomas Doherty: "Next to Buchenwald, Dachau, and Auschwitz, the once terrifying trio of movie horror-Frankenstein, Dracula, and the Wolfman—seemed … almost laughably harmless." (Doherty 116) Alongside this was the increasing influence of liberalism that reacted against America's conflicts in Asia as well as racial tensions within the U.S. itself, and so *Star Trek* navigated the territory between both creating something of an ideal rather than a reflection of contemporary national tensions, and as Christine Cornea notes, "it also presented audiences with a kind of utopian future in which conflicts had been resolved and peaceful relations had been made possible under the 'melting-pot' governance of a liberal humanist government." (Cornea 180) Though as Cornea further comments, it rarely loses the traces of either:

> On one level, the Enterprise's mission "to explore strange new worlds; to seek out new life and new civilizations" can certainly be read as an allegory enabling the series to engage with the international political manoeuvres of the period. On another level, engagement with internal racial conflicts was also neatly displaced onto conflicts between humans and alien beings from other worlds (read nations), in a kind of two-phase denial of contemporary America's domestic disputes [180].

Consequently, the Federation's—or the United Federation of Planets—quest to explore struggles to rise above the amoral impetuous of the conquest of America itself through imposing its will on those that already inhabit the "strange new worlds." This further complicates the Federation's Prime Directive, as seen in *Star Trek Into Darkness* (Abrams 2013), to not interfere with alien life forms when, as shown by the new Captain James Kirk, played by Chris Pine, human ideological preferences and imperatives outweigh those of others—as shown when Kirk decides to save Spock over the possibility of changing the destiny of the primitive inhabitants of planet Nibiru by revealing the starship *Enterprise* to them. When combined with the earlier remnants of Cold War vilification that saw invaders from outer space as ideological parasites who replicated themselves within the bodies of the "host" population, then the Federation embody all that they say they are not, just as the democracy of America itself is seen to be more equal for some and totally absent for others. The ongoing explorations of the Federation then are not so much about bringing order in outer space but maintaining it within their own areas of control so reflecting the problems of the contemporary American empire in achieving the same internal control, often by projecting its anxieties outside of its borders onto perceived enemies abroad.

Written at the end of the 19th century, *Dracula* manifests the anxieties of another Empire that feared for its survival from outside forces. As observed by Stephen Arata, Stoker's vampire can be seen to embody a form of "reverse colonization" (Arata 623), where peoples from the colonies begin to populate the heartland of the Empire itself. As noted by Tabish Khair, outsiders became increasingly visible on the streets on London:

> By the eighteenth century, their numbers [ ] appear to have started swelling in a visible manner: thousands of black soldiers from the United States who had fought for the British in the American War for Independence, slaves, servants, ayahs, lascars as well as the occasional non-European nobleman or business partner [Khair 8].

This appearance of otherness on the streets of the "home" nation caused increasing fears over miscegenation and declining purity of the nation's blood. Count Dracula perfectly represents this as an entity that makes manifest a set of ideological imperatives that are in stark opposition to that held dear by Imperialist Britain; and even more so he achieves this nefariously and under cover of darkness by replicating himself through the medium of blood. Exactly as the anxiety around identity seen in films like *Invasion of the Body Snatchers,* the vampire's converts look just as they did before but have a new ideological agenda, as noted by Dr. John Seward on seeing Lucy Westenra not long after she was turned into a vampire: "There lay Lucy, seemingly just as we had seen her the night before her funeral. She was, if possible, more radiantly beautiful than ever; and I could not believe that she was dead," (Stoker 221) subsequently suggesting that all those that were once considered as "us" inherently possessing the possibility of suddenly becoming one of "them." A fear which is perfectly summed up in Count Dracula's threat: "And you, their best beloved one, are now to me flesh of my flesh; blood of my blood; kin of my kin." (Stoker 311) While this transformation is shown to be unholy and diabolical, it accomplishes little more than the British colonial imperative itself as further noted by Arata:

> The fear generated by the Count's colonization of his victims' bodies—a colonization appropriately designated monstrous—modulates into guilt that his practices simply repeat those of the "good" characters.... And since the colonizations of bodies and territory are closely linked, the same blurring of distinctions occurs when we consider more closely the nature of the Count's Invasion of Britain. Just as Dracula's vampirism mirrors the domestic practices of Victorian patriarchs, so his invasion of London in order to "batten on the helpless" natives there mirrors British imperial activities abroad [Arata 633].

The main difference between *Dracula* and *Star Trek* then is not the intent of their respective adventurers, but the packaging they wrap that up in. This sees the vampire completely and openly embodying/mirroring the Empire's colonial intent, while the Federation pretends to promote equality and inclusivity as a way to consume all that they come into contact with.

Resistance Is Futile

Dracula, to paraphrase Montague Summers, has spawned many "kith and kin" but largely with no official connection to the original text or the author—though one could include the 1924 stage adaption by Hamilton Deane, its American rewrite by Jon Balderstone, and the 1931 Universal film by Tod Browning as they had an official permission by Stoker's widow. In contrast, the *Star Trek* franchise has continued to "boldly go" in its own right and includes an increasing amount of connected texts that still retain some form of direct connection to the original franchise. Over time, the *Star Trek* universe has evolved in its moral positioning, as observed by Timothy Sandefur:

> Over nearly 50 years, Star Trek tracked the devolution of liberalism from the philosophy of the New Frontier into a preference for non-judgmental diversity and reactionary hostility to innovation, and finally into an almost nihilistic collection of divergent urges [Sandefur 10].

Though Lincoln Geraghty feels there is still an overarching vision beyond the generational changes of moral stand point, "[e]vident in all of the Star Trek sequels is Roddenberry's utopian future, a depiction of what humanity will achieve if it fulfils its potential and stops infighting and starting war." (Geraghty 8). However, this does not exclude forms of ideological totalitarianism that make everyone the same, even if seemingly achieved with their agreement. This kind of "socialization" is seen in various figures throughout the films and series that once represented sworn enemies of the Federation but have now been accepted and converted to become acceptable members of this galactic collective. Two of the more obvious examples are the Klingon crew members, Worf from the series *The Next Generation* and *Deep Space Nine* and the films *Star Trek: First Contact*, *Star Trek: Insurrection* (Frakes: 1998) and *Star Trek: Nemesis* (Baird: 2002), and B'Elanna Torres from the series *Voyager*.

Worf still carries many of the aggressive features of the original appearance of the Klingons in the original *Star Trek* series—dark skinned, with black hair and bushy eyebrows with a joined beard and mustache, but with the added ridges on the front of the forehead, revealing him to be very different, at least in appearance, to his fellow human/Federation crew mates. However, this form of otherness constructs an idea of acceptable inclusion that affirms the ideological superiority of the Federation as well as the perimeters it sets for that inclusion or permission. B'Elanna Torres, as a later version of Klingon inclusion into the Federation, has become further assimilated. Half Klingon and half human, a pairing that would have been unthinkable in the original series, B'Elanna is much paler than Worf in complexion, with far less prominent ridges on her forehead, and indeed looks more human than Klingon. She is an interesting example as this humanizing factor is equated with sexualizing the character, which is also seen in another, possibly more famous example of assimilation (re-assimilation) into the Federation, that of Seven of Nine. Originally named Annika Hansen, Seven of Nine was assimilated into the Borg collective but later became isolated from them before encountering the crew of SS *Voyager*. She briefly works with the crew to survive an attack from a more violent species trying to kill them both, but then tries to assimilate the Federation members. The crew manages to sever her neural connection to the Borg and the ship's Doctor begins to remove much of the Borg implants in Seven of Nine's body, and Captain Janeway of the *Voyager* decides to try and "integrate" her into the Federation. As various commentators have noted the Borg are constructed as both characterless and sexless:

> The members of the Borg Collective have been "assimilated" against their will; a process that removes their individuality and allows for swift, telepathic communication and extreme efficiency in carrying out their colonising expansion into the universe … individual Borg are visually indistinguishable [Cornea 230].

Trudy Barber concurs, "In episode 'Q Who' (1989), Q first describes the Borg as "not a he; not a she. Not like anything you've seen before." (Barbar 136) and further notes what is distinctive about her integration (re-assimilation) is that it makes much of her newly found (restored) sexual identity, "In their understanding then, to be Borg is to lose identity, and according to this definition of Seven as Borg, there is a loss of physical sex through the loss of genitalia, but nevertheless the breasts are kept." (Ibid) However, they are not only just kept but emphasized with a skin-tight suit that makes obvious her curvaceous figure and large breasts. Barbar feels this is expressive of the irrepressible humanity in this gesture, "This is a stark reminder of the unpredictability of "human nature" and confronts our attitudes to notions of the "other" in terms of revulsion and fascination, responses also associated with notions of sexual fetishism" (*ibid.*); and yet when considered with B'Elanna's integration into the Federation (also seen in *Voyager*) a different agenda emerges. As mentioned earlier B'Elanna's only indication of her Klingon roots is some slight riding on her forehead, equally for Seven of Nine, her Borg past is only shown through a few pieces of technology around her left eye—giving the appearance of facial decoration rather than mechanical grafts. Otherwise both women have long flowing hair (though Seven of Nine usually wears hers tied back) and large, full, voluptuous, lips, giving the overall effect that to be integrated into the Federation, at least for the female characters, is to be overtly sexualized, something which is also seen in Stoker's *Dracula,* when women join the company of the Count.

The first women encountered are those that have been integrated by the vampire and live in his castle, also identified as his "brides." There is no clue as to what they were like before becoming part of the Count's household but once part of it they are shown as overtly sexualised, even predatory, as shown in their encounter with Jonathan Harker:

> All three had brilliant white teeth, that shone like pearls against the ruby of their voluptuous lips. There was something about them that made me uneasy, some longing.... The fair girl went on her knees and bent over me, fairly gloating. There was a deliberate voluptuousness which was both thrilling and repulsive, and as she arched her neck she actually licked her lips like an animal, till I could see in the moonlight the moisture shining on the scarlet lips and on the red tongue as it lapped the white sharp teeth. Lower and lower went her head as the lips went below the range of my mouth and chin and seemed about to fasten on my throat [Stoker 41].

A similar transformation is seen in the girls that Count Dracula encounters once he has arrived in England, Lucy Westenra and Mina Harker. Christopher Craft describes this transformation in regard to Lucy as follows:

> Kissed into a sudden sexuality, Lucy grows "voluptuous" (a word used to describe her only during the vampiric process), her lips redden, and she kisses with a new interest. This sexualization of Lucy, metamorphosing woman's "sweetness" to "adamantine, heartless cruelty, and [her] purity to voluptuous wantonness" (252–53), terrifies her suitors [Craft 89].

Even the "sexually reticent Mina," (Senf 3) as Senf describes her, while never fully integrated, acts very differently with Dracula than she does with any of the other men in the novel:

> With a mocking smile, he placed one hand upon my shoulder and, holding me tight, bared my throat with the other, saying as he did so: "First, a little refreshment to reward my exertions. You may as well be quiet; it is not the first time, or the second, that your veins have appeased my thirst!" I was bewildered, and, strangely enough, I did not want to hinder him [Stoker 310].

While the Borg are portrayed as evil through removing individuality from those it assimilates, it actually reflects the same processes undertaken by the Federation, as too does the subjugation demanded by the vampire reveal that of the British Empire, as Cornea notes re *Star Trek*:

> However, what is interesting in the case of this film [First Contact] is that the cosmetic individualism exhibited by the Enterprise is rarely echoed in the performance of these characters. It is not unusual for key crew members to be shown collectively working through a crisis situation, to the point where each performs a line of dialogue in a long sentence. Even when lapses occur in the normal presentation of this "regulated" self these are quickly recuperated or used to display how each crew member freely returns to being an instrument of the Federation, once more aligned with the collective "mindfulness" of the "modulated" self. So, the Borg's extreme vacuity actually mirrors the subjugated self required by the Federation, while simultaneously making the mode of being presented in the crew of the Enterprise appear more desirable [Cornea 230–231].

The almost exact same process happens in *Dracula* where the forces of the Empire are collected together in the "Crew of Light"—Jonathan and Mina Harker, Arthur Holmwood, Dr. John Seward and Quincey Morris—who are lead by Professor Abraham Van Helsing who demands complete loyalty from all of them, so that although they occasionally act individually, they are more often his collective to be controlled and directed. As observed by Fred Botting:

> Under the unifying and priestly command of Van Helsing the men of middle-class Victorian England reinvigorate their cultural identity and primal masculinity in the sacred values that are reinvoked against the sublimity of the vampiric threat. In the face of the voluptuous and violent sexuality loosed by the decadently licentious vampire, a vigorous sense of patriarchal, bourgeois and family values is restored [Botting 105].

This mirrors the control demanded by the vampire who equally requires patriarchal dominance and the enforcement of his version of "family values." One result of all this mirroring between the Federation, the Borg, the Crew of Light and Count Dracula is that, on one level, they all become equivalent and although they "sell" themselves as being oppositional, they all configure different faces of the same forces of control and regulation. Another correlation of this, which links the opposing forces in both texts but which also joins them, is shown in certain readings of *Dracula*'s only American character,

Quincey Morris, that intimate a connection between the rising American Empire—which can equally be seen to be the rise of the Federation—and the vampire.

As suggested earlier the equivalence between the Federation (United Federation of Planets) and America (United States of America)—in their various historical moments—is one that is almost taken for granted by critics, either as an example of the current state of the nation as it is, or is not dealing with internal and external affairs. In relation to this Barbar observes, "The Star Trek series is well known for its explorations and explanations of society and is often read as a mirror reflecting social attitudes to challenges facing ethnicity and race, or sex and gender, for example." (Barbar 135) It can equally be read as an escape from current American culture and this even while reflecting it. As noted by M. Keith Booker, "the escape is not from what many saw as the leftist drift of global politics but from the soul-destroying nature of life in modern capitalist America." (Booker 14) The America at the time of the publication of *Dracula*—the end of the 19th century—was possibly even more imbued with the exploratory spirit of the Federation and saw it gaining territory in the north, by purchasing Alaska from the Russians in 1867; increasing influence in the Pacific region when it annexed Hawaii in 1898; and victory in its conflict against Spain, which brought it control of The Philippines, also in 1898 (the year after *Dracula* was published). How much Stoker knew of America's own imperialist agenda is unclear but he must have felt they were natural successors to Britain as the major world force as seen in the description of Quincey Morris made in Dr. Steward's diary: "Mr. Morris, you should be proud of your great state. Its reception into the Union was a precedent which may have far-reaching effects hereafter, when the Pole and the Tropics may hold allegiance to the Stars and Stripes." (Stoker 263) Arata, though, intimates that the author might have seen this handover of power as not one that was wholly desired, and equates the American spirit of adventure with that of the vampire itself:

> There is even a suggestion that the American is at times leagued with Dracula against the others. Morris leaves, without explanation, the crucial meeting in which Van Helsing first names the Count as their enemy; a moment later he fires his pistol into the room where they are seated (pp. 288–289). He quickly explains that he was shooting at a "big bat" sitting on the windowsill,but this very brief and easily missed tableau—Morris standing outside the window in the place vacated by Dracula, looking in on the assembled Westerners who have narrowly escaped his violence—suggests strongly that Stoker wants us to consider the American and the Roumanian together [Arata 642].

This further suggests a line of equivalence within the texts considered here that sees the anxiety over the loss of the colonial imperative of Britain to the vampire in fact revealed the fear that it would pass on to the Empire's unruly offspring, the Americas, whose own "democratic" imperial intent can be seen to be represented by the Federation in *Star Trek*.

Live Long and Prosper

Star Trek, not unlike a vampire, has died/ended and risen again in many forms, and even though its most recent television reincarnation, *Star Trek: Enterprise* finished in 2005—there has been an announcement by CBS of a new series to begin in 2017—the cinematic adaptations have been re-vamped by director J.J. Abrams, with his *Star Trek* from 2009 and with an expected third film in the series, *Star Trek: Beyond*, expected in July 2016. Dracula ends, at least as a novel, with both the American and the vampire dead and, intriguingly, the former is responsible for killing the later, as related by Mina:

> But, on the instant, came the sweep and flash of Jonathan's great knife. I shrieked as I saw it shear through the throat; whilst at the same moment Mr. Morris's bowie knife plunged in the heart. It was like a miracle; but before our very eyes, and almost in the drawing of a breath, the whole body crumbled into dust and passed from our sight. I shall be glad as long as I live that even in that moment of final dissolution there was in the face a look of peace, such as I never could have imagined might have rested there [Stoker 409].

This is quickly followed by the last words of the American, and it is worth mentioning those before looking at what occurred in the final moments of the vampire. Quincey, wounded and bleeding out, takes Mina's hand and in the light of the newly risen sun sees the change in her appearance that has been brought about by the death of the Count. He says, "Now God be thanked that all has not been in vain! See! the snow is not more stainless than her forehead! The curse has passed away!'" (Stoker 410) Mina then continues, "And, to our bitter grief, with a smile and silence, he died, a gallant gentleman." (*ibid.*) The American draws attention to the fact that the "vampire's" hold over Mina, and by extension the future of the Empire, has been broken allying the anxiety caused by the monster's intrusion into the social order of middle class Victorian society. But one might also feel that he tries to hard to make this point, and that for "final words" he is going to great pains to make sure his audience believe that the threat of the vampire has passed. Alongside this is Count Dracula's death which is also most peculiar, for it is unlike the earlier killings of vampires in the novel. Professor Van Helsing had earlier instructed Arthur Holmwood on how to kill the newly vampiric Lucy which, according to his many years of research, involved pushing a wooden stake into the creature's heart and then severing its head, none of that happens in this final scene. Harker's blade only cuts the vampires throat and Quincey uses a metal knife to stab his heart and so, according to the earlier incidents, although this might incapacitate Dracula, it certainly would not kill him. In fact, the crumbling of his body bears more relation to the kind of corporeal transformations that Dracula has undergone before in the narrative, some of which are described by the Professor, when warning the "crew of light" about the nature of their opponent:

> He can transform himself to wolf, as we gather from the ship arrival in Whitby, when he tear open the dog; he can be as bat, as Madam Mina saw him on the window at Whitby, and as friend John saw him fly from this so near house, and as my friend Quincey saw him at the window of Miss Lucy. He can come in mist which he create—that noble ship's captain proved him of this; but, from what we know, the distance he can make this mist is limited, and it can only be round him-self. He come on moonlight rays as elemental dust—as again Jonathan saw those sisters in the castle of Dracula. He become so small—we ourselves saw Miss Lucy, ere she was at peace, slip through a hair-breadth space at the tomb door [Stoker 258].

This is suggestive—at least in the aspects regarding mist, dust and "so small"—that Dracula did not die at all, but transformed into some other form, something also hinted at by his look of content, just before he crumbled to dust, knowing he was about to elude his tormentors once again. There is also in this closing tableaux an implication, that if both the Count and Quincey are of the same order, then their joint "death scene" was just a means for them both to transcend the position they found themselves in; so that they could regroup and strike again. A notion that is supported by Dracula's earlier pronouncement: "My revenge is just begun! I spread it over centuries, and time is on my side. Your girls that you all love are mine already; and through them you and others shall yet be mine—my creatures." (Stoker 333) This seems to come to possible fruition in the novel's second ending, when the surviving members of the crew of light meet once again in Transylvania. The final pages of the novel, though meant as a final postscript to celebrate the crew of lights conquest over evil, remembrance of companions lost and hope for the future, it also has a distinct air of unease about it. Written by Jonathan Harker the "terrible memories" (Stoker 411) from their journey "through the flames" (*ibid.*) cling to every word. The only positive from the events is the birth of Jonathan and Mina's son, Quincey, named after the American they called comrade, but in light of what was mentioned above, casting doubt on his true intentions, as such even the hopeful words of Harker below are tinged with foreboding:

> It is an added joy to Mina and to me that our boy's birthday is the same day as that on which Quincey Morris died. His mother holds, I know, the secret belief that some of our brave friend's spirit has passed into him. His bundle of names links all our little band of men together; but we call him Quincey [*ibid.*].

This spirit might not be as benevolent as the boy's parents believe, and may in fact be the vampiric essence that left both Count Dracula and Quincey to be reborn in a future that will boldly go on to assimilate all worlds it comes into contact with. Just as the undying flame of the Federations ideological conquest of space is passed from Captain to Captain and generation to generation so to does the vampire move from one continent to another and from an ages old European aristocrat to a Wild West adventurer. In this sense then Roddenberry's space opera does not so much mirror or replicate the spirit of Stoker's novel but is in fact something of a sequel to the undead adventures of the Transylvanian Count as his spirit seeks to assimilate "new worlds and new civilizations."

Note

1. Arguably there have been many sequels to Stoker's novel in many formats including films, novels, graphic novels, etc., but none of these have had the involvement of the original author. Even the official play by Hamilton Deane or Tod Browning's 1931 film, whilst having copyright permission, where never seen or agreed to by Stoker himself.

Works Cited

Arata, Stephen. "The Occidental Tourist: 'Dracula' and the Anxiety of Reverse Colonization." *Victorian Studies*, Vol. 33, No. 4, Summer 1990, pp. 621–645.

Barbar, Trudy. "Kinky Borgs and Sexy Robots: The Fetish, Fashion and Discipline of Seven of Nine." *Channeling the Future: Essays on Science Fiction and Fantasy Television*. Ed. Lincoln Geraghty. Lanham, MD: Scarecrow Press, 2009, pp. 133–148.

Booker, M Keith. *Alternate Americas Science Fiction Film and American Culture*. Westport, CT: Praeger Publishers, 2006.

Botting, Fred. *Gothic*. London: Routledge, 1996.

Cohen, Jeffrey Jerome. *Monster Theory: Reading Culture*. Minneapolis: University of Minnesota Press, 1996.

Cornea, Christine. *Science Fiction Cinema Between Fantasy and Reality*. Edinburgh: Edinburgh University Press Ltd, 2007.

Craft, Christopher. *Another Kind of Love: Male Homosexual Desire in English Discourse*. 1850–1920. University of California Press, 1994.

_____. "'Kiss Me with Those Red Lips.': Gender and Inversion in Bram Stoker's *Dracula*." *Representations*, Vol. 8 Autumn, 1984, pp. 107–133.

Doherty, Thomas. *Teenagers and Teenpics: The Juvenilization of American Movies in the 1950s*. Philadelphia: Temple University Press, 2002.

Geraghty, Lincoln. "Living with *Star Trek*: Utopia, Community, Self-Improvement and the *Star Trek* Universe." Ph.D. Dissertation, University of Nottingham, March 2005. http://eprints.nottingham.ac.uk/10982/. Accessed 5 January 2016.

Invasion of the Body Snatchers. Director Don Siegel. Los Angeles: Walter Wanger Pictures. 1956.

Khair, Tabish. *The Gothic, Postcolonislism and Otherness: Ghosts from Elsewhere*. London: Palgrave Macmillan, 2009.

Sandefur, Timothy. "The Politics of Star Trek." *Claremont Review of Books*, Vol. XV, No. 3, Summer 2015. http://www.claremont.org/crb/contributor-list/390/. Accessed 5 January 2016.

Senf, Carol A. "Rethinking the New Woman in Stoker's Fiction: Looking at Lady Athlyne." *Journal of Dracula Studies*, Vol. 9, 2007. https://kutztownenglish.files.wordpress.com/2015/09/jds_v9_2007_senf.pdf. Accessed 5 January 2016.

Star Trek. Creator Gene Roddenberry. Desilu Productions and Paramount Television, 1966–1969.

Star Trek. Director J.J. Abrams. Hollywood: Paramount Pictures, 2009.

Star Trek: Deep Space Nine. Creators Rick Berman and Michael Piller. Los Angeles: Paramount Television, 1993–1999.
Star Trek: Enterprise. Creators Rick Berman and Brannon Braga. Los Angeles: Paramount Television, 2001–2005.
Star Trek: First Contact. Director Jonathan Frakes. Los Angeles: Paramount Pictures, 1996.
Star Trek: Insurrection. Director Jonathan Frakes. Los Angeles: Paramount Pictures, 1998.
Star Trek Into Darkness. Director J.J. Abrams. Hollywood: Paramount Pictures, 2013.
Star Trek: Nemesis. Director Stuart Baird. Los Angeles: Paramount Pictures, 2002.
Star Trek: The Next Generation. Creator Gene Roddenberry. Los Angeles: Paramount Television, 1987–1994.
Star Trek: Voyager. Creator Rick Berman. Los Angeles: Paramount Television, 1995–2001.
Stoker, Bram. *Dracula* (1897). London: Signet Classics, 1996.
Summers, Montague. *The Vampire: His Kith and Kin.* London: Studio Editions, 1995.
The Thing from Another World. Director Christian Nyby. New York: RKO Radio Pictures, 1951.

About the Contributors

Suzan E. **Aiken**, Ph.D., has worked in post-secondary and secondary education in the Midwest. Her research often focuses on strong female characters and silence as a strategy. This time, she pursued her love of *Star Trek* and Captain Kirk as an opportunity to study historic feminism.

Simon **Bacon** is an independent scholar based in Poznan, Poland. He has contributed articles to many publications on vampires, monstrosity, science fiction and media studies, and has coedited several books, including *Undead Memory* (2014), *Seductive Concepts* (2014), *Little Horrors* (2016) and *Growing Up with the Undead* (forthcoming). His monograph *Becoming Vampire* was published in 2016.

Andrew M. **Butler** is a senior lecturer at Canterbury Christ Church University. He is the author of *Solar Flares* (2011), *Eternal Sunshine of the Spotless Mind* (2014), "Human Subjects/Alien Objects?" in *Alien Imaginations* (2015), "Sleeping/Waking" in *Endangering Science Fiction Film* (2015), as well as books on Philip K. Dick, cyberpunk, Terry Pratchett, postmodernism and film studies. He is also an editor for the journal *Extrapolation*.

Teresa **Cutler-Broyles** teaches at the University of New Mexico in the cinematic arts department, and is a visiting professor at the Umbra Institute in Perugia, Italy. She is pursuing a Ph.D. in American cultural studies with an emphasis on performance theory and film theory. She has written fiction, nonfiction, travel essays, and chapters in academic publications on performance, media, and cultural analysis.

Eleanor **Dobson** is a doctoral researcher at the University of Birmingham. Her research interests include the Gothic and science from the nineteenth century to the present. She has published on representations of Oscar Wilde's ghost, and x-rays, electricity and ancient Egypt in Victorian literature.

Nadine **Farghaly** has a Ph.D. in American studies from the University of Salzburg. Her research focuses on gender representations within popular culture. She is the editor or coeditor of several books, including essay collections on *The Big Bang Theory*, *Resident Evil*, *Sherlock Holmes*, and many more in progress.

Haley M. **Fedor** is a Ph.D. candidate at the University of Louisiana at Lafayette, and is a Fulbright Scholarship recipient and Pushcart Prize nominee. Her fiction and nonfiction have appeared in or are forthcoming in *The Fem, Guide to Kulchur Magazine, Literary Orphans, Crab Fat Literary Magazine,* and *Dispatches from Lesbian America.*

Jack **Fennell** is a lecturer and researcher in English literature, and is a former Irish Research Council scholar and Visiting Fellow at NUI Galway. His research interests include science fiction, the gothic, narrative theory and gender. He is the author of *Irish Science Fiction* (2014), and was a contributing translator to *The Short Fiction of Flann O'Brien* (2013).

Derek **Frasure** is a Ph.D. candidate in the department of English Language and Literature at the University of Michigan, Ann Arbor. He has presented his work at national and international conferences on topics ranging from Foucault's concept of madness as ontology to lesbianism in comics. His dissertation focuses on the paradigmatic concept of infinity in postmodern American novels.

Ericka **Hoagland** is an associate professor at Stephen F. Austin State University where she teaches courses on travel writing, the African novel, and science fiction. Her research and publishing focuses on the intersections between science fiction and empire, including a study of colonialism in Gwyneth Jones' Aleutian trilogy and *Science Fiction, Imperialism, and the Third World* (2010).

Andrew **Howe** is a professor of history at La Sierra University, where he teaches courses in American history, popular culture, and film/television studies. His published work includes book chapters on fan-generated art involving *Game of Thrones*, the transformation of the Mohican myth in *Avatar*, and the anticipation of the late–20th century culture wars in the time travel television show *Voyagers.*

Ken **Monteith** is an adjunct professor at the American University of Armenia. He earned a Ph.D. in English literature from Fordham University in 2005, and after a career as an assistant professor in New York City, ran away to become the spouse of a diplomat—the closest thing there is to Star Fleet in the United States.

Lorrie **Palmer** is an assistant professor of film and media studies at Towson University. Her scholarship, teaching, and conference work includes genre (science fiction, action, horror, the Western) and gender in film and television. Her published work has appeared in *Film and History, Bright Lights Film Journal, Camera Obscura*, and the *Journal of Popular Film and Television*, as well as in several anthologies.

Michael **Pringle** is a professor and former chair of the English Department at Gonzaga University. Although an Early Americanist by training (with publications on Hawthorne and Equiano), he introduced the first science fiction English courses at Gonzaga. His research explores the link between philosophy and science fiction.

Kevin J. **Wetmore**, Jr., is a professor and the chair of Theatre Arts at Loyola Marymount University, and he also teaches in the film and television studies program. He is the author of several books, book chapters and articles on Godzilla, lightsabers, Norman Bates as a juvenile delinquent, exorcism cinema, Guillermo del Toro, Greek tragedy and genre cinema, and vampires in Shakespeare.

Zara T. **Wilkinson** is a reference librarian at Rutgers University–Camden. She has presented nationally and internationally on female characters in *Star Trek*, *Doctor Who*, and *Orphan Black*. In 2014, she organized Buffy to Batgirl: Women and Gender in Science Fiction, Fantasy, and Comics, a two-day academic conference held on the campus of Rutgers University–Camden.

Index